LUTHER'S WORKS

LUTHER'S
WORKS

VOLUME 6

LECTURES ON GENESIS

Chapters 31–37

JAROSLAV PELIKAN
Editor

HILTON C. OSWALD
Associate Editor

CONCORDIA PUBLISHING HOUSE · SAINT LOUIS

Contents

General Introduction

THE first editions of Luther's collected works appeared in the sixteenth century, and so did the first efforts to make him "speak English." In America serious attempts in these directions were made for the first time in the nineteenth century. The Saint Louis edition of Luther was the first endeavor on American soil to publish a collected edition of his works, and the Henkel Press in Newmarket, Virginia, was the first to publish some of Luther's writings in an English translation. During the first decade of the twentieth century, J. N. Lenker produced translations of Luther's sermons and commentaries in thirteen volumes. A few years later the first of the six volumes in the Philadelphia (or Holman) edition of the *Works of Martin Luther* appeared. Miscellaneous other works were published at one time or another. But a growing recognition of the need for more of Luther's works in English has resulted in this American edition of Luther's works.

The edition is intended primarily for the reader whose knowledge of late medieval Latin and sixteenth-century German is too small to permit him to work with Luther in the original languages. Those who can, will continue to read Luther in his original words as these have been assembled in the monumental Weimar edition (*D. Martin Luthers Werke*. Kritische Gesamtausgabe; Weimar, 1883 ff.). Its texts and helps have formed a basis for this edition, though in certain places we have felt constrained to depart from its readings and findings. We have tried throughout to translate Luther as he thought translating should be done. That is, we have striven for faithfulness on the basis of the best lexicographical materials available. But where literal accuracy and clarity have conflicted, it is clarity that we have preferred, so that sometimes paraphrase seemed more faithful than literal fidelity. We have proceeded in a similar way in the matter of Bible versions, translating Luther's translations. Where this could be done by the use of an existing English version — King James, Douay, or Revised Standard — we have done so. Where it could not, we have supplied our own. To indicate this in each specific instance would have been pedantic; to adopt a uniform procedure would have been artificial — especially in view of Luther's own inconsistency in this regard. In each volume the translator will be responsible primarily for matters of text and language, while the responsibility of the editor will extend principally to the historical and theological matters reflected in the introductions and notes.

Although the edition as planned will include fifty-five volumes, Luther's writings are not being translated in their entirety. Nor should they be. As he was the first to insist, much of what he wrote and said was not that important. Thus the edition is a selection of works that have proved their importance for the faith, life, and history of the Christian Church. The first thirty volumes contain Luther's expositions of various Biblical books, while the remaining volumes include what are usually called his "Reformation writings" and other occasional pieces. The final volume of the set will be an index volume; in addition to an index of quotations, proper names, and topics, and a list of corrections and changes, it will contain a glossary of many of the technical terms that recur in Luther's works and that cannot be defined each time they appear. Obviously Luther cannot be forced into any neat set of rubrics. He can provide his reader with bits of autobiography or with political observations as he expounds a psalm, and he can speak tenderly about the meaning of the faith in the midst of polemics against his opponents. It is the hope of publishers, editors, and translators that through this edition the message of Luther's faith will speak more clearly to the modern church.

J. P.
H. L.

Introduction to Volume 6

LUTHER's lectures on Gen. 31–37 (Weimar, XLIV, 1–304; St. Louis, II, 608–1159) carry the patriarchal narratives through the death of Isaac into the story of Joseph and his brethren. The last of the volumes of the *Lectures on Genesis* to appear in our edition, Volume 6 completes the English translation in eight volumes.

As was the case with the other volumes, we are obliged to reconstruct the chronological development of Luther's exposition from very meager data, some of them contained in *obiter dicta* that occur within the printed version and some of them available from other sources. Following the precedent set by Volume 5, we shall arrange these data in the order of the chapters of the Book of Genesis on which the lectures are based:

31:22-24 (p. 40): Luther refers to nine imperial diets that have taken place since the rebirth of the Gospel. The first of these would undoubtedly be Worms, 1521. It was followed by: Nuremberg, 1522; Nuremberg, 1524; Augsburg, 1525; Speyer, 1526; Speyer, 1529; Augsburg, 1530; Regensburg, 1532, moved to Nuremberg on account of the Turkish threat; Regensburg, 1541; Speyer, 1542; Nuremberg, 1542–1543; Speyer, 1544. Thus the "ninth" to which Luther refers would be the (third) Diet of Speyer, which opened on Feb. 9, 1542, and adjourned on April 11, 1542. The tenth would be the (third) Diet of Nuremberg, which met from July 13 to August 26, 1542, and from January 31 to August 23, 1543. Luther would then appear to have been lecturing on Gen. 31:22-24 after April 11, 1542, and before July 13, 1542.

34:1 (p. 187): In his discussion of the chronology of the story of Jacob, Luther mentions his earlier views regarding Jacob's return to Isaac, as these views were reflected in the first edition of his work on chronology, *Computation of the Years of the World* (1541). He indicates that he had changed them in the second edition (1545). If this quotation is accurate, it would have to fall into 1545. As we have shown in the "Introduction to Volume 8," Luther's last lecture on Genesis was delivered on Nov. 17, 1545.

35:2 (p. 228): As he had many times before, Luther speaks of the possibility that a general council of the church is to be convened, and he criticizes a conception of its agenda that would concentrate on the reform of church structure, ritual, and morality rather than on "the Word and doctrine." The Council of Trent was convoked by Pope Paul III (whose pontificate extended from 1534 to 1549) in a bull dated May 22, 1542, but it was aborted by the political and military situation. On Nov. 19, 1544, the pope issued a new bull, summoning the council for March 15, 1545. It did not actually begin until Dec. 15, 1545. The indefiniteness of Luther's language would suggest that the council, often announced and as often postponed, did not seem to be in immediate prospect at the time. It would fit well into the winter of 1542/1543 or the following spring.

35:5 (pp. 243–244): Discussing current events, Luther reflects on the battles of the Turks and on those of the Holy Roman Emperor, Charles V, who is now in "Belgium," viz., the Low Countries. Charles departed Spain for the campaign in Gelderland on May 12, 1543; the document granting freedom to Gelderland is dated September 1543. It seems plausible that these comments on Gen. 35:5 came sometime between those dates.

36:20-30 (pp. 296–302): A fragment from the *Lectures on Genesis,* the portion dealing with these verses, is preserved in a manuscript from Greifswald. The heading contains the date "October 16, 1543," which, as Meinhold points out, was a Tuesday, one of Luther's regular days in the classroom.

37 (pp. 313–407): On Dec. 17, 1543, Luther interrupted his exposition of Genesis to give a special series of lectures on "the Christmas Gospel from Isaiah," that is, Is. 9. In his introduction to these lectures, he stated: "Therefore if my health permits, I am suspending my lectures on Joseph and speaking during these days about the incarnation of the Son of God." As noted in the "Introduction to Volume 7," there is also external evidence that Luther was about to begin his exposition of the story of Joseph in September 1543.

37:12-17 (p. 349): Luther refers to an imperial diet that is now going on. In the light of the chronological information just listed, this can only mean the (fourth) Diet of Speyer, which was opened by Charles V on Feb. 20, 1544, and adjourned on June 10, 1544.

As we have noted in the appropriate place (p. 188, n. 1), the words put into Luther's mouth at Gen. 34:1 cannot be squared with the other information and must therefore be attributed to his editors. This would yield a chronology that is sparse but quite consistent: Luther began the lectures presented here in the spring of 1542 and continued them until early 1544. (In the light of this analysis, our suggestion in the "Introduction to Volume 7," that some of the material contained there could have come from November 1543, seems to have been mistaken.)

The basis of our translation has been, as always, the Weimar edition of the works of Luther. We have once more made corrections wherever they were obviously necessary, noting only those where the typographical error in the Weimar text would also have led to a Latin word. We have made conjectural emendations where they seemed to be called for either by other editions or by the sense of the passage; each of these is indicated in a footnote. And we have sought to identify quotations and allusions from Biblical, classical, patristic, and contemporary sources, amplifying or correcting references in the Weimar notes without explicitly calling attention to the changes. For the citations from Lyra, the *Glossa ordinaria,* and Paulus Burgensis we have used *Biblie iam pridem renouate pars prima* (Basel, 1502), referring to both page and note numbers, so that most references can be verified in other editions.

J. P.

LECTURES ON GENESIS

Chapters 31–37

Translated by
PAUL D. PAUL

CHAPTER THIRTY-ONE

1. *Now Jacob heard that the sons of Laban were saying: Jacob has taken all that was our father's; and from what was our father's he has gained all this wealth.*

UP TO this point Moses has related those events which happened in the six years after the birth of Joseph. From that time Jacob began to take thought for the government and support of his household, for which he had made no provision at all in the previous 14 years. But after he had become the father of so many children, it occurred to him, almost too late, to make plans for the welfare of his household. But even as he suffered all the worst hardships with great endurance under a greedy master during the 14 years, so during this period of six years, by marvelous skill and by the blessing of the Lord, he gained property that was not to be despised. But not without envy. For he could not keep his wealth secret from his father-in-law and the latter's sons. Accordingly, when the six years had run their course, he made preparations to return to his fatherland, although without making haste. Perhaps he would even have remained longer had not a call from God intervened.

But to that mass of miseries which he endured in the house of Laban for so many years was added the malice and envy of the sons of the household, who accused him quite openly of plundering their father's property. "He heard," says Moses, "that the sons of Laban were saying, etc." He also saw that the countenance of Laban himself was changed and that his brow was wrinkled and sad. All these things he understood as signs of an estranged and hostile disposition. Listen, then, to the extraordinary false accusation of the sons of Laban as they reproach Jacob for this wealth, the reward of such long and hard servitude, and you will say that the whole world of iniquity had joined forces with greed. This is the reason for that statement in Ecclesiasticus (14:6): "There is nothing more wicked than a greedy man." And from the heathen we have the excellent saying of the actor Publilius Syrus: "A greedy man does nothing right except when he

dies." [1] The unanimous voice and consensus of all of nature and all
nations detests and condemns greedy men.

This is because they have idolatry and a general ungodliness implanted in their hearts, directed not only against outsiders and
strangers but even against those belonging to their own household
and those of their own flesh and blood, yes, daughters, grandchildren,
and son-in-law. What could be thought more wicked and execrable
than such a man, one who does not favor his own daughters or his
wife with one morsel of bread? What will he do to a stranger and
to one who is without any tie of relationship? Therefore nothing is
more satisfactory, and a greedy man can do nothing better, than to
die, because by living he lives neither for God nor for others nor for
himself. Nothing else can he do but sin against God, against men, and
against himself, for he never benefits even his very own body.

The sons of Laban, therefore, employ very full and strong words
to express their envy. "Jacob has taken all that was our father's," they
say. Don't kill yourselves by lying! It is an exaggerated charge!
"What wretched men we are!" they say. "We are ruined; what are
we going to live on in the future? This fellow has pillaged all the
property of our father; he has all but sucked us dry and completely
consumed us." This is how Moses depicts Laban and his sons: the
sons followed in the footsteps of their father. "He has taken all," they
say. Yet Jacob served for 14 years and took no reward at all but
slender fare and clothing. Everything else he yielded to Laban.
Indeed, the latter would never have attained to such great wealth
if Jacob had not come to him, as Jacob said above (cf. 30:30). Besides,
he never stole anything, but with exceptional devotion he separated
a very large flock of lambs of one color from his own flock of mottled
lambs, which was much smaller and had been collected only with difficulty by diligence and divine inspiration. Nevertheless, in the meantime the other flock of Laban, which was quite numerous even before
this, was also increased. Jacob separated only the fruit of his own
toil, and from this he saved up those resources — slender enough, if
they are compared with the enormous property of Laban.

From this speech of the sons of Laban, then, we gather what is
the disposition and character of the greedy men. For they do not
consider what they have in hand, their numerous flock, their abundant
increase, but they only consider that Jacob has obtained a few sheep

[1] Publilius Syrus, *Sententiae*, 23. The original reads: *Avarus nisi cum moritur
nihil recte facit*, but Luther quotes it as: *Avarus nihil recte facit, nisi cum moritur*.

from their flocks, which he had increased with such great devotion for so many years previously. Jacob had demanded only one part of the flock as a reward for his labors. This they see; indeed, they see it with the greatest of grief and envy. How, then, could Laban add anything when he envies and offers with very ill grace what was owing to his faithful servant by every right and according to an agreement? Such a pestilential plague, to be sure, is avarice! It is not content with being able to devour everything alone, but it also demands that all others should be in want, suffer hunger, and perish from poverty and starvation. It cannot be satisfied even when all its income and treasures are safe and sound unless it sees that others have nothing at all.

Envy, however, is a very fair penalty for greed. For while the greedy man wants others to be in need, he does not enjoy his own property either, as the saying of Jerome in an introduction to the Bible testifies: "The greedy man lacks what he has as much as what he does not have." [2] A poor man lives more agreeably on his daily bread than the greedy man does on all his resources. I myself have seen a master in the University of Erfurt who had abundant resources but was so niggardly and tightfisted that in the course of a whole year he would not drink a pint of wine to preserve the health of his body. What is more wretched than to thirst, hunger, and suffer want in the midst of such great abundance and then to be tortured by the desire that one wishes that all others should be most wretched and to grieve and groan if one sees another man in possession of even one gold piece? See, then, whether avarice is not the foulest monstrosity of all monstrosities!

This cupidity and ill will of the sons of Laban outstrips all other examples. For Jacob, excellent man that he was, had served for so long with great toil and distress and had supported his wife and children by the sweat of his brow and had increased and enriched not his own property but the house and flocks of Laban, and yet he must still endure and hear this charge: "He has taken away all the property of our father." Like the name of Euclio,[3] the example and name of Laban certainly deserve to pass over into a proverb to denote immeasurable and boundless desire for wealth. For how much was it that Jacob had acquired during these six years by his skill? Certainly, he would have been worthy of a much richer increase. But

[2] Jerome, *Epistles*, 53, 10, *Patrologia, Series Latina*, XXII, 549.
[3] Euclio is a miser in the *Aulularia* of Plautus.

what shall we think that Laban would have paid to his son-in-law for such faithful and long service if this agreement had not been drawn up between them? He would have paid him what Jacob will mention later when he says: "You would have sent me away empty-handed" (v. 42), or he would always have remained a servant whose toils and afflictions would have been a source of profit to Laban as they had been previously.

For we see how greedily they gaze at this property of Jacob and how odious it is for them to increase it, as though they wanted to say: "What would Jacob have if he were without the property of our father? He would be a beggar and a stranger." But why do they not rather say: "What would our father have had if Jacob had not come here?" For what his services were he indicated to Laban above when he said: "You had little when I came to you" (cf. 30:30). His daughter Rachel was the keeper of his cattle and tiny flock. There was no need of a shepherd or any servant because they were so few. But they turn things upside down and ask: "What has Jacob brought to us? He came here empty and naked, therefore he should so depart again." But from where will he receive remuneration for the services which he rendered to this house for 20 years? "He has earned nothing," they said, "because he is a servant. We are free and are the master's sons. Let us therefore enjoy what Jacob has produced and push him out poor and destitute, or let him serve us gratis forever." For they thought that they had a right to make such a demand for themselves, that this service was owed to them, and that no mention of a reward could legitimately be made. Indeed, they also thought that it was not becoming to a servant to possess such splendid resources.

For this reason they employ the special term כָּבֵד, which, properly speaking, signifies "to be heavy." But metaphorically it denotes glory. Above, in Gen. 13:1, 2, we read: "Abram went up from Egypt, positively burdened with cattle, silver, and gold." So also the earth is said to be "weighed down" by hunger, pestilence, etc. Likewise, Pharaoh's heart was "weighed down" (cf. Ex. 7:14). It signifies that the things are present and that it is not a vain and empty matter. From here the meaning is transferred to "glory," because wealth and an abundance of all things produce glory and magnificence. So the sons of Laban speak enviously and say: "He has obtained all this 'weight' from our property, that is, this glorious and magnificent substance." They do not want to say fruit, possession, resources, property, etc., but they say כָּבֹד in a hateful and slanderous manner, as though

they wanted to say: "He came here as a beggar, but he has heaped
up great wealth at our house."

These matters, then, should be unfolded more accurately because
it seems that Holy Scripture wanted to set up an exact description of
avarice by this example, namely, that avarice is the home and training
ground of all vices and crimes (cf. 1 Tim. 6:10) and that the greedy
man is one who wishes neither God nor himself well. For he can
painfully exaggerate what does not serve his own advantages, and he
grieves that he is not able to gain possession of these things. Therefore what is said of ungrateful men will be much more correctly said
of a greedy man, namely: "If you have charged a man with ingratitude, you have charged him with every fault." The reason for this is
that ingratitude is a sin of omission but avarice is a sin of commission
and a matter of the greatest cruelty. Thus it exceeds the former by
far because it does serious harm to both public and private affairs.

2. *And Jacob looked at the face of Laban and saw that it was not the
same toward him as it had been previously.*

The first reason for Jacob's departure was the complaints and
charges of Laban's sons; the second was the change in the face of his
father-in-law. There was the same envy and greed in the father as
there was in the sons. He could not look upon the property of his
son-in-law without great ill will and grief; he wanted him to be
a pauper and a servant forever so that his wretchedness could be
a source of profit for Laban. He does not see that he had already
prospered previously on account of Jacob and that instead of one
daughter there was need of several shepherds for such a numerous
flock. But he sees that his son-in-law and daughters have one or two
sheep, lambs, and goats, and he is angry. He does not wear a clear
brow as previously, when he alone prospered and Jacob was in no
way concerned about private property.

Moreover, since the master of the house was displeased and angry,
the sons also and the rest of the household arranged their countenances
according to his nod. They also kept their sisters Leah and Rachel
under observation with hostile intent to see if even with their little
finger they should touch anything that belonged to the property of
Laban. Often, too, they devised abuse, insults, and accusations and
hurled them at wretched Jacob, hated by the head of the family.
Everything was sad, adverse, and troublesome for him in this house.
Nor did this envy and hatred endure only for one or two months, but it

is likely to have begun right away in the second or third year, as soon as Jacob began to prosper. But what could be a sadder experience for a man than to spend his life with a family group where the head of the family, his wife, children, servants, and maids scowl, grumble, and vent their displeasure? Yet Jacob fulfilled those six years. At last, however, he thought: "It is now time for me to leave this house, seeing that six years have been spent in the midst of the worst hatred and the most bitter slander." But he does not hurry, and he would not have withdrawn even now. But by divine command he is to return to his fatherland.

3. *Then the Lord said to Jacob: Return to the land of your fathers and to your kindred, and I will be with you.*

From this it is manifest what great troubles and annoyances Jacob endured, if, indeed, it is necessary for the Lord to have regard for him and to rescue him from these straits. For the Lord does not speak in vain, nor does He offer His Word to the lazy and smug, but to those who are in need, who toil, who are afflicted and are undergoing a very difficult conflict against the flesh and all external appearances, that is, against those things which according to human sense and reason fight against faith, as Heb. 11 says, so that the afflicted can rely on the sole protection of the Word of God and be sustained by it. Wisdom does not live "in the land of those who live pleasantly," says Job (cf. 28:13), because it is a word of the cross and despair. It pertains only to the troubled and mortified, the despised, those driven into despair, and the oppressed. Such was Jacob in his exile in the house of his unjust and greedy father-in-law, who wanted to give nothing and tried to snatch and strip everything from him and whose sons persecuted him very bitterly. All of them had the design to keep him bound in continuous servitude and to enrich themselves by his sweat and troubles.

In these straits the Lord speaks to him when he would have nothing else but faith and prayer left, embraces him when he is kept at arm's length and hated by all men, and supports his plan to depart: He orders him [4] to leave a family group that is so hostile to himself and to his wives, and to take thought for his own house. By this word God testifies that the whole life of the patriarch Jacob and all its activities are pleasing to Him.

Therefore this passage should be carefully noted. For Holy Scrip-

---

[4] The Weimar text has *iubeti,* but we have read *iubet.*

ture does not only preach about great miracles but also testifies that
God has a concern for service and household matters, and this is the
equivalent of the greatest of miracles and a sign of the special grace
and favor of God. This consolation has often been repeated above [5]
and in the whole Scripture, and it should be dealt with often. For
he who believes as Jacob did must be certain that all his thoughts and
all his footsteps are the object of God's care just as if there were
nothing else for God to do but to protect and guide him. For Moses
is preaching nothing about the kingdom of Egypt or Babylon, nothing
about the whole world. He is only relating how Jacob, troubled and
tried, was prepared to return to his fatherland. Therefore there is no
reason why we should be distressed and concerned about how the
kingdoms and empires of the world are governed. But let us give
thanks to God that we know that we are the object of His care in
such a way that He even knows all that we do, suffer, and think.

But men should be individually certain about this, that they are
the people of God, or members of the church. Above all things this
faith is necessary which firmly apprehends the following syllogism.
The whole people of God is blessed, holy, pleasing, and acceptable to
God in such a way that it cannot be torn from the hands of God.
We are the people of God. Therefore God exercises care for us. The
major premise is eminently true, because even the death and blood
of the saints are precious in the sight of the Lord (cf. Ps. 116:15); all
they do and suffer is pleasing to God. On the contrary, their errors
and lapses have been covered and forgiven, as Ps. 32:1 testifies.

But about the minor premise there is some question. For also the
Turk, the pope, and the Jews boast that they are such a people,
pleasing and acceptable to God. And so we must see to it that we
are certain about the minor premise, namely, that we are the sons
of God, members of the flock and people of God, under the one Shepherd, Christ. If you can firmly and surely determine this, then you
are blessed. Therefore be of good courage and do not be disturbed
or fearful even if the whole world should crash into ruin,[6] for, indeed,
you are sure that you are under that Shepherd who is Lord of heaven
and earth.

It is difficult, however, even for the sheep and the godly themselves,

[5] See, among many examples, *Luther's Works*, 4, p. 21.
[6] Horace, *Carmina*, III, 3, 7; see also p. 344, n. 21.

to give firm assent to this proposition. We must engage in a continual struggle against doubt and unbelief, such a great and difficult matter is faith! But the Turk, the Jews, and papists do not experience this struggle and do not fight, but they are absolutely sure and boast of their smugness that without any doubt they are God's people. The godly, accordingly, continually have need of consolation in order to believe the minor premise. Then the major premise will not fail you because the Holy Spirit testifies both by this example and many others that God's people please God even in the least and most trifling matters. For He will be working all things through you; He will milk the cow through you and perform the most servile duties through you, and all the greatest and least duties alike will be pleasing to Him. But by what arguments will one have to prove the minor premise? How am I to know for certain that I belong to the people of God? Before the incarnation of Christ the fathers had the promise, the Word, and the voice of God. They also had the sign of circumcision. We today have the Keys, Baptism, the Eucharist, and the promises of the Gospel. From this source you are to gather arguments and demonstrations by which you may become certain that you are a Christian, that you have been baptized and are walking in a godly and holy calling. See that you do not blaspheme but love the Word and serve God in some honorable employment. If this remains fixed in your heart, even though there will have to be a fight against doubt, you may nevertheless conclude and infer that you are a person whose deeds are all the object of God's care and please Him. You should think as follows: "I shall follow my calling and perform a servant's, master's, child's duties with Jacob. For I know that all these things are held in honor and are precious before the Lord our God."

It is necessary for these matters to be repeated because of the continuous struggle against doubt. For the opposite of the Word and divine comfort is thrown up to our senses. The flesh has a different experience, so that all things seem to be inflicted on the godly in an adverse manner, since, indeed, the ungodly are fortunate and the godly are afflicted. Therefore faith is a matter of invisible things until the final outcome proves the truth of the promises. For this reason the Lord addresses Jacob a second time not only to comfort him but also to strengthen him and help him in this struggle, which he undoubtedly suffered in all its bitterness.

But is it necessary to take careful note of what God says to Jacob.

"Return," He says, "to the land of your fathers," as though He wanted to say: "You have suffered much and long enough in the house of that greedy scoundrel, who is plundering you and skinning you. Go, therefore, and become the head of a family in your own fatherland." This is the voice of God consoling and encouraging Jacob. After accepting the consolation, he musters up courage and dares what he would never have dared otherwise. Without the knowledge of his father-in-law and his sons, he dares to leave the house with his wife and his children and with all his possessions in full confidence. Because the Word orders it, he is not fearful but proceeds in the name of the Lord, for these are the words of God, who is liberating Jacob from distress and promising to defend him in the future. "Go and gather together all that you have and move to your fatherland!" "But Laban will pursue me," Jacob could have said, "and drag me back into servitude. For he is mighty in strength, power, and number of his friends and relatives. I shall not be able to escape unknown to him or in safety." And so it turned out later, when Laban pursued him as though he were a fugitive and thief and threatened him with death. Therefore the Lord says: "I will be with you. Even though all the devils with Laban were against you, nevertheless I will be with you. Then let him come!" It is certainly a matter of importance that Jacob was able to believe this word. But he was a man exercised in faith and proved by many temptations. Yet he also had his weakness, even as the other fathers were at times exhausted by so many temptations and struggles. But they forthwith recovered their courage and strength. There was always this alternation of temptations and consolations.

4. *So Jacob sent and called Rachel and Leah into the field where his flock was,*

5. *and said to them: I see that your father does not regard me with favor as he did before. But the God of my father has been with me.*

6. *You know that I have served your father with all my strength;*

7. *yet your father has cheated me and changed my wages ten times, but God did not permit him to harm me.*

8. *If he said: The spotted shall be your wages, then all the flock bore spotted; and if he said: The striped shall be your wages, then all the flock bore striped.*

9. *Thus God has delivered the cattle of your father and given them to me.*

I wonder why he did not consult with his wives in the house and the tents. He was the son-in-law and the husband of the daughters. He could therefore have conferred with his family and wives in the house sometime and made known his plan to them. Perhaps Laban and his sons had forbidden him the house, so that he did not dare to enter the tents of his wives. So they had to be summoned and had to go out into the field where he was pasturing his own flocks and those of his father-in-law. Laban was undoubtedly suspicious, and so he did not easily let Jacob confer with his wives, lest he withdraw them from the house. Whatever it was, Moses seems to point out the malicious and suspicious nature of Laban.

But what spite it is for him to break the compact the moment he sees Jacob prosper! What are we to think that he seized during the previous 14 years, when he forcibly changes agreements and compacts in such a wicked manner? This the Holy Spirit is careful to report to amplify the wickedness and the greed of Laban. For he changed a condition whenever and as often as it pleased him. If he saw spotted cattle being born, he would say after they were born: "In the future I want the spotted ones to be mine." Again, when he saw that offspring of one color was being produced, Jacob not applying his rods, he would choose the white or black cattle. So he made sport of Jacob's skill and deceived him year after year, or rather, every half year, since in six years he made 10 changes. In the first year he kept the agreement, but in the remaining five years he changed it 10 times. This was extremely unjust! Therefore Jacob thought: "What are you to do with him? I will make no progress here. Therefore I will go away and leave this utterly godless man." This is an example of the outstanding faith and patience of Jacob, who was able to endure and suffer this treatment. Neither the agreement with his father-in-law nor the magic which he employed as often as Laban changed the condition at his pleasure would have profited him, had not the blessing of God been added, as he says: "But God did not permit him to harm me. God set me free and increased my flocks. Indeed, He has delivered the cattle from your father and given them to me" (cf. v. 7).

There is special emphasis on the expression "He has delivered." He does not say that God "took possession of" or "removed" but that

He "delivered." This expression is also used when the psalmist says: "Deliver me from my enemies" (cf. 31:15; 59:1; 143:9). God has delivered, that is, set free and saved. The Holy Spirit wants to indicate that this property belonged to Jacob and his wives by every right; it had been granted to them by the blessing of God and produced by their toils because Jacob had served for 14 years and during these six years was deceived 10 times. Therefore Holy Scripture states that it was delivered and removed by force, because it was owing to Jacob and his family. "God had to intervene with His might. The skill and cunning shown to me and approved by God would not have helped had not God with special might and power delivered and set free, as it were, the captive property of your father, the property Laban had previously snatched out of our mouths. What he held was completely ours, and what we have now I have not acquired by my skill or industry but by divine power, inasmuch as He, with a strong hand, has taken it away from the hand of this robber and scoundrel." This is what Moses wanted to indicate by the word יַצֵּל, namely, that the Lord by taking away conferred a blessing on Jacob. For in this way the hand of the Lord is with His saints to protect them and set them free from the fraud and the ill will of the ungodly.

10. *In the mating season of the flock I lifted up my eyes and saw in a dream that the he-goats which leaped upon the flock were striped, spotted, and mottled.*

11. *Then the angel of God said to me in the dream: Jacob, and I said: Here I am!*

12. *And he said: Lift up your eyes and see, all the goats that leap upon the flock are striped, spotted, and mottled; for I have seen all that Laban is doing to you.*

13. *I am the God of Bethel, where you anointed a pillar and made a vow to Me. Now arise, go forth from this land, and return to the land of your birth.*

These words imply a synecdoche, and on account of the brevity Moses employs they sound as if Jacob saw nothing in his dreams but goats of one color leaping upon the flock. The text must therefore be understood distributively, not collectively, that is, in one breeding he saw them leaping on those of one color and in the other on those of various colors. A part is to be taken for the whole. For he understands it to mean all the males in the flock of sheep and goats. Whenever he said: "This time you will have עֲקֻדִּים," עֲקֻדִּים were born, and so also with respect to the other kinds. It agrees with what he said above: "If he said, 'The spotted sheep will be your wages,' such were produced (cf. v. 8). If he assigned black or white offspring to me, black or white were born." In this way he wishes to indicate that God assisted him and in a wonderful manner thwarted the deceptions and wiles of Laban.

Furthermore, Moses seems to set forth additional proof of greed, no doubt that greedy Nabal,[7] as though endowed with a special prerogative and not in accordance with the agreement, took forcible possession of all the flocks of one color, in whatever breeding they were brought forth. Then he also left Jacob only one sort from among the spotted litters. If in one brood many spotted ones were born, which he had previously assigned to his son-in-law, he claimed the spotted ones in another brood for himself when he saw that a large number of them were produced. So he constantly employed change, and in the individual litters he never gave Jacob more than one kind of mottled offspring. All the rest he kept for himself. So there was need of the special power of God to repress the boundless greed of Laban, which even exceeds all the rapacity of the Turk.

"But God so comforted me," said Jacob, "that He sent an angel to strengthen me as I was struggling and found myself in a state of confusion on account of the remarkable wickedness of my father-in-law and to say: 'Laban is deceiving you in leaving you nothing but the spotted offspring. But the Lord has blessed you so that all offspring in the flock are born spotted.' Likewise, in another year Laban said that the mottled flocks would fall to me. Then again the angel comforted me and said: 'All the flocks will produce mottled offspring so that the one kind which is the only one Laban leaves you may surpass the rest in multitude and number, yes, that all offspring may be born such as he has assigned to you from the one species of those of more than one color.'" If God in this way had not lightened the poverty of Jacob, Laban would have left nothing at all to him. For it was an act of utterly wicked tyranny to concede only one species from the whole flock against the terms of the agreement. Accordingly, Laban is again depicted as a horrible and execrable plunderer and tyrant against his daughters, grandchildren, and son-in-law.

[7] On the name Nabal, cf. *Luther's Works*, 5, p. 285, n. 19.

We have not yet had the word בְּרֻדִּים above. It is derived from the word בָּרָד, meaning hail, and from this etymology the meaning of this word can easily be understod. For just as נְקֻדִּים means variegated with one or two spots, so בְּרֻדִּים are flocks spotted with small marks like hail, as though they had been spotted with many hail marks and were dappled, so to say. They were just like the young goats described in Vergil: "Kids whose skins were still sprinkled with white." [8]

The same word occurs in the sixth chapter of Zechariah, in the vision of the chariots (cf. Zech. 6:2-3): "The horses in the first chariot are red horses, chestnuts; in the second one, black; in the third one, לְבָנִים, white; in the fourth, strong horses and בְּרֻדִּים, dappled." In the first chapter (v. 8) there is another term, שְׂרֻקִּים, from שָׂרֵק, which signifies a very fine vine, a brown vine. שְׂרֻקִּים are horses that are not red or black but chestnut browns, like grapes on the vine. But בְּרֻדִּים in German signifies apple-gray, gray, because on their haunches such spots shaped like apples or mirrors appear scattered.

14. *Then Rachel and Leah answered him: Is there any portion or inheritance left to us in our father's house?*

15. *Are we not regarded by him as foreigners? For he has sold us, and he has been using up the money given for us.*

16. *All the property which God has taken away from our father belongs to us and to our children; now then, whatever God has said to you, do.*

The complaint of Jacob is followed by the complaints of Rachel and Leah. For it is godly and just for a mother to be moved by worry and concern for her children. For according to God's command it is the duty of a mother or wife to assist her husband in nourishing and bringing up the children and in attending to the administration of the household. These two wives complain in wretched fashion about the cruelty of their father, inasmuch as they are already the mothers of 12 children and they are still deprived by their greedy and unjust father of the things necessary for nourishing such a numerous household. Perhaps he was also reluctant to supply them with bread and milk, since he seized for himself everything that they had acquired by their toils. However, they did not have the opportunity or the

[8] Vergil, *Eclogues,* II, 41. The original has *albo* where Luther quotes *albi.*

permission to complain about their troubles. For they were not
allowed to do or say anything without the knowledge of their father
or against his will.

Therefore they say: "Is there any portion or inheritance left to us
in our father's house?" It is as though they were saying: "What shall
we do in this situation? We have a large household, two maids and
12 children. But our father is quite unconcerned how these are to be
provided for. Not so much as a farthing does he supply. He treats
us as though we were strangers who have no share in our father's
goods and inheritance." Such words seem out of keeping with the
respect of daughters to their father. This is a very hard and bitter
speech. But to whom does a share and the inheritance in the home
belong? Does it not belong to the daughters? They should have been
able to hope for a certain part of the inheritance, if not all of it.
"And yet our father conducts himself in such a way towards us,"
they say, "that we cannot even hope for anything from him or expect
it from him. The longer we live here, the harder and more cruelly
we are exercised in continuous slavery, which is even more intolerable
because he pays us no reward but in addition claims for himself and
consumes the money produced by our toil. Not only does he despoil
us of our legitimate portion and inheritance, but he has even sold
us as though we were slaves. He has added no dowry but demands
from us and takes from us what we have saved, a thing which does
not usually happen even to maidservants and slaves."

These are truly extraordinary complaints, and yet the words seem
harsher than is becoming to daughters. They do not seem to honor
their parents since they say such impious, horrible, and almost mur-
derous things about their father. For the Fourth Commandment
charges us to treat our parents with honor and to esteem them in
word and actual deed. But what could be said that is more atrocious
than this complaint which they raise: "Our father does not acknowledge us as daughters; he does not love us; he does not acknowledge
us as offspring born from his own flesh and bowels"? He has no
στοργὴν φυσικήν,[9] that is, that natural affection and love of parents
toward their children implanted in all men by nature, examples of
which occur very frequently in every life and in the histories of all
nations. Indeed, concerning the harlot who was carrying on a law-
suit before Solomon about her son it is stated in the Book of Kings

[9] The Greek term στοργή, which recurs often in these lectures, refers to the
natural affection between human beings, especially between parents and children.

(1 Kings 3:26): "Her heart yearned for her son." She would rather be deprived of the fruit of her womb than see the slaughter of her son. This affection, I say, accords with man's nature in particular. Yes, it is even present in beasts, who, the fiercer they are, the more they rage with affection and love for their whelps. Wolves, bears, lions, and pigs fight very fiercely and savagely for their young. So great is the force of nature.

Is it not therefore a horrible thing that avarice should so change not beast but man, who is the most distinguished in character, that he completely forgets natural inclination and love toward his children? This monstrosity of avarice in Laban could not have been censured more bitterly than when these excellent matrons, his daughters, complain that they are born of this father and are yet not regarded as daughters. For this means that the natural στοργή ("affection") and the love of parents toward offspring is overcome and driven out by avarice. They clearly demonstrate this when they say: "He has sold us and has devoured our money."

This, to be sure, is in conflict with nature. For it is natural that a father should provide for food and clothing for his daughters as for the weaker sex. And he should provide not only for these but also for the dowry, the inheritance, and other necessities. Indeed, the little birds and the beasts nicely follow nature as their guide; they provide nests, protection, and food for their chicks or their young. This Laban does not do but he regards his daughters as foreigners so that they are compelled to complain that the condition of maidservants is better, for by all rights, human and divine, wages and food for her labor are owed to a maidservant.

"To us nothing is paid," they say, "but we are regarded not as maidservants but as strangers and as if he were not our father and we were not his daughters." Here, indeed, the Fourth Commandment could cease to apply. For what paternal quality does Laban have that is worthy of honor? He is a beast and a monster! But how will you honor him as a parent who does not want to be a father and who disdains to regard you as a son but has stripped off all paternal feeling and affection and has degenerated into a tyrant?

But this tyranny the excellent matrons endured for 20 years on end. I would never have thought that such madness could enter human nature if it had not been attested in Holy Scripture. "He has sold us," they say, "that is, he has handed us over to you in return for your toil and all the good things that have been produced by you. By the blessing of God it was our good fortune to find a buyer who cares for us, nourishes us, and protects us. But cursed be the seller! On our account you had to be a slave, my dear Jacob, and all you earned in 14 years by very hard toil you had to pay for us. If we had not found a buyer so godly and generous, we would have had to perish of hunger, or he, becoming tired of his servitude and poverty, would have fled, leaving us with his father-in-law."

The complaints are certainly very serious and unheard-of, and you will hardly find another example like them. For it is incredible for a man to be so altered and to degenerate not into a beast but into an abortive monstrosity of nature. This is what the common saying means: "When an angel becomes a devil, he really becomes bad." The devil has become exceedingly corrupt and bad because he has degenerated from a preeminent, angelic nature. Thus a virtuous virgin, after she has once prostituted her virtue, no longer has any respect for anything but casts off all sense of shame for disgraceful acts of every kind. So also, if a Christian becomes an apostate, no other enemy of the church and godliness will be more bitter.

In the same manner, after Laban had been given over to greed and the worship of mammon, he lost the sense of propriety, which is characteristic not only of men but especially also of all beasts and is given in nature. From a parent he became a tyrant and the robber of his daughters. "He has given us nothing," they say, "not even a hair or a morsel of bread, and the wages he agreed to he has changed 10 times. Whatever we have, whatever we are, our whole life we owe to our purchaser, who nourishes and sustains us by his toil. Indeed, what is even greater and more atrocious, he is consuming our money. Our husband has paid for us with a very hard servitude of 14 years. But he was not content with seizing and taking away also the fruit and wages of our labors. What was owed to us for our labors and those of our husband he himself enjoys and applies to his own use."

Now then, ask whether these daughters sinned in detracting from their father's merits and disparaging him. I certainly shall not praise them, but I readily concede that there is a certain weakness and impatience, indeed, a sin in the saints, but one that is venial and tolerable. For what good can be said of a dog? I certainly would have said: "In what a currish and wolfish manner my father treats me! My father treats me just as though I were a dog." It is impossible to say anything human about such dog's madness. Then, too, they did not spread these matters among strangers but poured them into their husband's lap. Before him they were certainly permitted to complain about their difficulties without sin. "It is surely to be deplored that our father has shed all humanity and love towards us to such an extent that he not only neglects us but even takes away what we have produced by our own labors." No one will have the right to excuse, honor, and defend these faults, but he will be more correct in censuring them and finding fault with them, that other men may learn to acknowledge and flee the disgraceful example.

Although, therefore, we shall acknowledge that this mentioning of the faults of their father is a weakness of the flesh and a mark of the weaker sex, nevertheless, truly speaking, Laban is a dog. He is an example which all men should execrate and flee. However, the daughters in turn console themselves for their sorrow and wretchedness with the blessing of God, to whom they attribute it that He is the Author of the whole property and all the good things they now possess. "If the Lord had not been at our side," they say, "no other women on this earth would be more wretched." This blessing of God they acknowledge with grateful hearts, and they proclaim that God did not leave them in such great wretchedness and poverty but compensated richly for what their father had plundered: "Praised be God, who has heard our groans and counted our tears; all the resources that God has taken away from our father are now ours and our sons'."

So their answer to the complaint of Jacob about the injuries received from his father-in-law and in regard to his plan for setting out is: "Whatever God has said to you, do." It is as though they meant to say: "There is no reason why you should fear that you possess these blessings and are taking them with you unjustly. It is as you have said: 'God has taken away the possession of your father, and given it to me.'" Thus they repeat the same word which Jacob used above, as though they meant to say: "These resources which God has given to you by a kind of miracle were held captive under the hand of mammon and the greed of our father. He owed them to us by divine and human right, but because of his malice it came about that up till now neither you nor we have had possession of them, although they were acquired by your labors of 20 years. At last, however, God has come and liberated, or delivered, the resources from their greedy and unrighteous owner and assigned them to us."

This example, moreover, agrees beautifully with the deed of the Israelites in despoiling the Egyptians. For the Lord ordered this. It is stated in Exodus 11:2-3: "'Speak now in the hearing of the people that they ask, every man of his neighbor and every woman of her neighbor, jewelry of silver and of gold.' And the Lord gave the people favor in the sight of the Egyptians so that they might oblige them." They despoiled the Egyptians, namely, the Lord taking away and liberating the captive wealth, as it were, the silver and the gold from Egypt. They despoiled them not as a result of their lusts but by God's will and authority, inasmuch as He did the taking away and despoiled Egypt by issuing instruction that they should receive a loan and depart. "Because they owe you wages," He said, "for your labors of so many years. You have served gratis, and they have repaid you nothing. Therefore I am repaying you, and I am taking away from them what has been torn from you and retained and am paying it back to you as a debt."

This is a picture of all the blessings which God confers on the church to nourish and sustain it. Lazarus suffers hunger at the door of the rich feaster. So the church is afflicted in the world and suffers want. Godly pastors with their wives and children suffer hunger or, if they have anything, the envy and malice of men is so great that they want to wrest it from them by fair means or foul and often also, when they can do it with a show of right, they rob and plunder the ministers and the ecclesiastical revenues in the parishes in such a way that it can truly be said: "Whatever the church has it has in spite of Satan's and the world's disapproval, opposition through violence, and hindrance through stratagems and fraud." What the church has are the spoils, as it were, that God tears away from the world because the burghers and peasants do not deserve to have liberal hands to cherish and nourish the ministry of the churches and schools, but whatever good they confer are spoils, as it were, which God has torn from the jaws of wolves and the claws of lions.

We see how unworthily and shabbily the parishes are treated by the magistrates and the tax collectors. When they complain about their need and poverty, men immediately reproach them with avarice, saying: "The parsons are greedy!" And if there are any at the courts and in the cities who devise new ways of plundering the parishes and of harassing the priests, they are praised for their thriftiness and are rewarded with offices only because of their ability to censure and oppress the ministers of the church. If the rich are admonished to subsidize the education of students, it takes work and toil. To be sure, there is need of the eloquence of Pericles to relieve them even of a little, and even this is offered with much ill grace, great displeasure, and disdain. Therefore we have rightly stated that we live from plunder, or spoils, of which God despoils the world against its will and resistance. For it is not worthy of contributing any support to nourish the poor, afflicted church.

At this time, indeed, we are experiencing the liberality of certain princes who voluntarily supply what they can, as, for example, the illustrious prince John Frederick, duke and elector of Saxony, does.[10] But even in this state as well as in others there are a large number of harpies, namely, officials and tax collectors whose envy and ill will is such that only with the greatest difficulty can you force from their hands what has been contributed for the support of the ministers of the church by the open hand of the prince. We simply live from spoils not derived from our greed but from God's kindness and liberality, inasmuch as He in a wonderful manner takes things away from the hands of the harpies so that the churches and schools may be preserved and their ministers do not perish from hunger and lack of food. These then are divine seizures and spoliations, as these matrons state concerning their possessions in this passage.

But he who wishes to become rich from the ministry of the church should not censure or scold the vices of the mob or of the magnates and tax collectors, but he should deal lightly with them, flatter their greed, and say what pleases them. But sincere teachers serving the church or schools with good and pious zeal are hated and scorned by all, nor will they ever make money, because the Labanites are not liberal with their own property or anybody else's.

Often one Abimelech nourishes an Abraham or an Isaac, as we have heard above (cf. chapters 20; 21; 26), but all the others are enemies of the church. Often also a land has one or two good and pious tax collectors, but the rest are Labanites to whom parishes and ministers seem unworthy of living even one hour or of eating one morsel of bread. Nor do they conceal their opinions but openly state that villages and cities could not do without a swineherd or a shepherd or an executioner, but that there is no need for a parson or a schoolmaster. At the present time, therefore, many good men are suffering harsh treatment from these harpies. For often they extort their income from those in charge of the ecclesiastical revenues only with much toil, inasmuch as the harpies pay out grudgingly even what they themselves have not contributed. Therefore we must learn to endure these

10 John Frederick was elector of Saxony from 1532 to 1554.

wrongs and this envy with equanimity and to acknowledge the wonderful government of God, who pastures and nourishes us just as He
did Jacob when he was in the employ of Laban. Sometimes also He
gives us one godly tax collector or official who does some good, though
all the rest are envious and adverse.

Moses, therefore, relates how the two wives approved of Jacob's
opinion about the property that had been taken away from his greedy
father-in-law, how they approved of the deed itself, and how they
encouraged their husband to proceed. "Whatever God has said to
you, do!" they say. It also came about by the special kindness of God
for Jacob's consolation that he had the consent of his dear wives, who
had no other support left to them except their one husband and who
had been treated by their father in such a way that they desired nothing more than to leave their father's house. Their wishes and feelings
towards their cruel father are in agreement, and they are happy that
they have been offered an opportunity to depart. "Dear Jacob," they
said, "we have seen your wretched servitude for a long time already
and have wished that you would take us away much sooner. For we
are certain that God is with you and that what you have spoken are
the words and commands of God. Therefore, as soon as you can, follow the orders of God."

However, as I stated before, it is a very dangerous matter to leave
the father-in-law's home and to take away the wives with the sons and
flocks if the tryant is unwilling. Nor, to be sure, would Jacob ever
have dared to do this if he would not have had the Word, although
previously also he perhaps took counsel with his wives how they might
be liberated from this captivity and prison. For when he saw the
agreement being changed so often by Laban, the fear entered his
mind that sometime later he might find cause or a pretext to despoil
him of all of his property, as Jacob will indicate below when he says
(v. 42): "You would have sent me off naked." For as envious and
greedy men are accustomed to do, Laban undoubtedly often thought
to himself: "I see that he is becoming rich and prosperous against my
will, and this in some secret and wonderful manner. Something must
be thought up whereby I may reduce him to his former servitude and
claim these flocks for myself."

Because of Laban's boundless lust for plunder Jacob undertakes
his departure from this prison not without great danger, especially
with such a large household and the large quantity of baggage he
takes with him. But he dares it in the name of the Lord, and his wives

consent for the sake of the Word. For the Lord has said: "I have seen what wrongs Laban has done to you, but I have collected all your tears in a sack (Ps. 56:8). Therefore depart under My orders and protection."

Jacob could safely rely on this consolation and trust it; otherwise this was difficult and dangerous for human counsel or judgment. For when Laban pursued him, he could not only have taken away all his property but also have demanded a penalty from him for abducting his daughters secretly. But the command of God breaks through everything and brings it to pass that the wives follow him in all readiness, together with all the baggage. Indeed, later Laban will rage and pursue him for seven days, but in vain. Jacob takes with him the divine spoils. Therefore his departure and the whole journey is good and holy.

17. *So Jacob arose and set his sons and his wives on camels,*

18. *and he drove away all his cattle, all his goods which he had gained in Mesopotamia, to go to the land of Canaan to his father Isaac.*

Again the text confirms that this plundering was truly divine and a reward owed for the toils of Jacob. For he does not call it spoils, theft, or rapine, but he calls it goods, or possessions, clothing, gold, silver, flocks. "All this is yours," the wives said; "it is spoil given to you by God which you are tearing away from the jaws of greedy Cerberus in the manner of theft and plunder, although it is your own substance."

The text adds: "to go to his father," as though it meant to say: "He did not plan to run away like a kidnapper, thief, or robber, but he was undertaking a legitimate journey to his father Isaac, where he could live in greater safety and render an account of his journey and his goods to all men, whether Laban or others, who wanted to drag him into court and accuse him of theft, if, indeed, it seemed unjust to depart in secret and to withdraw all his property unbeknown to Laban."

Thus we, too, can enjoy the spoils of the world with a good conscience, although we must snatch our food from the claws of harpies, the world, and the devil. For they hate us and say that they have no need for pastors and ministers. But God says to the contrary: "I have need of the church, and you are My ministers. Therefore endure wrongs and tyranny for My sake. I will take care to distribute some

spoils among you; I will give you a good prince to offer you lodging.
I shall not give you the world as I have given it to the Turk, and likewise to the Epicureans and usurers, before whom I must set the wealth
of the world and whom I must fatten for the eternal fire. But to you
I shall give a small portion which will be like spoils. If it involves you
in great trouble and toil, consider that I have torn it away from the
world like the possessions of Jacob and the spoils of the Egyptians." [11]

19. *Laban had gone to shear his sheep.*

It is to be observed carefully that Jacob does not tempt God but
seizes an advantageous occasion to avoid the offenses which he could
escape. For dangers are not to be invited but avoided. Although we
have the Word of God on which we can and should safely rely, nevertheless, of itself it loads us with many great dangers, and so other
unnecessary dangers are not to be invited. Nor should we snore in
ease and smugness, but natural wisdom and industry should be used,
and likewise human counsels and help, so that we do not seem to
tempt God.

Jacob could have said: "I have the Word and the command of God.
Therefore I shall go forth from this house and care nothing about
Laban's fury and indignation. But under his very eyes, and while he
is in a rage, I shall leave his house and take along his daughters with
all of my property." This would have been rashness and unnecessary
presumption and tempting God. If, therefore, you have the Word,
you do well when you obey it. But prepare yourself to use those
things which are at hand, according to the Word. Thus Jacob has the
command about leaving this land and returning to his fatherland.
He also has the promise concerning God's protection, that he should
not fear, however great the dangers would be and however varied
the difficulties that would be thrown in his way, concerning which
mention will be made below. Nevertheless, he waits for an opportunity and a time when Laban is a three days' journey from home to
shear his sheep. He argued as follows: "During these three days he
will not be able to reach me, nor will he easily make the discovery
that I have left. In the meantime, I shall complete so much of the
journey that he cannot reach us on the first or the second day and
cause a disturbance." So Jacob seized a very fine opportunity with
singular prudence and wisdom. For so God has given us reason and

[11] On "the spoils of the Egyptians," see Augustine, *De doctrina Christiana,*
II, 42, 63, *Patrologia, Series Latina,* XXXIV, 64—66.

all creatures and all our temporal blessings to serve our uses. The man who wants to travel will require provisions for his journey from which he may secure food and lodging for himself. But he would act very foolishly if he thought that he had no need of money or food and that everything would be offered him on all sides by the providence of God. God has created all things that are necessary for this life not that you should expect them from Him directly but that you should enjoy those things that are at hand and in the order which He Himself has prescribed. By no means therefore should the use and the ministry of creatures be despised since, indeed, God has created them to serve us.

And Rachel stole her father's household gods.

This is another crime. Rachel steals the תְּרָפִים from her father. But please behold the ingenuity of the woman! She argued as follows: "Everything we possess has been violently taken away from us and retained by our father, and now it has been torn away from him by God as though it were spoils and handed over to us. Therefore it is permissible to take away all that he still owes us. But to me as the lawful bride he should have given some golden or silver ornament. But because he has not given it, I shall take secretly what he should have given of his own accord and by every right."

In the first place, the holy women and Jacob sinned gravely against the Fourth Commandment by accusing their father and father-in-law of neglecting the duty of love towards his daughters. This was a very hard charge, and Moses himself in a way seems to be in conflict with himself, since he says in the Fourth Commandment that parents should be honored and also that their eccentricities and weaknesses should be endured. But in this place he relates an example of the patriarch Jacob and his daughters that is plainly contrary. They seem to have forgotten all respect for their father inasmuch as they show themselves so hard and ill-disposed towards their father in their vehement and fierce accusation.

The second sin is that Rachel steals her father's תְּרָפִים. The Holy Spirit does not shrink from the word steal but clearly says that Rachel, a holy woman and wife of a holy man, while believing God's Word and exhorting her husband to depart according to it, stole the תְּרָפִים. He does not simply say: "She took away, removed" but "she stole" contrary to the Seventh Commandment: "You shall not steal" (Ex. 20:15). But if it is not permitted to steal from a neighbor or a stranger,

how much less from a father? And she steals what her father considered most precious and dear at his house, the gods which he worshiped.

Although it has been previously stated that much weakness adheres
to all the saints, which I do not like to excuse, yet it must be added that
Rachel's father ceased to be a father because of every kind of cruelty
and tyranny. For he regarded his daughters as outsiders and deceived
his son-in-law so often and, indeed, thought of keeping his son-in-law
and daughters in perpetual servitude. Therefore Rachel had a very
just cause by civil and natural law for seizing the תְּרָפִים, as has also
been stated above concerning Jacob. But there is also the First Table,
which establishes degrees between the commandments relating to
God and those of obedience in accordance with Christ's statement
(Matt. 10:37): "He who loves father or mother more than Me is not
worthy of Me." Accordingly, Jacob and Rachel are righteous not only
by virtue of the Second Table but also by virtue of the First Table.
For when obedience is to be rendered to God in the Second Table,
then obedience to parents and the obligation to all precepts ceases.
Much more is this so when the authority of the First Table is involved,
that is, when God orders something by a new word. Thus the saintly
people had a word of God announced through the angel, and Rachel
and Leah rely on it when they say: "All the property which God has
taken away from our father belongs to us and to our children" (v. 16)
and "Do according to the word which God spoke to you when He
testified through the angel that He knew all that Laban did to you."

Moses, moreover, says in the blessing of Levi in Deut. 33:9: "Who
said of his father and mother, 'I regard you not' . . . they observed
Thy Word and kept Thy covenant," that is, he who wants to serve
God is not obliged to obey the precept of the Decalog concerning the
honoring of parents. What is this? Why then does Moses make this
law if in another place he ordains the opposite? For these matters are
diametrically opposed and are real ἀντιλογίαι ("contradictions"). The
answer is that when the First Table gives instructions concerning the
worship of God and obedience to Him then the Second Table must
yield, and one must say to father and mother: "I do not know you;
I do not obey you." Men complain that in this way political and
domestic obedience is destroyed, and for this reason the Gospel gets
such a bad hearing [12] and is called a seditious doctrine, just as the

---

[12] The original text has *audit,* but we have read *auditur.*

title of the cross of Christ indicated (John 19:19): "Jesus of Nazareth, the King of the Jews," that is, a seditious King. In the same manner also, the doctrine concerning this King is called seditious and contrary to the Second Table, because it says that obedience should not be rendered to the magistrate and parents and, indeed, gives orders to speak ill of them, just as Rachel says of her father: "He is our foe and our enemy." What could be said that is more seditious? Or, "I shall not obey the magistrate, parents, etc."? What dissipation and confusion in all things will arise from this?

I reply that the obedience which God enjoins in the Second Table must certainly be shown, but there are degrees of rendering obedience and careful regard for them must be maintained. For if the First and Second Table come into conflict, the simple and correct method is that by which the Second is ordered to yield to the First, for God is the Creator, the Head, and the Lord of father and mother, the state, and the home. All these must be subject to the Creator. And when the question is asked, which of the two should be abandoned, the Creator or the creature, I reply that the creature should be abandoned. For the First Table takes precedence, and when it has been obeyed, then also the Second Table has its place; then you should obey your parents and bear and suffer wrongs from them, "but for Me," says God, "not against Me and against the First Table."

Therefore the simple and plain reply about Rachel's theft is that the First Table repeals the Second Table. It is rightly enjoined in the Second Table: "You shall not kill" (Ex. 20:13). But if the First Table orders killing, the commandment of the Second Table yields. So also the Seventh Commandment about not stealing becomes invalid when God orders you to take what is your father's. So also the Eighth Commandment prohibits the desire to curse and defame, especially in the case of parents, but the rights of the First Table must be preserved. For if it orders these things, you should hate and rebuke parents, as Rachel does.

This distinction is necessary and very useful. It often happens that the heretics abuse it and boast that they have the First Table and under this pretext abolish the Second Table. Here there is need of careful judgment. For in this way the pope also boasts that he has the First Table and argues from this that no one is bound to obey the magistrate but that all owe obedience to the Roman see, to which even emperors and kings are necessarily subject. But see whether he teaches the First Table correctly and for what reason he cancels the Second

Table! For in regard to the monastic profession they said that one should run to Christ, disregarding and scorning parents; the spiritual fathers should be listened to. There is extant, for example, a word of Jerome: "If your father and mother met you as you were about to enter the monastery and they showed you her breasts and wanted to draw you back by their tears, despise the tears and trample your parents under foot; flee naked to the cross of Christ." [13]

This is an ungodly and diabolical word, because they abused sound doctrine to establish monasticism and the doctrines of demons (1 Tim. 4:1). The matter itself and the doctrine is quite true, but see that you are a good dialectician and that you distinguish rightly between the First and the Second Table. Likewise you should see if monasticism is truly a divine matter, or God's cause, for which the Second Table should be canceled. If it is a matter, or cause, of God, then it is rightly stated: "Trample a mother's breasts under foot; despise her tears." But if not, remember that obedience should be shown by you with all reverence and that likewise their faults and infirmities should be endured, provided only that they are not in conflict with the First Table. Rachel had the First Table on her side, for she was called by the Word of God to leave her father's house. Her father sins not only against the Second Table but also against the First, for he is an idolater. All things that he has done hitherto he has not only done with infinite cupidity and greed, but he has also sinned by idolatry, and these two are the most serious sins of all. For although greed of itself is idolatry, there was still the additional worship of the idols, or תְּרָפִים.

Rachel therefore prudently concluded (she was a woman of about 50 years of age): "In accordance with the First and Second Table I am called to leave; accordingly, I have the Word of God. My father is sinning against both, because he is an idolater and a greedy man. For up till now he has not given me a farthing of those things which he should have given me by every right, human and divine. He owes me wages and gifts even by virtue of the Second Table, and not only of the First, because I am his daughter. Accordingly, I shall steal something, yes, something that is going to cause his idolatry some difficulty; I shall steal the תְּרָפִים. He is too grasping and mean to cast other images readily. Therefore, in regard to the First Table, I shall act rightly in taking away idols and in overthrowing false worship,

---

[13] Cf. *Luther's Works,* 4, p. 181, n. 80, for one example of such language in Jerome.

and in regard to the Second Table, I shall be exercising forethought for myself in carrying off what was owed to me by every right." Holy Scripture, however, calls it a theft, just as Christ mentions hatred of father and mother (Luke 14:26): "He who does not hate father or mother . . . or his own life, etc.," which is forbidden in the Law, although this is not really hatred.

In the Second Table it is rightly stated: "You must not hate another, neither hate or kill yourself." But in the First Table God commands: "I order you to hate your life contrary to the command of the Second Table, where I have enjoined that you should love yourself." So also murder is prohibited in the Fifth Commandment, but God orders the magistrate to use the sword in the First Table, saying, "Vengeance is Mine, I will repay" (Rom. 12:19; cf. Deut. 32:35). The magistrate, therefore, kills not by virtue of the Second Table but by virtue of the First Table, nor is his killing unjust, although it is really homicide. Thus this is called theft, or robbery, because it has reference to Laban and the Second Table, but in accordance with the First Table, it is a just and permissible work and a reward due him. It is called theft because Laban regards it as theft. We are not able to change the name, for Holy Scripture speaks in this way. So also robbing the Egyptians is robbery in accordance with the Second Table and as far as the Egyptians are concerned. But in accordance with the First Table it is a debt. Rachel, therefore, did not steal, but she secretly recovered wages that were owed to her.

However, there is need of careful distinction and accurate logic so that we do not confound these things, or, as the pope and the fanatics do, abuse this distinction. For they, with great danger to the church and state, arrogate the First Table to themselves, although they despise it and really trample it underfoot. But they want to take advantage of it, so that under this pretext they may dissolve all precepts and laws of obedience, those of magistrates as well as those of parents. The pope bellows: "I am the teacher and head of the church; therefore I should be obeyed. I am in the First Table; therefore I dissolve everything that belongs to the Second Table."

But here there is need of accurate judgment so that the distinction is correctly applied and the commandments and teaching of the pope are weighed in accordance with the true meaning of the commandments of the First Table. For I, too, teach that our prince does not have to obey the emperor, and I absolve him from obedience not only to the pope but also from obedience to the whole empire and the emperor. But by what right? Here it is necessary for me to see that I rightly define and distinguish obedience. I do it by this right, namely, because the emperor and pope give orders and issue instructions contrary to the First Table. Therefore neither the prince nor the people are bound to obey commandments contrary to their obedience to God. The pope also absolves men from obedience to the emperor, and he has often removed emperors from their realms and empires. Why? "Because they do not obey me," he says. "I sit in the First Table!" But he is a hypocrite who misunderstands and perverts the teaching of the First Table, and he falsely arrogates to himself what he does not have. But we rightly absolve, because the emperor and the pope do not embrace the Word of God but enjoin those things which are diametrically opposed to the Word. Therefore we teach that this obedience should be abhorred. But it is necessary to learn to distinguish rightly between the Word of God, by which God is worshiped directly, and human obedience, such as obedience to parents, teachers, masters, and magistrates. For these are creatures, but the church has no other teacher but God, and therefore it has no other obedience. Accordingly, when the Creator says directly: "Render this to Me, obey Me alone, regard Me as God, and believe in Christ and hear Him," then no one else should be heard. When you have heard this, only then descend to the obedience of creatures and obey your parents and the magistrate, and these acts of obedience cease when worship must be offered to the Creator. But they remain firm and intact after satisfaction has been rendered to the Creator.

In this manner, the despoiling, or theft, of Rachel retains this name in the Second Table, but in the First Table it is a very just recompense of works. And yet it is the same matter. The vengeance of the magistrate is murder in the Second Table; in the First Table it is justice. Disobedience towards parents and speaking ill of them is rebellion in the Second Table, but it is respect and worship in the First Table. The logic of the Holy Spirit teaches this distinction. Careful attention must be paid to it so that we may truly have the Word of God and not the traditions of men under the appearance and pretext of the Word, as the pope has imposed on the whole world and has regarded the rule over the world as subject to his tyranny.

Accordingly, all depends on this, that we have preachers, or teachers, and students who learn these things. We must pray to God to give us pastors such as He has hitherto given us, who teach this distinction clearly and rule by the light of the Word. For what is the world if it lacks this heavenly and spiritual light which we have from theology? The teaching of the jurists and physicians has its place, and it is excellent, necessary, and very profitable. But if all are given to these studies, where will that heavenly light remain when scholars and students of theology are lacking? Of what benefit are gold, silver, good health, and for that matter, this whole life if this lamp of the Word has become extinct? And yet it is now fostered by few, although it really has need of the diligence and interest of very many and although it is retained only with difficulty, for the devil and the world hate it. Thus Jacob is a star which shone in the house of Laban because of his knowledge and study of the Word, but we see how he is treated by Laban. But the whole world is in darkness and horrible blindness without this lamp. What is the pope, what is the Turk without this light? They are certainly rich, wise, and powerful, but because they are destitute of the light of life, they are most unfortunate.

Therefore let us study and carefully exercise ourselves in theology; let us preserve our schools and parishes, for this is the highest worship of God in the whole world. If things are bad, and if we must steal, let us steal in the name of the Lord! If it is necessary to take away from an ungrateful world by robbery the rewards owed to us, yes, our food and the things necessary for this life, it is the robbery and liberation of those things which belong to us. Let Laban and Nabal eat the rest; let him have a good year! We live on spoils which are nevertheless not spoils in the First Table, although the burghers and peasants think that they are giving us these things as though we were thieves and robbers. But let us not worry about these judgments but rather be satisfied with what Paul says in Phil. 2:15-16: "That you may be blameless and innocent, children of God without blemish in the midst of a crooked and perverse generation, among whom you shine as lights in the world, holding fast the Word of life." Let each one in his place be eager to advance the teaching and study of the Word for his own salvation and the glory of God and let him regard as a blessing those all too slender spoils by which God wants us to be supported in this life. For if the light of the Word is destroyed, then all will again be wrapped in the horrible darkness of the Turk or the pope or other heretics.

This is what is to be said about the theft of the תְּרָפִים, which the excellent woman Rachel seized as a reward, as it were, for her service or in place of her due inheritance. For she had no further hope of having even a small portion of the goods of her father with the good will of her father. Accordingly, that she might not leave her father's house empty and devoid of her whole inheritance, she takes with her the golden idols, because there was no longer anything human about Laban, but he was a rapacious beast who had plundered his son-in-law and daughters in a most unjust manner. Hence it was not unjust for him to be despoiled in turn by the rightful owners and heirs. Rachel, moreover, acted without the knowledge of her husband Jacob, as will become evident below. It is likely that he would hardly have permitted this if he had known it. But she dares it in reliance on the Word and her services towards her father, whom she had served for 14 years, although she was already married. For this reason it would have been fair for him to reward her liberally. Furthermore, something must be said about a grammatical question which is stirred up in this passage. This is the first passage in which the word תְּרָפִים is used. It is certain that it signifies idols, because Laban was an idolater. It is a strange thing, however, that Jacob, a holy man, with his holy wives and his whole church dwelt in an idolatrous house. In that house, therefore, there were at the same time God and the devil, sons of God and sons of the devil, as often happens. The whole world even now consists of sons of God and sons of the devil, just as Cain and Abel were joined together in Adam's home, Ishmael and Isaac in Abraham's home, and Esau and Jacob in Isaac's home. And so to the end of the world the false church will be joined to the true church, and false brethren to godly and sincere brethren. We today teach the Gospel purely and faithfully, but we have an admixture of usurers, papists, heretics, and sectarians, for the tares always remain mixed with the wheat (cf. Matt. 13:25); it cannot be otherwise in the world. At that time Jacob scrupulously taught the heavenly doctrine and the promises concerning the Messiah; this his wives and his household embraced, and it is credible that some were also converted from idolatry to the true worship of God. But the church of Jacob was in an ungodly and idolatrous home.

The Jews, however, talk much nonsense about the word תְּרָפִים. We shall touch on this briefly that we may not seem to have been ignorant of their madness. Lyra describes תְּרָפִים as having been the head of a firstborn boy who had been killed and sacrificed to a demon.[14] It was preserved in salt and spices so that it should not decay, and

---

14 Lyra *ad* Gen. 31:19, p. 94 recto, note "o."

under its tongue it had a golden plate on which was written the name of the demon from whom oracular responses were sought. He uses the same interpretation in regard to Micah in Judg. 17:3. But I do not believe any of these things. For תְּרָפִים is a common word in Holy Scripture, and the interpretation must be taken from other passages as, for example, in the history of the Kings in regard to Michal, who placed תְּרָפִים in the bed in place of David, namely, an image, adding a pillow of goat's hair (cf. 1 Sam. 19:13) to represent the image of a man lying sick in bed. Here it cannot be taken as the head of a boy, but it was the image of a man placed in bed instead of David.

Likewise in Hosea 3:4 it is stated: "The children of Israel shall dwell many days without king or prince, without sacrifice or pillar, without אֵפוֹד or תְּרָפִים." Here it does not seem fitting if you translate תְּרָפִים as idols, as though the people of God had had idols. But whatever it is, in my judgment and according to grammar the word seems to indicate in general a similitude or image of divine worship, whether true or false. Laban had idolatrous images. But Hosea seems to have included all symbols of divine worship, namely, the tabernacle, the table, the veil, the candelabrum, and the bread of the Presence, etc., all of which they lacked in the exile and in the captivity. Therefore, as the heathen call their idols by this name, so Hosea applies it to the furniture of the tabernacle, for it makes no sense that the prophet considers it punishment that they will dwell without idols. But he wants the sacred furniture, such as we have mentioned previously, to be understood, so that it signifies in general a certain image of formal worship in signs and symbols.

But the statue which Michal placed in the bed in place of David, I think, was an image which had been preserved somewhere from among the relics of superstition and idolatry. Among us, too, many statues are left which are preserved in one place in memory of the old idolatry, in another place as exhibits and objects of amusement for children, not for worship. In David's time such idols lay hidden away in the corners of buildings. Now when Michal had nothing else at hand, she quickly pulled out the statue and put it in David's place. Undoubtedly, there remained even at that time many vestiges of superstitions and idolatries from the kingdom and religion of the Jebusites as well as cries that could not be completely abolished. Of this the worried complaints of many of the psalms testify, in which David with great grief prays and fights against idolatry.

Concerning the city of Lachish Micah says that it was the beginning of the sin of the daughter of Zion and that the transgressions of Israel were found in it, so that even among the people of God idols could never be completely destroyed (cf. Micah 1:13). Indeed, look also at the time of Moses in the desert! Concerning this Amos and Stephen in Acts declare: "Did you offer to Me slain beasts and sacrifices forty years in the wilderness, O house of Israel? And you took up Sakkuth, your king, and Kaiwan, your idol" (cf. Amos 5:25-26; Acts 7:42-43). It is certainly strange that this should be stated of the people under Moses. On the contrary, however, Balaam says in Num. 23:23: "There is no enchantment against Jacob, no divination against Israel." But this is said by the synecdoche common in Scripture.

For the wheat of the church has always been mixed with tares. But it is sufficient that in David's time the kingdom and the ministry were pure and that both were so constituted that nothing ungodly or idolatrous was taught or commanded. Likewise in the desert under Moses the doctrine was pure and the magistracy was holy, ordaining nothing but holy things, without any ungodliness or idolatry, so that Balaam would have been correct in saying (Num. 23:23): "There is no divination against Israel" and likewise (Num. 24:5): "How fair are your tents, O Jacob, your encampments, O Israel." But that there were remnants and certain vestiges of idolatry among some there is no doubt.

In the same manner, when the pastor of our church [15] teaches rightly and fights against idolatry and likewise censures the faults of men, I can truly say: "There is no idol or ungodliness in Wittenberg." The church is therefore holy because the ministry is pure and the civil magistrate does not order or defend idolatrous practices. Duke George,[16] for example, ordered the papal religion to be preserved in his land, and he had obsequious pastors. The church was not true and pure there, but where there is a church in which the heavenly doctrine is purely taught and the magistrate does not oppose sound doctrine, there the tabernacles of Jacob are pure and beautiful. The body of itself is sound, firm, and strong, but it is not lacking in filth, matter, ulcers, spittle, and excrement. Still it is said to be sound by synecdoche. In the same manner תְּרָפִים remain in the world, yes, in

---

[15] The pastor of the church at Wittenberg was Johannes Bugenhagen (1485 to 1558), often called "Pomeranus."

[16] George "the Bearded" had been duke of Albertine Saxony until his death in 1539.

the church and the home of Jacob right up to the end. So much about the meaning of the word.

Furthermore, there are disputes about the etymology.[17] For some derive the word from רָפָא with א, some from רָפָה with ה. The former word means to heal or cure, and from this is derived רְפָאִים, "giants," "doctors," as though you were to say "helpers," or "saviors," that is, "gods." The latter word means to cease, to be unoccupied. It seems to me that תְּרָפִים is more correctly derived from this word, from the idea of being unoccupied, and that it alludes to the Sabbath, or to worship, because they had to be still, serve God, and keep the Sabbath, as is stated in Psalm 46:10: "Be still and know," that is, "listen to Me, leave your work, stop, and let Me have My way." So also those idols had their sabbaths and celebrations, and from this celebration they were called תְּרָפִים, for celebrations had to be held for them.

20. *And Jacob stole the heart of Laban the Syrian in that he did not tell him that he intended to flee.*

This is another crime and a far more serious theft than Rachel's, for Jacob did not steal Laban's idols or his goods but his heart. But to "steal the heart" is an idiom of the Hebrew language for frustrating and deceiving a hope that has been conceived, to make all plans useless and idle without any hope of gaining those things which you have tossed about in your mind. For Laban came to the following conclusion: "I have a son-in-law and daughters and grandsons and maidservants. By their effort I shall become quite rich. For they are subject to me by every right, and they shall increase my household property. Their faithfulness is evident. For Jacob is good and honest and will do me no wrong, nor will he find it easy to change his condition against my will and knowledge, and it will not be safe for him to do this. But if he steals anything or inflicts a loss, then I shall find special cause to keep them bound to me in perpetual servitude."

These are the magnificent hopes and thoughts of Laban, his very cunning and, in his own judgment, very sure plans. But in one moment they are suddenly confounded, and they vanish. Holy Scripture calls this "stealing the heart," that is, to make hope vain no matter how sure and without any doubt it may be, even while the heart is unaware of it. Laban feared no such thing but without doubt promised himself that Jacob would remain and that he could set in motion anything

[17] Lyra *ad* Gen. 31:19, p. 95 recto, "Additio."

rather than his departure. Yet Jacob withdrew in secret, not without great loss and much displeasure on Laban's part. On this account Laban will weave a long series and catalog of the worst villanies, as we shall hear below.

21. *He fled with all that he had and arose and crossed the river and set his face toward the hill country of Gilead.*

It should be carefully noted that Holy Scripture calls all the actions of Jacob by the names of the greatest crimes and vices. Previously it was stated that Jacob stole the heart of Laban the Syrian. Here it says that he fled without his father-in-law's knowledge and contrary to his will, taking along his substance and disappointing every expectation about a perpetual servitude. All these acts are referred to with the terminology of crimes, as Laban a little later will enlarge on them in rhetorical fashion. As Christ speaks of "hatred" of one's own mother and father, which is the name of an offense, even though it is the highest virtue (cf. Luke 14:26), so this act is not really a theft, but Holy Scripture speaks in the manner of men, who habitually make such an inference about acts of this kind. In the ears of Laban it is theft and desertion, but by divine law and justice it is regarded as a reward and wages due by virtue of the highest law. So also he who hates father and mother for Christ's sake does not hate them but loves them, as he who denies himself and loses his own life finds it.

The river of which mention is made here is the Euphrates, dividing Mesopotamia from the land of promise. Jacob, accordingly, reaches the point that he is now crossing the Euphrates, being confirmed in the strong hope that Laban cannot any longer overtake him and his family. But greed is a restless, indefatigable, rapacious, and eager monster, and it does not allow Laban to rest. But after Jacob has crossed the river, he travels on [18] to Mount Gilead.

22. *When it was told Laban on the third day that Jacob had fled,*

23. *he took his kinsmen with him and pursued him for seven days and followed close after him into the hill country of Gilead.*

24. *But God came to Laban the Syrian in a dream by night and said to him: Take heed that you say not a word vehemently to Jacob.*

In this place Moses only touches on the pursuit of Laban in passing; he will deal with it more fully later. Laban is raging, and his

[18] The Weimar text has *perro*, but we have read *porro*.

wrath is seething, and in his heart he is collecting a mountain of the worst shameful and criminal acts of Jacob. "Now it is clear," he thinks, "what kind of man he is. Now I have him caught and enmeshed in his own crime. This is a perfectly just reason to drag him back with all his goods and his whole family and to bind his faithfulness to me with an oath in perpetual slavery. For he is a plunderer, a thief, a kidnapper, a cattle stealer, a temple robber, and a traitor; and each of these crimes is worthy of eternal imprisonment and torment."

Thus Laban's rage is burning, and he imagines the most righteous reasons for exacting punishment from this most outrageous of all scoundrels. He certainly would have raged against the excellent man in most cruel fashion had he been permitted to indulge his fury. But I stated above that Jacob departed by divine inspiration and a command delivered through an angel; otherwise it is a matter fraught with peril to run away without taking leave of any of the people in the whole household and in the whole land, and even against the will of the father-in-law, and to take along daughters, grandsons, and the whole flock at which Laban as well as his sons used to gaze greedily. Therefore, if God had not hindered these mad attempts, Jacob would have been treated in a shameful manner by these men.

These factors, then, must be weighed rather carefully, so that we may understand with what great rage Laban was inflamed and how greatly he desired to avenge this wrong. For many shameful sins are coming together, and we shall hear below how they are exaggerated by Laban in dramatic fashion. Perhaps he would have spared his life but only for his own gain, that he might have Jacob subject to himself throughout his whole life. However, this is an outstanding example by which we are taught how God can restrain the furious assaults of Satan and his members so that they may not rage according to their liking. For God breaks and restrains the angry mood of Laban in such a way that he does not even dare to murmur against Jacob.

This is set forth for our consolation that we may have a sure hope in the goodness and mercy of God, who, Paul says, is faithful and will not suffer us to be tempted above that which we are able to bear but along with the temptation give an end so that we are able to bear it (cf. 1 Cor. 10:13). God places a limit on temptation so that we are not tempted above our strength or beyond His will and counsel. The devil and Laban had definitely determined that Jacob had merited the death penalty. But they would have mitigated the punishment, but only under the condition that he with his whole family would have consigned himself to perpetual servitude. This servitude would have been more bitter than death itself. But while they are thinking about overwhelming Jacob, God is present and scatters their counsels and cruel attempts.

"You will by no means do this, Laban," He says; "no, not even a harsh or bitter word will you exchange with him." In this way He puts a limit on his rage, just as God says to Job concerning the billows and storms of the sea (cf. Job 38:10-11): "I prescribed bounds for it and set bars and doors and said, 'Thus far shall you come, and no farther, and here you shall dash to pieces your proud waves.'" For the sea swells when it is tossed by the wind and storms, and by its swirling billows it threatens the dike, as it were, or the shore surrounding it, just as though it were about to flow out over all the lands of the earth. "But I have set a limit for it," says God. So the shore does not fear the threats and the swelling of the sea.

In this way the devil rises up against the church and hurls dire threats at the godly and stirs up violence and destruction for them. But He who has set a limit for the sea calms also these billows so that Satan cannot rage according to his liking. In this manner God checks the whole force and fury of Laban's rage by one dream and renders him as quiet as a sheep, no matter how unwilling and loud he is. For God does not permit those who believe and have His Word to be afflicted and tempted beyond their strength. He is the faithful Guardian of those who guard and keep His Word. Jacob had the Word: "Depart and return to the land of your fathers," and likewise: "I have seen all that Laban has done to you." This Word he obeys, and he takes everything with him, although he seems to commit very serious sins. God moves the hearts of his wives to follow and obey their husband and the Word, yes, even to urge him to leave.

Persecution follows this obedience. The devil tries to drag him back and to tyrannize him with his whole family. And it stands to reason that Jacob with his wives was in great distress. For the thought undoubtedly occurred to Jacob: "Behold, Laban is pursuing you with the intention of killing and destroying you and taking away all your goods. How foolish I was to run away and conceal my plans! What reason shall I give him for my secret departure? It was unwise of me to throw myself and my family into this danger, etc."

This was an internal temptation, which tormented [19] his heart.

19 The Weimar text has *auxit* but we have read *anxit*.

Thus he was assailed outwardly by Laban and inwardly by thoughts of despair. His wives, as well as his maidservants and the whole household, felt the same temptation. "How much better it would have been," they said, "to remain in Mesopotamia than to perish wretchedly here or to be led back into our former servitude and a much more severe one. We certainly could have been content with our former condition; even if we would not have been permitted to abound in wealth, we would nevertheless have enjoyed peace and been without danger. It is a pity,[20] in one moment to lose life itself or this small property and all hope of liberty."

Such without a doubt were the thoughts that entered their minds. Moses, to be sure, did not express the feelings of their hearts, but he gave sufficient indication of them, because he says that God came to Laban the Syrian in a dream, etc. In the meantime, however, Jacob supported himself by the promises given to him by God, namely, that he had departed by God's command, and by the same promises he encouraged his household and wives, because God had appeared to him in Bethel and had said: "Return to the land of your birth." "Hold on, my dear wives and children, God will not desert us or cast us off," he said.

In this way Jacob struggled and overcame temptation by faith. For this is a contest of faith. In the time of peace, when he is free of temptation, he does good works; in the hour of temptation he cries out, yes, he roars with a loud cry, so that all the angels may clearly hear him. For he is brought down to hell and undergoes the perils of death. Here he begins to struggle and shout, and by this shouting both heaven and earth are taken by storm. Therefore God comes in dreams by night to Laban as he is considering most cruel plans in his heart, and He puts an end to the persecution. Then those threatening billows and furious storms in Laban's heart are calmed. For He said to him in a dream: "I see that you are raging and burning with wrath and that all your endeavors and thoughts are intent on this, that you may do violence to Jacob; you think that you have a perfectly just reason to persecute and tyrannize him. For in your judgment Jacob is the worst scoundrel alive. In your heart you have thought up a huge mass of accusations and charges to vomit out against him. But I order you not only to keep your hands off him but not to offend him even by a word."

[20] The Weimar text has *mirabile,* but we have followed the Erlangen text and read *miserabile.*

Thus God does not forsake believers, especially when they cry to Him in true faith. We, too, have very often experienced the wonderful goodness of God and His protection. How many and cruel counsels of kings, popes, and cardinals have been wondrously restrained, not by our strength or counsel but by God's might; for He has smitten them with terror so that they would not dare to do anything, or if they have dared to do something, He has thrown their counsels and endeavors into disorder.

Nine diets have been held since the time when the Gospel began to spring up again and to shine on Germany while our adversaries raged in horrible fashion and made dire threats.[21] Indeed, at Augsburg men openly declared that they were prepared to pledge their property and blood. And they would have swallowed us alive, as is stated in the psalm (cf. Ps. 124:3), had not God preserved us and made their counsels vain. How often we have seen an incendiary causing a commotion and stirring up the worst of troubles until he was thrown out of his land! They will also make more attempts in the future and will not rest until the Turk scatters them.

Let us therefore remember this example of the liberation of Jacob from Laban, his fierce and cruel foe, by means of the Word which he believed. For where the Word is, there faith is also; and where faith is, there is also a cry because of temptation. It is impossible for this cry not to be heard. Once heard, this cry breaks all the might of heaven and earth as well as that of all the gates of hell (cf. Matt. 16:18). Accordingly, that catalog of accusations which Laban gathered together is suddenly scattered. Indeed, Laban congratulated himself that he was warned by God only with words and not by some blow or cross because of the greed and envy towards his son-in-law of which he was conscious.

He was so terrified and stung by the danger of death that he did not again wish to devise danger for his son-in-law but desired to avoid the punishment and evil which he feared, although he was not improved by the warning. He was, indeed, astounded by the judgment of God, but he soon returned to character, as we shall hear. He restrained his hands from doing anything evil, but he did not abstain from cursings and revilings. It was a gallows repentance, or Judas repentance, just as the pontiffs and their satellites, the kings and princes, are held in check and hindered in their plans against us.

---

[21] See Introduction, p. ix.

"Their spirit is taken from them," as it says in the psalm (76:12), but they do not recover their senses. This is the repentance of hypocrites and unbelievers who repent like Laban or Esau. It is not serious or voluntary repentance; they are not changed for the better. But they are only frightened from their purpose so that they do not accomplish what they were trying to do.

I have stated elsewhere how dreams are to be distinguished.[22] True dreams bring impressions with them which move the hearts with terror and a certain consternation, as it were, so that they cannot be despised. Such were the dreams of Pharaoh and Nebuchadnezzar. But others are ἄσημα ("without a distinctive mark") and, so to say, vain hopes and imaginations that should be despised.

But let us apply the example before us for our doctrine and use. For it is set before us for this reason, that we may see that God is present with His own although they are wretched and weak. Laban is far more powerful than Jacob, who finds himself in the greatest of danger unarmed and poor. But Jacob has the Word. Accordingly, GOD and His host of angels are present with believing Jacob as he prays. For just as God led the patriarch out of his father's house, so He leads him back, employing the protection of the angels. In the same manner, if we believe the Word and adhere to it in firm and steadfast faith, He will also help us and set us free, even in the very midst of plague, death, and war. For it is impossible for the man who believes God's Word to be forsaken and not defended.

The following story about angels will bear very strong testimony to this same fact. For their power overcomes the strength of all enemies, as the example of the siege of Jerusalem under Sennacherib teaches. Christ says (Matt. 26:53): "Do you think that I cannot appeal to My Father, and He will at once send Me more than twelve legions of angels?" Accordingly, when we are under the protection of God, there is no doubt that we are also under the safekeeping and guardianship of the angels, who are present with those who are encountering dangers in life and who conduct the dead to the place of peace and rest. For David says (Ps. 91:11): "He will give His angels charge of you, etc.," and likewise (Ps. 34:7): "The angel of the Lord encamps around those who fear Him."

These things should admonish and stir us up gladly to hear and love the Word but even more gladly to believe the Word in this

---

[22] See *Luther's Works,* 3, pp. 10—12, and 5, 237—240.

confidence, that we are covered by the protection of the angels. So much about the commandment of God whereby Laban is forbidden to make any trouble for Jacob in word or deed. For this pronouncement of God throws into disorder the catalog of accusations Laban has gathered, as well as all his calculations. The Hebrew idiom puts it this way: "Do not speak with Jacob from good to evil," namely, "by beginning at the good and resorting to the evil." But Laban did not obey in all respects, although he was compelled to abstain from action. But the catalog is completely rejected. "Your cruel counsels and thoughts," said the voice of God, "are nothing but a mere dream, vanity, error, and lying, and so you must not indulge your fury." Yet he does not restrain himself from inveighing against Jacob with altercations and revilings. There follows a very bitter complaint.

25. *And Laban overtook Jacob. Now Jacob had pitched his tent in the hill country, and Laban with his kinsmen encamped in the hill country of Gilead.*

After the reproof and admonition which Laban had heard in the dream, namely, that he should not say anything harsh to Jacob, he still proceeded, even though all his counsels and fierce passions were confounded. Although he can do no harm, he adopts a posture of violence and rage by threatening harm. He does not want to appear frustrated in his counsels, nor does he want to depart without achieving anything. He thought it disgraceful for himself to boast in this way to no purpose and to breathe forth slaughter and empty threats (cf. Acts 9:1). So he puts on a show of great indignation as if he wanted to pursue his own purpose and disregard the divine will.

In short, this is an excellent picture of hypocritical and feigned repentance. In this way even the wicked are sometimes pricked in conscience, as they used to say formerly in the schools,[23] not that they are truly pricked or are seriously repentant, but they pretend repentance and grief for their sin. I also held this opinion at one time. Therefore David's word to Nathan (2 Sam. 12:13), "I have sinned," must be understood altogether differently than the word of Saul, who likewise said to Samuel (1 Sam. 15:24): "I have sinned." It is indeed the same word, the same voice and face of compunction or repentance, but the hearts are very different.

For the repentance of the wicked is such that they grieve more

---

[23] The verb is *compungere*, from which the English word "compunction" comes; see, for example, Thomas Aquinas, *Summa Theologica*, I-II, Q. 79, Art. 4.

about the prohibition of their evil desires and sins than about the mortification of their corrupt desires and sins. These are acts of repentance according to the Law, which we usually call the repentance of the gallows. For if he were free of the fear of the cross and punishment, the thief would much prefer to steal than to abstain from another's property. Therefore he grieves that he is restrained by the fear of punishment. In this way Laban is also described not as truly repentant nor as coming to his senses, but he grieves that by the power of God a curb has been placed on his lusts and furious passions. It is a superficial repentance, just as Saul says (1 Sam. 15: 30): "I have sinned; yet honor me now before the elders." He is concerned about a bad reputation and disgrace among the elders, not about the fact that he has offended God.

But a truly repentant heart is so affected that it dreads nothing else but the wrath and indignation of God, taking no account of disgrace among men, provided it knows that God is propitious, even as David expresses this feeling and sense of sin in Ps. 51. But it must be observed that hypocrites remain true to form and when they are not permitted to vent their anger according to their liking, they nevertheless make a show of their rage and special power, lest they seem inferior to those whom they hate and persecute.

Mount Gilead was not so named at that time, but by anticipation it is here called by the name given to it for the first time later. Now, Moses seems to indicate that Laban took possession of the top of the mountain but that Jacob pitched his tent at the bottom of the mountain, to the effect that the former made the point that he was the greater and the more powerful. But immediately a rhetorical exaggeration and a piling up of Jacob's sins follows.

26. *And Laban said to Jacob: What have you done, that you have stolen my heart and carried away my daughters like captives of the sword?*

27. *Why did you flee secretly and without my knowledge? And why did you not rather tell me, so that I might send you away with mirth and songs, with tambourines and lyres?*

28. *And why did you not permit me to kiss my sons and my daughters farewell? Now you have done foolishly.*

29. *It would be in my power to do you harm; but the God of your*
father spoke to me last night, saying: Take heed that you speak
no harsh word to Jacob.

30. *Granted that you desired to go to your own people and that you*
longed for your father's house, but why did you steal my gods?

If Laban had been truly repentant, he would have believed and
given his assent to the Word of God which pronounced Jacob righteous and innocent and therefore undeserving of suffering wrong.
For he hears that Jacob has been absolved by God from all the
crimes for which he was pursuing him. But to promote his own
glory and to defend his own righteousness, he finds fault with Jacob
that his own wrath might not seem to have been empty and without
strength and that Jacob in terror might confess his sin. This is what
the proud hypocrite and very cunning self-righteous man wanted.

First, therefore, he says: "What have you done to me?" as though
he meant to say: "All the things you have done are the worst sins;
you are guilty of the worst crimes, for which I could punish you
according to my righteousness and right." But he does not dare to
harm him; he only pretends a certain fortitude and an utterly empty
righteousness. Previously it was stated that he was a greedy man;
now we see a very proud hypocrite and self-righteous man being
described. But he was reminded by the Word of God in a dream
that Jacob was righteous and good. He does not acknowledge his own
sin or the virtues of Jacob, indeed, he even exaggerates the sins of
Jacob heavily, saying: "You have stolen my heart." This is really
an atrocious crime.

The first sin he invents is the crime of lese majesty. He says:
"I was your father and father-in-law; you were my servant. But you
forgot all respect and filial obedience and, indeed, all piety towards
me. You had the audacity to depart in such a disrespectful manner
without taking leave of me, your parent, father-in-law, and master,
and, in addition, you dared to take away my daughters like a robber,
a bandit, and a kidnapper." But Laban is lying most impudently. For
although Laban's heart had certainly been stolen, Jacob nevertheless
had just cause for fleeing in secret; otherwise he would not have
been able to obtain permission to withdraw from his greedy master.

The second lie is that he says: "You have carried away my daughters
like captives." Are they not his wives, whom you, Laban, betrothed
to him, and did this marriage not cost him a great deal? Is it a matter

of driving off by violence and sword when a husband takes with him his wife, who is obliged to follow him by every right and who consents of her own accord, too, and exhorts her husband to depart? You see, therefore, what a poisonous and diabolical tongue Laban has, one that glorifies and whitewashes his own sins and converts virtuous acts into slander. For the wicked hypocrite invents all this and puts together these lies to dishonor Jacob with his household and to exalt his own righteousness and glory. But when were they driven off or captured with the sword? When did Jacob drag them off like a thief or robber? Are they not lawful wives who were not dragged off but who followed their husband of their own accord and willingly, as they were bound to follow him?

Therefore it would have been fitting for Laban to say: "Since you wanted to leave my house, you did well because you did not desert your wives but took them with you. And although it is hard to bear that you stole my heart, nevertheless, I give you credit for this, that you wanted my daughters to be companions of your flight." This would have been a more honorable speech, worthy of a good man. But he is an impious hypocrite, and so he turns everything upside down, and what should have been praised and commended in his son-in-law he censures and reviles in a most hateful manner. But see whether he observes what had been commanded, namely, that he should not say anything harsh against Jacob. He heaps up carefully chosen poisonous insults and what is most disgraceful, false and fictitious ones. For he knows that they are Jacob's wives and that he had committed no sin by taking them away, especially since they followed him of their own accord. Indeed, he would have been in duty bound to compel them to accompany their husband if they had been unwilling.

Therefore he is a detestable hypocrite who with the most poisonous reproaches dares to burden and attack so great a man, a man equipped with such great virtues. Moreover, by saying: "Why did you want to flee from me in secret?" he repeats what he has already said: "You have stolen my heart." He cannot forget this wrong; this is eating his heart out. He does not grieve concerning the sin, which is nonexistent, because Jacob is righteous and holy, but this torments the man, that he could not detect the plan to depart by any sign or power of judgment. "Here you stole not only my heart," he says, "but me myself with all my goods." For Jacob had augmented his property with a great increase. It grieves him that this choice morsel has been snatched from his jaws, and he thinks: "If I had known it, I would have left nothing untried to detain you. For now my very well-being and the increase of all my goods is lost to me."

But now after he has vomited forth almost all his wrath and indignation by accusing Jacob in a most atrocious manner and by justifying himself, he proclaims his own love and good will both toward his son-in-law and toward his daughters to increase the unworthiness of the accused and makes a great show of love, kindness, and στοργή ("natural affection") toward the children. "I have loved you and my daughters so much," he says, "and honored you with whatever services I could that you can wish for nothing from me but have always felt that I am most friendly to you. So also now, after calling together all my friends and the inhabitants of this land, I would have sent you on your way in honor and splendor, with joy, with music, and with tambourines, etc." To be sure! For what would that joy and those tambourines have been? Shackles, chains, imprisonment, and perpetual servitude!

If Jacob had indicated that he was contemplating departure with his wives, he would never have been dismissed. For that is how Laban was accustomed to bless his friends, as has been stated [24] previously. He would have dragged him back into perpetual servitude and misery if God had not prevented it. He revealed his cruelty well enough when he changed Jacob's wages 10 times and compelled him to serve 14 years for his daughters and six years for the cattle without receiving due wages. Accordingly, if God had not restrained his cupidity, he would have defrauded his son-in-law of all his goods. These are the tambourines, the joy, and the lyres!

However, he relates all this to encumber the excellent and holy man Jacob and to embellish and cover up his own tyranny, cruelty, and avarice. These are unadulterated and most frivolous lies; in fact, the smoother his speech is, the more bitterness he has shut up in his heart, and the individual words are composed with special care to calumniate and censure the excellent virtues in Jacob. For how could he dismiss the man whom he wished to keep at his house even for a thousand years? And he was especially grieved that he was losing a faithful servant and one so suitable for the promotion of his own profits. This is what that stealing of the heart means.

He makes a further addition and replies as though to an implied objection: "You have not permitted me to kiss my daughters, etc., to

24 *Luther's Works*, 5, pp. 296—298.

let me know most emphatically that your wives have been my daughters, and yet you are to be censured, because you have deprived me of every courtesy of love and parenthood that I might have shown my children and grandchildren in accordance with my love and natural good will for them. For it is common practice according to the customs and usage of all nations that daughters who are about to leave their father's house take leave of their parents and claim kiss, embrace, and blessing from their father. This I had the hearty desire to do. They are your wives, it is true, and you had the power legally to take them with you, but you should have been influenced by my love and have let me first kiss my dear, dear daughters and grandchildren; you should not have taken them away so cruelly from the embrace and bosom of a fond parent." "That is the source of those tears." [25] O iron heart, that does not groan at them! This desperate scoundrel should have been pope or bishop of Mainz,[26] inasmuch as he can cover a most cruel heart with such pious and honorable talk! "For how would you kiss your daughters? With the kiss of Judas (cf. Matt. 26:49)! Or, if you wished to kiss your daughters and to show your paternal love to them, why did you not nourish them and clothe them and attend to them with due kindnesses when they still served you?" But no, at that time he took everything away and regarded them as strangers and sold them like captives. If they had not taken thought for their own interests by flight, they would have had to perish of hunger. Such was the love of this most dutiful, no, most cruel and detestable, father Laban. But now, when he sees that he is being accused of manifest lovelessness toward his daughters and that his son-in-law has been compelled to flee with his daughters because of his cruelty, he wants to cover his barbaric conduct by accusing his son-in-law of abducting his daughters against his will and without taking leave of him, not because he is moved with concern or love for them but to cover his greed. For the thing that troubles him is what he mentioned at the beginning, the theft of his heart, obviously his advantages and the growth of his property derived from the servitude of Jacob.

For what would the cruel tyrant do in the actual moment of the departure, when in the previous 20 years he has done nothing kind or worthy of paternal love? But if there had been left in him even a little drop of love or paternal good will, he would now have shown

[25] Terence, *Andria*, 126; cf. Horace, *Epistles*, I, 19, 41.
[26] A reference to Albert, Bishop of Mainz (1490—1545).

himself different. He would have forgotten all offenses and injuries
or spoken as follows: "Come, I acknowledge that you have been too
harshly treated by me and that you have received no gift or wages.
Therefore I now hand over to you and your children this part of
my flocks or of those treasures which I regard as most precious, rings
and golden ornaments. Let them be pledges to you of my perpetual
love and good will!"

But what would the greedy hypocrite give? We shall hear below
how he searches and examines everything and would gladly have
taken away even those things which they held from the spoils assigned them by God. In the meantime, however, he decks himself
out as though he were righteousness personified and a great lover
of his children but Jacob were ἄστοργος ("lacking in natural affection") and cruel toward his father-in-law. This is incredible and
unheard-of ill will, hypocrisy, and cruelty! Profane men and heathen,
who follow nature and reason as their guide, shrink from crimes of
this kind. It seems impossible that such great cruelty should befall
a human heart, that a man is rash enough not only to neglect his
daughters and grandchildren but even to deprive them of all the
kindnesses and advantages that are their due. Moreover, it is detestable hypocrisy and pretense that can cover such a great crime with
a beautiful show of kisses, embracing, and paternal love. For Laban
wanted to kiss and embrace them for this purpose, that he might clasp
and enclose them in bonds of perpetual servitude.

These, then, are the virtues of the excellent and saintly Laban, and,
on the other hand, the crimes and sins of Jacob which he reproaches
in him. For so it usually happens in the world. Righteous men are
regarded as sinners and vice versa. No one in the whole world is a sinner except the man who has the Word and believes in Christ. But
those who persecute and hate the Word are the righteous ones. As
Christ says (cf. John 16:2): "They think they are offering God a service." Now, it often happens that men ignorant of the Word hate and
persecute the saints. But Laban is not such a good man that he sins
in error; he knowingly persecutes a righteous man. Similarly, the cardinals, bishops, and others also knowingly rage against the godly, and
yet they want to be regarded as holy.

The last and most atrocious crime with which he charges his son-
in-law is the theft of the gods. Here behold extravagant and dramatic
exaggerations! "The things which I have recounted up to this point,"
he says, "are serious and unworthy of a good man; but I pass them

by and pardon them. For it is possible that you stole away secretly, overcome by a kind of longing for your fatherland or some other desire. But this is the worst of all evils, that you have stolen my gods. What will you reply now? It may certainly be that you were moved by a certain levity or impatience, or by curiosity, although you could not have lived better elsewhere than with me, not even in your fatherland. But why did you take away my gods, that is, my divine worship? For this is a great sin. It was not sufficient for you to show yourself a scoundrel towards me; in addition you also polluted yourself and yours with sacrilege."

Here, therefore, he found a different pretext, one that was more holy by far, namely, religion and the worship of God. Yet there was no interest in godliness in him, but he had a heart obsessed by pure greed and the worship of mammon. Such are our adversaries Eck [27] and the bishop of Mainz. They are not influenced by the glory of Christ and the truth of the Gospel, but they hanker after prebends, revenues, or other prerogatives. Laban also cares nothing about worship but about the gold and silver, from which the idols were cast.

Nevertheless, he pretends he has a passion for piety and divine worship, as though he meant to say: "I would not care about the gold and silver; for I could easily procure other statues. But this is what makes me grieve, that you have violated my devotion, my worship practices, and my prayers. See, therefore, how greatly you have sinned by taking away from the Lord God His worship and ceremony and all the rites of devotion in my whole family. These are violations and sins against the First Table. You are making every effort to rob me and my house of our religious life, and you are opening a window to impiety and the devil, who wants us to be smug despisers of God and divine worship."

Thus what he interprets as sacrilege is not this theft of the statues but the violation and overthrow of the worship of GOD. For no nation was ever so stupid as to pray to the wood, the stones, the gold, and the silver from which the statues had been made. But they added the First Table and supposed that God in heaven has regard for this worship and hears the prayer made at this statue. Jeroboam, for example, after erecting two calves, added this proclamation: "These are your gods, who brought you out of Egypt" (cf. 1 Kings 12:28). He himself and the people knew that the calves which had been formed in this way were not in themselves that deity which had led the Israelites out

[27] Johann Eck (1486—1543).

of Egypt, but they believed that the worship of God at these statues was pleasing and acceptable.

It pleased the king to fashion this likeness because a bullock or a calf is the special material for sacrifices; he could not have had a more fitting image. So he does not say that this bullock or calf is God, but he ties the worship of God to the figures of the calves, where prayer, worship, and sacrifice were to be offered to God. Therefore the container is taken for the content by synecdoche, namely, that God is to be worshiped in the calf, just as God also had promised to hear the prayers of those calling on Him in the tabernacle at the ark and the mercy seat.

In this way all the nations have retained the worship of their fathers and have adorned, or rather, perverted, it by their idolatry. At Ephesus there was an image of Diana in which men imagined a deity to be present that heard and received prayers. Laban, therefore, accuses Jacob not of stealing gold or silver but of robbing him and his church of their entire divine worship and, to the extent that he could, of the kingdom of heaven. For what else is robbing men of their religious life and their worship of God than to rob them of God Himself, life itself, and eternal salvation and to give them up to Satan and hell? This sin is so atrocious and abominable that it can never be excused or expiated by any words or sacrifices.

But Laban exaggerates this in such a dramatic manner not because of his regard and zeal for religion, as though something had been taken away from salvation or the grace of God, but that he might heap on Jacob the envy and implacable hatred among his own relatives and brethren, who perhaps knew that Jacob had been rather harshly treated and that the chief factor in the increase of his household property had been this faithful servant. Accordingly, that he might cover up Jacob's merits and his own greed and disgraceful cupidity, he gathers together whatever virtues there are in the First and Second Table and adorns himself with them so that nothing may seem more holy according to all the commandments of God than most holy Nabal. But on the other hand, he turns back all imperfections and heaps them on Jacob, when in reality he is seeking nothing else but gold and silver. So also today, the papists boast of the name of church and that they want the true religion of the fathers preserved, Christ and faith unimpaired, and religion and obedience towards the laws and toward the church and the civil magistracy pure; and yet they worship and care for nothing but their belly.

Accordingly, this is a striking description of a notorious hypocrite who boasts that he himself is the greatest of saints and overwhelms the excellent and holy man Jacob with every kind of abuse, outrageous crime, and deceit, and as one who should be subjected not only to human punishments but to the torments of hell. He calls him thief, robber, kidnapper, housebreaker, unfaithful, ungrateful, sacrilegious, and a subverter of religion. He could not have traduced and reviled him more harshly. From this it is sufficiently clear how Jacob stood with Laban, and how Laban treated Jacob like a slave and in a shameful manner so that he abused him like a piece of property, or rather, an ass and the vilest of beasts, for the acquisition and increase of his holdings. Nevertheless, he paid him no reward but bread and water and now, in return for his great industry and toils, he reviles him with the greatest of lying insults. Surely this is not obeying God, who forbade him to speak anything harsh against Jacob, is it? No, this is a most bitter thing to do, to charge him with all the crimes and sins that can be thought of and mentioned.

But these matters are described for our instruction and example (cf. Rom. 15:4). For this is the perpetual rule of the ungodly that they obey God in appearance and confess Him with words but deny Him in deeds and despise His commandments. Laban abstains from open violence and does not lay violent hands on Jacob. But if it had been permitted, he would not have spared him, because he is all on fire with the desire to harm him. But the ungodly are humbled and kept in check by the fear of punishments. So they put on an appearance of repentance, but with a fictitious and deceitful humility, just as Laban did everything in pretense and secretly raged because he did not dare to fulfill his desire for vengeance.

The second rule of the ungodly is this. All outrages which they are turning over in their own heart and wish to perpetrate they impute to the saints. On the other hand, all things that the saints do and the virtues proper to them they arrogate to themselves. This is the universal rule of all hypocrites and ungodly men. Laban himself is an idolater, a thief, a robber, a kidnapper, a greedy man, a portentous monstrosity of that age. Yet to himself he seems the most honorable and excellent of men, and he accuses Jacob, who is the very embodiment of innocence and honesty and who is full of the most beautiful virtues and their remarkable consequences, which he brings forth for the advantage of the church, state, and home. But no one sins except Jacob, and no one is holy but Nabal.

These things are certainly offensive and undeserving, but they are written in this way so that we by steadfastness and by the encouragement of the Scriptures might have hope (cf. Rom. 15:4). No one sins in this world except the only-begotten Son of God. On the other hand, no one is righteous but the devil. Whatever he says or does is right and just. And so the heretics and papists always arrogate to themselves righteousness, holiness, and wisdom as the ones who alone protect and defend the catholic faith. But the true church bears this disgrace, that it is heretical, straying, scandalous, and seditious and, as Paul says in 1 Cor. 4:13, κάθαρμα καὶ περίψημα ("refuse and offscouring"). But since it thus seems good to God and it cannot be otherwise but that there should be a flock which for God's sake is a κάθαρμα and a reproach of men and rejected by the people (cf. Ps. 22:6), we are certainly not reluctant to be regarded as such in the world. For we have His richest consolation, which has said (cf. Matt. 5:11-12): "Blessed will you be when men hate you and when they cast you out, insult you, and utter your name like an evil omen on account of the Son of Man. Be glad on that day and rejoice, for behold, your reward is great in heaven." It is a matter of a short time. Life is brief and wretched, but the joy and glory we await is eternal. Since, therefore, it pleases God that we should be a little flock, insignificant and despised, let us bear the troubles of this life with a calm and joyful heart, just as Jacob bore reproach, abuse, and contempt from the proud Labanites and hypocrites.

It is true, we may be regarded as sacrilegious and as disturbers of religion and civil governments, and indeed, the greatest sinners of all men alive. But it will not be difficult for us to bear these reproaches, and we will conquer because of our Leader and Lord, the Son of God, who Himself bore the same reproaches and conquers in all His saints. Only let us be counted among the Jacobites and not among the Labanites, and let us not be disturbed because the devil together with the ungodly hypocrites is regarded and worshiped as God and as holy and righteous in the judgment of the whole world.

Furthermore, there remains a question concerning the word אַל where Laban says: "It would be in my power to do you harm." But I cannot adduce anything certain to bring out the meaning of this idiom. So I leave it to the rabbis and Hebrew grammarians, although I am of the opinion that they do not have perfect knowledge of Hebrew grammar, at least, not in this word. So great is Babylon and the confusion of interpretations! To be sure, they heap up about 20 forms of diction by which they make efforts to explain this one form, and not one of them agrees with another. But there is no doubt that when the Hebrew language still flourished many words in popular and daily discourse meant something far different than they do now, when we take them from books only. It is one thing to speak grammatically, it is another thing to speak Latin. Hence account must be taken not so much of grammatical and regulated discourse as of idioms. Moreover, I am afraid that the grammar of the Jews is mutilated. Accordingly, the rabbis often have idle dreams, at least, in some modes of expression.

At one time אֵל meant God, and in this passage the meaning is: "My hand is according to God." The grammarians and those who follow rules strictly say that it signifies "according to ability," and I readily concede this. For a passage in Micah 2:1 agrees with this: "They do evil because GOD is in their hands," that is, they have the power, they are powerful. It is likewise stated in Deut. 28:32: "There will not be לְאֵל, 'strength,' in your hand." Accordingly, it must be taken as a special idiom, even as in the Latin language many words have degenerated by usage into a meaning different from the grammatical rules. Examples are: *amabo* ("if you please"), *obsecro* ("pray"), *quaero* ("please"), *age* ("come on"), *apage sis* ("begone"), *Edepol* ("indeed"), and *Hercle* ("by Hercules"). Here there would certainly be great confusion if you should want to interpret these expressions in accordance with strict grammar. *Amabo* has passed over into an interjection in usage.

Such changes take place in all languages. The Germans say: *"Gelt* ("Not so?"), I will pay it to you." The German word *Gelt* ("money") is employed adverbially.[28] The Germans also say: "God, you should leave it alone!" Here the word *Gott* ("God") takes on the nature of an interjection. Now, I do not credit myself with judgment in Hebrew grammar, except that I see that the grammarians are toiling and sweating but have not yet worked it out because of the diversity between the idioms which the Hebrews were accustomed to employ in daily usage and the logical analysis of the grammarians. Those who have no experience of the language pull the meanings of words to pieces and cause ambiguities and confusion, as in the expression שֵׁבֶט in Gen. 49:10, where an infinite sea of opinions has arisen.[29] Some explain it

---

[28] Luther seems to be confusing *gelt* (*Geld* in modern German), "money," with *gelt* (*gilt* in modern German), "that's so."

[29] See *Luther's Works*, 8, pp. 240—241.

as a rod, others as a scepter, and others in a different way. Therefore
the Hebrew language has largely been ruined, and it is not yet entirely restored. If it were not for the New Testament, our rabbis
would nowhere be able to derive certain meanings from the Old Testament. The New Testament has contributed a great deal to the restora-
tion and elucidation of the Hebrew language and the Old Testament.

But I shall not oppose it if anyone takes אֵל for "ability" or for
"God." This is certain, that אֵל is derived by syncope from אֱיָל, which
means "strength." From this abstract noun they derive the denomina-
tive, or adjective, אַיָּל, "strong." So we have translated in Is. 9:6:
"Mighty God," "Might." Absolutely, without לְ, or prepositive particle, it signifies "might," "strength," or "God," so that God is, as it were,
denominatively called אֵל from the idea of "might." About this there
is no doubt, that this name is rightly assigned to God, as is clear from
Ps. 22:1, where אֵלִי אֵלִי occurs: "My God, My God, why hast Thou
forsaken Me?" From this comes אֱלֹהִים. This is approximately what
the Hebrew grammarians say of this passage, and if they have obtained
its meaning, it is well. If not, it is the surest of arguments that they
have not yet attained to the true and certain knowledge of the Hebrew
language. From the Old Testament they cannot confirm this interpretation, but from the New Testament (cf. Matt. 27:46) it is proved that
אֵל signifies God.

In this passage, moreover, the prepositive particle is added, לְאֵל,
that is, my hand "is present," or "is in readiness." Therefore, whether
this signifies God or only strength, or whether it is an abstract and
the divine name has degenerated into an interjection and signifies
ability, about this I am not going to quarrel, but I leave it undecided.
In the German translation we have translated approximately with
this meaning: "And I, with God's help, would have enough strength
to be able to do you harm." [30] So much about the grammar. "My
ability is present," he says, "or my power from God." But whatever
a hypocrite says or feels about God's name is wholly simulated and
deceitful, because hypocrites do not have God. "I could avenge this
wrong," he means to say, "that you took away my daughters and
gods, but the God of your father has under threats forbidden me to
do violence to you."

What wrong? "That you were not willing to be a slave and an ass
forever; that you refused to endure servitude so that you might sweat

---

[30] From 1534 on, Luther's translation had read: *Und ich hette, mit Gottes
hülffe, wol so viel macht.*

day and night and run and toil and bear the insults of my sons as well as my insults. This is the greatest sin! You should not have robbed me of this servitude, in which I wished to detain you and my daughters." This, to be sure, is an atrocious crime, not to be willing to consign oneself into the most abject servitude of a most cruel tyrant. But this is characteristic of hypocrites, to accuse others because they stand in the way of their lusts. But enough of the description of Nabal, which is a perfect picture of a pope and hypocrite. A real pope and a false hypocrite! Now we want to give ear to a pious man as well.

31. *Jacob answered Laban: Because I was afraid, for I thought that you would take your daughters from me by force.*

32. *Anyone with whom you find your gods shall be put to death in the presence of our kinsmen. Point out what I have that is yours, and take it. Now Jacob did not know that Rachel had stolen them.*

33. *So Laban went into Jacob's tent and into Leah's tent and into the tent of the two maidservants, but he did not find them.*

This is a brief excuse for that mass, or rather, wagonload, of insults and reproaches which Laban hurled against the holy man. "What was I to do?" he asks. "I was afraid!" He makes a humble confession and does not clear himself carefully concerning the theft, but he buries all the insults and injuries within himself and only says that he was afraid. If he had been more vehement, even as many men are exceedingly impatient about injustices, he could have attacked Laban in turn and thrown back all the denunciations. "Stop speaking ill of a man who has deserved very well of you," he might have said. "For in the judgment of God and that of all men you are sacrilegious, a robber, a tyrant, and an avaricious monster, for you have sold your daughters and regarded them as most abject slaves and beasts of burden, and in return for their hard toils and sweat you have no thought of repaying them with due rewards but with permanent imprisonment." This would have provided endless material for disputes and quarrels. Therefore we are reminded that we should also patiently bear the insults as well as the contempt and pride of our adversaries. But the truth, nevertheless, must not be passed over in silence. Nor will the lust for speaking ill in our adversaries pass by with impunity, even though we throw back none of their denunciations. For there is One who will look into these things and judge them.

Therefore Jacob says: "Whatever I did of these things, I did with a certain amount of fear and trepidation." So he does not accuse Laban, and yet he indicates that Laban must be severely blamed and accused because he had to fear that his father-in-law might take away his daughters, whom he had given him as wives. This is assuredly most atrocious! Quietly, therefore, and with a fine figure of speech he charges Laban with the worst crimes in such a way that by excusing and clearing himself he accuses him more violently than he could have done by any invective. For so the apologies of the godly are generally the most serious accusations against the ungodly.

In this way the pope and his accomplices are at the present time accusing us of heresy, blasphemy, arrogance, and sedition. But if I reply: "I am not a heretic; I am not seditious," as Christ clearly and expressly replies to the Jews (John 8:49): "I have not a demon" — and this should certainly be done, for we should not assent to revilings against the doctrine and truth of God or be silent in such a case — then, in my brief refutation, I am charging the pope himself with all the crimes and reproaches of which he has accused us.

This is therefore a splendid apology. For he quietly appeals to the conscience of the hypocrite and on the basis of all his deeds he charges him with cruelty and tyranny. "Your conscience," he says, "is our witness that you treated us unkindly, so that I had just cause to consider flight. For I thought to myself: 'Once Laban has found out that I am fleeing, he will seize my wives and all my goods and throw me into prison.'" Does it become a good man so to treat a faithful, saintly man, one who is industrious and careful in looking after the family property, that he is compelled to fear violence and injury from his father-in-law, lest he, forgetful of the closest ties, deserts, and στοργή ("natural affection") toward his son-in-law or his daughters, take the wives away from their husband? Is this to be praised or excused? No, it is most disgraceful, and it conflicts with all reason and honor. For a daughter who has been handed over to a husband is no longer in the power of her father; the father does not have the right of demanding the daughter back or of taking her away. It was therefore horrible cruelty that this excellent man should find himself involved in the danger that he might again lose his dear wives or children.

It seems that the tyrant threatened him with this on several occasions, saying: "If I knew that you were meditating flight and administering my affairs with too little fidelity, I would soon tear my daughters away from you." Moses, indeed, did not expressly say this, but it is quite reasonable; and the Holy Spirit seems to indicate that it was not without cause that Jacob adduced this reason to excuse his flight, namely, that he was afraid. Therefore, most holy Laban, with what praises shall we extol you? Evidently this is the way a father or father-in-law ought to feel towards his son-in-law and his daughters, who obey their husband and who in the household of their father are regarded as slaves by whose services the family property has grown in excellent fashion — that you should think of tearing them away from their husband! That hypocrite is assuredly the most horrible of all monstrosities, surpassing all beasts and tyrants with his cruelty; indeed, he is more cruel than cruelty itself.

But if there had been ever so small a spark of humanity or kindness in him, he should have been influenced and moved by such goodness, deference, faithfulness, and patience on the part of excellent and patient Jacob, but he is in no way moved by all these. So he pursues his son-in-law to bring him back to the imprisonment of his servitude or to take his daughters away from him. This, therefore, Jacob feared and he wanted to say: "You yourself are at fault; you oppressed us with such a slavish fear, and you threatened that you would take away all my goods if I were to go away. Therefore I was afraid."

"In the second place," he says, "in regard to your accusation of sacrilege against me, I will act as follows: 'Anyone with whom you find your gods shall not live.'" Here the Holy Spirit describes the human side in the saints. For however sublime they are in faith and spirit, they nevertheless not only err and are ignorant of many things, but they even take a fall according to the flesh. Jacob thinks that he is beyond all blame, suspicion, and danger, and that in this respect satisfaction had already been rendered to Laban. So he makes the offer that the one with whom Laban finds the idols should be killed. But in this manner a very dear wife is handed over to death by her husband. For if God had not intervened and prevented it, Jacob would thoughtlessly have offered his dear wife Rachel to be slaughtered. That is going too far, and Jacob concedes too much. But he acts in ignorance. Such are the sins of the believers, who are sometimes according to the flesh overtaken by tumbles due to ignorance and error. Thus Rachel also will vigorously tell lies later to save her life.

But upon this reply that most saintly Laban should by all rights have been satisfied, and he should have said: "Why should I make inquiries or conduct a search? I hear and accept the testimony of your innocence. They are my daughters and grandchildren, against whom I was previously too hard and harsh; I will not trouble you anymore, nor shall I accuse you of theft." This would have been proper for a father-in-law and a good man, but he cannot be satisfied, because he is full of demons. This apology would have satisfied anyone else if he had heard Jacob saying: "I have nothing to do with your idols." But to avoid any suspicion of trickery, Jacob added more and said: "I give you permission to search and unpack everything." This permission no one else would easily have given him. I would certainly have said: "I do not have your idols." I would not have given him permission to search all my goods, or at least, I would have conducted the search on my own. It was therefore quite out of place to concede such a privilege to this monster. Or was it not sufficient to hear that Jacob did not have the idols and that he offered the death of the one who had stolen them?

But behold that he has no sense of shame. For he goes and searches each tent. I cannot help being deeply moved and I am sorry that I cannot measure up to these things with words and paint them adequately in fitting colors. I would not have made further concessions if he had not been content with my confession, so frank and firm. Jacob yielded altogether more than he should have.

First, then, he enters the tent of Jacob himself. It would have been enough if he had found nothing there. But he goes also to the tent of Leah and, in addition, to the tent of both maidservants. In the end, one still remained, Rachel's; he had to cackle his way through this one too. And here the wellbeing and life of Rachel was in serious danger. So the Holy Spirit is at hand and finds a remedy against the permission which Jacob had given when he had said: "Anyone with whom you find your gods shall be put to death." Too much had been yielded! But the correction will follow. For God and His angels keep watch when Jacob sleeps.

This is the work and skill of God, to correct and emend what had been ruined by Jacob's error. He can make evil matters good when we have spoiled and harmed matters. And so, in the great infirmity characteristic of human affairs, not even the saints can be without many great lapses. Certainly, I have often done many things imprudently and foolishly, concerning which I was much disturbed later. Nor was I able to see how I might work my way out and extricate myself from matters that were being hampered by my folly. But the Lord found a means and a way that the error might be corrected.

Similarly, for Rachel a monstrous and specific danger was begotten from the inconsiderate permission granted by her husband. For the savageness of this worthless hypocrite was such that he would either have vented his rage on his daughter or he would have wanted his son-in-law to be consigned into slavery for her rescue and life. But God so governs His saints that even though they err and stray, the outcomes are nevertheless salutary or without great loss. For all things work together for good to the elect and those who believe (cf. Rom. 8:28), even errors and sins, and this is absolutely certain. For God is accustomed to make all things out of nothing, and so He can call forth and produce good from evil. Augustine especially is delighted by this thought. "So great is God's goodness," he says, "that He permits no evil to be done unless He turns it to good." [31] Jacob erred very imprudently, and, as far as he was concerned, he had thrown his beloved wife into danger of death, or at least, of disgrace. But a plan is shown him by God that is so cunning that both Laban and the devil himself are deceived.

33. *And he went out of Leah's tent, and entered Rachel's.*

34. *Now Rachel had taken the household gods and put them under the camel's litter and sat upon them. Laban felt all about the tent but did not find them.*

35. *And she said to her father: Let not my lord be angry that I cannot rise before you, for the way of women is upon me. So he searched but did not find the household gods.*

Here Satan is aiming at Rachel's throat. For Laban enters her tent and searches each thing very carefully. Nor could she hide the gods in her clothing, sleeves, or bedding; nothing was left but her own body with which she covered the idols. Therefore she hides the תְּרָפִים in the camels' litter. Not that they could be concealed there with sufficient safety, for Laban could easily have searched what was spread out. But in addition, she covered them with the most shameful part of her body, for she sat on the litter. However, not even this is without danger, for he could have suspected, as avarice and hypocrisy is usually suspicious, that there was some hidden trick. He might have said: "It is not without reason that I do not find you sitting in your customary place. What if the תְּרָפִים are hidden here?" But if he had

---

[31] Augustine, *Opus imperfectum contra Julianum,* V, 50, *Patrologia, Series Latina,* XLV, 1495.

ordered her to rise so that he might shake up and roll back the litter, the theft would have been made known and discovered.

But she devises a very fine lie. She pretends that she is suffering from menstruation, according to the custom of her sex. But it is becoming and reasons of health demand that at such a time a woman should not sit on the ground but rather on a bed, or on a bundle of straw, if a bed is lacking. In her extreme need and danger, she suddenly finds a helpful strategy, and experience bears witness that women have great ability to devise strategy on the spur of the moment. Therefore Rachel is assisted by nature, or by the character and industry of women with which this sex has been endowed. Although it has not been destined by God for government of the state or church, where the greatest strength of character and wisdom is required, they have nevertheless been ordained for the care of the home. For the longer they deliberate about important and difficult matters, the more they complicate and obstruct the business. But the first impulse of their nature in sudden dangers is usually excellent and very successful.

The father is therefore deceived by a womanish lie and is deluded by what appears to be a very honorable way of thinking. For he does not dare to search what nature itself has hidden, nor does he have anything further to say, but he is deterred by natural shame. But God had a part in this; for He turned off his understanding and smote him with blindness so that he should not search too carefully. Laban believes that what his daughter says is true, namely, that she wanted to sit by herself because of her sickness. Then, too, it was not likely that she would sit on idols, for he did not think that this was possible because of her state of health. But nothing did he believe less than that his daughter, brought up in his house, would steal the gods and divine worship of her father and treat them so shamefully as to place them under the camels' litter and sit on them. "My daughter would not hold my religion in such slight esteem," he thought, "the religion in which she was brought up from her tender years." So he deceives himself beautifully. His daughter added the lie not in fun or maliciously but as a very serviceable and necessary lie to offer her father an opportunity to deceive himself.

This, therefore, is the work and government of God in the dangerous emergencies and deeds of the saints. For if He Himself did not smite their adversaries with avarice and blindness and deceive their faculties so that they do not think the thoughts that should most of all be thought, often even their most crafty thoughts would profit

nothing. Indeed, it is a surprising thing that Rachel was so resolute
that she was able to despise the idols she had previously regarded as
most holy, paying no regard to the danger that threatened her from
her angry father. For we, indeed, treat temples, images, and our
altars with greater reverence than that with which Rachel treated the
idols of her father. She hid them in the litter and placed them under
her body. Moreover, the speech in which she excuses herself to her
father for not rising for him is strange. She addresses her father, and
yet she does not call him father but "lord," saying: "Let not my lord
be angry, etc." This is certainly a grave sin, because she does not respect and honor her father as she should have done according to the
Fourth Commandment. Nor are women so weak when they suffer
their menstrual periods that they cannot rise or walk.

Moses does not relate this without purpose. It seems almost to
mean that she ridiculed her father as an idolater who is searching for
his statues so anxiously and furiously. But I make no affirmation on
the matter. She could also have done it for this reason, that there
might be a greater pretense and outward show, as though she was not
only quite prepared to rise for her father like a most obedient daughter but also that she might conduct herself like a maidservant towards
her master with servile fear and concern for being hindered by her
adverse health from being able to show due respect to her father.
For women in the Holy Scriptures are accustomed to call their husbands lords, but children do not act likewise. "My father," said Elisha
to Elijah (cf. 2 Kings 2:12). But whatever the reason for this appella-
tion was, it was very suitable for beautifying and adorning a lie.
Laban, however, raged in vain both by making threats and by searching the individual tents. Accordingly, Jacob will set against him
another sharp and lengthy refutation of his insults, for he in turn will
pile up his own merits and the ingratitude of Laban.

36. *Then Jacob became angry and upbraided Laban; Jacob said to
Laban: What is my offense? What is my sin, that you have hotly
pursued me?*

37. *Although you have felt through all my goods, what have you found
of all your household goods? Set it here before my kinsmen and
your kinsmen, that they may decide between us two.*

At long last Jacob is kindled to anger, and he relies on God's admonition and the rebuke made to Laban. For he is moved with indigna-

tion at the matter, and yet he has more confidence in God's judgment than in his own innocence. From this he derives courage and consolation. This is what he wants to say: "God has seen my lowliness and affliction and has chided you on account of the tyranny you have exercised against me. For if I had been guilty of some sin before God, I would have borne that blame, not you. But as matters stand, I am certain of my innocence, and I know that the toils of my servitude have been approved by God but that your ingratitude and all your actions have displeased Him." This is the confidence and glory of Jacob, that he has on his side the judgment of God, who justifies him and condemns his adversary. Moreover, there is the additional factor of the very firm testimony of Laban's experience and conscience, for he describes the whole course of his own life and of that of his father-in-law and proves that by this also Laban is convicted of injustice and cruelty:

Accordingly, he answers "a fool according to his folly" but in such a way that he also observes what Solomon adds: "Lest he become like him . . . lest the fool seem wise in his own eyes" (cf. Prov. 26:4-5). For Solomon orders us to instruct, censure, and upbraid sinners and fools in season and out of season that they may not seem wise to themselves, that is, that they may not remain in the opinion that they did the right thing by sinning. But God's rebukes are to be set forth, and their life and evil deeds should be disclosed that they may feel that they have sinned and may repent. But who upbraids a fool in such a way that he becomes like him? If I, for instance, should want to contend with him by means of lies and false accusations, then I would become like him. But he should be rebuked in such a way that he is confounded in his folly. But this is God's judgment: "Your conscience and your whole previous life has proved you guilty; see that you acknowledge your guilt." Jacob employs this kind of reproof against Laban. "What did I do?" he asks. "What is my transgression; what is my sin? You have heaped up against me great wagonloads of insults and accusations; you have called me thief, cattle stealer, temple robber, and subverter of your religion. Show and prove only one of these, and I will pay a fitting penalty. But if you cannot, then you betray your fickleness and inordinate desire for lying, for by your silence you confess that you have lied and, indeed, you are convicted both by the testimony of God and by that of your own conscience. You can bring forward nothing in which I have sinned or omitted any of those things which I should have done. All of your accusing has been slanderous, pure lies, and the raging of a madman; you are confounded and condemned by your own judgment. I have God as the witness of my innocence, and your conscience as well." In this way one must delouse a fool with a club.

Where are now those pretentious words and fabricated charges, "You stole my heart, you fled," such as he hurled forth above in great rage? They have vanished like smoke. But stupid Laban refuses to understand this, although God reminded him in a dream not to say anything harsh against Jacob. So Jacob adds a gloss here and explains the Lord's words, saying: "You have charged me with such great sins unjustly and foolishly. All these things of which you accuse me apply more correctly to you, for God has said so, and your conscience testifies to it."

So stupid Nabal had to be given a beating that he might see that he had erred. This is answering a fool according to his folly, lest he seem wise to himself. For one should not pretend not to hear the revilings of Satan invented against godliness and God Himself, but they must be exposed and refuted. Such refutation is not sin; it is not unjust or reprehensible anger but holy and just and godly jealousy, which is angry at ungodliness and sin.

Such rebukes, moreover, are useful so that men may not persevere in errors and sins and remain slaves of Satan, who has driven them on and beset them; but their sins must be made known, that men may be converted and liberated from the tyranny of Satan. We, too, are attacking the pope as the Antichrist and seducer of the whole world; we expose and condemn ungodliness and idolatrous madness of every kind. We are incited to anger against him not by personal ambition but by righteous jealousy and fervor of conscience to vindicate and protect the glory of GOD.

Jacob, moreover, brings pressure to bear on his father-in-law and stops his mouth by asking: "What sin have I committed? What have I become guilty of? What is my iniquity?" Here I commend to the experts of the Hebrew language that they inquire into the difference between the two words פֶּשַׁע and חַטָא. For the rabbis gather together 13 words which all signify ungodliness and transgression and which do not belong to this place. These two, however, which Moses employs are usually distinguished by saying that פֶּשַׁע signifies the guilt of omission and חַטָא a sin of commission, and they comprise original sin. פֶּשַׁע signifies omitting things that should be done, חַטָא doing things that should be omitted.

So in 2 Kings 3:5 it is stated: "Moab rebelled against Israel," for the Moabites were tributaries of the people of Israel. But he rebelled, that is, he ceased rendering obedience and paying tribute. Likewise in Is. 1:2 we read: "They have rebelled against Me," that is, "They ought to have respected Me and obeyed Me as a Father, but they neglect due obedience to Me. I have adopted them as sons to serve Me, but they fall away from Me and choose strange gods. What they should have done least of all they do, and they omit what they should have done as a matter of duty." Likewise in Jer. 2:13 it stands written: "My people have committed two evils: they have forsaken Me, the Fountain of living [32] waters, and hewed out cisterns for themselves," that is, "they should have worshiped Me as a living fountain, but they omit doing so; they let Me go. Then they seek other fountains. This they should not have done."

So also Jacob says here: "There are two things for which you could have censured me. If I have committed anything that I should not have done, or if I have omitted doing what would have been a part of my duty, show me one or the other of these! You say that I have cast off obedience, stolen your idols, taken away your daughters; these are manifest lies. You yourself are compelled to acknowledge my innocence by word and deed. Add to that the testimony of God and your conscience. Indeed, you yourself are guilty of both sins. For you have sinned by omitting what belonged to the regard and remuneration of myself and your daughters; you gave them neither dowry nor any portion of their inheritance. Then you perpetrated a sin of commission by pursuing us and plotting evil against us. These are very grave sins, which you certainly ought to acknowledge and for which you should seek pardon."

And so Laban's honor is turned into the greatest disgrace. Now Jacob enumerates his outrageous sins in particular. "You have been all aflame against me," he says, "for you have not simply persecuted and pursued me, but you are inflamed and raging with anger." For this is the meaning of דָּלַק elsewhere, as in Ps. 7:14: "He has made his arrows fiery shafts"; that is, he wants to shoot fire, to set fire to a city. So he increases Laban's guilt not only extensively, by enlarging on it, but also intensively. "You have pursued me," he says, "with a crowd of relatives and friends, burning and raging, and you would have been glad to use swords and fiery darts (cf. Eph. 6:16) against me like a man possessed by a demon."

[32] The Vulgate text reads *aquae vivae*, but Luther quotes it as *aquae vitae*.

He rebukes him quite severely, as though he meant to say: "Since you found in me neither a sin of omission nor one of commission, you should certainly not have pursued me so furiously and ardently, but you should have recalled our relationship, that I am your son-in-law and your daughters are my wives. But without any regard for family loyalty you have raged against us so madly that you have forgotten that you are the father of your daughters. As for me, even if I were not your son-in-law, I am nevertheless your sister's child, for you are my uncle and not only my father-in-law. Therefore, a closer bond of relationship could not have existed between us, unless I were your own son. (If Jacob [33] had died, Laban would have been the legal father.) So we are related both by blood and by marriage. But contrary to all the duties of family ties, you not only honor us with no gift, but on top of it all you try to rob us of those things which have been granted to us by God."

So he correctly says: "You are not angry or furious in a human way, but you have plainly been disturbed by a diabolical and infernal madness, you are saturated with the fire of hell, and you flare up against innocent people who are your closest kinsmen." If it were my lot to have an honest and honorable son-in-law and my son were degenerate, I would certainly transfer all my substance from my degenerate son to my son-in-law. But Laban inverts and perverts the whole natural order of all duties. He robs honorable daughters and an excellent man, his son-in-law. This was the first thing.

But Jacob makes an addition and piles up more. "You have felt through all my baggage, that is, all my property," he says. This, too, does not become a wise man endowed with a noble character, especially in reference to matters concerning his son or daughter. For it is disgraceful to scrutinize each individual thing, to feel and to examine people almost to the living skin, as if they were the worst enemies. Indeed, even against an enemy no one would have a right to act this way. "But come, what did you profit?" he asks, "or what did you find by your careful examination except that you showed that you were angry without a cause? If you are too little moved by my judgment and cannot determine whether you or I am mad, let the matter be referred to judges and let our brethren judge between us." He makes him the offer of a decision at law. But con-

---

[33] This is how the text reads, but "Jacob" may be a misprint for "Isaac," for the names are confused elsewhere (see p. 204).

victed and confounded in his own judgment, Laban does not dare to make even a sound.

This is obviously how the ungodly hypocrites should be treated. The righteous man is absolved and the ungodly man is handed over in his place. For the evil that he was devising for others has rebounded on his own head. In Ps. 7:16, for example, it is stated: "His mischief returns upon his own head, and on his own pate his violence descends."

But there is a question concerning the brothers, namely, what does Jacob mean when he says: "Set it before my kinsmen and your kinsmen"? From where does Jacob have brethren in this land of pilgrimage since, indeed, he served for 20 years alone? Below also he said to his brethren: "Gather stones" (v. 46). My opinion is this: When we do not have a clear text, we must resort to guesses and pluck out thoughts and meanings, be they as they may. All of Mesopotamia seems to have been pasture land and the inhabitants engaged in the pasturing of flocks, even as they are now. Therefore there were shepherds throughout all the villages and towns. It is likely that Jacob had many relatives in his household from the house of Laban who worked for him as well as his father-in-law. Their services were divided, some serving Jacob and some Laban. But those who went with Jacob were undoubtedly good and godly men, as is also stated above in the household of Abraham in regard to Hagar and Abraham's servant, who attached themselves to him because of the purity of his religion.

Therefore he means the brethren from the relationship of Nahor and Terah. They returned with Jacob to his fatherland, and he had need of their services in pasturing the flocks. For the two wives were occupied in nourishing and caring for the children, who were still of a tender age and weak. On his own, moreover, he could not pasture such a large flock. He had need of servants, male and female, and in this place he calls them brethren. "Come then," he says, "let us choose some on both sides from our relatives and kinsmen by whose decision this quarrel may be settled." It is a very fair proposition, and Laban is put to silence by divine authority, his own conscience, his previous life, and the public testimony of all men and even of his brethren to such an extent that, being convicted and confounded, he finds nothing further to reply.

38. *These twenty years I have been with you; your ewes and your*

*she-goats have not miscarried, and I have not eaten the rams of
your flocks.*

39. *That which was torn by wild beasts I did not bring to you; I bore
the loss of it myself; of my hand you required it, whether stolen
by day or stolen by night.*

40. *By day the heat consumed me, and the cold by night, and sleep
fled from my eyes.*

41. *These twenty years I have been in your house; I have served you
fourteen years for your two daughters, and six years for your flock,
and you have changed my wages ten times.*

Jacob not only rebukes his father-in-law, but he also incriminates
him and by means of all the details amplifies Laban's horrible ingratitude and his own cruel servitude. For he mentions and expands his
own merits and good deeds so that Laban's wickedness and ingratitude may loom larger. Moses sets forth the example and perfect
picture of an excellent and faithful servant the like of whom is nonexistent elsewhere in any stories. Today, how sad and all too common
the complaints of all fathers of households are regarding the treachery
and dishonesty of servants!

"With such care," Jacob says, "I served you that your ewes and
she-goats were never sterile." But can the shepherds bring it about
that the flock is not sterile? Much depends in every way on the
faithfulness and care of the shepherd. The worthlessness of our
shepherds is well known. They are able to bring it about, either
by evil artifices or by negligence, that the ewes of their masters die,
are sterile, and waste away, and on the other hand, that those which
they have as their own property supply much milk, cheese, and wool
and produce many lambs. Hence much importance attaches to the
merits and faithfulness of the shepherds, that they do not neglect
the breeding and care of the flocks; and if this is done, it comes to
pass naturally that the ewes bring forth offspring.

"Therefore your ewes were fruitful," says Jacob. "This was brought
about by my faithfulness and care that there might be a plentiful
offspring of the flocks. For 20 years they have never been sterile."
For in those regions, as in certain parts of Italy, the ewes produce
young twice a year, and to this end there is need of much care
that the breeding of the flocks is not neglected. Therefore this is

an example of a faithful servant that is quite incomparable. How could Laban escape being enriched even while snoring in idleness, seeing that his faithful servant did nothing else but increase the goods of his master?

In the second place, he says: "I have not eaten the rams of your flocks." It is permissible for shepherds to slaughter a sheep on occasion or at least to live on the milk and cheese and to clothe and cover themselves with skins and wool. But Jacob chose not to make use of these privileges; he preferred to let everything accrue to the advantage of his master, even at his own loss. So Rachel had good reason to say above that her father had devoured and used up her wages.

In the third place, he says: "That which was torn by wild beasts I did not bring to you." It was not permitted to do this, although in all fairness he should not have been required to enter in his accounts what had been torn by wolves or other beasts. "I could not have kept a flock so carefully," he means to say, "that a wolf could not at times drag off a sheep or two. So I should not have borne that loss. But because you kept on throwing it into my teeth that this had come about because of my carelessness, inasmuch as I allowed the wolf to attack the sheep, I was compelled to make restitution."

Accordingly, he inflicted no loss on Laban, neither by neglecting the breeding, nor by eating the flesh, nor by the ravage of wild beasts. "I was the one at fault," he said, "that is, I was guilty; I had to be the one who did it; I was compelled to make restitution and to pay back whatever was lost." This was assuredly very hard servitude and tyranny, even to pay for what cannot be preserved by the greatest watchfulness and care! However, it often happens that precautions cannot be taken within the walls of a house that a dog does not drag away something or devour it or cause some loss. Moreover, it is strange from what source Jacob had the means to pay back and restore what had been lost from the whole flock. We cannot gather this from the story, but we can make a guess. Either his father Isaac sent him money, or Laban paid him a small wage which he used up almost entirely on these needs so that this greedy master should suffer no loss.

In the fourth place, he says: "My theft by day, my theft by night." This is how it reads in the Hebrew, although the rabbis say that ' in this place is a superfluous letter. But I do not agree with the rabbis in all matters. The meaning is: "Whatever men stole by day and by night was regarded as having been carried off because of my neglect and carelessness. I was compelled to restore and fill up the number, whether the loss had taken place by wild beasts or theft. You never lost a thing, not even a strand of wool. Whatever loss occurred, I had to make it all good." So Laban became rich entirely by another's care, toil, and sweat and, indeed, by the injury and loss suffered by his faithful shepherd. But the substance which is acquired from another's sweat and by tyranny to others is cursed.

Therefore Jacob speaks in a fine rhetorical style and preaches the Law to lead him to a knowledge of his sin. But a hypocrite is exclusively righteous, and to himself he does not seem to be able to sin in any way. Therefore it is impossible to bring such men to a knowledge of sin and to true repentance.

In the fifth place, he says: "By day the heat consumed me, and the cold by night." This was somewhat more tolerable in the first 14 years than in the last six, when he was serving for himself and for his wives and children to increase his property and to make provision for his own home. It was certainly very hard to bear heat and cold and sleeplessness at the same time, for bodies have need of rest and sleep so that they are not too exhausted by too much fatigue. But why did he suffer so much? Because thieves and wolves pay no attention to heat and cold, to nighttime or daytime. "And so I was compelled to keep watch near the flock night and day," he says. "I did not dare to use the heat or the excessive cold as an excuse. I had to leave home! And all these things turned out to your advantage and gain, while I toiled hard and sweat that your flocks might increase while you were snoring."

But where will you find an example today that is the equal of this wonderful faithfulness? For both nobles and peasants who are involved in raising livestock all complain about the treachery of the shepherds, and so they say that the flocks of the masters are afflicted with the mange, sterility, and other maladies and are also torn by wild beasts; not so the sheep of the shepherds, because the care of the former is inferior and the shepherds provide and improve their own profits from the losses of their masters. Whether fable or true story, the following is told everywhere. A certain shepherd was dragged off by a nobleman for punishment on account of crimes and thefts. When he was about to be sent to the cross, he was asked by the nobleman whether he knew another honest and faithful shepherd whom he might place in charge of his livestock. He said that he did not know anyone, that they were all of the same stock and some were considerably worse. They say that the nobleman was moved by this response to grant the shepherd life and to retain him, since he could not find a better one.

Therefore, the practices of our times and our servants eminently illustrate the virtues and faithfulness of this shepherd Jacob. For it is a quite singular example, and it is clear what great difficulties there are today in the domestic sphere in the midst of such great treachery of men. But these disadvantages must be borne in silence until God calls us from this life into a better one and demands punishment for the sins of the wicked. No one can display such faithfulness as Jacob faithfully displayed to his unrighteous master if he does not believe in God and depend entirely on faith in the Word.

Jacob adds further: "After I served you 14 years and, in addition, six for the sheep which fell to me in place of wages, you changed my wages 10 times in this period of six years." He was not content with being enriched for 14 years by Jacob's services and faithfulness; in addition, he also wanted to rob him of his due wages. Therefore, Jacob expands his rebuke as much as he can to incite him to the acknowledgment of his sin; but he has a heart harder than a diamond and an anvil. From this it appears what great patience and faithfulness there was in the patriarchs. The martyrs also suffered very many atrocious things, but there is no comparison with the hard toils of the patriarchs and the dangers they encountered. For it was great patience to endure such tyranny for 20 years. But how this change of wages came about has been stated above.

42. *If the God of my father, the God of Abraham and the Fear of Isaac, had not been on my side, surely now you would have sent me away empty-handed. God saw my affliction and the labor of my hands and rebuked you last night.*

"God saw my affliction and rebuked you." In the Hebrew it is put absolutely, without an accusative: "God has seen it and has therefore rebuked." So cruel was Laban that he would not only have dismissed him empty-handed and naked but would even have dragged him back into slavery if the divine warning had not intervened, as has been stated previously. But this is an outstanding passage, the like of which we have not had previously, because of this name: "The Fear of Isaac." פַּחַד to the Hebrews is "to fear," "to be terrified." In Ps. 14:5 we read: "There they shall be in great terror, etc." The hypocrites fear where there is nothing to be feared, or, as it says elsewhere (Prov. 28:1): "The wicked flee when no one pursues." So it is commonly explained, but it must be understood of worship. What, then, does the Holy Spirit mean in making mention of the "Fear of Isaac"?

There is no doubt that he means God, for He adds: "the God of my father, the God of Abraham and the Fear of Isaac." "The Fear" is joined with God; therefore it is necessary that it is equivalent to God. "The Fear" simply signifies God here. If it signified anything else but God, Jacob would not have joined it with God. For the honor or worship of God must not be transferred to another. Infinite, however, are the questions and explanations why he calls God the Fear and Respect of Isaac and why he does not call Him the Fear also of Abraham but assigns this name to Isaac alone.[34] I shall follow the simple and common meaning, that he calls God by this name because of the outstanding and singular worship of his father Isaac, who feared and worshiped God with singular piety. This is the common meaning, and it pleases me well.

But in addition, one must take note of these expressions, which Moses set down with special emphasis, as I have often pointed out elsewhere.[35] In Gen. 2:22, for example, he says: "He took a rib and built a woman from it." There he could have used another and, it seems, a more suitable word, but by this richer word, as it were, he wanted to indicate that woman is God's building, not only because of the mystery of the church but also in a domestic sense, because all of Scripture employs this way of speaking about women, as is stated in Ex. 1:21 concerning the blessing of the midwives and their remuneration that "God built their houses." Rachel also said above: "Go in to my maidservant, to see if I may perhaps be built up from her" (chapter 30:3), that is, "that I may acquire the offspring and posterity of my house or family." For a woman has been especially created for this purpose that a house may be built up in her, that children and a posterity may be born.

Jacob likewise says in this place that Laban was rebuked. This also was said with significance, as also Rachel a little earlier spoke of the despoiling of God (v. 16). For the devil with the evil angels and wicked men is intent on hindering or overthrowing every good work. Accordingly, if any good is done, it is usually done by rebuking,

[34] Lyra *ad* Gen. 31:42, p. 95 recto, "Additio."
[35] See *Luther's Works,* 1, pp. 131—132.

by disputing, by contending, and by snatching it out of the jaws of
the devil and of evil men. These and similar expressions, which are
set down so distinctly, and if I may say so, so carefully, should be
diligently noted in Scripture. In this passage therefore I regard the
literal sense as that closest to the truth, namely, that God is called
Fear of Isaac on account of the excellent worship of the latter. Others
interpret it to mean that Isaac was afraid, since he was to be sacrificed.
But this is a foreign and wicked meaning, for Isaac was neither
afraid nor terrified, but of his own accord obeyed his father and
God. For not terror but spontaneous obedience and fortitude should
be attributed to the saints. For fear signifies that sin is ruling, and
sin was not ruling in Isaac, but an obedient spirit. Although the
flesh fought back, nevertheless the spirit, which subjected the flesh
to itself, conquered and gained dominion.

But besides this meaning, I think that Christ is also pointed to.
For the fathers regarded this blessing as being distinct from their
bodily blessing. "In Isaac shall your seed be named," says Paul
(Rom. 9:7), and he also stresses the emphatic word. For Ishmael's
blessing was bodily in the 12 princes. But "in Isaac shall your seed
be named," which is nothing else but Christ Himself. He is the true
Seed. For the fathers looked beyond the bodily blessing which
Ishmael and Esau had, chiefly to the spiritual blessing, which is
Christ Himself. Therefore I see the Trinity here, and elsewhere too,
wherever I can dig out that mystery from passages of the Old
Testament. Therefore "Fear" here signifies the Son of God incarnate,
whom the patriarchs and prophets beheld in the promises and whom
they taught. So, for example, it was promised in the beginning (cf.
Gen. 3:15): "The Seed of the woman will crush the serpent's head."
Likewise, it was stated: "In your Seed shall all nations be blessed"
(cf. Gen. 12:3). This One the fathers feared and worshiped as the
Jewel and the Kernel of the bodily promises, which were the shells,
or husks, given to strengthen their faith as they reared a posterity
for Christ's sake.

Therefore, the Holy Spirit signifies that Isaac waited for that Seed
with great longing and worshiped It. Jacob here glories in the future
Christ, whom his father worshiped. We should also carefully remember that these striking passages should be referred to Christ. We had
several of this kind in the promises above, and below there is mention
of the coming שִׁילֹה (Shiloh; cf. 49:10), who is the Son of the uterus,
the Son of the womb. We should not follow the interpretations of

the rabbis, who obscure Christ in horrible fashion, for the fathers carefully took notice of this Jewel enclosed in their bodily blessings and worshiped It. Otherwise Jacob would not have said here: "The Fear of Isaac." For He is the Son of God, Christ Jesus, incarnate in the Second Person. Nor does he speak in this way because He is another god from the God of Abraham, but to signify the mystery of the Trinity.

In this manner these emphatic words, which Moses scatters like jewels here and there in his writings, are wonderfully sweet, provided they are referred to Christ. For other explanations are cold and rotten, like the one about the sacrifice of Isaac.

These are also the truest and most beautiful adornments of these stories, with which the Holy Spirit describes acts of the saintly patriarchs that are so mean and trifling that they seem worthless and wicked to hypocrites and papists. But they represent the highest wisdom and faith. Therefore, whatever the saints do, however insignificant and sordid, it is great and glorious because they do it by faith and the Word, that is, in innocence and holiness. Christ says: "Believe, and you will be well" (cf. Luke 8:50), that is, "You will be clean and holy, and what you do will all be clean, holy, and useful, just as there is nothing useless in a sheep." For even the dung and the bones have their use, not only the milk and the wool. The murmurings in the saints are that dung; they do not injure the saints, however, but all things work together for their good (cf. Rom. 8:28) because they live, act, and suffer in their faith in the Word. "Thy Word," says Christ, "is truth" (John 17:17). Therefore he who apprehends and believes the Word is upright, holy, and righteous. On the contrary, all enemies of the Word, although outwardly holy, are worthless and damned.

These things should be carefully noted for our consolation and teaching and for that of the church, so that we may know that our life is pleasing and acceptable to God also in its humble duties. Reason and the world does not know this, for it is carried off to strange visions, manifestations, and speculations, as well as to horrid and monstrous works, fastings, watchings, etc. This is where the monks and the philosophers among the heathen came from. They wanted to gain preeminence over others by these monstrosities and to turn the eyes of the crowd upon themselves. But the wisdom of the world is foolishness before God.

Jacob, accordingly, lives without the outward show of works in

4

marriage and in slavery, and he appears worthless before God as he is most wretched in the world. For the world does not discern what faith is and what power faith has, such a hidden and unknown thing is faith to reason. According to the statement of Christ (cf. John 14:17), "The world cannot receive the Holy Spirit"; it neither sees nor hears nor perceives Him by any sense. But we should make it our aim that the godly are taught and stirred up to faith in the Word so that they may be found to be eager in the practice of the Word. For in that case, all the works, political and domestic, with which they are occupied are excellent works; whether you walk, whether you sleep, or whether you are awake, all your works are pleasing to God because the Word, faith, and the Spirit which dwells in you are good.

Finally, this also belongs to our consolation, that Jacob says that the God of his father had been on his side, etc., and that He had had regard for his affliction and the toil of his hands. For what else is the toil of his hands but the poor, weak, and sordid duties which have hitherto been described in him as in any shepherd? These things the Holy Spirit wanted set before the churches and the believers as an example and for their strengthening, that they may know for certain that God has regard for all the works of the saints and the godly, yes, that He even numbers their hairs one by one (cf. Matt. 10:30), as has been stated several times above. So great is His concern and care for those who hear His Word and believe it.

This consolation, moreover, is especially necessary for the church because the devil, together with the whole world and our flesh, in wretched fashion afflicts and harasses those who have the Word. Consolation or protection must not be expected from the world and the princes of this world, nor should carnal counsels be sought from ourselves, for they are vain. Indeed, those who seek or await help of this kind experience what is said in the psalm (116:11), "All men are liars," and again (Ps. 146:3), "Put not your trust in princes, in a son of man, in whom there is no help." But the whole world is carried along in its blind frenzy and perishes in its vain counsels and endeavors because it does not want to suffer the persecution of the devil, the ungodly, and the flesh.

Hence, God must have regard and care for His own, who, destitute of all help and counsel, have their eyes fixed on His Word. For they bear the cross and their troubles. So Jacob was tormented not only by the devil but by his own father-in-law, his blood relative. Therefore, we should learn and observe this, that God numbers all our actions and thoughts, however trifling and abject they may be, if only we believe in Him. For if we care for His Word, He in turn cares for us in all adversities which are thrown in our way by the world and Satan.

43. *Then Laban answered and said to Jacob: The daughters are my daughters, the children are my children, the flocks are my flocks, and all that you see is mine. But what can I do this day to these my daughters, or to their children whom they have borne?*

Up to this point Moses has set forth the example and picture of a saintly man, the excellent and faithful servant Jacob, showing what kinds of things he did and how much he suffered, how he tried either to win over his adversary to a knowledge of his sins in accordance with love or to lead him to repentance. In this way he performed the service of a holy and just man. But what he achieved we shall hear next.

For Moses describes the opposite example of the worst hypocrite. Although he has depicted him quite graphically above, namely, what kind of man he was towards his son-in-law, daughters, and grandchildren, nevertheless, let us now see how much he has improved in his behavior and life after the admonition and reproof of God and Jacob. First he says: "The daughters are my daughters, and the sons are my sons. What can I do to them?" O you holy man, St. Laban! Here there is not a word of penitence or confession. He does not say: "My dear Jacob, I acknowledge and confess my sin, for I treated you too cruelly and not at all like a father. Nor did I conduct myself towards you and my daughters as was becoming of me." This word you will never extort from a hypocrite, unless it is on a very rare occasion, for a hypocrite is such a monstrosity that he is simply sinless, if I may say so, and not to be converted. To a hypocrite it seems impossible that he should sin or go astray, even if he is admonished about his sin and error in such a way that he can feel it with his hands.

We have this picture set before us also in others, in Pharaoh and in Saul. Or, if ever they acknowledge a sin in words, they nevertheless do it rarely or definitely hypocritically and in pretense. The sinner is the only holy man, the only righteous man! Indeed, unrighteous men do not sin even on a civil level, especially if they are surrounded by authority or tyranny. Heinz the incendiary, the bishop of Mainz, Doctor Jeckel, and Grickel never do wrong; they are the righteous and holy ones among men! [36] This is indeed a great temptation and indignity which seriously offends and afflicts the flesh. But these examples are written to console and strengthen us so that we may know that it cannot be otherwise but that we must live with such hypocrites and with all the greater courage endure such perversity of carnal judgments. Jacob alone is the sinner, but Laban is just! So also we at Wittenberg are the only sinners! Even though we give an account of our doctrine and prove and defend it to everyone who asks us, and refute and convict our adversaries by their own judgment and conscience, we nevertheless achieve nothing. They are righteous, we are wicked. He who cannot bear and endure these things cannot be a Christian. They have to be in the right; Christ and Christians are in the wrong!

Let us now look at the words of Laban which we shall interpret not slanderously but sincerely, not according to the opinion of his own heart, according to which all things seem to be spoken proudly and scornfully. For his statement "The daughters are my daughters" is indeed true, but they had already been given to Jacob as wives. The flocks likewise were his reward acquired with much sweat. Therefore he is lying, and I could interpret his words more correctly in this way. But I shall not follow the harder meaning. Let us receive the words as having been uttered with a father's heart: "You have all things from me, my son! I am your father, why should I harm my own people? I have given you my daughters, sheep, and cattle; you have obtained all things by my favor. May the Lord bless you so that you may grow and enjoy what is yours in a godly and happy manner; may you be blessed!" In this way a sincere and good father is accustomed to speak to daughters, a son-in-law, and grandchildren. The hypocrite uses the same words, but they are all false and feigned. This we shall demonstrate by two proofs.

First, he does not acknowledge his guilt and the robberies that Jacob throws into his teeth. For Jacob has accused him of theft and other serious crimes as well as of cruelty towards himself and his daughters. He acknowledges and confesses none of these things but is righteous. Therefore, although such hypocrites use the words of honest men, as Laban gives a fine imitation of the words of a good

---

[36] Luther is referring to Duke Henry of Braunschweig (1489—1568), Albert, Bishop of Mainz (1490—1545), Jakob Schenk (1508—1546), and John Agricola (1492—1566).

and faithful father, nevertheless, they do not speak from the heart. They are not honest.

Secondly, it was becoming of a father to offer a small gift to his daughters and grandchildren, saying: "My daughter Rachel, here you have 10 gold pieces for a dress, etc. Here, Reuben, take this along as a remembrance of your grandfather, etc." But he does not confess his sin, nor does he bestow any gift in testimony of his paternal love and good will. The purpose of everything is to deceive and cheat an excellent man so that his wives and brethren may change their opinion of Jacob, forget all the wrongs, and praise the kindness of the father-in-law. But the fruits inform against the tree.

For, before all things, God requires a confession and a restitution of what has been taken away, and then that a man should show some proof of good will and unfeigned love. But nothing of this comes to pass; the righteous hypocrite perseveres in his righteousness and yet he produces no sign of righteousness, neither affirmatively nor negatively. So Jacob's reproach is vain and useless. This is the first thing which, as we stated, we interpret sincerely, omitting the harsher and odious meaning. But he proceeds and now also becomes religious and holy. He is not content to defend his own righteousness against unrighteous Jacob, as though he had not sinned against Jacob. Therefore he will now have to be raised to heaven, to the choirs of angels.

44. *Come now, let us make a covenant, you and I; and let it be a witness between you and me.*

The hypocrite repeats and very often emphasizes this clause: "Let it be a witness between you and me," as the whole narrative will show. For when they have no fruits, hypocrites are nevertheless accustomed to abound in leaves, like the fig tree that was cursed (cf. Matt. 21:19). With great tediousness he repeats this again and again: "Let God, the mountain, the heap, and the pillar, etc., be a witness between me and you." But there is neither fact nor truth behind this. Those who want to live in the world must accustom themselves to these artifices of the hypocrites.

He now begins to overwhelm the saintly man with ill will and suspicion. For he pretends that he fears God and that by his admonitions he wants to stir up Jacob to the fear of God, as though Jacob were not religious enough. He wants to make a treaty in the presence of God and erect a pillar, and he is very concerned in making a settlement with him about boundaries, lest Jacob should cross them and

inflict some damage on him. But what was the purpose of such solicitude in the case of a man whose faithfulness and diligence he had
learned to know excellently and very clearly in the course of 20 years?
What was the need of binding a faithful son-in-law by means of an
oath and such religious pomp in a treaty? Previously he had given
him his daughters as wives and had had faith in him in regard to
the administration of the family property. Why did he now fear
him when he was living in a foreign land?

It is nothing else but pretense and empty pomp, by which he
tries to dishonor a saintly man and render him suspect, as though
danger were threatening from him. He arrogates innocency and righteousness to himself and pretends great fear of wicked Jacob, as
though he were thinking of doing him harm. If he had been a good
and honest man, he would rather have said: "Go your way, my dear
Jacob! The Lord bless you with yours; if I can serve your interests,
I shall do it with the greatest readiness. If any danger or difficulty
is encountered, indicate it, and you will see that you are cherished
and loved by me in a fatherly manner. I shall never fail you and
my dear daughters and grandchildren." But he promises nothing.
Indeed, he oppresses Jacob with the additional burden of ill will,
inasmuch as he pretends that he is afraid of Jacob. For his aim is
that he be respected in his holiness and religion but that Jacob be
rendered suspect to all because of an eagerness to do harm. Therefore, since he cannot convict him and rebuke him for some sin, he
nevertheless tries to brand him with a certain stigma so that he might
depart under suspicion of wrongdoing and ungodliness.

But it also occurs to me that Laban was somehow alarmed after
the manner of the wicked, who have an evil conscience and have
a way of becoming terrified and alarmed at the sound of a leaf (cf.
Lev. 26:36), as Solomon says (Prov. 28:1): "The wicked flee when
no one pursues." The poets tell the story of Orestes when he was
driven by the Furies,[37] and there is an excellent description in Juvenal
of those who toil under the torment of conscience. He says: "Still,
why should you think that they have escaped punishment whom their
hearts, conscious of a foul deed, keep terror-struck?" [38] These are the
ones who are alarmed and who grow pale at every flash of lightning.
For this is the punishment which is joined to sin.

Therefore, although Laban knew that no danger threatened him

[37] Luther is thinking of the *Eumenides* of Aeschylus.
[38] Juvenal, *Satires*, XIII, 192—194.

from his son-in-law, whom he had tried and found to be good and faithful, it could also have happened that he was still afraid of others, the parents, or relatives, or friends of Jacob. But the chief factor was that by this outward show and hypocrisy he was eager to extol himself and to oppress Jacob. With such men, therefore, the godly have to do in the world, men who are deceptive materially and spiritually, and that, too, under the outward show of holiness, righteousness, godliness, and religion; and they triumph when they are able to overwhelm us with an impression of religion cultivated by them and violated by us. Laban alone is therefore righteous and holy in regard to the First and Second Table. This is the picture and image of the world.

45. *So Jacob took a stone, and set it up as a pillar.*

Jacob is ready to make a treaty for the sole reason that thereby he may be conveniently and quickly separated from this worthless hypocrite. For association with hypocrites is most irksome to all the godly. It is more tolerable for anybody to deal with an open enemy than with a hypocrite who pretends friendship and good will and inwardly nourishes hatred and ill will. Nothing is more grievous and troublesome than to associate, live, and eat with a man who at the same time is intent on all opportunities to criticize and harm you and who cannot be convicted of violence or fraud. But this hypocrisy and secret intrigue must be borne; to be sure, he swears by everything holy that he is one's greatest friend and completely devoted to true godliness. If you were to charge him with lying and reproach him for his evasive and crafty heart, he would still remain unconquered by dissimulating and making a complete denial. Jacob therefore simply accepts the proposition and hurries to make a treaty. He sets up a stone with his own hands as a pillar and memorial of the treaty, thinking as follows: "O that I might be removed from this worthless scoundrel!" Indeed, he encourages his brethren to heap up stones. We should do the same. We should flee association with hypocrites by whatever way this can be done.

46. *And Jacob said to his kinsmen: Gather stones, and they took stones and made a heap; and they ate there by the heap.*

47. *Laban called it Jegar-sahadutha: but Jacob called it Gilead.*

In the manner of Scripture, Jacob called the shepherds and his relatives who were descended from Nahor brethren. They could

both have been satisfied with the making of the treaty, but holy
Laban wants to give it greater strength. He is not satisfied to have
set up a stone as a memorial of the treaty, but he is the first to give
a name to the pillar in the Syriac or Chaldean language, for the sole
purpose of binding the conscience of his son-in-law. He wants to
say this: "Behold, we have made a treaty; we have heaped up stones;
we have made a heap and given a name to the heap. It will be your
duty to remember this treaty." Behold his wonderful religious scruples about keeping this treaty, when above he changed the contract
for wages 10 times! Indeed, if he had not been rebuked by God,
he would not have made any treaty but would have dragged Jacob
back into his former captivity. גַּל signifies a heap; עֵד, a witness.
Jacob has regard to the Eighth Commandment about not speaking
false witness. The Syriac word has the same meaning as the Hebrew
word, a mound heaped up of stones, a hillock of stones or earth.

It is not in vain that he calls it a mound of testimony, for he wants
to say: "Be mindful of the mound that has been raised up. Let it
be a perpetual reminder to you in your ears and heart not to forget
this peace-making. For if you violate it, it will stand against you
as a most solemn testimony in heaven and on earth. On my account
it would not have been necessary to heap up this mound of stones;
I am a righteous man. But danger threatens us from you." Thus he
pretends to be concerned about nothing but religion and righteousness, and secretly he brands Jacob with suspicion and the stigma of
treachery. These things cannot be read without a great amount of
righteous indignation; and yet it is not sufficient to have imposed the
name once; no, he repeats the same thing more often.

48. *Laban said: This heap is a witness between you and me today.*
Therefore it was named Gilead.

He proceeds to lay emphasis on the memorial and carefully attends
to everything. He designates not only the place but also the time,
and later he will also note the persons. He is a very good notary, and
he knows how to secure the instrument. Moses, however, added this
clause: "Therefore it was named וְגַלְעֵד." For it is a very celebrated
name in Holy Scripture, in Jeremiah (cf. Jer. 8:22) and elsewhere,
and it is even transferred metaphorically to Jerusalem, which is called
a mound of witness because it is a holy city and the city of God,
in which the worship and the Word and oracles of God sounded
forth. It is an elevated hill and mound of God on which many wit-

nesses of God lived who heard God speaking and testified concerning Him by their confession, preaching, and thanksgiving. In this manner the prophets transferred it as a common noun to Jerusalem and to the church universal. At Jerusalem there were congregations, and the testimonies of God sounded forth.

But Laban was not yet content with this repetition; he could not sufficiently fortify the treaty which had been made. This is usual with hypocrites and heretics. There is only empty talk in them. This is clear in the case of the Sacramentarians, who abound in their supply of words and cannot sufficiently magnify and extol what is their own, but they disparage and roughen up what is ours. Therefore he adds:

49. *and the pillar Mizpah, for he said: The Lord watch between you and me, when we are absent one from the other.*

This is also a celebrated place in Holy Scripture. Later it became the proper name for a city not far from Gilead, as is clear from Joshua (13:11). As a common noun, however, it signifies a lookout, a watchtower from where we look out for the coming of the enemy, fires, or other happenings, etc. "Therefore the mound of witness is not sufficient," thinks Laban. "But because he dared to depart from me once and carry off my daughters, he will perhaps return some time later and take my life. Hence there will be need of a watchtower." He even adduces the name and presence of God! "The Lord watch between me and you," he says. "Not only do I receive the mound on the earth and among men as a testimony, but I also make an appeal to the sight of almighty God, that He may be a witness and observer." Oh, what religion, sanctity, steadfastness, and truth in the worship and invocation of God!

In this way, such people dare to boast of God and godliness. They do not repent but are most stubborn and obstinate in their sins. For Laban is your impenitent and secure hypocrite over against the saintly and excellent man Jacob, and he overwhelms him with testimonies heavenly and earthly by which he wants to burden his conscience. What then should Jacob say or do? Laban is exceedingly holy and dares to invoke God as a witness and observer. "When we are absent," he says, "that is, when you have returned to your fatherland and I have returned home and you plot something without my knowledge and when I shall not be able to foresee your stratagems, then I shall leave this mound as a protection and fortification between

me and you, and then, too, as a watchtower between us and God."
So he calls both God and men to witness.

These are assuredly strong enough reminders of the treaty. Who
now denies that Laban is a saintly man, when he invokes God with
such great confidence and relies on God's help and protection? But
he does this only to terrify and burden Jacob. By all things holy
he puts him under oath whom he had previously found to be very
good and faithful. In this way hypocrisy extols itself and despises and
dishonors all others in comparison with self. Then, too, all hypocrites
are liars, and so he does not yet stop but adds another protest.

50. *If you ill-treat my daughters, or if you take wives besides my
daughters, although no man is with us, remember, God is witness
between you and me.*

Behold a poet who is most ingenious in the invention of cases!
"Do not ill-treat my daughters," he says. This is only a pretext and
the emptiest of fictions. But the case which he adduced above is
nearer the truth, namely, that neither Jacob himself nor his relatives
should harm him. Again, he burdens the excellent man and in a veiled
manner accuses him of adultery, as though he had previously regarded
him suspect of adultery and is now compelled to fear his desertion
or departure from his daughters.

Alas! what should the saintly man have done who loved his
wives and children so much that he had served 14 years for both
women and endured a heavy servitude so long? He had also married
the one whom he did not love and whom he did not seek as his
wife and had performed many services for his father-in-law beyond
the usual services of a son-in-law and servant. Who would accuse
this man or hold him suspect of treating his wives with too little
kindness?

But Laban makes a boast of paternal affection and στοργή ("natural
affection"). "Ah! what will become of my daughters when they are
carried away so far from my sight? See to it that you remember this
treaty and do not offend them in word or deed!" Thus he oppresses
Jacob with poisonous slander, and yet he pretends and lies in every
respect. Nor do you hear any word by which he testifies that he
acknowledges his sin or wants to render satisfaction to his son-in-law
and grandchildren for wrongs inflicted. He pretends that he is moved
by paternal concern and solicitude regarding his daughters. But he

shows himself in no way milder or more generous than he was
previously.

He also adds: "No man is with us," that is, "we two stand alone
near the heap." Concerning this a question can be asked, namely,
whether they conversed alone, with witnesses removed, or in the
sight of all the relatives who were present, but with strangers excluded. It can be understood in both ways, although the meaning
more acceptable to me is that he excluded foreigners and strangers.
"Although we are alone," he says, "and men whom you fear are not
present, nevertheless, God is present as an observer, and He sees and
is a witness between me and you." Everything tends to burden an
innocent man, if not with infamy and the mark of manifest disgrace,
at least with suspicion and ill will. Such are the characters of
hypocrites. From the one criminal person learn to know all of them,
as we read in the poet.[39]

51. *Then Laban said to Jacob: See this heap and the pillar, which
I have set between you and me.*

52. *This heap is a witness, and the pillar is a witness, that I will not
pass over this heap to you, and you will not pass over this heap
and this pillar to me, for harm.*

He repeats the same things and amplifies them in rhetorical fashion.
But in the end he betrays the real reason for such anxious peace-
making after he has poured out such thunderous words against Jacob.
He makes no mention of his daughters but shows that he is afraid
that Jacob may devise some evil against him or that his relatives,
who may eventually wish to avenge these wrongs, may do so. "If
I will not pass over." This is a Hebrew way of speaking; "if" is
used instead of "that." He means to say: "I shall not cross over to
you. Even if in extreme necessity you have need of a drink of cold
water, I shall not be at your side to offer it to you. But if you cross
over to me for harm, this heap and this pillar will punish you."
Conscious of the evil in himself, he fears all things safe, trusts no
one, and yet extols himself under the name and title [40] of religion and
the treaty.

But in reality this trepidation and terror is the greatest punishment

[39] Vergil, *Aeneid, II,* 65—66.

[40] The Weimar text has *a titulo,* but we have followed the Erlangen text and
read *et titulo.*

of the hypocrites and the ungodly. For an evil conscience cannot rest or be quiet. It is like a little dog, in German called Remorse;[41] if it is quiet in life, it is nevertheless present at the time of death and barks. Now, Jacob had the best and surest testimony of conscience, even by the silent testimony of Laban himself. But Laban is conscious of the wrongs and treachery he committed against his son-in-law in return for his great services and by which he increased his property. For he was content with small wages; he allowed himself to be sent away empty-handed. Therefore Laban thinks: "What if he causes trouble for me at some time with his friends, mindful of this wrong, and seeks to get back from me what remains his due of the inheritance and wages?" He wants to fortify himself so that he should not cross over and cause confusion and trouble. But if he should return to his former servitude and misery, he would bear it more easily. "But I shall not cross over to you," he says; "I shall not come to you or be enriched or benefited by you as you have come to me."

53. *The God of Abraham and the God of Nahor, the God of their father, judge between us.*

How can the rascal make things so hot? With this thunder, as it were, he tried to terrify the saintly man and to disgrace him as an unrighteous and ungodly scoundrel but to display his own positively angelic holiness. But he is taking the name of the Lord in vain (cf. Ex. 20:7). This garrulity betrays the heart of hypocrites and their contemptible malevolence, according to the statement in Prov. 14:23: "Where words are many, there is frequently penury." Laban, however, understands the god of his father to be the one Terah and Abraham worshiped when he was still an idolater in Ur of the Chaldees. He is referring to that idolatry of his fathers of which mention is made in Joshua 24:2: "Your fathers lived of old beyond the Euphrates, Terah, the father of Abraham and of Nahor; and they served other gods."

Up to here, then, we have the picture and image of a hypocrite and idolater, who pretends everything and takes the name of God in vain. But even as we have heard only the empty sound of words in the hypocrite, so, on the other hand, Jacob pays attention to brevity, and he is full of godliness and excellent fruits. Therefore he attends to everything with the very few words. For he had previously re-

41 See p. 369.

proved Laban heavily enough, but because he perseveres in his smugness, pride, and ungodliness, he lets him go. For the hypocrite prattles nothing else but blasphemies against God and revilings against righteous and saintly Jacob.

53. *So Jacob swore by the Fear of his father Isaac,*

54. *and Jacob offered a sacrifice on the mountain and called his kinsmen to eat bread; and they ate bread and tarried all night on the mountain.*

55. *Early in the morning Laban arose and kissed his grandchildren and his daughters and blessed them; then he departed and returned home.*

Jacob does not swear by the God of Nahor or Terah, but he swears by a God who is closer, that is, by the God whom his father fears and worships, by Christ, according to the commandments and promises of God. For hypocrites also serve God but by the commandments and tradition of men. It is as Isaiah and Christ say (Is. 29:13; Matt. 15:8): "This people honors Me with their lips, but their heart is far from Me." No one comes closer to God with the lips, no one employs the name of God more frequently, than hypocrites. But God proclaims that their worship is idolatrous. "I indeed hear My name," He says, "I am called Creator of heaven and earth by them, but contrary to the Second Commandment. For they do not call Me so from the heart; no, they corrupt their worship by the commandments of men. 'They ask of Me righteous judgments,' says Is. 58:2, 'they delight to draw near to God.' I do not want to be worshiped with human acts of worship and doctrines but in the fear of Myself, that is, that you may embrace My Word in faith. As stated in the last chapter of Isaiah (66:2): 'To whom shall I look, if not to him who is humble and contrite in spirit and trembles at My Word'; by them I want to be worshiped. It is also stated in Is. 8:13: 'But the Lord of hosts, Him you shall regard as holy; let Him be your fear, and let Him be your dread, and He will become your sanctification.'"

If Christ, then, is to be our fear, that is, when He should be worshiped by us, it is necessary that we have the Word and promise of God. Such fear or dread is true worship, which brings it to pass in us that we despise all other dread and terrors, as Isaiah says (8:12-13): "Do not fear what they fear, nor be in dread. But the Lord you shall regard as holy." He will protect you well, and you must consider that He is to be feared, revered, and worshiped, who speaks with you. "If you do this, then I the Lord will be your fear," He says. For you have a certain and firm Word, and when you retain it, you will not err in your divine worship.

In this manner Isaiah understood this passage when he calls God our dread or fear, namely, on account of the worship which is offered to God according to His precepts and promises, not only with the lips, as hypocrites fear and worship, without the Word and on the basis of the commandments of men. Jacob, accordingly, sacrifices with this faith and confession, which a hypocrite does not do. It seems to the latter that he is too good and too holy to have need of making a sacrifice and invocation to God, for he justifies his iniquities. But Jacob gives thanks to God; he sacrifices and prepares a banquet, which was required for a sacrifice; he calls his friends together and undoubtedly preaches a sermon here. Laban paid no attention to the sacrifice, although, perhaps, he joined the others in the banquet. But Jacob praises God and the Fear of his father, that is, Christ, because he was liberated from that scoundrel. When the banquet was over, Laban departed. We are also now rid of the miserable rascal!

But before he departs, the hypocrite kisses his sons and daughters not with a paternal love and affection but with a certain show of humanity and attachment observed for fashion's sake in the customs and conventions of all the nations. For he dismisses them without any remuneration. He takes his leave of them in words, but inwardly in his heart he nourishes ill will and the most bitter hatred, in which he cannot even refrain from begrudging them the things which they had acquired by God's blessing and without his gift. These, then, are two contrary pictures, that of a most cruel hypocrite who sins without end and is an example of all crimes, idolatry, hypocrisy, avarice, and final impenitence, and that of an excellent and saintly man, who had a conflict on his hands for such a long time with a monster of this kind.

CHAPTER THIRTY-TWO

1. *Jacob went on his way, and the angels of God met him;*

2. *and when Jacob saw them, he said: This is God's army! So he called the name of that place Mahanaim.*

AFTER Laban had left, the holy patriarch Jacob, freed from the heavy and long misery of servitude under his father-in-law, rejoiced that peace and consolation had finally been restored to him after the completion of his tribulation. He then proceeded on the journey he had begun, that he might return to his dear father Isaac, who already for a long time had been weakened by old age.

But Moses says that as he went, the angels of God met [1] him and on seeing them he recognized them with great joy as God's army and God's host and called the name of this place מַחֲנָיִם, for he said: "This host is God's host." But in Latin we cannot render the Hebrew word in the singular number. For it is a plural noun, or rather, a dual, a number which is also employed in Greek. מַחֲנָיִם means "two camps." These are words of joy and triumph for the patriarch with great confidence and a feeling of security because of the peace given to him by God, just as though he meant to say: "Now the angels are appearing, heaven is laughing, the stormy winter has passed, and now the clear and serene light of day is shining forth."

To this quiet joy of having now brought to an end all his troubles and difficulties there also comes this addition, that he has angels and God's army meeting him. But Moses also testified before this that the patriarchs frequently enjoyed appearances of angels, as he related above concerning Abraham, Hagar, and Jacob's ladder with its angels ascending and descending; also when Jacob was told to return to his fatherland. Yes, they often saw angels, and indeed, the excellent and holy fathers had special need of the sight of them. But here he sees not one angel but a host of angels. Luke also says (Luke 2:13): "Suddenly there was with the angel a multitude of the heavenly host."

The angels are called hosts, soldiers (στρατιῶται), watchmen,

---

[1] The Weimar text has *factus,* but we have read *factos.*

guides, and governors over God's creation. For this is their lower
office. Their higher office is to sing: "Glory to God in the highest."
Their lower duty is to watch and govern us and the creatures, and to
fight not only on behalf of the godly but also on behalf of the ungodly,
as is clear from Daniel (10:20), where the angel says that he is returning to fight against the prince of the Persians. But a good angel does
not resist a good angel, and so the prince of the Persians was an evil
angel of the number of those concerning whom Christ says (John
12:31): "Now shall the ruler of this world be cast out." Satan, the
god of this world, has very large hosts of devils, and there is a kind
of monarchy among the evil angels.

The matter speaks for itself, and Scripture demonstrates it quite
clearly since, indeed, we see the world horribly embroiled, disturbed,
confounded, and struck by horrible outrages. This comes about because the evil angels rule everywhere in the courts of the pope, the
emperor, kings, and princes, yes, even in private homes. These are
and are called works of the devil, which we see and experience, but
the world does not see that murders and other infinite crimes are committed under the authority and at the instigation of the devil. All
see the effect, but they do not see the cause. It is certain, therefore,
that the leaders among the good angels fight against the leaders of
the evil angels, for experience testifies to this. The heathen also retained a vague shadow of this knowledge when they invented their
household gods [2] or good and evil genii. God is the Creator and Ruler
of all men, and through the angels He controls the empires even of
the ungodly, such as the Babylonians, Assyrians, and Persians, as
Daniel testifies. The same is clear in our courts and their rulers. As
a result of this, it comes to pass that the very best of causes are often
hindered, disturbed, and protracted at the courts in various ways and
yet at length favorable outcomes are obtained under the leadership
and counsels of the good angels. These are the wonderful counsels
of God, concerning which there can be no dispute why He governs
the world in this or that manner.

But it is a matter of great and wonderful wisdom that Jacob can
recognize the angels who meet him and that he can call them God's
hosts, our Lord God's troops. Surely God does not have armies and
hosts on earth? Yes, this is what Jacob calls all the angels. And he
did not have this knowledge from his father-in-law Laban, who was

---

[2] A reference to the Roman *lares* and *penates*.

an impious idolater and not a teacher of such sublime and heavenly matters. But as stated above, such knowledge was handed down in a direct tradition from the fathers.[3] For Abraham saw Noah for more than 50 years; Shem also lived beyond the age of Abraham, and Isaac and Jacob saw and heard him. He was a great teacher, a prophet and priest of the Most High, who took this doctrine from Enoch, the grandson of Adam.

These men were the teachers and hearers who preserved this doctrine and handed it on to their posterity. At the same time, however, there were the additional factors of experience and tribulation. He who has such leaders and masters will easily make much progress. Jacob not only learned from his forefathers, but he also had experience as a teacher. He saw the angels ascending and descending, and likewise in Mesopotamia with his father-in-law he saw and heard the angel in his sleep. In this place he sees a host and armies of angels. Thus fact and words combine, or knowledge and fact and experience. Otherwise this doctrine and wisdom is too sublime for it to be comprehensible by human reason, which does not know that angels exercise care over empires, kingdoms, the household, men, beasts, and, in short, all creatures.

The Epistle to the Hebrews (1:14) describes them in the words: "Are they not all ministering spirits sent forth to serve, for the sake of those who are to obtain salvation?" They are not gods or goddesses but ministers who serve the world, and who do so on account of those who will inherit eternal salvation. For whatever is done in this life is all done on account of the godly men and those who are to be saved. For their sakes the sun shines, kingdoms are preserved and established, the earth is made fruitful, and marriages are contracted. In short, all things in heaven and earth are ordained to this end, that the righteous should be gathered together and the number of those who are to be saved should be filled up.

Accordingly, this is a truly heavenly doctrine and not a matter of human reason and wisdom that in this life empires, states, and households, and, in short, whatever this world has are all governed by the ministry of the holy angels.

But a question now arises. If these things are true and certain, as they assuredly are, then the opinion of Erasmus and of all the Epicureans is completely false. For they, moved by the infinite ine-

---

[3] See *Luther's Works*, 2, p. 116, n. 27.

quality and confusion of matters in this life, where they see wicked men more fortunate than good and godly men, descend to such a level that they deny this protection and ministry of the angels, and, indeed, the very providence of God. But both common experience as well as the complaints of the saints testify that the greater scoundrel anyone is, so much the more fortunate he is. Cicero says: "What is most excellently thought out falls out worst." [4] Also extant are the complaints of Julius Caesar, Demosthenes, and others who were outstanding in wisdom, doctrine, virtue, and ability, concerning the unfortunate result and outcome of their counsels. To be sure, the deaths of these same men were very sad in comparison with their very great services to the state. If godly men are oppressed, the church is afflicted and severely disciplined. The ungodly come forth, flourish, and abound in wealth and power. What, then, is this service of the angels? Who cannot see that all things are borne along and confused by chance and at random and that this government is rather Satan's? Christ calls him the prince of the world (John 12:31), and Paul calls him the god of this age (2 Cor. 4:4). How then does the administration of the angels stand? My reply is that this, as I previously stated, is the wonderful and incomprehensible wisdom of God which human reason does not grasp. However, if we should want to open our eyes, we would be able to perceive this and form this conclusion, that the devil is bound and held captive as though fetters and manacles had been put on him to such an extent that he cannot touch even a hair of our head except by God's will and permission. If something adverse occurs, it must not be attributed to neglect on the part of the angels in their ministry, but it must rather be referred to the temptation by which the godly as individuals and the whole church are accustomed to be disciplined in this life. For the power of the devil is not as great as it appears to be outwardly; for if he had full power to rage as he pleased, you would not live for one hour or retain safe and intact a single sheep, a crop in the field, corn in the barn, and, in short, any of those things which pertain to this life.

But now ponder in your heart the whole course of nature and of this whole life and survey every kind of men, cattle, birds, and fish, and you will find more good than bad things and you will also see that a very small part is subjected to the power of the devil. For

---

[4] In the form quoted here, *Optime cogitata pessime evenire,* this proverb does not seem to appear in the extant writings of Cicero, but there are similar formulas in places such as *De divinatione,* I, 24.

he is compelled to leave the fish in the rivers, the birds in the air, the men and animals in the villages and cities, which he would not do if it were not for the protection of the angels. At times, however, he causes great disturbances, brings kingdoms and monarchies into conflict with each other, and throws provinces, states, and households into confusion. To be sure, he causes disturbance, and yet he is not able to carry out what he most desires, to overthrow all things and to mingle heaven with earth. So strong are the walls, fortifications, and hedges of the angels round about us and all things.

Therefore, if the evil things which happen in this life are compared with the good things, the number and abundance of the good things will be far greater than that of the evil things, with the exception of those things which pertain to temptation or the punishment and chastisement of sinners if ever sins prevail and kingdoms, states, and princes are handed over for punishment and destruction, as God destroyed Sodom and the neighboring cities. In that case the walls and armies of the angels cease their activities. But in the state and all orders of life the devil stirs up various tumults; he impels men to adulteries, thefts, murders, and perjuries. But for all that he does not seduce or subvert all people, for he is put under restraint so that he is not even able to kill whom he wishes from among the evil. For if all things were in his power, he would even destroy the ungodly, although they have been already previously enmeshed in his fetters.

Therefore God tolerates even the wicked and sinners to declare His great goodness and tolerance, but only up to the time which has been set for punishment. When their iniquities have been filled up, He withdraws His hand.

In this manner a reply can be given to the question: If the angels are the armies of God and spirits who serve, why do so many evil things happen which are displeasing to God? Things go well with the ungodly; they are given life, honors, offices, and they abound in wealth. All these things are certainly given to the very worst of men by the good angels. But I reply that there should be no discussion about the counsels of God as to why He bestows good things also on evil men and scatters His gifts among the good and evil alike, on the ungrateful and grateful, as Christ says in Matt. 5. For this comes to pass that He may show that He has not only a human goodness circumscribed by its own limits but rather immense, infinite, and incomprehensible goodness.

Therefore let us leave God's administration of matters to Him and praise His great mercy since, indeed, it is manifest that more good happens than evil, also in the case of evil and blasphemous men, who also have their own bodily blessings. For if God were not to govern the world through His angels even for one day, the devil would certainly strike down the whole human race all of a sudden, plunder it, and drive it off, destroying it with famine, plague, wars, and fires. These things would have to be endured not only by the evil but also by the good. But that we can be secure and safe from such great perils under the protection of the armies and hosts of heaven, this we should determine for certain. At times the angels even permit some evils to happen. But they do this so that we may be tried and that our faith may be proved and exercised and that in this way we may learn to recognize God in His wonderful counsels and works and give thanks to Him for His wonderful government, as this example of the patriarch Jacob teaches us. For he goes on his way joyfully and confidently because the sun has dawned on him and heavenly hosts have met him. But some time later the sun will set again. Now he reigns and triumphs full of faith and spiritual joy, but soon he will be thrown into the greatest misery and confusion.

In the same manner, God leads and governs both the godly and ungodly. When all things already seem to be at the point of crashing into ruin, all hope and confidence is still not to be completely cast off. Wait, endure, and hold out! God is still living; the angels are ruling and defending. However much they seem to have forgotten their duty and the protection entrusted to them, in actuality they are nevertheless not remiss in their duty. But there is such a thing as temptation and trial, by which God exercises not only the godly but also the ungodly, although the ungodly certainly do not understand this. Similarly, in sudden wind and rain storms flashes of lightning threaten heaven and earth with the conflagration or ruin of the whole earth. But when the storm dies down, the earth sprouts forth and shows that the storm was of great benefit to fertility, however wild it was.

This, then, is the doctrine which is taught in this passage, that the angels are ministering spirits and servants of creation. They fight for the safety and welfare of the world and the godly, and this is their lower office. Their higher office, however, is to sing "Glory to God in the highest" and "We praise Thee, O God, etc." In heaven likewise they see the Father's face (cf. Matt. 18:10). This they do to the glory of God and to their own joy and that of all the believers. They also well understand that wondrous government of this life, namely, how the good fortune of the ungodly agrees with the adverse fortune of the godly, which we cannot understand in this life of the flesh. But at the end of the world and after this life we shall see the most beautiful harmony and concord of this administration.

Just as the rustic does not understand the wonderful symphony of so many sounds in organs or the lyre because he is ignorant of the whole science of harmony, so also we judge that all things are being carried along haphazardly, and we think that God is asleep and the devil awake and reigning. At the same time, the judgment of reason makes its presence felt. It determines that neither God nor man is the ruler of this world but that human affairs take place by chance. This is the wisdom of the flesh, not that heavenly and inestimable knowledge of God's government which shows that the number of those things which are preserved is greater than the number of the things which perish in the world, and likewise, that God's goodness is greater than the devil's ill will. But fleshly reason still remains fixed in the saints and causes them to waver when they see such great confusions and the dissimilarity of fortune. This comes to pass because we are not yet in that light which the angels enjoy and do not yet perceive how sin and righteousness, death and life, darkness and light come into agreement.

Let us therefore learn that the government of the angels is certain and that the devil's ill will is overcome by the boundless mercy of God, who preserves this natural order of things against all the raging and every assault of the devil. For this we see in all areas of this life. The father of a household at times incurs the loss of cattle, poultry, and money, but he retains his house and fields and the most important part of the property.

Thus the great ornament of this town is its university and the assembly of learned men who are engaged in the study of heavenly doctrine and liberal arts. But mixed in with these there are scoundrels who do not recognize that they should live soberly and modestly in the midst of this assembly, in the shrine of the Muses, as it were, yes, in the sanctuary of God and the angels. But as though they were in the midst of the Cyclopes and Centaurs they raise a tumult and dishonor the excellent assembly of teachers by their depraved morals and scandals. But God and the angels see in what manner this dissimilitude is in agreement. Perhaps if the time for punishment and the destruction of the school is not yet at hand, it is a kind of temptation which will cease shortly, and the Lord [5] will grant us other fruits and a blessing from those who live a godly and moderate life and who obey the admonitions of their teachers.

So far concerning the protection of the angels. Knowledge of this and confidence in it is especially useful and necessary for the godly, even as Jacob has caught sight of these heavenly hosts with great joy and now rejoices and exults because of the conquest of all the troubles and devils under his wicked father-in-law Laban. He is joyful and secure in the Lord, and he has the angels as associates and witnesses of this joy.

But the common vicissitudes and changes in the life of the saints should be carefully observed. At one time they are confronted with happy and enjoyable experiences, at another time with sad and troublesome ones. Alternations of this kind occur also in all of nature, as, for example, those of day and night, light and darkness, mountains and valleys, as is stated in the Psalm (104:8): "The mountains rose, the valleys sank down to the place which Thou didst appoint for them." Sometimes we hear what delights us, if not in the world, at least in heaven through the Word of God. At other times temptation and affliction of the spirit return. To these alternations the godly must become accustomed, for a wonderful change will follow immediately.

Furthermore, I take the noun מַחֲנָיִם not as a common noun but as the proper name of a place in the Holy Scriptures. This is to be especially noted because this is where David borrowed the thought of Ps. 34:7: "The angel of the Lord encamps around those who fear him," that is, the angel marks off a camp and builds a rampart around the godly. This is one of the special and most memorable consolations in the psalms and should be applied to our advantage. "And yet I do not see that I am surrounded by the ministry of the angels," you will say, "in fact, I feel the contrary, and it seems to me that I have been handed over to the power of Satan and brought down to hell." By no means should you come to this conclusion! For if you had been handed over to Satan, he would not allow you to survive even for an hour but would drive you headlong into all outrageous crimes

---

[5] The Weimar text has *Dominum,* but we have followed the Erlangen text and read *Dominus.*

and, indeed, he would not even grant you the time to involve you in crimes and sins but would kill you immediately. But the fact that you are alive you owe to the defense and protection of the angels. But if you must depart from this life and succumb to the fury of Satan with God's permission, it is still a great blessing because you have God comforting and consoling you through the Word.

This consignment into Satan's hands which is held up to your eyes and heart is a temptation for an hour and a moment of time, not for your perdition but to try you, for your salvation and endless gain. It is as Christ says in John 12:24: "Unless a grain of wheat falls into the earth and dies, it remains alone; but if it dies, it bears much fruit." For so Christ was also delivered into the hands of robbers, but only for an hour and for salvation. Accordingly, if you feel that you are being vexed and tempted by the devil, pray and give thanks that you have not been consumed but only tried and proved, according to the statement in Lam. 3:22: "It is of the Lord's mercies that we are not consumed, because His compassions fail not." Likewise we read in 2 Cor. 4:9: "We are persecuted, but not forsaken; struck down, but not destroyed, etc."

Job's example teaches the same thing. The devil at first takes all his property from him with his children and leaves him a peevish, irksome, and abusive wife. He also afflicts his health with a terrible ulcer. Nevertheless, the devil says to God: "Have You put a hedge about him?" (Job 1:10) Here he complains that the godly, and the ungodly too, are surrounded by a wall. With silent indignation he threatens destruction to body and property, as though he meant to say: "If Job were in my hands, I would show what I could do and how he should sound forth Your praises. I would bring it to pass that he would curse You to Your face." But the Lord permits him to torture Job's body and to take away his goods but not to take his life.

Accordingly, examples of this kind teach us that all the malice and vexation of the devil is only instruction and chastisement, by which we are aroused so that we do not snore and become listless and are thus overthrown among those who are half asleep. At the same time, however, this doctrine is confirmed and remains sure and certain, that the angels are God's armies regardless of the fact that many evils occur in this life because of the evil angels.

3. *And Jacob sent messengers before him to Esau his brother in the land of Seir, the country of Edom,*

4. *instructing them: Thus you shall say to my lord Esau: Thus says your servant Jacob: I have sojourned with Laban, and stayed until now;*

5. *and I have oxen, asses, flocks, menservants, and maidservants; and I have sent to tell my lord, in order that I may find favor in your sight.*

מַלְאָךְ is the same word he used for naming the angels above. It is the name of an office and not of a nature. For according to their office they are messengers; they are soldiers at a post and on guard for the whole world, but according to their nature they are spirits.

Jacob is still exultant and he proceeds with joy. He is not afraid or alarmed because he is returning from Mesopotamia at the order of God, who strengthened him in a dream through an angel who chided Laban and checked him. And he has here seen the hosts of God. Accordingly, he decides that he must deal with his brother Esau in a kindly and friendly manner, and it is reasonable that he had an earnest and heartfelt desire to see his brother. For he thinks that Esau has become reconciled to him during these 20 years, and so he sends messengers to greet him so that he may know that he is honored and loved as a brother. But later he will send gifts when he hears that Esau is coming to meet him with 400 armed men. That will be rather hard and beyond Jacob's expectation.

The trivialities of the Jews which Lyra seems to have followed in this place are worthless and silly.[6] For they say that Jacob was alarmed because he had stayed too long with idolatrous Laban and had contracted a stigma from him. They likewise think that Jacob thought the promises were conditional and required due service towards God. But such a view should by no means be held concerning the fathers, although it is a true distinction to say that the promises were twofold, conditional and simple without a condition, as, for example, the promise of the Law is conditional and the promise of grace is simple. When wages are promised to one who works, there is a condition which demands the service and duty specified, and if this does not follow, the wages are not paid.

But we should renounce such promises when we have to do with God in a matter of conscience. For we will soon be confounded if we do not attend to our duty for even a single moment. So it is a false

---

[6] Lyra *ad* Gen. 32:3-5, p. 95 verso, note "d."

and a very bad gloss of Lyra that he has taken from the Jews, who make the nonsensical statement that Jacob could not determine that it was a simple promise of grace and without a condition and that his conscience was terrified because he had contaminated himself with the idolatry of his father-in-law. But it is not right to say this about the saintly patriarch Jacob. No doubt he detested and fled idolatry as much as it could be done.

The saints are certainly not without the flesh, but they repress their carnal impulses, lest they break out in action, according to the statement: "Those who belong to Christ Jesus have crucified the flesh with its passions and desires" (Gal. 5:24). For they are mortified through the Spirit, who exercises dominion over them. There are lusts of the flesh here, which does not cease to grumble, but they are not brought forward into effect and deed. The saints do not war according to the flesh (2 Cor. 10:3).

But the promise of grace is this, when God says: "You have done nothing; you have merited nothing. But I shall do this for you and present it to you by mercy alone." Such promises are unmerited, and the promises of the patriarchs Abraham, Isaac, and Jacob were like them. They have been recounted above: "May your mother's sons bow down to you" and "I have established you with oil and wine." [7] Here no condition is attached: "If you do this, you will be blessed," but "You have this promise and blessing gratis." Moses, to be sure, is full of legal promises, but the patriarchs have simple, unmerited promises. Thus Jacob is confident and joyful in accordance with these; he congratulates himself on the very rich consolation and very strong protection of the angels. A similar emotion is expressed in David's case in Ps. 30:6: "As for me, I said in my prosperity, 'I shall never be moved.'" God is laughing, the angels leap in joy and exultation, the spirit rejoices in the Lord, and therefore Jacob does not fear. He is persuaded [8] that his brother's wrath has cooled off after such a long time, especially since none of his power and wealth had departed in the meantime and he had remained at home in his homeland, whereas Jacob himself had endured wretched slavery in banishment and exile and was still wandering without a definite abode. For Esau held the whole property and land of his father. Therefore Jacob feels secure and is certain that his brother has been placated. So he lovingly

[7] See *Luther's Works*, 5, pp. 137—147.

[8] The Weimar text has *Sed*, but we have read *Se*.

and kindly greets him by means of messengers, not in alarm or suspecting any evil.

The form of greeting is according to Hebrew idiom and custom, by which a person calls himself the servant of another, superior person in order to declare one's respect. The greetings of the Italians are also of this kind, very polite.[9] But the words of Jacob's greeting are not the words of a man who is afraid but words of respect and courtesy.

Although Esau recalled the theft of the blessing, the thought immediately came to him: "What is it that he has stolen? I am in possesion of all things in my father's house; he is a foreigner and an exile. He has served an ungodly and idolatrous man for his two wives; I exercise dominion in this land. I have powerful neighbors, relatives, and close friends; Jacob is very wretched. Let him have that blessing, since, indeed, it offers nothing but the worst misery and servitude in exile. I abound in wealth and power; I have no wants."

So his flesh rejoices in the losses and miseries of his neighbor. "Come! what has my brother taken from me? God has assuredly repaid it in an excellent manner if he has taken anything away," he means to say. "It appears, in fact, that the order has been reversed in such a way that my brother is neglected and has fallen from divine grace but that God is taking care of me and increasing my dignity and wealth." The same thought could have occurred to Jacob, inasmuch as he clearly perceived the arrogance and smugness of his brother. So he greets him respectfully and humbly.

6. *And the messengers returned to Jacob, saying: We came to your brother Esau, and he is coming to meet you, and four hundred men with him.*

7. *Then Jacob was greatly afraid and distressed; and he divided the people that were with him, and the flocks and herds and camels, into two companies,*

8. *thinking: If Esau comes to the one company and destroys it, then the company which is left will escape.*

So far, Moses has related how the patriarch Jacob on his return from Mesopotamia, filled with gladness and joy, triumphed, as it were,

---

[9] See the earlier reference in these *Lectures on Genesis, Luther's Works,* 4, p. 272.

because he had been liberated from a very severe trial at Laban's house and had at the same time been met by the hosts of God to increase his joy and sense of security and to arouse firm confidence in God's protection. But clouds and tempests again get the better of that brightly shining sun, and from heaven Jacob will sink right back into hell.

Moses is very obliging and generous in his description of this trial. For it is a memorable example of how God exercises the saints by various trials and consolations. Many examples of this are set forth in Holy Scripture. It is testified in Psalm 93:19: "When the cares of my heart are many, etc." Such is this life, full of griefs and troubles! The life to come has been promised so that by steadfastness and by the encouragement of the Scriptures we might have hope (cf. Rom. 15:4). In the meantime, these two are mingled, steadfastness, or encouragement, and tribulation. For if encouragement is present, all is prosperity and joy; again, when darkness and tribulation break in, the devil reigns and Christ is crucified.

Therefore we are instructed by these examples not to despair but to expect the best and hope for a certain and rich redemption from evils and the end thereof, even though in these evils we can see neither their end nor God's presence, which is hidden to the understanding of the flesh. Accordingly, the Word must be learned, and a person must exercise himself in it and get to know these continuous alternations which are customary in the life of the saints and of all believers who wish to please God. Paul says (2 Tim. 3:12): "All who desire to live a godly life in Christ Jesus will be persecuted." In Acts 14:22 we read: "Through many tribulations we must enter the kingdom of God." "But God is faithful, and He will not let you be tempted beyond your strength" (cf. 1 Cor. 10:13), however different it appears to human reason and however much every temptation seems to be beyond measure and intolerable. Thus Paul says of himself in 2 Cor. 1:8: "We were so utterly, unbearably crushed that we despaired of life itself," but there is no need for you to fear that you will be burdened by God beyond measure, because the statement stands firm: "God is faithful, etc."

These matters often recur in these stories, and so they must be often repeated; it is a serious and difficult matter. They are not just empty words, but it is a matter of death and eternal life. Nor is there anyone who has perfectly exhausted this wisdom in such a way that he has no further need of practice or instruction. For we must always learn and grow, and in truth, this wisdom must be learned from the Word; it cannot be perceived with the eyes or understanding of the flesh.

Therefore, after we have seen the triumphs and glory of Jacob with the heavenly armies and hosts, let us now also descend with him into hell and see his sadness and terror. The messengers return and report to Jacob what they have seen. "We bring a gloomy report," they say. "Your brother is coming to meet you with 400 men." At this point Jacob is greatly terrified, although there is no danger, as we shall hear later, as to how he will escape from these difficulties. There would have been great danger if, by God's permission, these armed men had been permitted to attack the flocks and Jacob's company, and at this moment this is the only thing that is observed by Jacob's eyes and heart, namely, that the armed men can do harm and that they are coming to slaughter him with his wives and children. But God thinks far otherwise, and there will be another ending which Jacob does not foresee.

The flesh cannot help being alarmed because Jacob was conscious of the enmity between himself and his brother. Therefore he had no doubt that certain destruction was hanging over him. He thought: "Why does he want to be surrounded by so many armed men? Why does he not greet me with a single word or through his messengers express his good wishes at my return?" So he puts the worst interpretation on matters. This is what the flesh usually does, for it immediately casts off all hope and becomes alarmed. It cannot experience any other emotions. For Paul says of himself (Rom. 7:23): "I see in my members another law at war with the law of my mind." The law of the mind says: "Hope, trust, do not doubt, do not fear! God lives and reigns; the angels are on guard!" But I hear another law in my members which says: "It's all over; the case is hopeless; you are undone!" This is the law of the members. The flesh is unbelieving and prone to despair; it cannot promise itself liberation and believe in it.

Therefore the same thing happens to the patriarch Jacob; he trembles and is terrified after hearing that his brother is coming with such a large multitude to fight against him and his wretched unarmed throng of women, shepherds, and little ones, and that he is breathing forth not only battle but also murder (cf. Acts 9:1). As he says below (cf. v. 11): "Lest he may come and slay me and the mother with the children."

But how does this alarm of the patriarch suit such a saintly man, that he is cast down from such great triumph and the joy in which he had exulted into such deep despair? Does it become him to waver and doubt so? To be sure, had we been there, we would probably have done worse things. These are examples that instruct us. Peter, ordered to walk on the sea, at once hurries to Christ and exults in his great boldness as though he were lord of the sea, the billows, the devils, and the whole world. But when a stronger wind blows he begins to doubt. So Christ reproves him, saying (Matt. 14:31): "O man of little faith, why did you doubt? I ordered you to come and you are coming. But because you feel the wind contrary to the Word and experience, your faith wavers and you sink."

In the same manner, a man placed beyond temptation seems to himself to be quite well and strong enough, and he dares to despise the devil and trample him underfoot and also to strengthen others. It is stated in Ps. 30:6: "As for me, I said in my prosperity, 'I shall never be moved.'" I don't give a farthing for all the devils and for death itself! But when a storm arises and the wind becomes stronger or an unusual apparition confronts us, we cry out: "Woe to me! It is all over with me! Death will devour me! 'Thou didst hide Thy face, I was dismayed'" (Ps. 30:7).

The same thing happened to Moses at the Red Sea. The children of Israel had gone out with great joy. Egypt had been humbled and punished; they had taken away spoils; all were shouting: "The Lord God is with us, etc." Everything is absolutely capital! But when they see Pharaoh pursuing with his army and that they are hemmed in on both sides by mountains, they say: "Were there not graves in Egypt, etc.?" (cf. Ex. 14:11). Fear of death and hell follows such a great triumph. Indeed, look at Moses himself, to whom God says: "Why do you cry to Me?" (cf. Ex. 14:15). His heart was also ready to drop out of him and to be shattered into a thousand pieces! For he had led the people of Israel out of Egypt, and when they had scarcely come forth, he saw them exposed to very cruel butchery. "I will be the one responsible for such a great disaster and so many slaughters," he thought. "What have I done? I have provoked the king of Egypt." So he cries out, and his heart is terrified and alarmed. But God replies: "Why are you crying out? I shall curb this tyrant." "And yet the sea is before us, and we are shut in by mountains on both sides. How shall we escape?" The Lord says (cf. Ex. 14:16): "Lift your rod and stretch out your hand over the sea and divide it that the children of Israel may walk in the midst of the sea over dry ground." This is what our Lord God can do!

These matters should instruct and confirm the church in all adversities. For they are set forth in this way that the church may believe and trust when all things seem impossible and lost and no place is left anymore for counsel and help. It is stated in Ps. 107:27: "All their wisdom has been devoured." In such a case you should learn to come to this conclusion: "Although all things are done in great weakness and already seem lost, nevertheless, for God nothing is impossible." For thus the angel says to Mary: "With God nothing is impossible" (cf. Luke 1:37). For He once created all things out of nothing; He still retains this ability and in the same manner still preserves and governs all things. What is nothing for us is everything for God; and what is impossible for us is very easy for Him. By the same power, on the Last Day He will raise the dead who from the foundation of the earth have lain in the dust of the earth. So much about the alarm of the patriarch Jacob in very great peril. This is a proof that the flesh is alive and flourishing even in the saints. For this reason the saintliest man, even after such great promises and consolations, very nearly slips into despair.

Now look at the condition of the whole household and of this household church of Jacob. After they see the head and father of the household himself tottering and becoming alarmed, what were they to do? The bishop, the teacher, the comforter of the church wavers and becomes afraid; what hope should those have who depend on this teacher and their leader? Accordingly, there was wretched grief among the wives of Jacob himself and among those of the shepherds or his kinsmen. For he had a great throng attached to him on this journey because of his numerous flock. To drive it there was need of about 100 or 200 shepherds. Perhaps these also, smitten by fear and impatience, said: "Why is it that he has led us out of Mesopotamia? Would that we were still with Laban! There we would be living safe and secure, and there would be no danger from armed men." Such complaints usually afflict and torment a disturbed heart more than the danger itself does. Therefore, even if Jacob had had no fears on his own account, his heart was nevertheless crushed by the cries, wailing, and tears of this kind that came from the women, and the alarm of his flesh was increased, as will be evident below.

This is just what Moses means. Not only did he fear but he became anxious. He describes a very weak faith. צַר means "anxiety"; he was scared. His heart was at a loss for advice, nor did any method of escape or safety suggest itself. Scripture elsewhere calls this room, as in Ps. 4:1:[10] "Thou hast given me room when I was in distress," that is, "Thou hast made space for me in distress." For Scripture places narrowness and space opposite each other, that is, the confusion of the heart opposite consolation. So also Jacob, when he found himself involved in great straits, became alarmed because, in accordance with the psalm, "his wisdom had been devoured" (cf. Ps. 107: 27). Therefore, this is a pitiable description in which that victorious conqueror is depicted as though he had descended into hell and become quite forgetful of so many glorious promises and consolations that had preceded.

But these matters are set forth in this way "that we may not rely on ourselves," according to the statement of 2 Cor. 1:9. For Paul also had experienced various perils and various liberations. Occasionally, however, he showed such courage and composure that he seemed to despise all perils and difficulties easily and without any fear. So he says in 2 Cor. 6:11-12: "Our mouth is open to you, Corinthians; our heart is wide. You are not restricted by us, but you are restricted in your own affections, etc." Here his heart is transported with joy, and he wants all to open their hearts and to rejoice with him. All things in heaven and earth are smiling at him. But on the other hand he says: "We were so utterly, unbearably crushed that we despaired of life itself" (2 Cor. 1:8). And then: "We felt that we had received the sentence of death; but that was to make us rely not on ourselves but on God, who raises the dead" (2 Cor. 1:9). What is this? Why do you not rejoice, Paul? Why do you not gladden others? Is Paul, the great apostle, to be humbled in such a way that he chooses to die rather than to live? He who a moment ago was full of the Holy Spirit now seems to be devoid of any spirit.

The first and foremost example of such a struggle we have before us in the picture of Christ sweating blood in the garden. Such, indeed, is the life of all the saints, whose examples are set before us that we may be instructed and learn not to trust in ourselves but in God. For this is the knowledge of the godly, not to trust in themselves and to trust in God, and such a God who makes the dead alive and calls into being those things which are not (Rom. 4:17), for these are the works of God. Therefore, if you want to be a godly man and wish

[10] The original has "Ps. 18."

to acknowledge and worship God as your Father, remember that you have to fight it out with the devils, with the world, the flesh, sin, and the Law. Among these the world is the slightest foe, although to the tribulations of the world there are always added the mad assaults of the devil, who assists the world and terrifies the godly. For we suffer not even the slightest tribulation without Satan's being present.

Accordingly, let us remember that we should do and learn this most of all, to trust in God in all temptations. For it is His special work to make the dead alive, to render those who are completely confused peaceful and tranquil, and to make those who are wretched happy and those who are in despair joyful. Therefore Moses has his reasons for being so copious and accurate in describing this temptation, for he wants us to fix this example carefully in our hearts.

But what does Jacob do while his faith is in difficulties and being overwhelmed, while the flesh predominates in his law, which doubts, despairs, and blasphemes? First, he does "what is in him," as the papists usually say, but in another sense.[11] For they do not rightly understand nor do they rightly apply this phrase. For above we stated that although we have God's promises and commandments, nevertheless, God must not be tempted, that is, means must not be neglected, but we must use those we can use since, indeed, God has not given us reason and the counsels and help of reason that we should despise them. This is what those men do who are either presumptuous or in a state of despair. When they say: "Whatever I do, I shall not hinder what must necessarily come to pass by a kind of fate," this is the voice of those in despair. But the presumptuous are accustomed to make this boast: "If I have to live, I shall live even if I do not eat. God has promised life, therefore it does not matter whether I eat or do not eat." But since we have God's promises, we must take careful precautions not to tempt God by presumption and not to sin by despair. When you have a ladder, there is no reason for throwing yourself out of a window, nor should you go through the middle of the Elbe when you have a bridge. But each one should do what reason instructs him to do and commend the rest to God. He will grant fitting results.

Here we have a very beautiful example of this. For Jacob omits none of those things which he is able to do. He divides the people who were with him and sends gifts. He himself hurries ahead and attends

---

[11] Luther is referring to the familiar scholastic formula, *facere quod in se est.*

to all matters that are in his power. Another man in despair would have said: "You can do nothing! If it is foreordained that you should be slain, you will not be able to take precautions against it." This is exactly the way others argue from predestination: "If I am predestined, I cannot perish, whatever I do." These are voices of Satan which should be avoided. It is, indeed, true that whatever is foreordained will come to pass, but it should be added that this is unknown to you. You do not know, for example, whether you will die tomorrow or live, and it is God's will that you do not know this. It is therefore foolish for you to search out what God by His special counsel has concealed from you. But because you do not know how long you will survive, you should use the things necessary for life. If it is foreordained that you should die after a month, nevertheless, God should not be tempted since, indeed, you are uncertain about that, but you should use the things necessary to sustain life.

Therefore, it is necessary to censure the foolishness, or rather, the ungodliness, of those men who refer all things to predestination, which embraces the hidden counsels of God and His government unknown to us.[12] If you were God, it would be permitted to proceed according to this. But because God wants you to be ignorant of this, therefore remain in your calling and within the limits of the Word, and use the means and counsels which God has ordained. I cannot foresee the fruit of my doctrine, namely, who is to be converted and who not. If I now wanted to say: "Those who are to be converted will be converted without my efforts, and if some are not to be converted, what point is there in my toiling to no purpose?" this would be absurd and impious. For who are you to ask this question? Do your duty and leave the outcome to God. It is not for you to say: "If these things are to happen, they will happen." In His Word God has issued instructions through Paul saying: "Go and do your duty! Preach the Word; be urgent in season and out of season, censure, beseech, rebuke in all patience and doctrine" (cf. 2 Tim. 4:2). This commandment must necessarily be obeyed, idle curiosity being disregarded.

These matters are to be taught carefully for the refutation of that impious wisdom of the Turks by which many today are delighted.[13] For the Turks enter battle in this spirit: "If I have to die, I shall die;

[12] This is a recurrent warning in these *Lectures on Genesis;* see, for example, *Luther's Works,* 4, pp. 143—145.

[13] An allusion to the interest in Islam that had developed among Christians as a result of renewed contact with the Arabs and the Turks.

but if not, no dart will harm me." So they rush furiously at the foe at great risk even when they would be able to avoid danger. But it is God's will that we should use the opportunities and methods which have been shown us to avoid dangers. With the greatest care, Jacob follows up whatever counsel he can find, even though he is not helped or liberated by these measures which he thinks out and prepares. For if God had not changed Esau's heart, he would have achieved nothing. But in such a strait he tries everything he can. He does not cast aside his care and devotion to his family and its protection; his hands and feet are not relaxed; he does what lies at hand so as not to tempt God. He divides the people into two companies and likewise the cattle. מַחֲנוֹת in the feminine gender in this passage signifies a company.

But what kind of plan is it to say: "If Esau comes to the one company and destroys it, then the company which is left will escape"? This is simply a human plan and an invention of reason, not of the Holy Spirit, who then put a different plan into effect, obviously for the purpose of softening Esau's heart. Nevertheless, the Holy Spirit guided even this plan in such a way that Jacob did not tempt God. For he thought: "If my brother comes to meet the flocks, he will kill them all together with the shepherds and the whole family at the first furious charge. I shall therefore divide them into two companies, so that if he smites the one, he will be satisfied with that vengeance and spare the other one and cease from his rage." For it can happen that the human heart becomes satiated by so many slaughters committed on the one side. So the cruelest victors have often curbed the rage of soldiers after victory. When Hannibal saw the Romans slaughtered after the battle of Cannae, he ordered his soldiers to stop the slaughter.[14] There are human considerations which Jacob puts together in his heart — that an enemy, however savage he may be, could be satiated by the slaughter of half the people. So he guards against tempting God and yet offers one half to destruction and plunder and hopes that the other half will be preserved.

But that he imagines such atrocious acts to come from the fury of his brother arises from the flesh and the devil. God allows Jacob to have such suspicions of Esau, but He Himself in the meantime thinks far differently. This, accordingly, is the first excellent counsel, as far as human wisdom and the judgment of reason are concerned,

[14] Livy, *History of Rome*, XXII, 58, 1—4.

by which Jacob tries to mitigate the wrath and indignation of his brother.

The second is that he turns to prayer, and thereby he also takes precautions not to tempt God. For here his faith, although weak, shines forth, though almost overwhelmed by troubles and terrors inasmuch as he is afraid that he will be slaughtered with his whole company and flocks. This is the right action, especially necessary in tribulation. He does not presume that something miraculous and beyond his strength must be done with his sword, and he does not tempt God by despairing and casting off all suggestions of reason, but he begins to rouse himself to invocation. Nevertheless, he still has a struggle.

We have often said that when faith is weakest, it is strongest. So wonderful are the works of God. Isaiah says (60:22): "The least one shall become a clan, and the smallest one a mighty nation." Paul says likewise in 2 Cor. 12:9-10: "I will all the more gladly boast of my weaknesses . . . for when I am weak, then I am strong." Jacob here is very weak in his terrors and troubles, amazed, and dejected above measure. Yet his faith was never stronger, because faith which struggles against unbelief draws, as it were, the last and deepest sighs.

But this sighing no one understands, neither Jacob nor anyone else. It is the ineffable groaning of which Rom. 8:26 says: "The Spirit Himself intercedes for us with sighs too deep for words." It is not the voice of triumph, but in reality it is a groaning by which the afflicted heart only sighs and seems to draw breath with difficulty. Isaiah calls it a smoking flax and a reed which is not whole but crushed and shattered (Is. 42:3). But although there is nothing weaker and more feeble than this groaning (for it is, as it were, the last breath), it is nevertheless ineffable.

These are contrary, or contradictory, modifiers, and yet they are true; nor is there anyone who can grasp or explain in words how much this groaning is able to do. "For My power," says God's Word, "is made perfect in weakness" (2 Cor. 12:9). The flesh, to be sure, cries out that it does not understand this; in fact, it feels and experiences the contrary. This, however, is sure: weak power is perfect, and on the other hand, perfection is weakness. Who ever spoke in this way? Beware of "I cannot!" When the devil has brought you to the point that you cannot do anything, he has already lost. Only do not add your agreement by despairing, because it is an ineffable groaning. So Scripture speaks. For when despair is not added but there is a sighing, then there is the most perfect power in the weakest weakness.

The Lord says to Moses in Ex. 14:15: "Why do you cry to Me?" Moses was not crying, but he had become dumb with fear; no sound of any voice was heard; he was like a dead man. But the Holy Spirit, who understands that groaning, utters what is a prodigious cry. And how does He cry? "Abba! Father! O my dear God!" Here despair is not yet complete, but there is left a spark of faith, a little sigh, a little groan which is very small in your eyes but very large in God's ears — a shout that rises above all shouts and fills heaven and earth so that God cannot bear not hearing it and replying: "Why do you cry to Me?" Jacob therefore prays with ineffable groaning as follows:

9. *And Jacob said: O God of my father Abraham and God of my father Isaac, O Lord who didst say to me: Return to your country and to your kindred, and I will do you good,*

10. *I am not worthy of all the mercies and all the truth which Thou hast shown to Thy servant, for with only my staff I crossed this Jordan; and now I have become two companies.*

11. *Deliver me, I pray Thee, from the hand of my brother, from the hand of Esau, for I fear him, lest he come and slay us all, the mothers with the children.*

12. *But Thou didst say: I will do you good and make your descendants as the sand of the sea, which cannot be numbered for multitude.*

The languid and despairing faith of Jacob nevertheless does not completely despair. The flax smokes, but it is not extinguished (cf Is. 42:3). The reed is crushed but not cast off, according to Paul's statement (2 Cor. 4:8-9): "We are afflicted in every way, but not crushed; perplexed, but not driven to despair; persecuted, but not forsaken; struck down, but not destroyed, etc." Therefore, he begins to breathe a little, but with much hesitation.

It is, moreover, an outstanding example of an excellent prayer which has all the conditions that are required for a good prayer. O that one could do it! In the New Testament the doctrine and promises concerning prayer are set forth in great abundance, but who can carry it out? No, not even Jacob could! But he is so disturbed that he first arranges everything before he comes to prayer, although this should have come first (Ps. 51:1) "Have mercy on me, O God, etc." But the flesh, taking us captive to the law of sin, brings it about that we turn the order around. It is therefore a fault that he turns to prayer more slowly than he should have, but it is the weakness of the flesh that first carried him away to the suggestions of reason.

In this manner he began his prayer: "O God of my father Abraham, etc." In Hebrew it is "Gods." It is a glowing prayer, in keeping with that spark of struggling faith; it is the cry of Moses at the Red Sea. But first Jacob's faith appropriates the God of Abraham and Isaac, and later he also calls Him his own Lord. Thus he reminds God of the promises made to Abraham and to Isaac but especially to himself. These greatly increase and kindle his prayer and arouse and warn his struggling faith and smoking flax. "You said it to Abraham. You spoke to Abraham and to Isaac and to me; You will not lie," he means to say. And yet he still struggles. It is, assuredly, a wonderful thing to have such great strength and such strong pillars of consolations and promises on which to lean and still to be alarmed.

But he says: "You said to me, 'Return to your country.' You led me into this tribulation, temptation, and dangerous life." It is truly a great consolation when anyone can say: "Lord God, it is not by my rashness that I became involved in this calamity nor by the advice of any wise or foolish man. But You spoke; You ordered it. Therefore I did the right thing in leaving Laban, and now Your matter is at stake; Your promise and truth are in difficulty; Your faithfulness must be rescued, not mine."

This is that humblest faith and that sighing concerning which mention has been made. This moves heaven and earth and is the most pleasing prayer: "You are the One who said it. I am under Your obedience; I must return to my fatherland on Your authority and orders, O Lord. But see what hindrances are placed in my way. I have been driven into these troubles and difficulties, from which I cannot struggle clear by my own strength and devices. Therefore, I have need of Your help." The others perhaps did not pray but offered the objection: "If we had remained with Laban, we could have been safe." But Jacob does not trouble himself with those thoughts. This is a very strong prayer. But why does he say further: "AND I WILL DO YOU GOOD"? Jacob meant to say: "This is, after all, Your word; it is Your word that You do not want to destroy and harm me but to do me good in my fatherland, to which You have ordered me to return." From this it is clear that he was tempted and troubled not only by the devil because of the message of the coming of his brother but also by his wives, sons, and the whole household with its cry: "Ah, dear father, where are we to turn now? My father, my husband, my master," they cried, "what have you done; why have you brought us into this critical situation?" These complaints forced from him the strong words: "Lord God, hear, I beg you, how these people are alarmed and are also tormenting my heart, although I know that You have promised me help and salvation."

Thus faith shines forth and makes itself heard, even though it is weak. For he undoubtedly addressed them thus: "Why are you alarmed? Surely you will not despair? The hope of rescue should certainly not be cast off. I will not lose heart even if you have despaired." In this manner he encouraged himself too and checked the tears and groans of his people. "God did not order me to return," he said, "in order to harm me; things must still turn out well. God will be with us; only let us use the remedies at hand and cry to Him."

Such prayers, which are poured out in extreme despair and the greatest dangers, are very pleasing to God. These are the ineffable and vehement groanings by which the godly rouse themselves against despair. "It does not have to be that way in spite of everything," he means to say. "We shall still not perish; I shall not die but live, etc. (cf. Ps. 118:17). I have the promise. The Lord has said that He wants to do me good; do not weep, wail, and become alarmed! God has ordered us to go out of Mesopotamia and to return to my fatherland."

This is the struggle of the godly, in which they awaken faith powerfully by the remembrance of the promise and the divine command and by trust in it. I must and will preach, but the devil offers resistance. Very well, preaching there must be, even if the world should be torn apart! These are the men of violence who take the kingdom of heaven by force (cf. Matt. 11:12). Carnal men read such things sleepily and understand nothing, because they are unskilled and inexperienced in such temptations. They do not know what emotions the man has who is struggling in extreme necessity. Here the devil urges that all is lost. "Why do you cry out?" he suggestively asks the afflicted man. "It is all over with you and time to give up." But the Spirit says in opposition: "All is not lost; quite the contrary! It is by no means all over! I know that God has determined and promised something else in regard to me." This is the great fervency and power of the Spirit in weakness. It is a very pleasing sacrifice to God according to Ps. 51:17, for it is the sacrifice of mortification: "The sacrifice acceptable to God is a broken spirit, a broken and a contrite heart, O God, Thou wilt not despise." Thou certainly wilt not despise it, for it is a most acceptable sacrifice for a sweet-smelling odor which fills heaven and earth.

As is stated in the Song of Solomon (3:6): "What is that coming up from the wilderness, like a column of smoke?" It is certainly a slender column, but its smoke reaches up into heaven, and it fills our Lord God's nostrils to such an extent that He says: "Stop! I can no longer hear." It is a slight and insignificant groaning, but with its odor and crying it reaches into heaven into God's presence, and by it God is moved to give help.

Therefore, we should learn to be strong and unbroken in courage, whatever evils and dangers confront us and however much despair catches the attention of our hearts. We should give heed to what has been said by the heathen poet: "Do not yield to evils but proceed more boldly against them." [15] For he who does not yield and slacken his hands is safe and an excellent priest who has sacrificed the most outstanding and best sacrifice. Jacob was never a more holy priest than in this place, although he had previously been mortified by many temptations. That is why Moses is so copious and long in this description. Later he will relate the fight with the angel, and greater things will be done than Jacob had ever dared to seek or expect. In this manner God wants our faith to be exercised and aroused that we may grow from day to day and become stronger.

So far, then, the promises which are required for prayer as it is taught in the New Testament, and also the command. For prayer should not be made in the manner in which the monks sound forth their empty mumbling and βαττολογία ("idle talk," Matt. 6:7) of their prayers, paying no attention to the promises or the command and not thinking of urgent necessity. That is not praying. In former times, when I was a monk, I also used to pray in this way. To be sure, I used to pray in temptation, but the promises and the command I did not know. We were only mumbling words. But true prayer should proceed from a believing heart and one that sets before itself both the necessity and God's command, by which the heart is fired up to present its petitions in faith. Here the individual words are pondered, not as the monks or nuns are accustomed to mumble their prayers absentmindedly and without understanding.

[15] Vergil, *Aeneid*, VI, 95 (also quoted in *Luther's Works*, 1, p. 214).

Nor does true prayer worry about the number or multitude of words, but it multiplies and increases the sighs, to which no words answer except very feebly, as appears in this prayer. For Jacob prayed not only these words which Moses relates, but he sighed the whole night through and the whole day. It was a long prayer as far as groaning is concerned, although the words were very few. Then, too, gratitude and remembrance of past blessings are required for prayer. If these examples are assembled, they stimulate faith in a wonderful manner, and it is very pleasing to God.

Therefore Jacob says: "I am not worthy of all the mercies and all the faithfulness which Thou hast shown to Thy servant," that is, "You have shown me the greatest steadfast love and faithfulness." This is gratitude, or a sacrifice of thanksgiving (εὐχαριστικόν), just as previously it was a sacrifice of mortification. By this groaning he is killed and despairs of his own strength and that of all creatures. Moreover, among the rest of his blessings, he lists the following: "I crossed this Jordan with only a staff. Now I have divided my whole crowd into two companies. So have I grown rich at the home of Laban, though at the beginning I had nothing but my staff when I left my father's house, that is, I was alone. Of course, I had provisions for the journey and a little money (for he was not so destitute that he had not been given provisions for the journey by his parents), but I was alone, without a companion." This is a Hebrew idiom which Moses employs in Ex. 21:3: "If the slave has entered with only his own body, he shall go out with only his own body," that is, alone. It signifies only solitariness, not lack of money.

"Therefore, I acknowledge," he says, "that it is not my work that I acquired such great substance but Thy mercy and truth, since I crossed the Jordan alone on my staff. For 14 years I served for nothing at Laban's, poor and needy, and I scarcely had bread to eat. And Thou, my God, in six years hast enriched me in such a way that I grew into two companies in this short time. This is a manifest and palpable blessing, O God." For it is a great thing for a shepherd to grow in this way on milk, wool, cheese, and butter without avarice. And Jacob had four wives, 11 children, and a large number of slaves.

Therefore, with beautiful words he amplified this sacrifice of thanksgiving, which is otherwise described in a very few words here, just as he also completed it in a few words above. For his prayer was continued day and night. It is recounted only once in this passage, but Jacob did not pray or think these words once; he prayed without ceasing.

This phrase, however, is well known: "Mercy and truth." For these are always joined in Holy Scripture, in Micah 7:20, for example, and elsewhere in the Psalms. "Mercy" signifies the specific act of kindness or the quality of kindness, as Christ, quoting Hos. 6:6, says in Matt. 9:13: "I desire mercy and not sacrifice." חָסִיד refers to him who loves his neighbor and does good to him, and it also refers to the one to whom good is done, to the one who is blessed with many mercies and kindnesses by God. Jacob says: "There is no count of Your mercies and kindnesses toward me. And now there is also this addition, that in six years You enriched me, a pauper, so that I have grown into two companies."

Truth is promise, as Paul says in Rom. 15:8-9: "For I tell you that Christ became a servant to the circumcised to show God's truthfulness, in order to confirm the promises given to the patriarchs, and in order that the Gentiles might glorify God for His mercy." Christ was promised to the Jews, and so truth was kept with them. He was not promised to the Gentiles but was given to them by mercy. None of our fathers had the promise. God, indeed, promised that He is determined to be God to all men, and this knowledge has been implanted in the hearts of men, as Paul testifies in Rom. 1:19. The works and worship of all the nations testify that to be God is nothing else than to do good to men. For that reason men pray, one to Jupiter, another to Mars, etc., with no other thought except that they want to be helped. Thus all men naturally understand and come to the conclusion that God is some kind of beneficent divine power, from whom all good things are to be sought and hoped for. God is One who promises, and He is truthful, that is, He makes promises to all men in the law of nature, which says: "Call upon God, or worship Him."

Accordingly, even though they err in the Person of God because of idolatry, the devotion which is owed to the true God is nevertheless there, that is, invocation and the expectation of blessings and help. But to this people the promises concerning God were given; truth was expressed to them, and the definition or knowledge of God without idolatry and error. This is truly a great and inestimable blessing of God, and so Jacob praises the mercy and truth of God. "You promised and also showed forth this truth, especially during these six years," Jacob means to say. "You likewise promised that You want to bless me as I return to my fatherland. For the sake of the mercies and the evidences of truth which You have shown and are about to show, I ask You to rescue me."

Furthermore, this gratitude includes the third virtue of prayer, which also belongs to mortification, namely, that it is heard without merits on its part. For one must not pray: "Have regard for me, O God, because I am a holy monk, I am a chaste virgin, I am an excellent bishop," like the Pharisee in the Gospel with his: "I fast twice a week, I give tithes of all that I get" (Luke 18:12). That monstrosity must be far removed and expurgated from prayer; otherwise prayer is corrupted, and both sacrifices, that of mortification and that of thanksgiving, are defiled by such dung.

Therefore, one should by no means speak in this manner, but we should follow the example of Jacob, who says: "I am not worthy of all Your mercies. I am not worthy, no, not even of one act of mercy or truth which You have ever shown me, are even now showing me, or will show me hereafter without any merit on my part. For it is impossible that I should merit anything. Therefore I do not rely on my worthiness but on Your promises and mercies." This is a truthful heart and a true prayer, for this is really God's judgment concerning us, to which Paul gave expression somewhere when he said (1 Cor. 4:7): "What have you that you did not receive? If then you received it, why do you boast?" So you must pray in this way: "Lord God, what You have hitherto shown me is Your promise and mercy. There is no worthiness in me. Accordingly, as You have done hitherto and have given me all things even though I am unworthy, so also hear and help me hereafter in my unworthiness." Otherwise God will reprove you, saying: "Why are you proud, you who are dust and ashes? You are earth, and to earth you will return. Did I not create you from dung? Who has preserved your life? All that you have is Mine pure and simple."

Therefore, there are those three conditions of a good prayer, which make it very pleasing and a sweet-smelling odor before God which cannot fail to be heard. The first is that you should take hold of the promise. The second is that you should be mortified in your distress. The third is that you should give thanks and acknowledge that you are not worthy of one act of mercy but are seeking and hoping for help through mercy alone. These virtues — chastity, sobriety, and kindness in helping the poor — are indeed praiseworthy and commanded by God, but confidence should not be placed in them. Our confidence should not rely on the Law and its works, although they should be present, but on the mercy and truth of God. Then prayer and groaning is a golden sacrifice.

Now follows the petition. "Well, what are you asking for, Jacob? You acknowledge that you are unworthy of My mercy; you acknowledge that I am One who makes promises; you confess that you receive all things from Me out of pure grace. Then what are you asking for? What do you lack?" The child must have a name if one is to baptize it. As though God did not know what things we are in need of! He is assuredly not ignorant. For Christ says (Matt. 6:8): "Your Father knows what you need before you ask Him." Why, then, does He want me to sigh, cry out, groan, knock, and acknowledge that I am unworthy of His help? He wants it for this reason, that you also may remember what you are lacking. Otherwise, we snore in our smugness and dream that we are the most fortunate people when we are the most wretched. But we do not know this, nor do we learn in any other way except in a time of temptation. Jacob had his life by God's blessing; he had two companies. But in this moment he loses both and is reduced to nothing. Formerly he did not know this when he gloried and exulted. But now he is instructed what and how much he can do, so that we should learn to place our confidence not in ourselves but in God and so that we should rejoice in His gifts in such a way that we do not boast in connection with them. For this is exceedingly difficult on account of the corruption of nature, which is corrupted by the contagion of original sin so that when we are afflicted, we easily slip into despair. When all things are prospering and favorable, we are smug and proud. So at one time the saints are cast down, at another time they are raised again that they may learn to observe the common saying: "By the middle way you will go in greatest safety." [16] This does not come to pass except through temptation. Therefore we should not be presumptuous in regard to ourselves but trust solely in the mercy and truth of God. These are immovable and eternal; they do not perish or deceive our hope and our confidence.

But what does Jacob lack? All things are lacking. "My brother will slaughter me, my wives, and my companies," he thinks. He fears this. But where is God's promise, apprehended in faith? Or do you not know that God can change Esau's heart? God promised and

[16] Ovid, *Metamorphoses*, II, 157, which had become proverbial.

showed His mercy and truth to Jacob, and yet his flesh is alarmed and groans and he flees mortification. This comes to pass through the fault of original sin. He looks only at the danger. "I do, indeed, have two companies," he thinks, "but I see that in a short time it could come to pass that I lose everything and that even I myself will escape the danger of death only with difficulty." For he says: "Lest he come and slay us all, the mothers with the children." Again, he becomes alarmed, and his faith grows weak, and yet he does not despair. This is how it usually happens in temptations; faith struggles with the flesh, and thoughts of despair and hope clash (cf. Rom. 2:15). There are contrary winds, those of faith and of unbelief, of hope and of fear. "The mother with the children, etc." These words indicate his distress and anxiety. Suddenly, on receiving the message about his brother's coming, he has lost everything. All his property and hopes are unexpectedly ruined and fall to the ground. Nevertheless, he clings to the promise, saying: "You said, 'I will do you good and make, etc.'" This he sets over against his doubt and despair as expressed in the words "lest he come, etc." For they were words of the militant flesh and of very weak faith. But he took hold of the Word, saying: "May Your truth sustain, arouse, and console me, by which You promised that You want to do me good and bless me and my seed. But this will not be done, and You will not bless me and my seed, if Esau destroys me."

God could have produced a seed and promoted a blessing even with Jacob destroyed. The promise of seed and posterity also depended on Isaac, and yet orders were given to offer him in sacrifice, and Abraham had to hold on to this faith, that God could have produced seed for Isaac even from the ashes, as has been stated above.[17] That, to be sure, was a very heavy temptation. Now, Jacob in his state of confusion would surely have forgotten what God had said, namely, that He would be his God, and he began his prayer as indicated above: "O Lord, who didst say to me, etc." But he did not only pray in this way; he also delivered sermons and exhorted his household along these lines. Often he said to Rachel: "Be of good courage; hope in God and His Word! But will he slaughter us? No, he will not do it! I have asked the Lord to protect us and rescue us. Reflect that God has spoken to me and promised help!" With such exhortations, sermons, and prayers he encouraged himself and his family.

[17] See *Luther's Works,* 4, pp. 91—98.

These are striking passages and very memorable examples in the stories of the fathers which teach us that before all else God's Word is to be apprehended and firmly retained, lest we lose it or reject it even though all other things are lost, and even though Esau kills our sheep. However much our enemies threaten us with whatever is atrocious, we should nevertheless not allow faith in the promise to be taken from us but cling to it and live in it as the holy fathers Abraham, Isaac, and Jacob lived in it. For even though you are weak, do not for that reason throw away the Word; the matter will turn out well enough. But if you reject the Word or allow it to be removed from your eyes and heart, the devil will triumph and drive you to despair. Accordingly, Jacob spent the night at Mahanaim with this temptation and prayer. Mahanaim is a city beyond the stream Jabbok, to which David fled when he was thrown out of his kingdom by Absalom (cf. 2 Sam. 17:24, 27). It is a celebrated place in Holy Scripture. It is not far from the Jordan. For the Jabbok flows into the Jordan. Gilead, Mizpah, and Mahanaim are neighboring cities.

13. *So he lodged there that night and took from what he had with him a present for his brother Esau,*

14. *two hundred she-goats and twenty he-goats, two hundred ewes and twenty rams,*

15. *thirty milch camels and their colts, forty cows and ten bulls, twenty she-asses and ten he-asses.*

Above I have stated, and it must be stated often, that God must not be tempted but use must be made of the suggestions, means, remedies, and aids that are at hand, lest we become like the Turks. For it is the very worst of temptations to expose oneself to dangers with negligent hands and feet and not to flee them or avoid them when you can, and later to cast the blame on God's will. The godly should be reminded that the outcome of future events is unknown; God alone knows the future and what is impending. But even though we do not know it, we must nevertheless do what we can. This is the place for the statements that a man must do what is in him.[18] Not in respect to grace but in external matters and dangers the judgment of reason must be consulted so that we do not tempt God. Augustine says concerning this passage that we should be reminded

[18] See p. 104, n. 11.

by this example that although we believe in God, we should nevertheless do what must be done that we may not seem to tempt God by neglecting it.[19] So Jacob uses many devices. First, when he approaches the boundaries of Esau's realm, he sends ambassadors to search out his brother's heart and to seek to gain his goodwill and reconciliation. But this plan miscarries because his brother approaches with 400 armed men far more powerful and more alienated, as it appears, than before. Nevertheless, he acted rightly in sending ambassadors, and if he had not employed this means, he would have sinned.

The second device is that he divides the people and flocks into two companies to rescue at least one of the two, because he despairs of peace and fraternal goodwill. Nor did this help him, because God softens his brother's heart. But he could not have found a better plan to rescue some of his company from the cruelty of his brother. For Esau was very powerful and undoubtedly in league with the princes in Seir and the other neighboring nations; he had sons, grandsons, and sons-in-law, and, indeed, both brothers were centenarians at the time when they met, or at least 98 years old. Esau had been married for 60 years, and in such a long time his family had multiplied greatly, and he had increased in the resources and power of his relations and close friends. Jacob was in his 84th year when he married two wives. He brought with him little ones of 12 or 14 years of age. Joseph was six. What was this wretched throng in comparison with such a great army, or at least in comparison with the children and grandchildren of Esau, who were inflamed with both anger and indignation against Jacob? So Jacob acted wisely in dividing his company, although that also would have failed if Esau had been able to indulge his fury.

In this manner we should remember that in dangers we, too, must try out and do what reason and the diligence of human ingenuity point out to us, even though at times even the plans that are very well thought out become useless. This we should also do so that we do not later accuse our carelessness or stupidity, as such complaints are often heard when men say: "If I had tried this or that first, these evils would never have happened." Too late, after the event, they take counsel and even burden their conscience that they did not apply any remedy in time. Therefore, we must deliberate and with the greatest pains do whatever can be thought out by human

---

[19] Augustine, *Quaestiones in Heptateuchum*, I, 102, *Patrologia, Series Latina,* XXXIV, 574.

counsels so that with a tranquil heart you may be able to say that you looked ahead beforehand and thought and did all that was possible.

The third device is the one concerning the sending of gifts. But although that also is not very successful, it is nevertheless very well thought out, and Moses carefully describes the individual events, even as he is more copious in this whole narrative than is customary. For it is a strong and hard temptation and a very serious mortification. Therefore, after two plans have failed and Esau's enraged heart could not be appeased by the ambassadors sent by his brother, Jacob thinks that he will send a gift and deck it out in fine fashion with words and a festive procession so that the enraged Esau may be softened to some extent. This is carefully recounted by Moses. For he does not send animals of one kind, as is usually done today when a prince is presented with a hundred oxen and two hundred sheep, etc., and it is a very precious gift. But he chooses a certain number from the individual kinds and so sends him a herd of various animals as a gift. But gifts of themselves have the property of placating men, as even the heathen poet testifies, saying: "Gifts, believe me, placate both men and gods." [20] Therefore, a better method could not have been found than an offering of gifts. For these two, a personal prostration, humiliation, or apology and gifts, have the greatest power in reconciling embittered hearts. First, therefore, he sends the she-goats with the he-goats, and thus, in order, the specified number of the individual kinds, as they are enumerated in the text.

But Moses says: "He took from what he had with him." Jerome translates: "He separated." The meaning is that he did not select the best from the flock but passed through the whole flock in which individual animals were well fed and fat, and from that portion he separated whatever crossed his path.

מִנְחָה signifies a gift. Above (4:3-5), it is employed of the two brothers Abel and Cain. It is a sacrificial gift which is offered. It not only signifies an offering offered to God but also a gift which is donated to men. עִזִּים and פָּרִים are related to the German words *Gaiss* ("she-goat") and *Farr* ("bullock"). We have taken them from the Jews. It is, therefore, an excellent gift and distinguished in very clear order according to the individual species that belong to animal husbandry.

16. *These he delivered into the hand of his servants, every drove by*

---

[20] Ovid, *Ars amandi*, III, 653. The original has *capiunt* where Luther quotes *placant*.

*itself, and said to his servants: Pass on before me, and put a space
between drove and drove.*

See with what care he arranges all things that he may the more
easily soften the heart of his embittered brother by confronting
him with a pleasant sight! He separates the herds and attaches a special shepherd to each one and arranges matters in such a way that
there is a space between each drove so that Esau as he comes up
may not see a disorderly flock but that the she-goats should meet him
first, then the he-goats, then the ewes, and so on in succession after
regular intervals. רֶוַח properly does not signify space or an interval
but, as men interpret it, a rest, as is stated in Ex. 8:15 concerning the
second plague of the frogs: "But when Pharaoh saw that there was
a respite." But I think that Moses wanted to use this word because
these herds of their own accord were crowded and massed together as
they put their heads close together, so that there could scarcely be
any breathing, as is stated in Ps. 49:14: "Like sheep they are appointed
for Sheol." His desire is not only that the gift be beautified by its
arrangement but also that the flocks be spared so that they may not
suffer harm or perish by being too tightly packed together. But in addition he supplies verbal embellishments.

17. *He instructed the foremost: When Esau my brother meets you,
and asks you: To whom do you belong? Where are you going?
And whose are these before you?*

18. *then you shall say: They belong to your servant Jacob; they are
a present sent to my lord Esau; and moreover he is behind us.*

19. *He likewise instructed the second and third and all who followed
the droves: You shall say the same thing to Esau when you meet
him,*

20. *and you shall say: Moreover your servant Jacob is behind us. For
he thought: I may appease him with the present that goes before
me, and afterwards I shall see his face; perhaps he will accept me.*

The words are brief but very rhetorical. He issues instructions to
them that they should embellish the gift with words and also address
him honorably. "Do not say," he says, "that these flocks separated
into five groups are your brother Jacob's. By no means say this, lest
the memory of the stolen blessing is scratched open again. But say:

'They are your servant's, of whom you are the lord.'" This is great modesty and humility by which an offended heart should certainly have been touched and softened.

These words he enjoins not only on one shepherd but on all of them so that they should speak modestly and humbly and call Jacob a servant but Esau a lord. The equipment of both of them also reflected this. For Esau was approaching with a great entourage, like a lord on horses and chariots. But Jacob comes on foot like a shepherd, and he offers no royal gift but that of a shepherd. By this he hoped to be able to move his brother to think: "What are you to do with a man who is unarmed and very wretched, who is bringing along an unwarlike retinue — children, wives, maidservants, and menservants? It is altogether necessary to spare them since they are suppliants." This is certainly a great debasement and humiliation of such a great patriarch, who was adorned with such great promises and visions of angels. But the mortification humbles him and at the same time reminds him to take counsel in regard to the present danger by whatever means he can.

He takes careful precautions not to annoy Esau anymore even by a single word. So he orders them to avoid the word brother, friend, or any other terms which seem to give a suggestion of any pride. Jacob was by no means inferior to his brother Esau, because he had been blessed by his father. It is expressly said in the blessing: "May your mother's sons bow down to you" (Gen. 27:29). Here, to be sure, the opposite of what is promised becomes apparent. And he will be humiliated even more. But I stated before that this is a time of mortification and that Jacob debases himself in this way to take thought for his own interests in the present danger and that it may not seem that he threw himself headlong into destruction.

He adds further: "He himself is behind us." "He does not flee but follows and trusts in your kindness. He hopes that he will find favor and peace." These words are also very friendly and winning and should be able to heal and soften any heart, however sore it may have become. He is careful to remind them that they should speak with his brother according to these words: "Take care that you do not say that his brother is following or that I have become rich at Laban's and have a large household. Do not be proud or make me hateful but humble yourselves and say: 'Your servant is coming after us.'"

"For I will appease him with gifts," he says, "and see him later.

Perhaps he will receive my face." This is Jacob's plan: "I want
to appease him with gifts. From this I shall easily gather whether
he is inclined to mildness. If he makes no reply to the first shepherd,
he will nevertheless reply to the second and third one, etc. And after
the gifts that have been offered, I myself will come and humble
myself." "Perhaps he will receive my face," that is, "receive me into
favor, be reconciled to me." This is a Scriptural idiom which means
to accept. "To receive the face of sinners" (Ps. 82:2) means to praise
their sins and not to reprove them. Therefore we see how a man
ought to do what is in him. For thus Jacob sends gifts to his brother
and arranges them very skillfully and finally embellishes them with
words to the best of his ability. This means doing what is in him
and not tempting God. For if he had not done this and a slaughter
had taken place, his conscience would have been forever plagued by
these thoughts: "Why did you not humble yourself before your brother
and address him respectfully? If he had seen that you were a suppliant, he undoubtedly would have spared you. But because you
were too negligent in devising plans and remedies, you deserve to
suffer such things."

21. *So the present passed on before him; and he himself lodged that
night in the camp.*

22. *The same night he arose and took his two wives, his two maids,
and his eleven children, and crossed the ford of the Jabbok.*

23. *He took them and sent them across the stream, and likewise
everything that he had.*

24. *And Jacob was left alone.*

After sending his ambassadors on ahead with the gifts, Jacob does
not follow instantly but stays with the companies that night so that
there may be a day's space between him and the preceding gifts
and that he may be able to discover his brother's heart from this distance. However, he does not yet find rest but is mortified more. For
during the night he rises and with his wives and children crosses
the ford of the Jabbok. This text seems to indicate that Jacob wanted
to cross the stream secretly in the middle of the night while men slept,
and it appears that he was afraid that if his brother came in the
morning, he would hinder his crossing. So he took pains to transport

his wives and children and all that he had, and this task he completed with difficulty in the space of two hours.

Moses says emphatically: "He sent them across." It sounds as if he first led his household to the stream and crossed over by himself and tested in what part it could most easily be crossed and later finally led his wives and children across. After he had crossed, however, he separated himself from his whole family in a lonely spot and prayed with great anxiety because he was still full of terrors and weakness. He chose a lonely spot because solitude is very well suited to those who are praying, also in the daytime. For when prayer is serious and ardent, we do not readily allow those words to be heard which we pour out before God in a rather inept manner.

At night, therefore, he arose and was occupied one or two hours in transporting his wives and property. He was engaged in wrestling for a like period of time. Nighttime, moreover, is especially suitable for temptations, as is stated above in chapter 15 (v. 17): "After sunset, when it became dark, there appeared a smoking fire pot, etc." Darkness of itself saddens and dejects the hearts of all men and cattle also. On the other hand, the dawning light of day gladdens all living things. Therefore it is correctly stated in the German proverb: "The night is no man's friend." It is a time suitable for tribulations and prayer, to which tribulation forces man. Therefore his ardor to pray increased, but in the greatest of infirmity.

We see, moreover, with what great care Moses, or rather, the Holy Spirit, describes even the most trifling actions and passions of the patriarchs, among which none of the showy and prodigious works such as the monks and the self-righteous boast of are prominent. But these passions are especially outstanding and golden because they have this promise, that not only their death and blood are precious in the sight of the Lord (Ps. 116:15), but that even the hairs of their head are precious and numbered (Matt. 10:30). Therefore the Holy Spirit did not deem it unworthy to linger over these domestic and pastoral works and passions. For faith is exercised very well in these matters, and there ensues a sacrifice well-pleasing to God.

Therefore we should continually fix our eyes on these examples of the patriarchs that we may learn that also our deeds which are done in faith, and likewise the afflictions which we endure in faith, are all acceptable to God and like a continual sacrifice. This is a great consolation for believers. The life of the godly appears to be an idle life and without any fruit and worth. But this is our great glory, that we know that our tears and each of the drops that fall from our eyes are numbered by God and that all things are written before the eyes of God and gathered in a golden vessel, so to say (cf. Ps. 56:8).

But monastic fasts of seven days or more, watchings, and celibacy, nothing of which comes from faith, are not so gathered. So the devil does not persecute these things but fosters them that they may be without danger. But they are very displeasing to God because they are all taken up and done contrary to the Word. But such doers of works are twice wretched because they are enmeshed in Satan's nooses and are afflicted much more violently than all the godly. For what is more wretched than to be subject to the devil and to render obedience to him?

It is also a wonderful thing that the patriarch had such an obedient household which endured so many dangers with such patience. Those messengers especially, who allow themselves to be exposed to the angry brother with equanimity, could have returned to Mesopotamia and there have been in safety. But they endure common dangers with their master, who made it his chief aim to keep them in faith and the knowledge of God, who Himself had given the promise which they awaited along with their master. Therefore Jacob is an illustrious and very practical high priest, who rescues and saves so many souls from Mesopotamia with the pure doctrine and worship of God. His domestics were true martyrs contending with such great difficulties for the sake of their master.

Today you would find very few people of that most corrupt class of men who would imitate this patience and constancy. But where the Word is taught, there faith is, and where faith is, there are such neighbors, servants, wives, and children, etc. There must be some also today. For as the rain does not fall for the sake of one stalk but for the sake of many fields so that they may become fertile and bear much fruit, so the Word is not given to convert only the one or two but on account of many men of all ranks (cf. Is. 55:10-11). You should not think that when I and Pomeranus [21] are removed, all good and godly men have been taken away. Our Lord God has more godly people. But for all that, the godly are miracles in the world and gifts of God because the greatest part is ungodly.

[21] See p. 34, n. 15.

24. *And a man wrestled with him until the breaking of the day.*

This passage is regarded by all as among the most obscure passages of the whole Old Testament. Nor is this strange, because it deals with that sublime temptation in which the patriarch Jacob had to fight not with flesh and blood or with the devil but against God Himself. But that is a horrible battle when God Himself fights and in a hostile fashion opposes His opponent as though on the point of taking away life. He who wishes to stand and conquer in this struggle must certainly be a holy man and a true Christian. Accordingly, this story is obscure because of the magnitude of its subject matter, and because of its obscurity all other interpreters pass it by. It would also be permissible for us to pass it by. But we shall still say what we can.

Lyra has given some kind of explanation of this contest, but he could not explain all things correctly.[22] Augustine resorts to allegory.[23] But bare allegories should not be sought in the Holy Scriptures. For unless they have a story and a certain fact as a foundation, they are nothing else but fables like those of Aesop. Secondly, even if we have a story, it is not the business of all men to form allegories from it. Origen was not too successful, and Jerome had even less success with them, for they did not have a perfect knowledge of the narratives, without which no one can handle allegories successfully. So before all else the historical sense must be dug out. This teaches, consoles, and confirms. Afterwards allegory embellishes and illustrates it as a witness. But the narrative is the author, so to say, or the head and foundation of the matter.

We shall therefore make an attempt to see if we can dig out the true sense and doctrine of this passage. If we cannot attain it perfectly, we shall nevertheless not be very far from the mark. First of all, however, the hindrances of various opinions must be removed. Hosea adduces this passage when he says (Hos. 12:3-5): "In his manhood he strove with God. He strove with the angel and prevailed, he wept and sought his favor. He met God at Bethel, etc." From this all the interpreters infer that the man wrestling with Jacob was an angel, but we always observe this canon, that whenever Holy Scripture makes mention of apparitions, as above in Gen. 18, when three men meet Abraham, and the word angel is not expressly men-

---

[22] Lyra *ad* Gen. 32:24, p. 96 verso, note "g."

[23] Augustine, *Quaestiones in Heptateuchum,* I, 104, *Patrologia, Series Latina,* XXXIV, 574—575.

tioned, there we do not interpret it as angels because it is clearly stated: "The Lord appeared to him," not an angel. But afterwards, in chapter 19, when two angels go on to Sodom, we concede that they were angels.

So also in chapter 28:12-13, when Jacob sees the angels ascending and descending and the Lord stands on the ladder. Here we understand the Lord not as an angel, as those who ascend and descend are called angels by name, but as the Son of God, who was to become incarnate, our Lord Jesus Christ, who is true God and true man. By the communication of properties we say: "Man is on high above all creatures, and God is the lowliest one." This is the mystery "into which angels long to look" (cf. 1 Peter 1:12), because on account of the unity of Person they see God below but man above. So also we say: "Man sits at the right hand of God the Father." Likewise: "God descends into hell and ascends into heaven." This is the communication of properties concerning which we spoke more copiously above.[24]

Wherever, therefore, the name of angel is not expressed, we do not understand it as angels. In this passage it is expressly stated: "You have prevailed with God," not only "you have striven with God" but "you have also conquered." Likewise, the statement follows later: "I have seen God face to face." But the passage in Hosea we interpret to mean that these words which the prophet relates are imitative, not that he may explain his own doctrine and viewpoint concerning this example but that he may reprove and reproach the false prophets who made a boast of such words and stubbornly tried to defend their idolatry against the temple at Jerusalem and the divine regulation of worship under the pretext and example of this patriarch Jacob. "There is no need," they used to say, "for us to make offerings at Jerusalem, as the priests demand to glut their avarice; they condemn our sacrifices as ungodly sacrifices because we are withdrawing the people from their worship and much of their income has departed." So they spoke evil of the true teachers and godly priests who retained the true worship of God, and they appropriated for their own case the testimony of this story since, indeed, God spoke with Jacob in that place, Bethel or Peniel, and had shown him both the ladder and the angels and Jacob had striven with God and the angel had wept and prayed to him. This last fact they themselves have invented.

[24] See *Luther's Works,* 5, pp. 218—223.

Such were the sermons of the false prophets, on the refutation of which the prophets, and especially Hosea, really toiled. For all his sermons have reference to the censuring of the idolatry of the kingdom of Israel because they chose special acts of worship and special places for themselves where God had formerly spoken to the fathers, where angels had appeared, or where places were outstanding for other reasons. But God through Moses had issued a most rigorous prohibition against the impudence of inventing new forms of worship, as when He says: "You shall not offer in every place but at the place which the Lord your God will choose out of all your tribes to put His name and make His habitation there; thither you shall go, and thither you shall bring your burnt offerings and your sacrifices" (cf. Deut. 12:4-6). At that time the place appointed for worship was the temple at Jerusalem. The ark of the covenant was there, and God had promised that He would speak from the mercy seat to draw the people away from the diversity of idols to a united worship of God, to which He wanted to gather all together, if not in bodily presence and external works, at least in heart and prayer, if any were too far away from this place.

But the false prophets used to fight against this viewpoint and say: "God is everywhere; therefore He can be adored and worshiped in every place, both in Bethel as well as on any other mountain." They did not have regard for the commandment of God. For when God fixes a certain manner and designates a certain place for His worship, it must not be said: "Wherever I will worship God, it will be pleasing to Him if only I do it in a godly and devoted manner," or, "I shall make offerings to Him wherever it pleases me." Isaiah, for example, censures this madness very severely, saying (Is. 57:5): "You burn with lust . . . under every green tree." The Turks and Jews are accustomed to speak in this manner today, claiming that they are able to serve God outside of the unity of faith and the church of Christ. Mohammed claims that anyone is saved in his own religion if he prays, if he gives alms, if he does other good works. It is not necessary for him to be a Christian or that he should be in the unity of Christ and the church. In the papacy also all corners were occupied with chapels, convents, and idolatry of every kind.

Therefore Hosea cries: "This example of Jacob by no means confirms your idolatry. He did, indeed, struggle with the angel, but you should have remembered that the Lord God of hosts led Israel out of Egypt through the prophet. But where is this God to be found? Where has He made a memorial for His name? Where is this memorial? Where the ark of the covenant is" (cf. Ex. 20:24).

This is true, indeed, that God is not bound, neither to Jerusalem nor to any other place, and that He is able to save also elsewhere. No one will deny this. But try it and see what you will get! If you invent forms of worship according to your own judgment, you will be in danger of God's wrath. By His almighty power God could save the human race without Christ, without Baptism, and without the Word of the Gospel. He could have illuminated men's hearts inwardly through the Holy Spirit and forgiven their sins without the ministry of the Word and of ministers. But it was not His will to do so. And God very strictly prohibited all erring forms of devotion and worship.

When hypocrites say: "Whatever is done with good intention is pleasing to God," those self-chosen devotions are to be condemned, and men should be reminded that they should direct their eyes where God has revealed Himself. We must not say: "Paul preached at Rome, therefore Christ is there. James is buried at Compostela in Spain, therefore God should be worshiped there by the invocation of Saint James." By no means! Yet many miracles are performed there? My reply is that God abominates and condemns all erring thoughts outside the one and only revelation made in the Word and sacraments, to which He wished to gather us and in which He wished to include us. For this reason Christ sent His disciples with this command: "Go therefore and teach all nations, baptizing them in the name of the Father and of the Son and of the Holy Spirit, teaching them to observe all that I have commanded you" (Matt. 28:19-20), and "He who believes and is baptized will be saved" (Mark 16:16). He wants us to be gathered in connection with the Word and Baptism as by a sure and infallible sign because He wants to save us and help us, just as He promised He would listen at the mercy seat among the people of Israel.

If you want to be absolved from your sins in this manner, go to your pastor, or to your brother and neighbor if your pastor cannot hear you; he has the command to absolve you and comfort you. Do not invent a special absolution for yourself. If you want to receive the Lord's Supper, go to the assembly of the church and the public congregation and receive it there. Do not devise a special administration and use of the sacraments. For God does not want us to go astray in our own self-chosen works or speculations, and so He gathers us together and encloses us within the limits of the Word so that we are not tossed about by every kind of doctrine (cf. Eph. 4:14).

This happened to us under the papacy when we despised Baptism, the Lord's Supper, and the remission of sins and made pilgrimages meanwhile to Saint James, Rome, and Jerusalem, as though God were not present in all the churches and congregations which have His Word and sacraments. Finally, there was an infinite variety of sects and orders, each of which had its peculiar, segregated ritual in distinction from the ritual and ordinance of God. Nor could those innumerable forms of fornication, as Holy Scripture calls them,[25] be prevented except by casting off our own works. So God wants all these things to be removed, and He sets forth His Word, which says: "Here you shall adore, worship, and make offerings. In the Word, in the Lord's Supper, and in Baptism you have the remission of sins. With these [26] you will have to be satisfied if you wish to be saved."

In this manner the prophets with great zeal inculcated upon the Jews a place chosen by God against the erroneous and misdirected pilgrimages [27] to idols and sacrifices in different places. But they were shamefully treated by their hearers, they were outlawed and slain. So also today the pope condemns, excommunicates, and kills those who censure the perverted lusts and whoredoms of idolatry. Nevertheless, those who are truly godly embrace this light of the Word with grateful hearts and like chicks take refuge under the wings of our hen, Jesus Christ, God's Son, and under them they find rest and protection against every onslaught of Satan and against his stratagems. So much concerning the passage from Hosea, the meaning of which is not to be taken as indicative or affirmative but imitative.

The gloss of the Jews should also be rejected. They imagine that the man wrestling with Jacob was the good angel who was Esau's guardian and that he opposed Jacob and fought with him in accordance with the duty which he owed to Esau. Moreover, they contend that the angel when conquered wept and asked Jacob to let him go. But there is the greatest absurdity in this madness. They dream that the angel did not know that the blessing belonged to Jacob; likewise, that God so strengthened Jacob that he conquered the angel and, on the other hand, the angel was weakened and therefore wept. It is a foolish and frivolous piece of imagination to suppose that the angel

25 A reference to such passages as Ps. 106:39 and Hos. 4:12.
26 The Weimar text has *in*, but we have read *iis*.
27 The Weimar text has *modus*, but we have read *motus*.

was ignorant of the promised blessing or so evil that he wanted to resist the ordinance of God. Lyra for once has come closer to the truth. He makes this angel a man, but in the person of God, and says that he wanted to flee but was detained by Jacob until he blessed him.[28]

But our opinion is this, that the wrestler is the Lord of glory, God Himself, or God's Son, who was to become incarnate and who appeared and spoke to the fathers. For God in His boundless goodness dealt very familiarly with His chosen patriarch Jacob and disciplined him as though playing with him in a kindly manner. But this playing means infinite grief and the greatest anguish of heart. In reality, however, it is a game, as the outcome shows when Jacob comes to Peniel. Then it will be manifest that they were pure signs of most familiar love. So God plays with him to discipline and strengthen his faith just as a godly parent takes from his son an apple with which the boy was delighted, not that he should flee from his father or turn away from him but that he should rather be incited to embrace his father all the more and beseech him, saying: "My father, give back what you have taken away!" Then the father is delighted with this test, and the son, when he recovers the apple, loves his father more ardently on seeing that such love and child's play gives pleasure to the father.

These games are very common on the domestic scene, but in the affairs and contests of the saints they are very serious and difficult. For Jacob has no idea who it is who is wrestling with him; he does not know that it is God, because he later asks what His name is. But after he receives the blessing, he says: "I have seen[29] the Lord face to face." Then new joy and life arises from the sad temptation and death itself.

This, therefore, seems to be the teaching of this story, if only I could expound it according to its worth, that, according to the example of Jacob, God at times is accustomed to play with His saints, and, as far as He Himself is concerned, with quite childish playing. But to us whom He tempts in this way it appears far different. However, it is excellent and very salutary exercise and perfect instruction, and this is blessed with a very happy end, namely, that one learns "what is the good and acceptable and perfect will of God" (Rom. 12:2). To the flesh it cannot seem otherwise than an evil, troublesome, and gloomy will, but when we are weeping, God is smiling

---

28 Lyra *ad* Gen. 32:24, p. 96 verso, note "h."

29 The Weimar text has *Vide*, but we have read *Vidi*.

in a most kindly manner, and He takes pleasure in those who fear Him and hope in His mercy (cf. Ps. 147:11).

Moreover, the temptation to despair which usually accompanies this experience increases the grief and agitation of the flesh when the afflicted heart complains that it has been forsaken and cast off by God. This is the last and most serious temptation to unbelief and despair, by which the greatest of the saints are usually disciplined. He who is able to stand and endure in this temptation comes to the perfect knowledge of the will of God so that he is able to say with Jacob: "I have seen the Lord, etc. I did not think that the Lord meant so well with me." But before we reach this stage, life may be a trying experience. Therefore the teaching of this story concerning the temptations of the greatest saints is open and clear. With great delight they taste how kind the Lord is (cf. Ps. 34:8). But even though not all grasp or understand these contests, they are nevertheless not to be rejected for this reason.

Concerning apparitions, however, I have spoken in a general way on several occasions above,[30] and it is necessary to know that not all of them are to be believed, but only if they are of the analogy of faith (Rom. 12:6). I shall cling to the Word of God and be content with that. By it I shall die, and by it I shall live. There is sufficiently abundant protection in the promise of God not only against the devil, the flesh, and the world but also against this lofty temptation. For if God sent an angel to say: "Do not believe these promises!" I would reject him, saying: "Depart from me, Satan, etc." (cf. Matt. 16:23). Or, if God Himself appeared to me in His majesty and said: "You are not worthy of My grace; I will change My plan and not keep My promise to you," I would not have to yield to Him, but it would be necessary to fight most vehemently against God Himself. It is as Job says: "Though He slay me, yet will I hope in Him" (cf. Job 13:15). If He should cast me into the depths of hell and place me in the midst of devils, I would still believe that I would be saved because I have been baptized, I have been absolved, I have received the pledge of my salvation, the body and blood of the Lord in the Supper. Therefore I want to see and hear nothing else, but I shall live and die in this faith, whether God or an angel or the devil says the contrary.

I think that this is the true treatment of this passage. For Jacob himself will explain it in this way in the end when he will say (v. 30):

[30] See, for example, *Luther's Works,* 4, pp. 125—130.

"And yet my life is preserved." This picture of the conflicts and struggles in the saints is full of consolation. Elsewhere the example of the nun Mechtild is recounted.[31] She was vexed by the devil, because she knew or experienced absolutely nothing about faith. This was a temptation to unbelief, which is a most bitter grief and torment of conscience. For hearts are consumed by trepidation and doubt, and experience alone shows what this grief is; it cannot be declared in words. Nevertheless, that temptation was not yet equal to this struggle of Jacob. For it was not God who was fighting against her, as was the case here with Jacob, but the devil, who can drive men to unbelief, despair, and blasphemies against the Holy Spirit. I myself, for example, have seen some, and especially women, who simply complained that they were damned and cast off, because they were vexed by Satan with the spirit of blasphemy.

Now, the nun held nothing else up against this temptation except this statement: "I AM A CHRISTIAN," that is, "I have been baptized in the blood of God's Son; I have been fed with the body and blood of Christ. These things I firmly cling to; with this consolation I am content, even if God Himself were to speak otherwise." Similarly, Abraham was ordered to kill the son of promise, and yet he believed very firmly that God would keep His promises.

These matters must be dealt with carefully for the sake of those who will be future pastors of the churches. For there will always be some who will suffer these temptations. They should be cheered up and strengthened by the voice of the pastors in this manner: "In like manner, have confidence, my son; believe that you have been baptized, that you have been pastured and fed in the Lord's Supper and absolved by the laying on of hands, not mine, but God's, who has said to you: 'I forgive you your sins; I promise you eternal life.'" If they grasp this in firm faith, temptations and the spirit of blasphemy will vanish. For Abraham, too, undoubtedly felt great trepidation and consternation in his whole person when he was commanded to kill his son. In the meantime, however, he retained this faith by which he firmly determined that even if his son were reduced to ashes, he would nevertheless be the father of a posterity according to the promise. "What? Has God become a liar? Will the Lord tell lies? Or, will He not keep His promises?" Such thoughts occurred to him. And yet he obeys the command, thinking: "Just as the Lord

[31] A reference to the medieval mystic, Mechtild of Magdeburg (c. 1208—1282 or 1294).

produced a son from my loins and from the womb of a worn-out and sterile mother, so also He will be able to revive him after he has been burnt and reduced to ashes."

In this manner, Abraham also fought against GOD, which is one of the most serious and difficult of all struggles. But in this, God demonstrates His most perfect and excellent will. Although this struggle is not understood and cannot be endured except by the saints, nevertheless, this teaching and consolation should be prominent to strengthen us so that we are not devoured by the devil, even though God is faithful, who will not let us be tempted beyond what we are able (cf. 1 Cor. 10:13). For that is what this example of Jacob teaches us. He was completely unequal to this great struggle and yet remained unconquered. But God conducts Himself in such a way towards him that he does not recognize that God is the wrestler. He thinks that it is an angel. But it is God who shows Himself as his adversary as though He wanted to kill him and deprive him of the promises and blessing and hand it over to his brother Esau. Nor can anyone adequately express in words what his thoughts were on this occasion. But such thoughts as these undoubtedly occurred to him: "What sort of poor wretched being am I? Have I been created only to bear evils? I alone without respite am seized and afflicted by one evil after another. Of all men living, there is none more unfortunate than I am. I see my brother Esau reigning in triumph and growing and increasing with great glory, wealth, children, grandchildren, and revenues. What if God has changed His viewpoint, rejected me, and received my brother into favor?"

These were Jacob's thoughts, but they still remained thoughts. For nature and weak faith cannot, indeed, abstain from these, just as it cannot easily divest itself of other emotions such as impatience, wrath, and concupiscence. But they should remain only thoughts; they should not become axioms that are fixed and speak the final word or are established by our judgment and conscience. I cannot prevent my heart from being disturbed by strange vexations. Hence one should follow the advice of the hermit to whom a youth complained that he rather often experienced imaginations concerned with lusts and other sins and to whom the old man replied: "You cannot prevent the birds from flying over your head. But let them only fly and do not let them build nests in the hair of your head. Let them be thoughts and remain such; but do not let them become conclusions." [32] It is the

[32] The same story from the *Vitae Patrum* is told in *Luther's Works*, 16, p. 311.

mark of desperate men like Saul, Judas, and others to make conclusions out of thoughts, saying: "My punishment is greater than I can bear" (Gen. 4:13) and likewise: "I have betrayed innocent blood" (cf. Matt. 27:4). These men throw away the Word, faith, and prayer. That is making judicial sentences out of temptation. But Jacob does not throw away his faith, although he experienced a very serious temptation and had innumerable thoughts which those who are inexperienced in these matters do not understand.

The chief significance of this story, then, is the example of perfect saints and of temptations in high degree, not against flesh, blood, the devil, and a good angel but against God appearing in hostile form. For although Jacob does not know who this man is, he nevertheless feels that he has been forsaken by God or that God is opposed to him and angry with him. Therefore we retain the grammatical, or historical, sense; and when this is fixed, the allegories offer themselves spontaneously.

We simply stick to the words of the text that it was the form or appearance of a man and not an angel. For Moses wrote the story as Jacob recounted it, like this, no doubt: "Suddenly he attacked, and a man fell upon me." This was a shape, or an appearance. But he does not discuss who that man was, because he does not know. But later, when he sees his back, he recognizes him and says: "I have seen the Lord face to face." That attack, accordingly, was the same as if a great strong man had fallen upon him and attacked him. Who it was, he did not know. Jacob himself was a man of regular strength with powers intact such as are usually found in a sound and strong body. Although he fought without sword and arms, he offered stout resistance. He still had a degree of faith in the promise. Although he was alarmed, his thoughts had not yet reached finality and become conclusions. His faith was, indeed, assailed and tried, but he still held to this conclusion firmly: "I have the promise." Relying on this, he does not decline single combat. He ventures forth thinking: "If he strangles me, he strangles me."

But what his distress of heart was in that struggle is not described. We infer that this selfsame temptation was a fight of faith against unbelief. For this man wanted to smite his soul and conquer it under the name of God so that he might cast away all hope of God's mercy and grace, just as Satan attacked Christ, saying (Matt. 4:9): "All these I will give You, if You will fall down and worship me." Here the devil transforms himself into the figure and majesty of God, and this is a great temptation which can only be felt and not told in words. Nor is it strange that a man in this crisis cannot take counsel or come to a conclusion on the basis of reason. For the spirit itself is fighting here, and the Holy Spirit is present, helping our infirmity (cf. Rom. 8:26); if He were not present, the temptation would turn out contrary to determination.

Moreover, it is likely that this man added some such remark as: "You must die, Jacob, for you are not the man to whom God gave the promise" or "God does not want to keep even the promise that has been given, etc." These were fiery darts (Eph. 6:16)! Yet the holy patriarch was the very man to whom the promise and blessing pertained. But here he is tempted to the last spark and right up to the smoking flax (Is. 42:3). But it is still smoking; it has not yet been put out, nor is the reed shaken.

These matters in the saints are too sublime for us to be able to understand them, although they should be read and heard. Moses does not expressly give the exact words which they exchanged in the struggle, and yet it is not likely that they were completely silent. Undoubtedly, the man sounded forth with terrifying voice, saying: "You must perish, Jacob; you are in for it!" To this Jacob would have replied: "No! that is not God's will. I shall not perish!" Yes and no there assailed each other very sharply and violently. Such things cannot be adequately expressed by word of mouth, especially when God Himself is saying: "You will perish!" and the spirit shouts back: "I shall not perish, but live, etc. I was pushed hard so that I was falling, but the Lord helped me (cf. Ps. 118:17, 13). I may be pushed, assailed, and thrown down, yet I shall not die." So they struggled with arms and words alike as two wrestlers usually do. But in the meantime, faith, too, joined the struggle by praying and crying the well-known cry of Moses at the Red Sea.

This was the crisis of the struggle, in which faith exerted itself more than the arms did by urging and repeating: "No, no, etc.! God has given me orders, called me, and sent me to return to my fatherland; I shall not believe you nor agree with you. Even though God kills me, well, let Him kill me, but I shall still live." In this manner they employed different words at different times during the two hours. They were undoubtedly keen and very vigorous words. Jacob did not know who the man was, and his reason could come to no conclusion or take counsel, because in such a struggle all the senses are disturbed, and reason is confused, as is stated in Psalm 107:27:[33] "They were at their wits' end." Jacob did not know what had happened to him except that his faith heard it being said: "The blessing does not pertain to you but to your brother Esau. You are nothing, etc." Therefore he lives by the Word alone. His faith is very weak and likewise very strong. For when the flax is smoking, it is very close to burning (cf. Is. 42:3). He himself was in the greatest distress, because he will say later: "My life is preserved," as though he meant to say: "My life was in the greatest distress, but now a breathing space has followed." For God does not tempt to kill but to renew, establish, and strengthen. This can be gathered from the text itself. This is Jacob's struggle described in a few words, which we leave to the experts to be explained at greater length.

The Hebrew word which the Seventy have rendered as "struggling" [34] is derived from אָבָק, which signifies "dust," and, indeed, stirred-up dust which is scattered in the air. It is not dust lying still but dust stirred up by those who are toiling and fighting, as in Is. 5:24: "Their blossom like dust." Therefore the word itself signifies to stir up dust by fighting. However, I think that it is one of the words not adequately known, because the Hebrew language has not yet been perfectly restored. The Jews by their ambiguous interpretations have introduced many perversions, especially in the dark passages concerning the Messiah.

25. *When the man saw that he did not prevail against Jacob, he touched the hollow of his thigh; and Jacob's thigh was put out of joint as he wrestled with him.*

Jacob is stronger than the man, not because he is really stronger than the Lord but because the propriety of character is preserved, for the Lord does not make use of greater strength than a man can customarily use. He wants to make trial only of the strength of one man, since the Lord Himself is truly the stronger one. And I, to be sure, would not readily be prepared to wrestle with a man of faith who has the promise, not even if I were a strong giant, for in this case nature is toiling above its strength. Therefore God does not display His power but the skill and ability which becomes a strong man. At the same time, He brings with Him a horrible temptation of the

---

[33] The original has "Ps. 104."

[34] The Septuagint translation reads: καὶ ἐπάλαιεν ἄνθρωπος μετ' αὐτοῦ ἕως πρωί.

spirit. This in the end strengthens Jacob so that he struggles above his strength. For no man, when he is sane and in possession of his reason, can do what suffering and oppressed nature does when nature is weakened and it struggles even unto death. In this case it can overcome all difficulties which it would otherwise not have the strength to endure. After such crises men are accustomed to say when they return to their senses: "How tired and weak I am!" There follows a weakness and languor of all strength because nature has toiled above its strength.

There is a story or fable told somewhere of five fingerprints made on a stone altar by a certain man who had requested that a host be given to him in the Supper as large as the priest took. When it was denied him, he struck the altar with his right hand, moved either by terror or a certain amount of indignation. From then on the marks of his hand remained impressed on the stone forever. For a man in temptations or smitten by terror does what would otherwise be impossible outside of temptation. In this way, therefore, that man,[35] who was Christ our Lord, struggled with Jacob in the same manner in which man engages with man. But when the Lord saw that Jacob was stronger, especially in faith, which God does not like to resist, He employed a special trick of wrestlers and touched the joint of Jacob's thigh.

The word כַּף signifies the hollow of the hand, that is, the hand curved like a shell. From this Moses makes mention of כַּפּוֹת, "shells," in German *Koten,* and on account of the resemblance, it signifies the joint or concave bone which the Greeks call ἰσχίον, into which the bone of the upper leg is inserted and in which it turns. But there are sinews surrounding it so that a joint is made of the two bones and that they do not part from each other. The foot is moved by that joint. Accordingly, Moses wants to say that the man moved the bone of Jacob's thigh from its place; he dislocated his hip so that his leg came out of its joint. But when a dislocation has occurred, the sinews are also moved and contracted, and very acute pains are caused on account of the pressing together of many sinews, and numbness of the member follows.

When this man could not conquer Jacob, he pressed his hand on his thigh and with that pressure the thigh and sinews were moved out of place. He gave him a hard press and wanted to make his leg

---

[35] The Weimar text has *viste,* but we have read *iste.*

lame. These are tricks of wrestlers. When I was in Patmos,[36] a certain man at Eisenach who merits belief recounted a similar example to me, saying that he had known a strong giant with a shaggy chest and uncombed beard, with hair hanging in knotty lumps and with head always bare, who was accustomed to bend and break iron, and he said that many such men were to be found among the Turks at that time. Moreover, at that time there was at the court of the Emperor Frederick a famous Jew who was a celebrated wrestler and who had beaten all the youths of the court nobility and had prostrated them in wrestling with the same trick which is described in this story. Perhaps he had here learned to touch the joint of the thigh and to weaken and conquer his opponent with pain which is usually very acute there. When that giant came to the emperor's court, the courtiers urged him to wrestle the Jew. Although he indicated that he felt a loathing for this race of men, he was at last persuaded by their pleas and entered the arena with the Jew. The Jew begged pardon in case he should treat the foreign antagonist, who was a guest, too harshly. The giant, on the other hand, urged him to put forth all the strength of his talents and body and not to spare him, saying that he, too, to the best of his ability would put on display his best exhibit of strength and agility. But the moment they engaged, the giant seized the Jew and slew him by breaking the bones of his neck.

I am telling this as an example to illustrate this story so that we may know that there are many similar tricks of wrestlers like pressure on the loins, the joints, and other parts of the body, by which those of weaker strength are often able to conquer those with outstanding strength. But Jacob in his great confusion does not feel that touching of the joint, because in a man who is under stress both sense and reason are disturbed and numb so that he cannot concentrate, nor hear or see anything. This usually happens especially when spiritual attacks are added such as Jacob experienced at that time. So he does not cease from the struggle even when his thigh is dislocated.

26. *Then he said: Let me go, for the day is breaking.*

If this wrestler is Christ, of what concern is the rising of the dawn to Him? My reply is that He assumed the character of a man and

---

[36] A reference to Luther's exile at the Wartburg Castle after the Diet of Worms in 1521.

retained the same until He disclosed Himself. So the dawn also rises for Him in this character, and in the manner of all nations He had to return to His usual tasks. But Jacob said:

I will not let you go, unless you bless me.

Why do you not let him go? Your thigh is hurt and you are already lame; what will you do? "I feel no weakness," says Jacob. Who is strengthening you? "Faith, the promise, and indeed, this weakness of faith." In this manner God is conquered when faith does not leave off, is not wearied, and does not cease but presses and urges on. So it makes its appearance in the Canaanite woman, with whom Jesus was wrestling when He said: "You are a dog, the bread of the sons does not belong to you" (cf. Matt. 15:26). The woman did not yield here but offered opposition, saying: "Even the dogs eat the crumbs that fall from their master's table." And so she was victorious and heard the excellent word of praise: "O woman, great is your faith!"

Such examples teach us that faith should not yield or cease urging or pressing on even when it is already feeling God's wrath and not only death and sin. This is the power and strength of the Spirit. Christ, while still wrestling with Jacob and with His omnipotence concealed, wants to be dismissed, but Jacob replies: "I will not let you go, unless you bless me." Why? "Because you said that I have been cursed, and for this reason my soul was confused. Therefore take back that sentence and bless me. You must provide me with a retraction, or I will not let you go. I have defeated you in strength of body. I will also overcome the words of your mouth, for my soul, which you said is lost and condemned, has toiled more vehemently than my body and arms. So I will not let you go unless you retract your judgment concerning me and give me the testimony that I have been blessed before God."

27. *And he said to him: What is your name? And he said: Jacob.*

28. *Then he said: Your name shall no more be called Jacob, but Israel, for you have striven with God and with men, and have prevailed.*

What is your name? Are you not Jacob? From whence then have you such great power and great strength? Now the temptation becomes somewhat milder, and Christ begins to lay aside His mask and to speak comforting and life-giving words. He now reveals

Himself just as He did in the Gospel towards the Canaanite woman
when He said (Matt. 15:28): "O woman, great is your faith." Her
faith was very sharply attacked when He called her a dog. But she
came back at Him, saying: "Seeing that You call me a dog, give me the
crumbs which fall from the tables of the masters and which belong to
the dogs." This was assuredly a beautiful and illustrious faith and an
outstanding example which shows the method and skill of striving
with God. For we should not immediately cast aside courage and
all hope at the first blow but press on, pray, seek, and knock. Even
though He is already thinking of leaving, do not cease but keep on
following Him just as the Canaanite woman did, from whom Jesus
could not conceal Himself but, as Mark says (7:25), she entered the
house and fell at His feet.

Even if He hides Himself in a room in the house and does not
want access to be given to anyone, do not draw back but follow. If
He does not want to listen, knock at the door of the room; raise
a shout! For this is the highest sacrifice, not to cease praying and
seeking until we conquer Him. He has already surrendered Himself
to us so that we may be certain of victory, for He has bound Himself
to His promises and pledged His faithfulness with an oath, saying
(John 16:23): "Truly, truly, I say to you, if you ask anything of the
Father, He will give it to you in My name." Likewise (Mark 16:16):
"He who believes and is baptized will be saved." These promises
will never disappoint you, unless you refuse to follow and seek. In
this case, through your fault, by snoring and sleeping, you lose the
most certain promises and Christ Himself, because you refuse to
enter this arena and take up the contest with God where the possession
of these promises is seen and flourishes. This Man exercises Jacob
until true strength and firmness of faith shows itself. For this reason,
He changes his name. He says: "Your name shall no more be called
Jacob. You were previously called a trampler because of your brother,
but they have not yet imposed your true name on you. Your name
will be ISRAEL. For your fortitude and the invincible strength of
heart by which you have conquered God and men have merited this."

The wrestler therefore reveals Himself when He says that Jacob
has fought with God and men, and from the fight He gives him a new
name. אֵל signifies God. Investigations have been made by all the
fathers what the signification of this word Israel was. Jerome makes
modest complaint that he is overwhelmed by the authority and learning
of very eloquent men who explain this word as meaning "A man who

sees God." [37] But he adds, nevertheless, that he prefers to accept the etymology of the angel or God rather than that of others, even if they are most eloquent.

שָׂרָה signifies to have dominion, to prevail, to be chief. In Is. 9:6 שַׂר שָׁלוֹם is "the Prince of peace." But when י is placed before a word, as in יִשְׂרָאֵל, the first "a" is absorbed, and the word becomes a proper name, as it does also in other cases because of the prefixed י, in Jehoshaphat, Jesus, and Isaiah, for example. יִשְׂרָאֵל is a fighter, prince, lord, or mistress, of God. But all men have sweated over the explanation of this word because it seems absurd that we are called lords and conquerors of God. And this is certainly true if we judge according to philosophy. But in the Spirit and in theology it is right and godly to say that God is conquered by us.

Yet He is not conquered in such a way that He is subjected to us, but His judgment, or His wrath and fury and whatever opposes us, is conquered by us by praying, seeking, and knocking, so that from an angry judge, as He seemed to be previously, He becomes a most loving Father and says (Matt. 15:28; Luke 7:50; cf. Matt. 8:13): "O woman, great is your faith. Your faith has saved you. As you have believed, so be it unto you. Oh, how you hurt Me with your cry!" It is the fullness of consolation that God exercises us in such a way and exhorts us to fight and shows that it is to Him a most pleasing sacrifice to be conquered by us.

But these matters must not be measured by the judgment of reason, which also tries to conquer God by its own strength and works. But God is conquered in this way as soon as He has surrendered Himself to us, so to say, and revealed Himself in His Word, promise, and Baptism. It remains that you should conquer those things which want to take this God away from you, namely, through the truth of the promises and faith. Or, if He pretends that He is unfriendly and angry with you inasmuch as He does not want to hear you and help you, then say: "Lord God, You have promised this in Your Word. Therefore You will not change Your promise. I have been baptized: I have been absolved." If you persistently urge and press on in this way, He will be conquered and say: "Let it be done unto you as you have petitioned, for you have the promise and the blessing. I have to give in to you. For a constant and persistent seeker and petitioner is the sweetest sacrifice."

[37] Jerome, *Liber Hebraicarum quaestionum in Genesim, Patrologia, Series Latina*, XXIII, 988—989.

It is very refined and pleasant in theology that Christians are called a שַׂר, or שָׂרָה, of God. שָׂרָה otherwise means a housemother, or mistress, who exercises dominion in a house. Accordingly, believers are princes and masters of God because they struggle with God and conquer. We do not spend time on the other etymology. For it has no meaning if you interpret: "Master with God." But it is expressly stated here: "You have striven, you have fought with God and men." The wrestler calls himself not only God but also man, as though he meant to say: "In conquering me you have conquered God and man." He joins both. "Previously you overcame one man by supplanting your brother, whence you obtained the name Jacob; but now you have come forth superior to God and man at one and the same time."

29. *Then Jacob asked him: Tell me, I pray, your name. But he said: Why is it that you ask my name? And there he blessed him.*

30. *So Jacob called the name of the place Peniel, saying: For I have seen God face to face, and yet my life is preserved.*

31. *The sun arose upon him as he passed Peniel.*

The Latin translator added the clause: "Which is wonderful." But it is not in the Hebrew, and so it has been omitted by us. But Jacob in his amazement and consternation does not yet understand what these words mean for him. For he has not yet completely surmounted the trial of the man which he has sustained until now in all its severity with no other idea but that he would have to perish and die. For such apparitions take place in the manner in which he who is tried feels or as the weak flesh thinks. For it is necessary that both things should be done and felt — the mortification of the flesh and the quickening of the Spirit, as is often stated in Holy Scripture (cf. Ps. 118:21): "I thank Thee that Thou hast humbled me and become my salvation," and likewise (1 Sam. 2:6): "The Lord kills and brings to life; He brings down to Sheol and raises up." These are works of God.

When Jacob therefore struggles with weakness of faith and does not cling to the promise firmly enough but wavers somewhat according to the flesh and has doubts about God's will, as the flesh is accustomed to do, then there appears to him the gloomy face of God, struggling with him and desiring to kill him. The same happens to all who are tried when they do not rejoice in the goodness of God which has been clearly perceived but shudder at God's wrath and are terrified. Here all things seem to threaten instant death, all things are black, cloudy, gloomy, unfavorable, and mournful in heaven and on earth. Neither the sun nor the moon shines forth because the heart, overwhelmed in the flesh, is dying, and when that is dead, all things fall into ruin. So Jacob, still having a spark of the Spirit left which is living in him, fights and strives in great weakness, which is nevertheless very strong, as has been stated above.

These are hidden and wonderful things and known only to those who have the promises, in which they are vexed and humbled. Nevertheless, in that humiliation they come forth as victors even over God Himself. For that man says: "I am God and man whom you have conquered." But in the struggle Jacob does not understand nor does he see his fortitude because of that weakness, but he begins to ask: "Who are you? Tell me your name, since, indeed, you say that I am the conqueror of GOD and men." Here the wrestler reveals himself as God and man. But Jacob does not yet understand, and he is still submerged in darkness, the sun not yet having arisen for him. He still adheres to the thought that his adversary is threatening him with death. Yet, because he hears that he is victorious, he says: "I would like to know who you are, for you have struggled with me to take my life from me and yet you acknowledge that you are conquered."

But the wrestler conceals his identity and leaves him in uncertainty and doubt. The image of this man is represented to Jacob in accordance with Jacob's feelings. Jacob does not understand, and so the man does not reply to the question about the name, as though he meant to say: "I told you already previously that you have struggled and prevailed with God and men, and from this you should have gathered who I am." He does not want to tell him his name but proceeds to tempt, vex, and instruct him. But if Jacob had had a grip on himself and clouds were not obscuring the light of the sun, he would have understood more easily what was meant by being a conqueror of God and men. To be sure, he understands the words, but he does not comprehend the matter itself because he does not know that this is the Lord. He thinks: "Well, who are you, in whom I have conquered God and man?" But at length there follow the epiphanies of the Lord when He blesses him. Then, laying aside the mask, He manifests Himself, namely, that the wrestler is God and Man, who would at length manifest Himself in our flesh and whom the Jews would crucify.

But what the blessing was Moses did not describe. Undoubtedly, it was that by which the fathers were blessed: "In your Seed all the nations will be blessed, etc. It is I, O Jacob, who have blessed you and will bless you." Therefore what Jacob could not see formerly when he was still a man but investigated and sought in doubt and uncertainty he understands and sees with great joy from the Word and blessing. "It is surely not You, my heavenly Father and Lord?" he thinks. "I thought that You were a specter or a man. Then You are the One who has blessed me, my father Isaac, and my grandfather Abraham?"

This is the joyful climax of this contest. For now Jacob returns from hell to heaven, from death to life. It was certainly a very fierce and difficult ἀγών ("contest") which he had hitherto sustained. So he gives thanks to God and confesses his distress. Now he no longer wants this place to retain its former name but calls it Peniel, as though he meant to say: "It should not be called a struggle or vision of hell but a vision of God." Therefore he says: "I HAVE SEEN THE LORD FACE TO FACE." "And now I see clearly," he says, "that the wrestler who tested me was God Himself. Why was I so terrified? Why was I so alarmed? I did not know that this was the Lord my God."

Without any controversy we shall say that this man was not an angel but our Lord Jesus Christ, eternal God and future Man, to be crucified by the Jews. He was very familiar to the holy fathers and often appeared to them and spoke with them. He exhibited Himself to the fathers in such a form that He might testify that He would at some time dwell with us in the form of human flesh.

This true explanation has not been discovered by us or taken over from others, but the man himself manifests himself by giving the name Israel to Jacob, and at this point Jacob says: "I have seen the Lord face to face." He Himself, our Lord Jesus Christ, tested Jacob not to destroy him but to confirm and strengthen him and that in this fight he might more correctly learn the might of the promise. Indeed, He added this strength and power to Jacob that he might conquer and joyfully praise the vision of the Lord.

In the grips of tribulation and the struggle itself he did not speak thus, just as others under the cross are never in the habit of uttering such happy and joyful words. But those who are godly and spiritual must nevertheless maintain the struggle and reach the point where they see the face of God, as was said previously concerning the woman of Canaan. She had seen and heard Christ, and when He withdrew into a house to conceal Himself, she followed Him there and pressed on until she succeeded in storming Christ's heart, which was too obstinate, it seemed, in repelling her. Having conquered in such a struggle, we can with the patriarch Jacob congratulate ourselves and boast that we have seen Peniel, that is, the face of the Lord. For in this way Jacob both attests the difficulty of the struggle which he had experienced and his joy; and he wants to say: "Good God, in what great troubles and difficulties I have been involved, and in what great consternation! But thanks be to God, for I have now withstood the struggle and am safe! My soul has been freed and rescued from these troubles, and now I give thanks to the Lord my God."

31. *And he limped because of his thigh.*

32. *Therefore to this day the Israelites do not eat the sinew of the thigh which is upon the hollow of the thigh, because he touched the hollow of Jacob's thigh on the sinew of the hip.*

When the struggle has ended, the patriarch feels the pain in his thigh. But consolation comes to him, the sun of heaven, or the face of God and the light of the sun, the natural light of day; heaven and earth is pure light for him. But in this place he speaks about the sinew, of which he made no mention above; for he only mentioned the joint. Here he adds the sinew because the joints are surrounded by very strong sinews. In German we have translated *die spanader* ("sinews"). The Jews do not eat them, but the Germans have no aversion for them; indeed, many regard them as delicacies.

But what the Hebrew word נָשֶׁה properly signifies I do not really know. The proper name Manasseh has been derived from this word, that is, "forgetting." Even among the Jews there is no agreement about the meaning of the word. Certain people interpret it as the "sinew of forgetfulness," as though you were to say that he forgot his place on account of the dislocation. But these are Jewish ideas, that is, inept and foul. For the Jews invent rocky and rough etymologies. Others have rendered it as "the sinews of contraction," which is a better explanation. For it regularly contracts and expands, and in this manner the foot is moved. I think that it is derived from the verb וַיִּגַע, which signifies to raise, so that it means the sinew raised over the thigh. But I make no firm statement on the matter. Jerome does not translate correctly when he says that the nerve withered away in the thigh. For Moses wants to say that it was moved from its place, and very acute pain usually follows a dislocation. But this is what Moses says, namely, that the sinew in Jacob's thigh was touched.

This is the story and simple meaning of this passage, which has been treated to the best of our ability, and I hope that it will also be plain to others. Now the allegorical meaning also should be touched upon. But I have often said that allegories are dangerous in the explanation of Holy Scripture because one man follows this procedure, another man another procedure; some men put down one foundation, others another, and sometimes they build gold thereon and at another time stubble (cf. 1 Cor. 3:12). Augustine has well said: "A figure proves nothing." [38] So in the asserting and confirming of the dogmas of our faith, allegories or other figures are of no avail, but there is need of proofs and testimonies which are taken from the sources of Holy Scripture themselves. For any man, according to his own liking, can either interpret or imagine figures and allegories. So they have nothing sure and certain. Nevertheless, they can be adduced as lights and ornaments to adorn and illustrate doctrine or the literal meaning, as Paul in Gal. 4:22 adduces the example of Abraham, Hagar, and Sarah to adorn and illustrate the doctrine of justification by faith and the doctrine concerning the two testaments. When the allegory agrees with the doctrine and its assertion,[39] it is a very beautiful adornment and, if I may say so, seasoning of doctrine.

However, in illustrating the example which is set before us in this story, we shall still wait longer before we treat the allegory. For first the literal meaning should precede as the foundation of the allegory. It is an outstanding and very salutary example, which should be set before the church with special care. For we are reminded here that in our life we should prepare ourselves in the same manner and learn to recognize the church of God in that picture of Jacob's struggle. For God hides the church and also our salvation under a dark and horrible cover, to which we must become accustomed so that we do

---

[38] Augustine, *De doctrina Christiana*, III, 59, *Patrologia, Series Latina*, XXXIV, 68—69.

[39] The Weimar text has *adfectione*, but we have read *adsertione*.

not despair or fall into unbelief even in the greatest dangers and adversities which are thrown in our way by Satan, the world, or God Himself. For Paul says in Col. 3:3: "Your life is hid with Christ in God." This is the sum and substance of this example. We do not live in the flesh, or, even though we have our habitation in it, we nevertheless do not live according to it. Nor do we render service to the wisdom and righteousness of the flesh and much less to avarice, wrath, and usury; such are not our arms. But while we have our habitation in the flesh, we live by the faith of the Son of God. For I know no other life but that I believe in the Father Almighty and our Lord Jesus CHRIST, His Son, who suffered for me, etc.

But these things are not seen? They are truly hidden in God, but in such a way that the devil is not able to remove this life or tear it away, however hidden it may be. For we are not praised, honored, or joyful in the flesh, but we are mortified, we die, suffer, and are perplexed, loaded with insults, spit upon and regarded as the worst of all men, whom, if they could, they would remove as heretics and criminals with fire and sword. Are not these experiences an oppressive lid on this life? But under these there lies concealed a beautiful and precious gem which is called: "I believe in the Son of God."

For just as our head, Christ, is hidden in God, so the church lies hidden under these lids, and in the world it is necessary for her to put up with being called seditious, error-ridden, heretical, the offscourings of the very worst men who have ever lived. These reproaches she endures; they are her beautiful precious stones which she wears on earth, her jewels and golden chain. These are her gems and her most beautiful and precious jewels, with which God adorns her in this life. So in this example a picture is drawn of how God tempts us privately and the whole church according to the example of Jacob. For He wrestles with her and conducts Himself like an adversary and enemy who wishes to forsake, cast away, and indeed destroy her.

For if you carefully consider the state of our church, we seem to have nothing but the pure Word and the sacraments, and we have an infinite number of adversaries — princes, nobles, citizens, domestics, and pupils, and finally our own flesh which we carry about with us. For this is our glory, to be vexed and laughed at even by those from our own midst, by those in our own household. Those are our lids, on account of which we judge that God by no means wants to recognize and regard us as His own. For nothing becomes the church less than this picture. When I saw such contempt, aversion, and hatred for the Word arising from men after the rebirth of the light of the Gospel, I myself often thought: "Why did I begin to teach? Or, why do I keep on when men rage against us more and more and become worse daily?"

But these things must be borne, and we must conclude that God is the One who is hidden. This is His peculiar property. He is really hidden, and yet He is not hidden, for the flesh prevents us from being able to look at Him. It murmurs, is sorrowful, rages, is angry, and cries: "I am most wretched, forlorn, and despised." It is certainly true that the pastors of the church together with the godly do not have the protection of princes, or kings, nor even the patronage of the citizens or peasants, which is the church's due. The patronage which it already has is often taken away, so much are the pastors and the godly exposed to plunderings and wrongs of every kind. So it seems that God is completely forsaking us and casting us away, because He is hidden to us and we are hidden along with Him. But in faith, in the Word, and in the sacraments He is revealed and seen.

Reason, wisdom, righteousness of the flesh, and this light of the sun God regards as dark and misty, but here the Word comes forward like a little flame shining in the midst of darkness and scattering its rays through its doctrine and the sacraments; these rays God orders to be apprehended. If we embrace them, God is no longer hidden to us in the spirit but only in the flesh.

Therefore, also when we are plunged into disasters and troubles and covered by darkness, things on account of which we cannot be sure that we are the church or pleasing to God, let us learn to take hold of the Word and let sink and fall what falls, and let us not be moved by the fall and defection of others. But let us reflect that we are in a dark place, with the lamp of the Word shining before us. "For he who believes and is baptized will be saved" (Mark 16:16). For that light is the only one which the sun and human reason do not see; but it shines in the heart. Besides this Word we should know nothing and see nothing. For if this Word alone is shining, there is no danger, and the hour will come when we shall come forth and say with joy: "I have seen the Lord face to face, and my soul has been saved."

Jacob, therefore, has supplied the church of God with a very useful and beautiful example of faith struggling in infirmity, so that we should not think, as the monks imagined, that the fathers and prophets were senseless rocks and logs in whom there was no infirmity.[40] Otherwise, we would have to despair, because we still experience the greatest infirmity in the flesh. For the flesh murmurs and does not want to suffer or to be trodden down. Therefore we complain and cry out that we are being treated unworthily. Let us then contemplate the holy partriarchs and comfort ourselves with their example since, indeed, they were not always firm and strong in faith.

Jacob was showered with the richest of consolations, not only with those he himself experienced but also with those that came upon his grandfather Abraham and his father Isaac. Nevertheless, he wrestles with the greatest infirmity. So you should reflect: "I am not alone in being tempted concerning the wrath of God, predestination, and unbelief. I am not alone! All the saints, as many as have ever believed or now believe in GOD'S Son experience these struggles of temptation, by which either they themselves or the whole church are disciplined. For what is this whole assembly which is called the church? It is a tiny little flock of the most wretched, forlorn, and hopeless men in the sight of the world. What is this flock compared with the whole world, what is it compared with the kingdom of the Turks and France, indeed, compared even with our adversaries, the papists?

So if you ask where the church is, it is nowhere in evidence. But you must not pay regard to external form but to the Word and to Baptism, and the church must be sought where the sacraments are purely administered, where there are hearers, teachers, and confessors of the Word. If the church is still not in evidence, you should remember that our blessings are hidden and that their magnitude cannot be perceived in this life. Man is still wrestling, but he is not in any danger; indeed, this contest obtains a very joyful outcome.

Let us compose a proverb from this history: when you think that our Lord God has rejected a person, you should think that our Lord God has him in His arms and is pressing him to His heart. When we suppose that someone has been deserted and rejected by God, then we should conclude that he is in the embrace and the lap of God. So Jacob feels and thinks nothing else but that he will be destroyed. But when he takes stock of matters, he is held fast in the embrace of the Son of God. The example of Job in his humiliation

[40] Cf. *Luther the Expositor*, pp. 76—77.

and affliction teaches the same. For in this wonderful manner the Lord treats His saint (Ps. 4:3), namely, when we think that it is all over with us, He embraces and kisses us as His dearest sons. This is what Paul means when he says: "When I am weak, I am strong; when I die, I live" (cf. 2 Tim. 2:11; 2 Cor. 12:10).

But we do not understand, and the reason is that the flesh stands in the way. It cannot endure the mortification of itself and hinders the spirit so that it cannot perceive the boundless love and goodwill of God towards us until it comes forth from this struggle and repels the hindrances of the flesh. But the same things are copiously handed down everywhere in Holy Scripture. For it is stated in Rev. 3:19: "Those whom I love, I reprove and chasten." In Prov. 3:11-12 we read: "My son, do not despise the Lord's discipline or be weary of His reproof, for the Lord reproves him whom He loves, as a father the son in whom he delights." These and other statements like them are very striking and memorable.

But is it taking delight in a son to strike him with scourges and blows? Scripture certainly teaches this, and experience testifies the same. For those who are good and faithful fathers chastise their sons severely. They cannot endure their becoming disobedient good-for-nothings. They do not do this with evil intent but that their sons may be instructed and corrected if there is anything improper in their ways so that they may turn out to be good men. But the boy who is scourged does not understand that his father has the best of intentions and true στοργήν ("affection"), but he thinks that his father is a tyrant and that he has given up all care and love for him. So also a good teacher hates the laziness or ill will of a pupil, and he takes care to correct him with discipline, not that he hates the pupil or is in the grips of a kind of lust for flogging boys, though I saw many of this kind in the schools years ago when I was a boy, but he loves the boy very much and is moved by this love when he chastises him.

Actual fact and experience teach that there is need of discipline. Our heavenly Father follows the same method in chastising the godly. Therefore the man who can endure this discipline and persevere will at length experience what is stated in Heb. 12:11: "For the moment all discipline seems painful rather than pleasant; later it yields the peaceful fruit of righteousness to those who have been trained by it."

We see the same thing happening in this story, where the curse has given way, temptation has passed, and blessing and joy follows:

"I have seen the Lord, etc., and my life has been preserved." So the godly man thinks when he has escaped from the temptation: "Ah, what a merciful God I have! I was just despairing and going down to hell. But now I see that this struggle has benefited me for my life. I would never have thought that God is so close to me." It is very sweet, accordingly, to experience the fruit [41] of discipline and chastisement in this manner. "O my heavenly Father, were You so close to me, and I did not know it? How good I feel now! Let Esau and all the devils come on! I will no longer be afraid, because I have the Lord God on my side. Before this I saw His back parts in the form and character of a man by which He seemed to threaten destruction to me, and my heart was distressed lest He might push me down into hell. But now I see His face" (cf. Ex. 33:18-23).

It is usual for that external form to appear which the internal imagination, or emotion, of a godly man feels, as happened to the disciples while Christ was walking on the sea (cf. Matt. 14:25, etc.). They were alarmed and distressed when they did not recognize the Lord, and so Christ seemed like a ghost or a devil to them. But when they hear Him saying "It is I," that form is changed, and their eyes are opened so that they recognize Christ with all fear removed. This is what seeing the Lord face to face means, namely, to be brought back from hell and to be conducted into heaven, so that the heart concludes: "I do not now have God cursing me in His anger but blessing me and propitious." But practice and experience are required for this knowledge of God, and it must be continually taught and dealt with. There must also be some practice and acquiring of the habit in life. Otherwise it is not understood since, indeed, those things which seem to us to be signs of God's wrath are most certain indications of His great love and goodwill.

I have often seen excellent men horribly vexed by terrors, afflictions, and the severest persecutions, so much so that they nearly experienced despair of heart. But these things must be learned so that we may be able to comfort such men and interpret the temptations as the special manner by which God is accustomed to wrestle with us in the form of a destroyer and that we may exhort them firmly to retain the promise, or lamp and spark, of the Word in the hope that the rescue will certainly follow. For God leads down to hell and brings back (cf. 1 Sam. 2:6). Now you see His back parts, and

[41] The Weimar text has *ructum,* but we have read *fructum.*

God seems to be shunning you, but sometime later you will see His front parts and His face. This is what it means for Him to love those whom He chastises. This love must be learned from experience, nor should chastisement be avoided and shunned. The story is told of a peasant who, when he heard this consolation from his pastor, that the afflictions and troubles by which God afflicts us are signs of His love, replied: "Ah, how I would like Him to love others and not me!"

This was a foolish and impious reply. We should not feel and speak like this, nor should God's works in us be interpreted and understood in this way. But we should know that mortification is very salutary. By it we are instructed for life and salvation, not for destruction, as Paul testifies when he says (Rom. 12:2): "That you may prove" (not only that you may learn by words but that you may also learn by experience) "what is the will of God, what is good and acceptable and perfect." For this is God's will, our mortification and sanctification (cf. 1 Thess. 4:3). But we cannot be sanctified unless the flesh and the body of sin is mortified, which in this life with all its force is driven into sins of every kind, adulteries, lusts, thefts, etc. God therefore judges, chastises, and scourges until we learn what is the good and acceptable and perfect will of God so that we sing with David (Ps. 119:71): "It is good for me that Thou didst humble me, that I might learn Thy statutes." I would gladly be exempted; my flesh shrinks from temptation, but I know that this is the excellent will of God. Likewise: "The Lord has chastened me sorely, but He has not given me over to death" (Ps. 118:18). "I was pushed hard, so that I was falling, but the Lord helped me" (Ps. 118:13), so that my soul should see the face of God and be saved. "I thank Thee that Thou hast answered me and hast become my Salvation" (Ps. 118:21).

So far, then, we have had the example of the holy patriarch which in a wonderful manner comforts the saints who are weak in faith. But just as they accepted the consolation and as the temptation redounded to their salvation, so also we should make efforts to become like them in the struggle and in the rescue. For then we shall learn what that means which is mentioned in Ps. 34:8: "O taste and see that the Lord is good! Happy is the man who takes refuge in Him!" In this we understand and feel how good and sweet the Lord is, when we return from the darkness and shadow of death, for then the light is most pleasing and pleasant. The child then kisses the rod! Dear rod, what pious children you make! So much about the example and the story.

I find no great pleasure in allegories, but I shall touch on them in a few words. Augustine set this down as the basis for his allegory, that Jacob is the body of his posterity. So far he speaks correctly. For there must be a person who is the figure of a whole congregation. But what he adds about the struggle with the man and about the victory after Jacob is blessed is too hard and far too artificial. For he thinks that the crucifixion of Christ is signified in the fact that Jacob prevailed against the angel, or God, and this had to take place through his evil descendants. These prevailed against Christ, that is, they crucified Him, and yet the crucified Christ blessed Jacob, namely, the better part of his posterity.

But this allegory is too hard and forced. It makes a twofold posterity, a good and a bad one. The bad posterity conquered, but the good one was blessed when Christ conquered death and those evil victors. This part we do not approve. It seems that the fathers who followed this view were deceived by a faulty translation in the Latin word *latitudo*. For with this word they translated the word פַּך, which, as stated above, signifies the socket, or the joint, of the thigh. From this word *latitudo* they devised a double posterity. Jerome and Origen composed many allegories of this kind, but with very poor success. So there is need of an accurate judgment in discerning the allegories which turn up among the fathers or are devised by others.

But to me it does not seem incongruent if we make Jacob a person and a body of good, and not of evil, posterity, as Scripture makes the distinction. "For not all who are descended from Israel are Israelites, not those who are the children of the flesh but those who are the children of the promise" (cf. Rom. 9:7-8). Otherwise, also the evil posterity would have received the blessing of God. But Jacob is a picture of the true posterity of Israel, that is, of all the saints and of us also who believe in Christ. Therefore Israel is in this temptation with Jacob when either the individual members are privately tempted or the whole church in general is tempted. In this struggle we conquer God, as previously stated, because we have the promise. Adhering to this in faith, we become stronger even in infirmity so that we conquer our heavenly Father and God's Son after the example of the woman of Canaan, to whom Christ says (Matt. 15:28): "O woman, great is your faith!" He also said (Mark 9:23): "All things are possible to him who believes."

This is a useful and good allegory, instructing and confirming consciences, which should always be put to use and kept before one's eyes so that we may conclude that the believer conquers God by his faith and prayer because God has promised that He will be his Defender and Savior and the Giver of all blessings. Therefore He is not willing to deny Himself and cannot do so (cf. 2 Tim. 2:13). But if He appears in another form or in another capacity and seems to be adverse to you, you should not be disturbed in heart, nor should you yield, but in faith you should offer resistance so that you may conquer and become Israel. How? Not with the strength or weapons of your flesh and nature but with confidence in the cause that intervenes between you and God, namely, that He has promised and sworn that He will be your God. With this confidence you will conquer, inasmuch as it arises not from nature but from the promise. If, therefore, He meets you as a wrestler and wants to destroy you or to hide His name and promise, be strong and hold firmly to the Word, even though you feel great infirmity, and you will conquer. Then in that fight you will also feel that the sinew, or joint, of the thigh is moved from its place and is becoming weak. This is a true allegory and agrees with the idiom of Scripture which often expresses posterity by means of the term thigh. So Augustine does well to apply the sinew of the thigh to posterity. For Moses says: "Therefore all the souls of those who came from Jacob's thigh were seventy" (cf. Ex. 1:5).

But the weakened and numbed sinew teaches those who are struggling and are believers that that carnal birth is of no avail at all towards this victory. For the thigh, which signifies the generation of the flesh, has been dislocated and has become weak. From this Christians know that they do not become the people or sons of God by birth or by the righteousness of the flesh, nor by carnal propagation or succession according to the statement (John 1:13): "Who were born, not of blood nor of the will of man, etc." All things are mortified. So hypocrites and Jews boast in vain concerning these things, inasmuch as they are still acting like mad men in the glory of the flesh and the righteousness of the Law. For that man pressed his hand on Jacob's thigh, and by this pressure the sinew was mortified. But the sons of God are born from God. The godly posterity of Jacob should therefore learn not to glory in the flesh nor to seek life in the blessings and glory of the flesh but in the blessing of God. This makes sons of God according to the promise: "In your Seed all nations will be blessed" (cf. Gen. 22:18). Likewise, it is stated in John 1:13: "Who were born from God, etc." This is a beautiful example for seeking allegories, for it teaches and consoles at one and the same time.

In agreement with this there is also the fact that the children of Israel do not eat the sinew, that is, they do not believe. For elsewhere to eat signifies to believe. "Unless you eat the flesh of the Son of Man, etc.," John 6:53. We do not eat, or believe in, that sinew raised above the thigh. We do not praise the sinewy wisdom, glory, righteousness, and power of the flesh but abstain from all confidence and glory in the righteousness of the flesh. But the good posterity of Jacob alone understands this wisdom and manifests it, for it alone has had its thigh moved. All others honor and eat the sinew of the thigh, which is tough and holds fast because it has not yet been mortified in them. Christians alone abstain from the dislocated thigh and sinews, because the New Testament teaches (cf. John 1:13): "Who were born not of blood nor of the will of man nor of the will of the flesh, but of God." This allegory is nearer the truth and in agreement with the doctrine of the Gospel, for God's people struggle with God and conquer, and after the victory they receive the blessing and reject the righteousness and wisdom of the flesh, yes, they crucify the flesh with its lusts. He who is godly and has the gift of composing allegories will easily find others.

CHAPTER THIRTY-THREE

1. *And Jacob lifted up his eyes and looked, and behold, Esau was coming, and four hundred men with him.*

T HE matters recounted in this chapter are clear and easy because they deal with moral issues, civil life, and human affairs. So we shall run through them briefly, since there is no obscurity either in the words or the story. For as an example for our faith and to strengthen it, Moses describes how God hears the groaning of a weak and struggling faith. These groans are, indeed, ineffable but not without great fruit. Thus Jacob belongs to the number of those of whom Christ says (Mark 9:23): "All things are possible to him who believes." For by faith he has come forth as the conqueror of God and men so that neither God nor man wishes to harm him or is able to do so. God has blessed him, but his brother Esau has experienced such a change that he not only does not want to harm him but even wants to help, love, and be good to him. His anger has been changed into brotherly kindness.

This is surely the hand of the Highest, by which an angry man is prevented from doing what he had purposed, for God has the hearts of all men in His hand, so that they cannot go beyond a fixed limit. It is just as is stated in Job 38:11 concerning the limits imposed by God on the sea: "Thus far shall you come and no farther, and here shall your proud waves be stayed." To those who look at the sea when it is tossed by billows and storms, it seems to be threatening the shore as though about to burst through the borders by which it is enclosed and to overflow in all directions. But the pressure of the waters and billows is checked and kept within limits. So also the hearts of men rage in horrible fashion when inflamed by anger, but God has set up limits to fury and anger which it is not permissible to cross. The same is evident in this example of Esau, and everywhere in the stories of the heathen many other examples are extant which testify that human power and wisdom can never advance beyond the limit prescribed by God.

Hannibal had advanced up to the walls of Rome, causing terror and alarm both in the city as well as in all of Italy so that he would have had the certain hope and opportunity to gain possession of both, if only he would have had the courage which he had previously displayed in battle.[1] But he retreated, God checking his attacks. So his friends cried: "You know how to conquer, Hannibal; but you do not know how to use your victory."[2] But they did not know that a secret, divine power was at hand which checked him. So also the pope has advanced to his limit. Nor will the Turks cross the boundaries set up by God. Indeed, the devil's ragings and efforts will last only as long as it seems good to God to let him loose for His glory and our mortification and well-being.

In the same manner, the Lord says concerning the king of the Assyrians in Is. 37:24: "You have said, With my many chariots I have gone up the heights of the mountains, to the far recesses of Lebanon; I felled its tallest cedars, etc." But the Lord replies (v. 29): "Because you have raged against Me and your arrogance has come to My ears, I will put My hook in your nose and My bit in your mouth, and I will turn you back on the way by which you came." He was not lacking in will and strength, but the power of God opposed him. It is as Is. 10:15 says: "Shall the ax vaunt itself over him who hews with it, or the saw magnify itself against him who wields it?" There is no reason for you to exalt yourself beyond measure because of your successes and power. For it is just as if the saw or the ax boasted that it cuts or splits the wood. For unless I put the saw into motion and cut the wood, the ax or the saw would never accomplish anything.

This victory, that he was about to overcome his brother, was promised to Jacob by God gratis and out of pure goodness. Esau is not conquered by strength, diligence, plans, evil tricks, or pretense but solely by the goodness of God, for his will is [3] changed. This is the most illustrious victory of all, when men are brought to such a point that their hearts and wills are changed. Nor was there ever a better victory than when willing men were made out of unwilling men who were offering resistance. But this is the work of the power and majesty of God alone, to change an angry and offended heart and

[1] Livy, *History of Rome*, XXIII, 16, 1.
[2] Livy, *History of Rome*, XXII, 51, 4; the words are attributed to Maharbal.
[3] The Weimar text has *mutantur,* but we have read *mutatur.*

mind into a quiet and kind one. For otherwise the human heart is so ungovernable that it cannot be changed by any might, whether of the devil, of death, or any other evil, however violent its power may be. It can be changed only by force and violence because man's will is unconquerable and obstinate and cannot be prevailed upon by any wisdom or any strength if it is not overcome by goodness.

This God alone can do, as is evident in this example. For Jacob deserved to be called Israel since he conquered God and had the experience of seeing Him smiling and rejoicing, whom he had previously regarded as an enemy plotting against his life. He conquered the wrath both of his brother Esau and of all who came with him in no other way but by faith and prayer, by which both God Himself and men are conquered. For this reason it is stated by Solomon in Prov. 16:7: "When a man's ways please the Lord, he makes even his enemies to be at peace with him." And we have experienced the same thus far. For under the blessing of GOD many have been converted to peace who bitterly hated and persecuted the Gospel. This was done not with violence but with the kind and beautiful victory by which man's will is changed of its own accord. So great is the might of prayer. It conquers both God and brother Esau: it has overcome both heaven and earth. Brother Esau now has no thought of harming him and cannot do so. For his whole capacity for feeling and his will have been changed, as we shall hear.

Accordingly, Jacob, free from care and joyful, congratulates himself on the victory which he has from God Himself and not from an angel. As he said previously: "I have seen the Lord, etc." This reconciliation of his brother testifies to two things, that the vision was true and not an empty specter. Then, too, it testifies that prayer and the ineffable groaning had obtained more than he had dared to ask or hope for, for he had never promised himself so much comfort either in God or his brother. He sought only this, that his brother would withdraw and let him go unharmed with his family. He did not expect that goodwill which he experienced in meeting, embracing, and kissing his brother and weeping on his shoulder.

One must believe and hope and persevere in prayer, and one must knock. He will certainly come and will not tarry! (Cf. Heb. 10:37) For it is impossible for urgent, instant, and persevering prayer not to be heard. But because we do not believe, we do not experience this perseverance, nor do we feel the magnitude of God's goodness and salvation. Let us therefore stir up our hearts to faith and prayer and know that God is delighted with that perseverance and has enjoined it when He says (Matt. 7:7): "Seek, and you will find; knock, and it will be opened to you." Nor is prayer ever heard more abundantly than in such agony and groanings of a struggling faith.

Thus far the church has obtained the mitigation of many of the worst evils that impended from the Turks and other adversaries. Altogether differently, therefore, and much more richly were our prayers heard than we either prayed or understood. Paul says in Rom. 8:26-27 and Eph. 3:20: "We do not know how to pray as we ought, but the Spirit Himself intercedes for us with sighs too deep for words. And He who searches the hearts of men knows what is the mind of the Spirit." For we always seek less than we should, nor do we hope for those things which God bestows in all readiness. We do not seek as is necessary, nor do we understand these things, for they are too great for us to be able to comprehend them with our heart, inasmuch as we think only small and tiny thoughts. The Lord is great and high, and therefore He wants great things to be sought from Him and is willing to bestow them so that His almighty power might be shown forth. This is the first part concerning the victory of Jacob.

Secondly, that Jacob may avoid tempting God and in his unrestrained joy and the elation of his victory might not exasperate his brother's heart, which was scarcely yet placated, he is not proud and does not behave insolently towards his brother as foolish men are accustomed to do. He does not say: "I have the promise of victory; I care nothing about your anger or threats." For with this contempt and pride the wound which had been healed with great difficulty would have broken out again. But he uses whatever courtesy he can to increase and preserve his goodwill. He decks out another beautiful procession with which he goes to meet him with his family. That is doing what lies within him [4] not to destroy the blessing of God. If by God's kindness we abound in comfort and joy, we should not be fierce or exalt ourselves immoderately but use God's blessing with fear, humility, and thanksgiving, according to the statement of Ps. 2:11: "Serve the Lord with fear, with trembling pay homage to Him," so that we do not slip into smugness, pride, and the tempting of God.

Jacob honors his brother, and he uses means to retain his goodwill.

[4] See p. 104, n. 11.

Nor is anything lost from that victory, even though he conducts himself in a humble manner as a friend towards his brother. He arranges
his family in the ranks with which he comes to meet his brother after
sending ahead the gifts, and he does this with all zeal that he may
display the gifts to soften and appease Esau, although he is now
certain of victory.

1. *So he divided the children among Leah and Rachel and the two
   maids.*

2. *And he put the maids with their children in front, then Leah with
   her children, and Rachel and Joseph last of all.*

3. *He himself went on before them, bowing himself to the ground
   seven times, until he came near to his brother.*

Here he divides his company with a far different heart and reason
than he had done above. For then he was uncertain about his brother's
intentions, and so he deliberated in alarm and despair and distributed
his company in two groups, thinking: "If he kills the one group, the
other one will escape." He himself remained alone on the shore behind
the front group and wrestled with despair. Then his flesh was unsure
and perplexed and because of the weakness of his faith inclined to
despair. But now he approaches his brother with a heart free from
care; he divides his household forces not with a downcast heart but a
joyful heart free from care. But he does it in such a way that he
may not tempt God or offend his brother again, whom he had conquered with that weak and struggling faith. This was therefore a
division arranged only for the procession and to indicate his goodwill;
no longer did he keep himself behind the front group, but he went
before them all and set out to meet his brother, for the temptation has
been overcome, and the sun of confidence and joy is rising for him.
It is a very beautiful procession. For his dear wives and lovely children and maids follow him as the father of the house, and when he
comes into the sight of his brother, he bows to the ground seven times
until he comes close to him.

Among the Hebrews the word for doing reverence which is used
very much in Holy Scripture is derived from the verb שָׁחָה, which
signifies to bow down, as in Ps. 38:6: "I am utterly bowed down and
prostrate; all the day I go about mourning." From that gesture of bowing down it has the name adoration, that is, reverence, which is shown

to those who are superior to us or to God. It is performed either by the bowing down of one who is standing or by bending the knee. For this gesture is an indication of reverence and humility, which is shown to those whom we acknowledge as worthy of honor and respect. According to our usages, we are accustomed to bare the head, which the Jews did not do, not even in the temple. We call adoration all our external respect towards superiors or equals, whether it is done with one knee bent, as in the presence of princes, or with both bent, as is usually done in the adoration of God. In this manner Jacob adores his brother seven times as his senior and ruler, whose goodwill and kindness he acknowledges because he has become reconciled to him, and he shows true brotherly goodwill.

A question now arises. How do these developments agree with the blessing promised above, that the greater should serve the lesser and that Jacob would be the lord of his brothers? For by this degradation it seems that the blessing has been inverted and completely changed, and this argument can be amplified and confirmed in various ways. For nowhere do we read that Esau adored Jacob and acknowledged him as his superior. But the contrary is done in this passage by Jacob, who is bowed down before Esau. Besides, Esau's power was far greater. Jacob is bringing his little children with him, among whom the oldest, Reuben, was 12 or 13 years old at the most; the others were younger. Esau, on the other hand, has grandchildren and perhaps even great-grandchildren, and among them leaders and princes. For he had married his wives when he was forty. From that time he fathered many children right up to the 77th year of Jacob, in which he received the blessing. Indeed, when Esau was still in the house of Jacob's father, and before Jacob took away the blessing, Esau already had numerous offspring. He was a lord and ruler, joined by affinity to the nations in the land of Canaan, and allied with the Ishmaelites and other princes.

Such a great leader did Jacob go to meet with his children and unwarlike company, returning from servitude and exile, far inferior to Esau, who is approaching with 400 armed men. Later Jacob will have to be an exile again in Egypt. In the meantime, Edom has gained many outstanding leaders and kings, and his power has increased daily. Indeed, on coming forth from Egypt, the children of Israel are prevented from touching the land of Edom, and the Lord says that He will not give them even a footbreadth of it. Surely that is not domination on the part of Jacob, is it? David was the first to subdue the Edomites, but before that they were free for 624 years. However, they did not remain under the rule of Israel for more than 120 years. For under Joram they threw off the yoke again and set up their own king and were no longer tributaries of the kings of Israel. It appears therefore that the blessing became useless and was inverted.

Some people reply that this blessing looks toward Christ, in whom it was finally fulfilled; but a reply must be given according to history.[5] For that subjection or humiliation of Jacob which lasted during the whole time of the exile is only a temptation, as has been stated above, just as we Christians are of all men the most wretched and subject to all. But it is not a rejection, only a struggle. For in reality we are and we remain lords of heaven and earth. Temptation is not a changing or overthrowing of the promised blessings, just as the captivity of Israel under the king of the Assyrians was a kind of temptation but not a changing of the people. So also in the terrors of sin and death, I do not exchange death with life, and Christ with the devil, although in the midst of temptation it seems like this. Abraham, although he was tempted on receiving the command to sacrifice his son, did not lose his son. Such in general are all temptations. At first sight they appear to be very gloomy, terrible, and quite different from the promises, but in the end the outcome agrees with the Word of God, which remains firm and unmoved.. As in the case of a storm which has suddenly arisen, the crash of the thunder and lightning seems to threaten heaven and earth and men and beasts with ruin and destruction. But so far is it from disturbing or changing anything that it actually fertilizes and irrigates the earth.

But as far as history itself is concerned, Israel was never really under the rule of Edom. Esau was never able to exercise dominion over the people of Israel. Indeed, in the time of David and right up to Joram, Edom was subjected to the kings of Israel. Therefore the blessing remained established and firm, and the kingdom lasted among the posterity of Jacob right up to Herod and the coming of the true Israel, the Messiah, as the prophecy states in Gen. 49:10: "The scepter shall not depart from Judah until Shiloh comes." When His coming was on the threshhold, the earthly dominion of Israel ceased, and then Herod seized the kingdom. But the blessing remained intact right up to the advent of the Savior, who wrestled

[5] See *Luther's Works*, 5, pp. 134—146.

with Jacob. Then a new and better kingdom was instituted, in which the true ISRAEL reigns over heaven and earth, and over angels and demons, since, indeed, every knee is bowed at the name of Jesus of things in heaven and things on earth and things under the earth (cf. Phil. 2:10). Here the blessing of Jacob was truly fulfilled, and yet under a figure it also remained preserved, so that Israel was never subjected to the Edomites, although it was often attacked and harassed by them.

However, the fact that Jacob in this passage humbles himself and bows down before his brother and calls him "lord" must not be understood as meaning that something was taken away from the blessing and from his rank but, as men commonly say, they are "merely honorary" words, which are not binding. And whether you call it respect or obedience, it does not bring with it the handing over of the property or dominion. Although Jacob calls himself a servant and Esau a lord, Esau does not possess the kingdom on that account, nor did he ever gain possession of it. The respect proceeds from a certain feeling of humility, so that Jacob might not seem to be puffed up by smugness and success; it does not proceed from the transfer of the blessing. It is only an honorary tribute. Then, too, it is a common occurrence in life that superiors address not only their equals but even their inferiors in a courteous and respectful manner and offer them their services. For thus love is accustomed to assist and promote even inferiors with every kind of service and respect. Thus a pastor, when he sees a man tempted and afflicted with terrors of conscience who seeks consolation from him, offers to the afflicted man even the lowliest and most servile services so that he may arouse and strengthen his weak and broken heart. But by this procedure he does not hand over the dominion or government of the church, but he himself retains the function entrusted to him.

These are the services of godliness and kindliness by which major offenses are often forestalled, and they are not forbidden by God. Indeed, it is commanded that we should be subject to equals as well as inferiors for the benefit and advantage of our neighbor. By this humility we lose nothing at all of our dignity, even though we accommodate ourselves to the well-being of another and, indeed, to the glory of God. Therefore the blessing of the patriarch Jacob remains safe and sound, and all these procedures by which he seems to be subjected to his brother should not be called a change but a temptation.

4. But Esau ran to meet him and embraced him and fell on his neck and kissed him, and they wept.

Moses employs full and significant words to describe the reconciliation of the two brothers so that no one can doubt that Esau is doing and saying everything from his heart and that he is really changed. He rushes up to his brother, embraces him, falls on his neck, and kisses him, and neither of them can contain his tears for joy. For their fraternal emotions are aroused, and the hearts of both are aglow with true goodwill so that they forget all offenses and injuries. No longer is mention made of the 400 men, nor does any sign of anger or indignation appear, but every act is full of true brotherly love and goodwill. For Moses uses words which show that these matters are done and said candidly and sincerely.

Although hypocrites can simulate love, nevertheless, both the gestures and the individual words indicate that there were burning emotions in both of them, and that Esau's heart was truly appeased and reconciled. For he thinks: "What are you to do with this man? He is my own brother. If it seemed good to God that he should receive the blessing from my father, I shall not envy him or regard him as unworthy. Let him have it and keep it for himself!" Others surely thought: "There is that wretched man Jacob, who 20 years ago used to boast about snatching away the blessing! Now he has to bow down before our prince and lord, Esau, in a most abject manner. Where now is the splendid fame and glorious hope of Jacob? We have the true blessing because Esau has the power of command according to the promise: 'By your sword you shall live, and there will come a time when you will break his yoke from your neck; of the fatness of the land and the dew of heaven you shall live' (cf. Gen. 27:39-40). That fatness of the land and also gold and silver we already have," they said. "Esau lives by his sword; he is an illustrious warrior who subjects his brother to himself, and he will also subjugate other people. He has shaken off the yoke of his brother." It is likely that Esau taught that the promise had been made to him in this sense. He undoubtedly magnified the promise with whatever diligence and seriousness he could, because the children of this age are wiser than the children of light (cf. Luke 16:8), and they can twist meanings in a wonderful manner if there seem to be any in their support. To be sure, from one little twig they can make a whole forest, from one little flower a whole meadow, and from one word a whole Bible!

We who have true and far more ample promises and blessings do not wonder so much at these things, we do not press these matters and enlarge on their greatness and magnificence as much as the ungodly do with the exaggerations and embellishments of their gifts. Look at the zeal with which the papists urge and amplify the one sentence "You are Peter, and on this rock, etc." (Matt. 16:18) in defense of the primacy of the pope. Whole cartloads of commentaries are extant on this one statement alone.[6] But as for us, how coldly we treat the doctrine of the Gospel! How carelessly we read or hear that Christ suffered for us and died for our sins! It is so also with statements like "The righteous shall live by faith" (cf. Hab. 2:4; Rom. 1:17). The teachers of other arts are also more diligent in the practice of their profession, and it is useful and necessary in life that the arts and abilities of men should be promoted. Thus in the case of merchants, we find the most careful and anxious solicitude concerning calculations. But in the embellishment and amplification of our blessings we are very lazy, and this sluggishness and carelessness arises from our flesh. Then also we are dealing with hidden, heavenly matters, not matters of experience, but they are dealing with present, visible, and palpable matters. So they are more wide-awake and more diligent.

In this manner Esau investigated this promise very carefully, for his experience corresponds to the promise. "To me the sword was promised," he said. "Therefore I am justly a warrior and a leader. My brother is a shepherd, a poor exile! The fatness and fruitfulness of the land belongs to me. I am not subject to any man, and I have now shaken off the yoke of my brother." This vainglory and insolence arises from the material blessing, for this is what meets the eye and has much splendor and pomp in the world. Jacob also had material blessings, but they were not so splendid. For Edom had kings and dukes before his brother Israel. The spiritual blessing is always covered with a very insignificant and wretched outward appearance.

This vainglory of Esau helped greatly in effecting a reconciliation. For he thought: "I am the lord, and since no danger threatens me from my brother, why should I treat him too unkindly? For I have not only words of blessing, as Jacob has, but the reality together with

[6] Cf. *Luther the Expositor,* pp. 113—119.

the words. For I abound in resources, power, and a large number of friends; I have been born from the flesh and blood of the holy patriarchs. Therefore God has not rejected me, even though Jacob stole my blessing." It is also likely that in the end Esau was saved. God made this distinction between Jacob and Esau and likewise between Isaac and Ishmael to show that His kingdom is purely spiritual. There is no doubt that many of the offspring and posterity of Esau were saved. For many of the Edomites were joined to the people of God in Israel and circumcised, and many came up annually to Jerusalem for the appointed celebration of the festivals and worshiped there. Accordingly, Esau hoped that he would participate in the grace of God and the spiritual blessing, and he noticed that he was also being blessed and enriched in a material way. Then he saw the humiliation of his brother, and all of this served to soften and mitigate his heart so that he became truly reconciled to his brother from the heart and came to this conclusion: "Why should I kill my brother? Why should I vent my anger on his lovely children and wives? God forbid that I should become a parricide!" Esau was just as delighted with the wealth and good fortune that had fallen to Jacob's lot as if they belonged to himself.

Finally, one must also add the serious and ardent prayer by which Jacob obtained mitigation. The wealth and material blessings which he had could not have healed an embittered heart, although at times they do soothe grievances. But the might and efficacy of prayer was greater. If we pray seriously and perseveringly, the only result can be that a friend is made out of an enemy. But let us only cry out and place our hope not on our worthiness but like a smoking flax (cf. Is. 42:3) on the goodness and mercy of God. Then God most certainly hears us. This is a true reconciliation of brothers and not a pretended one, just as Moses enumerates the surest signs of brotherly goodwill and love in both of them. Now the explanation of this chapter is easy.

5. *And when Esau raised his eyes and saw the women and children, he said: Who are these with you? Jacob said: The children whom God has graciously given your servant.*

This is a very beautiful and friendly conversation of the two brothers, full of godliness. Jacob still remains in his humility and captivating goodwill. For it is God's will that even political rank, or, as men commonly call it, the secular sanctity,[7] be honored in its

---

[7] See also p. 297 for the phrase *sanctum saeculare.*

order and manner. It has its own glory, its own preeminence, by which those who excel others should by no means be despised, but their own honor should be assigned to them in accordance with God's ordinance. The Hebrew word חָנַן and חֵן properly signifies to give with a prompt and kindly heart. In German one would use the word *begnaden,* that is, "whom God in His grace has bestowed upon your servant," *damit mich gott begnadet hat.* In this way he at the same time acknowledges the kind treatment of God and gives thanks. Moreover, he decks out his cause with whatever words he can to nourish his brother's goodwill and teaches by his example that we also should bestow due honor and respect on our superiors and should not be harsh, obstinate, and inflexible towards them but should be eager to lay them under obligation to ourselves by humility and service. These are ethical matters.

But why does Esau inquire whose children they are, as though he did not know? Had not messengers been sent ahead to offer gifts, from whom he undoubtedly made inquiries about Jacob's company and other matters? He asks the question to seize the opportunity to deal with his brother and converse with him in a pleasant and fraternal manner, for all suspicion of guile and pretense had to be removed. He does nothing in a hypocritical manner, and I hold the view that in the end he was saved, as I also feel concerning Ishmael.[8] Therefore Esau's will was truly overcome and changed; but with his will changed, all matters give way of their own accord. Esau's house stands open to Jacob and all his goods because the will is the queen which exercises dominion over wealth. When I know that I am loved by someone, I have no doubts that all things which can come from the friendly and well-intentioned heart are ready and at my disposal. Therefore, since Esau's heart was reconciled also by time, which softens grief and anger, as the saying goes, and then by the humiliation of his brother, it must be understood that nothing was done in a hypocritical manner, but that all gestures and words were candid and sincere, proceeding from love and goodwill, and were not colored. So Esau came to meet his brother and embraced and kissed his brother and wept, and now, by whatever manner he can, he seizes the opportunity to manifest his fraternal heart and love towards Jacob. This is that glorious and true Israelitish victory, by which through

---

[8] See *Luther's Works,* 3, pp. 161—162, for one such statement.

prayer and the struggle of faith the will both of God and of man is overcome.

6. *Then the maids drew near, they and their children, and bowed down;*

7. *Leah likewise and her children drew near and bowed down; and last Joseph and Rachel drew near, and they bowed down.*

8. *Esau said: What do you mean by all this company which I met?*

This procession Jacob also prepares to placate his brother. Although Esau had previously been reconciled by the power of God through the victory and struggle of prayer and faith, nevertheless, Jacob does not omit the external indication of his goodwill, lest it might seem that he is tempting God or disturbing the peace and concord which has been initiated and offending his brother's heart anew by a kind of pride. Accordingly, Jacob bows down with his wives, maids, and children before Esau, although he himself is the son and heir of a better blessing. For he had the spiritual blessing on account of the promised Christ joined with the bodily blessing. Esau did not have the promise that Christ was to be born from his flesh, and yet he who is greater subjects himself and conducts himself as if he were the lesser one.

In this manner we also should be subject to every divine ordinance for God's sake because it is God's creature (cf. 1 Peter 2:13). Superiors should therefore be honored by us with whatever respect we can, but in such a way that we do not reject or deny the Word of Christ and the promise of grace on their account and lose the spiritual blessing. For all respect, honor, and services of every kind are to be paid to magistrates with a good conscience and joyful heart if they remain within the prescribed limits, that is, provided that obedience to God and confession of the Word remain intact. But if they want to be made equal to God, they should be reproved and opposed with the word of the apostles in Acts (5:29): "We must obey God rather than men."

In this way, therefore, the greater one, who has been presented by God with the spiritual blessing, humbles himself towards his brother, who is the lesser one before God, just as we confer due honor on kings, princes, nobles, burgomasters, and councilors and call them, as Christ says (Luke 22:25), εὐεργέτας ("benefactors"), illustrious, noble, wise, etc. For there is a secular rank and a dignity ordained by God which God wants us to honor. But if they want to exalt their throne above the stars of God and become like the Most High, as Is. 14:13-14 says, they should by no means be obeyed. Otherwise we honor them with true respect and true love in the proper order, place, and measure. We do not flatter them when we call them "most kind," "most serene, etc.," but from our heart we respect the rank and person ordained by God for this office. In this manner Jacob does not flatter Esau as a superior, but he calls him a lord and himself a servant in true humility and out of true regard for his brother. It is a beautiful example of the civility peculiar to this language and people, one which equals and those of the same age employed towards each other when addressing each other. In our usage it is not the received thing that one calls himself the servant of another. The simple and common form is "My friend," "My lord," etc.

Esau again inquires what these companies are that he may have an opportunity to converse more familiarly with his brother and to emulate him in mutual love and goodwill. It appears that he had not yet received the gifts sent by Jacob. One cannot say what the reason was. Whether it was that he was still burning with hatred and refused to listen to the messengers sent before he saw his brother actually humbling himself, or whether he refused to accept the gifts, moved by special kindness and mercy since he had become milder and had seen the companies offered by his brother, I do not really know. But it seems that he refused the gifts more out of goodwill than hatred. "Why should I receive them from him?" he asked. "Why does he send these gifts when I, by God's blessing, am far richer than he is?" This was the reason why he did not listen to the messengers who were sent, although they did not yet understand how he was minded towards his brother.

I will interpret it so that it remains established that this victory worked the miracle that Esau's heart was changed and placated. So it can be that while his anger was still hot, he set out with the 400 armed men to terrify or kill his brother. But when he saw him humiliated and sending gifts, the Lord's hand intervened and changed his heart so that he said: "Why should I do violence to my brother? Why should I take anything from a good and upright man, a needy exile? The Lord has blessed me more bountifully than He blessed my brother; it would be fair for me to relieve his need by the abundance of my possessions. Why, then, should I accept gifts at his hand?"

8. *Jacob answered: To find favor in the sight of my lord.*

Jacob perseveres in fostering and retaining his brother's goodwill. Now their hearts become quite peaceful, with all hatred and ill-will extinguished. God works this inwardly through the Spirit, but outwardly through means, the respectful procession and the offering of gifts, although Esau does not seem to have accepted them because of the very great zeal and love with which he embraces his reconciled brother.

9. *But Esau said: I have enough, my brother; keep what you have for yourself.*

There is nothing colored or pretended in these words, but all should be taken as having been spoken sincerely and candidly. For Scripture invents nothing, but when it says that God and man were conquered by Jacob, it wants us to be convinced that Esau's reconciliation was serious and that he was completely changed. For Jacob felt that both were adversaries and enemies. But the wrestler said that Jacob had conquered him and changed the heart of God and man. So we understand that all Esau's deeds and words were without deceit and hypocrisy. I emphasize these matters with greater care because of the glosses of the Jews. They are accustomed to depreciate and disparage the deeds of the uncircumcised heathen and to exaggerate their faults but to praise and exalt themselves immoderately. So they hold the view that Esau pretended goodwill and that all his flatteries were suspected by Jacob, who was unwilling to have confidence in his brother.

But I think that Esau was truly changed in his heart, although he had a very just cause for hatred and indignation. For the blessing rightfully belonged to him as the firstborn, but he was a great man, a fine, brave man, undoubtedly instructed in the doctrine and sermons of Isaac and the other fathers among whom he was brought up, and he learned to curb his evil desires. Then, too, this procession drawn up to please him was an additional factor, and likewise the struggle and prayer of Jacob. Finally, there was the government of God, and all of these things drove his heart to forgetfulness of the wrong he had suffered. So he has done and said this with a sincere and upright heart, even as Jacob a little later will praise him highly, saying (Gen. 33:10): "To see your face is like seeing the face of God." For since it is a work of God, it cannot be pretended or colored; to be sure, God does nothing but what is right and true.

Therefore, with the supposition of guile and pretense set aside, we are right in praising Esau for refusing the gifts in a most honorable and friendly manner. "I have an abundance of all things," he says, "and so I shall not accept the gifts offered by you. I shall leave them to your little ones and your family to enjoy." All this has come from a friendly and brotherly heart.

10. *Jacob said: No, I pray you, if I have found favor in your sight, then accept my present from my hand; for truly to see your face is like seeing the face of God, with such favor have you received me.*

11. *Accept, I pray you, my gift that is brought to you, because God has dealt graciously with me, and because I have enough. Thus he urged him, and he took it.*

Jacob urges his brother to receive the gift offered. "For I am offering you this," he says, "from the blessing and the property which the Lord has given me. You should not refuse this favor of mine, moved by my poverty and need, because by the goodness of God I have enough. Nor do I offer it impelled only by necessity or fear but with all goodwill and burning love towards you. I ask you, therefore, not to reject it. For I am giving you the gift with no other motive but that you may understand that you are loved by me in a brotherly manner and that you may pardon it if anything was done which offended your heart. The gift, indeed, is small and unworthy of your exalted position, but you must have regard for my heart and my fondness for you." Above, the word מִנְחָה is employed of the sacrifice of Cain and Abel. It signifies properly a gift, *Geschenk*.

Jacob, moreover, adds a reason by which he tries to persuade his brother to accept the gift offered, namely: "This one thing is enough for me and equivalent to all my property, that I have found favor in your sight, for I have seen your face as if it were the face of God." This is wonderful and lovable rhetoric! Nor should it be thought that Jacob is lying or inventing anything, but he is speaking seriously from his heart. Not that I think that he should be flattered in his sins but that virtues and faults should be rightly distinguished. For it has often been said above that we do not excuse the saints everywhere, and we heard above that Jacob manifested his infirmity well enough when unbelief and the flesh fought against the spirit. This we do not excuse, for a saint who knows that his sins are forgiven him and that he is an heir of eternal life should not become alarmed, terrified, or unbelieving but he should fight with a steadfast faith in the promise and overcome doubt. But because we are still in the flesh, which is unclean and contaminated by sin, we are hindered from trusting, hoping, and praying with the ardor that we should, but there is still much weakness and imperfection adhering to us. But God patiently bears the smoking flax (cf. Is. 42:3) and the faith which is alarmed, provided that it does not fight against the Word or shake off the confession of God and faith in Him. Weakness is not harmful, but "God's power is made perfect in weakness" (2 Cor. 12:9). But precautions must be taken in both directions, that we do not excuse the faults and lapses of the saints or interpret their right deeds and words otherwise.

Augustine asks at this place whether Jacob is an idolater or whether he is flattering his brother when he says that he saw his face as the face of God.[9] He is really in trouble in finding an excuse. But it is an idiom of Scripture which must be understood rightly. For above the wrestler said: "You have conquered God and man," that is, "you had two backs turned against you, God's and your brother's," and this signifies wrath or an alienated heart, and this is an idiomatic way of speaking common to all languages. When I hate someone, I turn my face and eyes away and present the back of my head and my back to him, and this is a sign of wrath and indignation. In this manner, when God is said to avert His face and to show His back, it signifies that grace has been lost, or the knowledge of the grace, favor, mercy, joy, and thanksgiving, and that terror, sorrow, and doubt concerning God's will have taken their place, so that a troubled conscience says: "I do not know how I stand with God."

Therefore the face does not signify the sight of the divine essence, but it is what Ps. 67:1 says: "May He make His face shine upon us and have pity on us," that is, "speak with us in a winsome manner." Likewise Ps. 4:6-7 says: "The light of Thy countenance has been lifted up upon us, O Lord! Thou hast put joy into my heart." When, for example, I say to one who has been tempted: "Take heart, my son, your sins are forgiven you" (cf. Matt. 9:2), and likewise: "O woman, great is your faith" (cf. Matt. 15:28), then God's face is made to shine. When

9 Augustine, *Quaestiones in Heptateuchum*, I, 105, *Patrologia, Series Latina*, XXXIV, 575.

He addresses us in a winsome manner and shows His goodwill toward us by His words and deeds, then God shows His face. In this life this takes place only in the Word and the sacraments. But when, on the contrary, He says: "You have committed adultery, you have stolen, and you will most certainly die; whoremongers, adulterers, etc., shall not possess the kingdom of God" (cf. 1 Cor. 6:9-10), and likewise: "That no man transgress and wrong his brother in this matter, because the Lord is an avenger in all these things" (cf. 1 Thess. 4:6), and likewise: "And they will go into eternal punishment" (cf. Matt. 25:46), the heart becomes terrified and trembles at all these things, and so God's face is turned away.

Above, Jacob says concerning the turning of God's face to him: "My life is preserved" because the Lord addressed him with winsome words and gave him the richest consolation in the promise and the blessing. So with his brother a sun, light, and life arise for him from the Word and the testimony of his brother's best intentions. The meaning is: "My brother, I have seen your face turned toward me not otherwise than I previously saw God's face turned toward me, and while I am looking at your face, it seems to me that I am truly beholding the face of God." This is not flattery but serious speech. "I was as delighted by the sight of you as if I had seen that God had met me."

But God's winsome face must be recognized in His promises, in the sacraments, and likewise in external blessings and gifts, in a gracious prince, a neighbor, a father, and a mother. When I see that the face of my parents is gracious, I see at the same time the winsome face of God smiling at me. As Jacob had previously said that he had seen the Lord face to face, he now discerns the same face of GOD in the face of his brother Esau, for he sees the good pleasure of God's will in the goodwill and favor of his brother. In the same manner, the face of God shines forth in all His creatures because they are works of God and testimonies of God's will and presence. By these He coaxes us with an external aspect just as He shows His winsome and kindly face to us inwardly in our heart by the Word and the promises.

This is the true explanation of this idiom so that no one should interpret it as flattery and idolatry. He adds an explanation or proclamation of mutual love and goodwill in his brother when he says: "You have received me favorably, or you have wished me well." The word רָצוֹן signifies will, good pleasure, goodwill. In Ps. 51:18 we read: "Do good to Zion in Thy good pleasure, O Lord," and in Matt. 17:5:

"This is My beloved Son, with whom I am well pleased," and likewise in Luke 2:14 we have the phrase "goodwill (εὐδοκία) to men." This is what Jacob wants to say: "I see that you are pleased with me; you receive me graciously, embrace and kiss me, and weep with me. You refuse to accept my gift and are more ready to give than to receive (cf. Acts 20:35). And so you declare your goodwill and good pleasure towards me. Therefore receive a small gift, a pledge of our mutual love, so that it may testify that I acknowledge your goodwill." But he calls the gifts a blessing. He says: "Receive the blessing which I have brought to you and which God has given me; for God has dealt kindly with me, etc."

These are assuredly words of a heart overflowing with boundless joy and gladness. He rejoices with his whole heart and congratulates himself because he has won his brother's love. This serenity which followed the storm and darkness of the former struggle with his brother and the man is therefore very beautiful and pleasant. "I see," he says, "that God and my brother are appeased out of wonderful goodness." So it signifies great joy when he said above: "My life is preserved. It seems to me that I am now truly reviving from death and hell, because I have seen the kindly and friendly face of God." A wonderful modesty and humility shines forth in these words, for he wants to say: "I have not brought a magnificent and imposing gift which is worthy of admiration, but it is the blessing of God. I beg you to accept it on this account, that it may be a pledge and reminder of my gratitude and the blessing of God, by whose gift and grace I offer this to you, such as it is. Receive it, therefore, because God has given it to me, in the name of the Lord, just as if it had been offered to you by God, so that the blessing may also be with you and increase without end and that this goodwill and mutual brotherly love may continue with us forever."

Previously Esau said: "I have רָב," that is, "plenty." Jacob says: "I have כֹּל," that is, "everything, totality." He amplifies his blessing: "I not only have abundance, but I have everything." These are words of a person in exultation and transport over the joy occasioned by the face of God and brother shown to him in grace, mercy, and goodwill. "If only I have God's grace and yours," he means to say, "it is enough and more than enough for me, nor would I suffer any loss if I gave everything to you. I am losing nothing, and I shall never be in need since you have become reconciled to me. I am a rich lord because I have God and you as my friends."

All this shows how faith revived and was aroused in Jacob and how he now reigns and triumphs again. For Jacob has now come to the conclusion that his blessing is equal to all the wealth of the whole world. Previously he had nothing when he said: "My brother will come and smite me and my wives and the whole household." At that point he had nothing at all, because all was in despair. But heaven and earth are again filled for him with all the good things and resources of the whole world. For unbelief robs us of God's mercy and our brother's and of the abundance of all things.

Moses, moreover, adds that Jacob compelled his brother to receive the gift. For he said: "Do not despise the blessing of God and my gift lest it seem that you are not reconciled to me from your heart. For although I have no doubt, yet both of our families will suspect that your grace and favor are still uncertain. Therefore I beg you, for the sake of brotherly love and goodwill, not to refuse this little gift."

12. *Then Esau said: Let us journey on our way, and I will go before you.*

13. *But Jacob said to him: My lord knows that the children are frail, and that the flocks and herds giving suck are a care to me; and if they are overdriven for one day, all the flocks will die.*

Esau wants to be thankful and to do his brother a good turn. He offers to be the companion and guide of his journey right up to the crossing of the Jordan. Nor was this done craftily, although it is likely that there were still suspicions in both households. But Jacob was quite certain from the promise concerning his brother's change of will, and he understands that all this proceeds from a friendly and open heart. Yet he advises against this humiliation and service of his brother. "It is not necessary," he says, "for you to be humiliated in this way, and this would be too hard for you. For my lord knows that I have frail little ones, and flocks that are breeding, sheep, young lambs, and sucking calves that cannot follow without danger if we advance too quickly." Reuben was about 13 years old, not much more. Levi was 12 and Judah 10, and so on right down to Dinah, who had not exceeded her fourth year at the time of this crossing. So he brings a crowd of little ones with him with much trouble, but children so delicate cannot follow Esau's company of horsemen and men under arms. "And so we will be a hindrance and a burden to you, my brother," Jacob means to say.

It was an absolutely honest refusal. For it is much more difficult to lead an unwarlike and tender crowd of little ones than several companies of knights, since, indeed, many things happen which hinder progress and at times compel a halt for several days or hours. It takes infinite care to travel with a household, and this was especially true at that time, when wagons were not in use as is the case with us but the baggage and the little ones were placed on camels and asses. So Jacob is not making any pretense or lying when he says: "We will be a burden and a hindrance to you; we will delay your journey; we will burden you with this troublesome company," but he is serious in asking him not to take this trouble upon himself, lest Esau bring forward any other excuse — that he is willing to proceed more slowly or some such thing. He indicates in a veiled manner that this will be annoying to the armed men who were in Esau's company. Indeed, he also mentions the danger, if the sheep were driven hard for one day. This is what the Hebrew word "to knock" signifies, as we, for example, are accustomed to knock at a door. For flocks are driven with a rod or staff. He means: "If I were to urge them on or drive them in such a way that they would keep pace with the horsemen, all the flocks and little ones would perish on one day." In German the word is *übertreiben* ("overdrive"). "So it is more appropriate for you to go on ahead with your companies and for me to follow slowly."

14. *Let my lord pass on before his servant, and I will lead on slowly, according to the pace of the cattle which are before me and according to the pace of the children, until I come to my lord in Seir.*

15. *So Esau said: Let me leave with you some of the men who are with me. But he said: What need is there? Let me find favor in the sight of my lord.*

16. *So Esau returned that day on his way to Seir.*

The Hebrew word נָהַל properly signifies "to lead to," as in Ps. 31:3: "Lead me and guide me," and in Ps. 23:1: "He leads me beside still waters." In this passage Jacob says: "I will bring it to pass that they are led gently, step by step, as sheep are led to pasture or water, so that the cattle and children do not perish," for these are the duties of a shepherd. And concerning Absalom David says in 2 Sam. 18:5: "Deal gently with young Absalom." ·

But this addition, "according to the pace of the cattle which are before me," in Hebrew is "according to the foot of the work and the little ones." He calls his whole substance "the work" (מְלָאכָה), and the same word occurs in the Third Commandment of the Decalog (Ex. 20:9). From this comes מְלָאכֶת, "the work," or "power of heaven," which brings force to bear on things below to make the earth fruitful and to produce rich harvests of fruits. Christ, too, speaks in this manner (Luke 21:26): "The powers of the heavens will be shaken." But here he calls his whole household and substance "work," with the exception of the little ones and women. In the Third Commandment it is stated: "Six days you shall labor and do all your work," that is, care for your property. "But on the seventh day you must keep the Sabbath, rest and listen to the voice of the Lord your God" (cf. Ex. 23:12).

A further question is discussed here by others, whether Jacob lies when he says that he will come to Esau in Seir, when there is no record anywhere that he went there. I have often stated that I do not free the saints from all sins.[10] For we know that the greatest and most saintly men often fell in a horrible fashion and became contaminated not only with error and common weakness but also with the greatest sins contrary to faith, hope, love, patience, namely, with unbelief, doubt, disrespect, and murmuring against God. In this we are willing to have them as allies and examples to comfort us. Let us not think that they were statues, stones, or trunks of trees, but they were like ourselves. Elijah received an answer from God to his prayer that it should not rain for three years, but later he felt his flesh trembling and begging that he should be allowed to die (cf. 1 Kings 17—19). But their upright deeds and words which are beyond censure should by no means be interpreted captiously and slanderously. Accordingly, we should not suspect Jacob of acting in a hypocritical and guileful manner with his brother, but there is in him a heart that is absolutely open and filled with boundless joy because of the reconciliation that has been brought about. It is free from care and devoid of all fear and sense of danger, and so he has no reason for flattering or lying.

But why did he not go to Seir although he had promised it? My answer is that he did not promise that on this journey he wanted to go directly to Seir but told Esau to precede until he should follow him and come to Seir. But he went home to his aged father and visited

---

[10] Cf. *Luther the Expositor*, pp. 76—77.

him before he came to his brother in Seir. But it is likely that he traveled to and fro to his brother in Seir or in some other place on several occasions, and there is no doubt that both of them came together for the burial of their father.

Again, to show his goodwill, Esau says that he is willing to assign to Jacob the attendants whom he had with him as a guard. But Jacob refuses because the delay which he suffered on the journey on account of so many hindrances would be annoying to them. "I am quite satisfied," he said, "to know that you are friendly towards me." So they both go their different ways after saying farewell, Esau to Seir but Jacob to Succoth.

17. *But Jacob journeyed to Succoth and built himself a house and made booths for his cattle; therefore the name of the place is called Succoth.*

The city of Succoth was so called at this time from what was done. For Jacob erected a shelter there for his cattle and built a house for his household. The text sounds as if Jacob remained in that place for some time and it was not only a slight detour or lodging for one night or a day, but it makes mention of a building and so indicates that he stayed there for some time. Lyra bases his comment on the opinion of the Hebrews and says that he dwelt there for a year and a half and that this opinion gave rise to the question above, whether Jacob lied since he promised that he would come to Seir and nevertheless remained for a year and a half in Succoth.[11] But it is uncertain how long he remained there and whether he went to his brother or not. Yet it could have taken place, and it is human and ordinary that they should attest their love by mutual service, inasmuch as they were reconciled to each other. In the same manner it is likely that the brothers often came together and kept their friendship warm and also produced the same among their grandsons and relatives. This, it seems to me, follows more correctly from the fact that the text says that Jacob dwelt in Succoth in a permanent shelter and in a furnished home than that he lied and did not go to his brother.

Furthermore, to make this additional statement in passing, I once held the view that Benjamin was born in this year of the return from

---

[11] Lyra *ad* Gen. 33:17, p. 97 verso, note "c"; see also the *Glossa ordinaria* on this passage.

Mesopotamia.[12] But I have found out that this view is false and that he was born in about the eighth year after the return. For it is a useful and necessary precaution to examine and remember the chronological order in sacred history. Paul prohibits the genealogy of persons (cf. 1 Tim. 1:4; Titus 3:9), not the calculation of times, for this is very helpful for the knowledge of Holy Scripture. The former is uncertain because of infinite confusions and almost impossible in such a great variety of second and third marriages, etc., and likewise in such a great diversity of families which are mixed in various ways. For often, as Lyra testifies somewhere,[13] one man is named by two or three names, or several men are called by one name. Therefore, genealogy is an inexplicable and forbidden undertaking, and he who wishes to investigate these matters with too much curiosity undertakes a useless labor. But the reckoning of the times is necessary for this reason, that the Jews might be convinced about the coming of Christ, for which most illustrious testimonies can be drawn from chronology. Although even this cannot be gathered so exactly, it makes little difference even if the greatest precision cannot be obtained. Below, however, we shall have more to say about the reckoning of Jacob's years.[14]

Succoth, Penuel, and Mahanaim are cities situated beyond the Jordan, in the tribe of Gad. Later the Arabs occupied this land right up to the Jordan, and so it has obtained the name of Arabia. In the history of the Judges, chapter 8:16-17, we are told that Succoth and Penuel were overthrown by Gideon because they had refused to give bread to the exhausted army. At last, therefore, after his servitude, exile, and so many labors and temptations, God grants peace and rest to the patriarch Jacob so that he can live in safety and tranquillity with his family and flocks and care for his property in the domestic sphere as it becomes a father of a household. Accordingly, he builds a house, teaches, and governs. The Holy Spirit regards it as worthy to describe all such matters so carefully, first, that He might show this change in the life of the saints in which tribulations and consolations are accustomed to succeed each other in turn just as in nature there are changes of day and night, winter and summer. God exercises the saints with great kindness and mercy that they may not

---

[12] See Luther's *Computation of the Years of the World* (W, LIII, 60).

[13] Lyra *ad* Gen. 36:1, p. 100 recto, note "a."

[14] See p. 255.

become dull in peace and tranquillity and that they may not become heartbroken in adversity. The cross is necessary to humble the flesh so that it does not rebel and exercise dominion over the spirit. But affliction which is without an end or breathing spaces would shatter the spirit and drive it to despair. Therefore God in His wonderful goodness tempers these according to Paul's rule in 1 Cor. 10:13: "God is faithful, and He will not let us be tempted beyond our strength." Often, indeed, He allows temptation to reach its peak and the stage of ineffable groaning (cf. Rom. 8:26), but nevertheless with the temptation He also makes a way of escape, so that we do not succumb but are able to bear it, as Paul says in 2 Cor. 4:9: "We are struck down but not destroyed, etc."

This is the doctrine of the entire Holy Scripture, which is set forth in this passage in the example of Jacob, namely, that there are alternations of tribulation and consolation for this reason, that the body of sin may be mortified and that it may not be exalted by pride, and then that the spirit may not be devoured by sorrow and exhausted by terrors. It is God's will that precautions be taken against both courses, that we should not be proud according to the flesh and not despair according to the spirit but that we should proceed by the middle way between sorrow and joy, between boasting and disgrace. For in this way the patriarch Jacob had many temptations, but after all these he received consolation when he saw God's face and that of his brother appeased. For after he crossed Penuel, his life was preserved, the night was past, and the sun shone forth. A little later another temptation will follow. There is a second reason why the Holy Spirit set forth these matters, namely, to testify that all the works of the saints, however lowly and childish they may be, are pleasing and acceptable as good fruits in the sight of God. Included are not only those sublime theological virtues like contests with death, sins, and other temptations and the victories over the same fraught with great perils, but even those lowly, domestic, and humble services, so that we may learn to regulate our life in this manner that we may be certain that we are pleasing to God in all our acts of duty. I do not always pray, nor do I always meditate on the Law of the Lord and struggle continually with sin, death, and the devil; but I put on my clothes, I sleep, I play with the children, eat, drink, etc. If all these things are done in faith, they are approved by God's judgment as having been done rightly.

This should be carefully taught against the horrible hypocrisy of the monks which fascinates the eyes and minds of men by its marvelous outward appearance so that, captivated by admiration of this, they feel disgust for daily household activities as though they were worldly and scorned by God, even though, to be sure, the hypocritical monks have much that is silly and absurd in their life. But every idle word of the ungodly is displeasing to God, and their sacrifices and most splendid acts of worship are sins and abominations. But for the believers all things work together for good, even weaknesses, mistakes, and lapses, as Rom. 8:28 tells us. Reason and the wisdom of the flesh is ignorant of this, and so it does not judge correctly and cannot distinguish the works of hypocrites and saints.

From Succoth Jacob moves to Salem, buys a piece of land there, and erects an altar for the invocation of God and the preaching of the heavenly doctrine. I think that this part should be joined with the following chapter and that from this point the 34th chapter should be commenced.[15]

18. *And Jacob crossed over to Salem, to the city of Shechem, which is in the land of Canaan, after he returned from Mesopotamia; and he camped before the city.*

The first question of this chapter is a grammatical one concerning the signification of the words Salem and Shechem.[16] There is no agreement among the Hebrew grammarians or all the other exegetes concerning the force and proper meaning of these nouns. For I have stated on several occasions above that there are a large number of words whose meaning is unknown to the Hebrews themselves.[17] The use and knowledge of this language has declined to such an extent that it can never be restored perfectly. Not only in the words but also in the idioms and constructions is there manifold and varied obscurity, and by this it comes to pass that we do not know the force and figures or emphases of many forms of diction or statements. If it can by any method be restored to a state of integrity, this must be done through Christians, who have the true knowledge of Holy Scripture from the New Testament. The Jews obscure the genuine sense by their ambiguities, drawing words into varied and manifold

---

[15] At this point the original has "Chapter 34," but we have followed the usual division into chapters and begun Chapter 34 at p. 187.

[16] Lyra *ad* Gen. 33:18, p. 97 verso, note "d."

[17] See, for example, *Luther's Works*, 2, pp. 137—138.

meanings, and they do this with the set purpose of contriving questions and errors of every kind.

But a careful and good grammarian should make an effort to reduce the varied meanings to one which is certain, for it is necessary that for one word there should be one proper and genuine meaning. Therefore let him show the individual roots and their proper meanings, and afterwards let him bring together the figures, metaphors, allusions, and idioms. The rabbis do not do this, for when concepts fall, words and their meanings also fall, just as no one understands the discourse of lawyers, doctors, and theologians if the concepts are lost. Scholastic theology can be an example. For there is none among our hearers who understands Scotus, Thomas, and the like, for their concepts and their usage of words have become obsolete. The same thing would happen in other disciplines if usage and the practice of these concepts did not remain. For when concepts perish, also the understanding of words immediately becomes more and more obscure.

The question is also asked whether in this passage Salem is used descriptively in its force or as a proper noun.[18] Descriptively it signifies "peace" or "peaceful," and likewise "perfected," and at times even "retribution." If it is accepted adjectivally in this meaning, the sense will be: "Jacob crossed the Jordan intact, or peacefully and quietly, that is, without temptation and unharmed, and he arrived at the city of Shechem." This is not a bad explanation, for he now came forth as a victor over temptation and the conflict which he sustained with the wrestler; he received consolation, and all was safe and sound in his case. So he builds a house and devises shelters with a tranquil heart free from care.

Others make reference to the story of Jacob's dislocated thigh and interpret as follows: "Jacob came intact, that is, restored and healthy, so that he did not limp anymore." Neither do I find fault with this explanation. For it could have come to pass that his thigh was restored by medical skill, which was undoubtedly very well known to the fathers. For they had not only a knowledge of the best medicines but also a large supply of them. They had balsam and many other remedies which we lack today. Therefore I do not debate the matter, and I find it easy to believe that Jacob's thigh was restored and healed. But this is not the force and proper meaning of the word, and since the Hebrews had other words more suitable for expressing

---

18 Cf. the *Glossa ordinaria* on Gen. 33:18, p. 97 verso, note "c."

this sense, they would undoubtedly have used another more suitable word. For this passage seems to have a more genuine ring if you translate: "Jacob came quietly and peacefully," in an adjectival signification.

The third opinion, that it is a name of a city, cannot be easily proved. Jerusalem, too, is called Salem, as we heard above in chapter 14:18.[19] Nor can it be established that Shechem was called Salem by the ancients, as is stated elsewhere concerning Luz (cf. Gen. 28:19; 35:6), which was later called Bethel. For not all the names of places are extant among the Jews. But concerning this I will fight with no one. For our faith or religion is not imperiled by this whether you take it as an adjective or a proper noun.

The name of the city of Shechem, however, remained to all posterity, and it was very celebrated especially in the Books of Kings. Sirach calls the people who dwelt at Shechem a foolish people (Ecclus. 50:26), just as the Germans are accustomed to judge concerning the Swabians and the Bavarians. They were a proud people given to luxury. They say that the city was close to the two mountains Gerizim and Ebal. Others contend that it was situated close to Jericho. This much is certain, that Shiloh, where the tabernacle was, was very close to Shechem, and it is quite likely that Shiloh was this very place where Jacob lived and where Christ spoke with the Samaritan woman of John 4:7. The tabernacle was in the same place for a long time under Joshua and Eleazar right up to the time of Samuel. From this fact posterity took occasion for manifold idolatry, moved by the authority and example of the fathers, whom it wished to follow in making offerings and worshiping in the same place contrary to God's Word. Thus Jeroboam later rebuilds Shechem and transfers the worship of God there from the temple at Jerusalem, as we read in 1 Kings 12.

But although I have no firm reply to make in such a variety of opinions, since the Hebrew rabbis themselves disagree, nevertheless, the interpretation which I favor most is that Jacob, freed from so many troubles, full of faith and consolation, and with strength intact, is spoken of as having come to the city which is called Shechem either after its prince or after its founder. Indeed, many other cities have obtained a name from their founders, and it was a very distinguished place at all times among that people, as we have stated.

[19] See *Luther's Works*, 2, p. 381.

19. *And from the sons of Hamor, Shechem's father, he bought for a hundred pieces of money the piece of land on which he had pitched his tent.*

Hitherto the patriarch Jacob had nothing of his own on this earth; now at length he buys a portion of ground. Although the promise stood sure that God would give him the whole earth, he nevertheless bought this small portion, just as his grandfather Abraham had bought a field opposite Mamre and a double cave for the burial of Sarah (cf. Gen. 23:17). Therefore Stephen says correctly in Acts 7:5: "He gave him no inheritance in it, not even a foot's length," namely, while they were alive, but both of them bought a place, Abraham for burial purposes, and Jacob a place for a habitation, since he now had rest and had come forth from these storms of temptation. He paid a hundred pieces of money for that portion, and from this it appears that it was not very large. Others say that the price was a hundred lambs.[20] But whether you understand it as coins or lambs, it could not have been a large field acquired for such a small price, or fields were cheaper at that time than they are today. Therefore he now has his own abode near the city of Shechem, which is celebrated in Holy Scripture on account of this possession and is close to Shiloh, where the tabernacle was and where gatherings of the people were held.

20. *There he erected an altar and called upon the strong God of Israel.*

Jacob thought of staying here, and so he erected an altar. He had not yet returned to his father Isaac, but later, I believe, he visited his father fairly often as well as his brother, leaving his household and flocks in this place. Nor was Hebron a long way from Shechem, about 10 miles. Hebron was 5 miles distant from Jerusalem, Shechem 3 or 4 miles. It was therefore very easy to visit his brother and father. Although Scripture does not expressly state this, it nevertheless follows as a good conclusion since, indeed, a reconciliation was brought about between the brothers. I think that he lived in this place at least eight years.

Moses, moreover, describes the use of the altar that was raised when he says: "And he called upon the God of gods of Israel." For this is how it reads in the Hebrew. This is a remarkable passage, for Christ almost everywhere in the Old Tetsament is manifested to us under a divine name. In this passage Moses embraces the three

[20] Lyra *ad* Gen. 33:19, p. 97 verso, note "f."

Persons together, as he is often accustomed to do elsewhere. Above, the man wrestling with Jacob was our Lord Jesus Christ Himself, the Son of God, who wanted to be manifested in such a way that He might be a distinct Person from the Father and the Holy Spirit and that there might nevertheless be one God. Thus I here interpret the first אֵל as the Son of God, who was to become incarnate, but the אֱלֹהֵי as the Father and the Holy Spirit. These three Persons are the one God of Israel.

The Jews, however, read, and the text sounds that way, that he called the altar itself by this name. They also explain the passage in Jer. 23 and 33 in this way where it says: "Behold, the days are coming, says the Lord, when I will raise up for David a righteous Branch, and He shall reign as king and deal wisely and shall execute justice and righteousness in the land. In His days Judah will be saved, and Israel will dwell securely. And this is His name by which He will be called: 'The Lord, our Righteousness'" (cf. Jer. 23:5-6; 33:15-16). There the tetragrammaton יְהֹוָה occurs, that is the true God, our Righteousness. But this remarkable witness concerning the deity of the Son of God they make fun of with such statements as that the altar is called the God of gods. They proceed likewise with Jerusalem in Jer. 23:6: "In those days Judah will be saved, and Jerusalem will dwell securely. And this is the name by which He will be called: 'The Lord, our Righteousness.'" Likewise with Ex. 17:15: "And Moses built an altar and called the name of it 'The Lord is my banner,'" or, "my exaltation and strength." Likewise, Mount Moriah was called "reverence of GOD" (cf. Gen. 22:2).

By these statements they try to disparage the authority and weight of the testimonies concerning the deity of Christ. But Jerusalem or the altar is not the LORD nor exaltation nor our righteousness. Yet the Jews urge this argument against us persistently, nor do they suffer it to be torn from them. But for us there is an easy explanation from the doctrine of the New Testament, as is taught elsewhere.

Jacob, accordingly, on receiving consolation is safe and sound and freed from the terrors of death, and after the pain from his dislocated thigh has subsided, he raises an altar that he may give thanks to God for this restitution of his health. For he sets up the altar that the Word might be taught, that invocation, giving of thanks, and other acts of divine worship might be made there. For when Holy Scripture says that altars were raised, it is just as if it were saying that schools or churches were established where sacred things which belong to the worship of God might be administered. The altars were not erected in the interest of showing spectacles and processions, nor for the sacrifices of Masses, but for the preaching of the Word. In this way, then, Jacob is described as of a tranquil and joyful heart after his liberation. However, in his happiness, he does not forget God, his Liberator, but he erects an altar, he teaches his children, he rules his household and church, and exhorts them to invocation and thanksgiving. But this tranquillity does not last long, for already the day is inclining towards evening, and the black night is coming on.

CHAPTER THIRTY-FOUR

1. *Now Dinah the daughter of Leah, whom she had borne to Jacob,
went out to visit the women of the land;*

2. *and when Shechem the son of Hamor the Hittite, the prince of the
land, saw her, he seized her and lay with her and humbled her.*

THIS is a different and a much more severe trial than the former
one was, when he was alarmed at meeting his brother. That
was full of the greatest and gloomiest perils and disasters. For now
the excellent patriarch sits at home in the midst of his wives, children,
and household church and is very pleasantly contented with the
consolation recently shown him after a very heavy struggle. Nor
does he sit in idleness, but he does his duty as the father of the house
and a teacher with the greatest of care, governing, teaching, and
praying, and suddenly, contrary to all expectation, he is hurled into
a very sad trial. It is therefore an example written for our learning,
that we may learn patience in adversity (cf. Rom. 15:4). For if such
a great man is disciplined in such a severe manner, it will not seem
strange or unworthy to us if like experiences also befall us at some
time.

But first there is a question concerning the age of Dinah when
she was defiled. For it is not likely that she had reached marriageable
age when Jacob first came to Shechem, since she was not more than
three or four years at the highest. But she would have to be 11 or 12
years old when she was outraged. It follows from this that Jacob
dwelt in Succoth or in Shechem at least eight years before the birth
of Benjamin, whose nativity will first be described in the following
chapter. Therefore, what I wrote in the previous edition of my Chronology, that Jacob went to see his father Isaac directly in the
first year after his return, I changed later, and I think that he was
in this land for about 10 years after leaving Mesopotamia and stayed

in Shechem eight years.[1] Here he had his own property, on which he stationed his flocks and household. At times he made excursions to his aged father and his brother to visit them.

The story of Dinah compels us to decide on this number. It is necessary to set her age at 12 years at least, so that she could be given in marriage and might be able to consort with a man. But this also is very rare and almost impossible especially at the present time, when a girl of 12 cannot conceive and become pregnant. For in childbearing there is great labor and difficulty, and it is often connected with danger to life and so requires strength and maturer years. However, it is likely that at that time the nature and powers of men were stronger because of the temperate nature of the climate and air, and likewise because of the convenience of their situations and temperance in food and drink.[2] Civil laws assign 14 years to men but 12 to women as maturity for marriage. But at that age they do not even know that they are alive or that they are girls, and so today we do not observe these limits. Even though Dinah might then be regarded as quite mature for marriage, in the text she is nevertheless called a יַלְדָּה, a little girl, for it was not the custom to give girls in marriage so quickly. For above we heard in regard to Rebecca that she was about 30 years old when she married Isaac.[3] Then, too, the nature of men has not only become more languid and weaker in this extreme old age of the world, but intemperance in eating and the inclemency of the climate, air, and localities in which we spend our lives has also weakened it very much. So it comes to pass that we are old before our time and our bodies are afflicted by various diseases.

Moreover, many people debate the question whether there has been some abatement in the age of men and whether the strength and years of the human body have diminished.[4] Some think that there has been no abatement at all since, indeed, many are found today

[1] *Computation of the Years of the World* (W, LIII, 60). The second edition of this work did not appear until 1545. If the above statement were authentic, we would be obliged to suppose that Luther lectured on these verses no earlier than 1545. From other information (cf. Introduction) it is clear that this date cannot be correct. We must conclude, therefore, that these words do not come from Luther's own lectures on Gen. 34 but are the work of his editors, who had access to the second edition of Luther's work on chronology and who felt qualified to take such liberties with their material.

[2] For similar speculations, cf. *Luther's Works*, 2, p. 231.

[3] See *Luther's Works*, 4, pp. 335—336.

[4] See *Luther's Works*, 1, pp. 340—343.

who reach the age of 100 or 90. I myself have seen such. And although Moses says in Ps. 90: "The years of our life are threescore and ten, or fourscore at the most" (cf. Ps. 90:10) and although at that time those who were so many years old were regarded as having reached the extreme limit of life, it seems quite clear that the years and strength of the human body have not decreased in our time, when one may see many who reach the age of 70 or 80.

Others cite the statement of Ps. 102:25-26: "Of old Thou, O Lord, didst lay the foundation of the earth, and the heavens are the work of Thy hands. They will perish, but Thou dost endure; they will all wear out like a garment. Thou changest them like raiment, and they pass away." Here Holy Scripture testifies that heaven and earth wear out like a garment. So it is certain that the strength of heaven and earth and of all creatures that are in heaven and earth is decreasing, of animals, men, plants, and herbs. There is no longer as much strength and vigor in them as there was formerly. Adam lived 930 years, and in general the age of all the fathers before the Flood was greater. But after the Flood the age of men decreased, and all creatures and heaven and earth degenerated. The power of the sun and the fertility of the earth is not what it was formerly. All of nature has experienced a great decline and corruption since the Flood. Indeed, it even devastated and destroyed Paradise. The four rivers of which mention is made in Gen. 2:10 no longer flowed out of Paradise after the Flood. There was another face of the earth, another cultivation of it after that horrible destruction and devastation, and gradually the age and strength of all creatures are declining more and more.

Not until his 24th year does a man acquire the bodily strength suitable for marriage and to manage household affairs, but a girl is ready for bearing the pains of childbirth in her 17th or 18th year. In the time of David the average age of a man was 70, and today such men are also to be found, but they are very few, and it is almost tantamount to a miracle if any reach the age of 70 or 80. The most common span of life is 50 or 60 years, and those who exceed this surpass the usual limit.[5] But Moses in his prayer in Ps. 90 speaks of the common limit of life. For the life which is left after 70 or 80 years is useless for accomplishing anything, for producing children and also for household administration. When David was 70, he died.

[5] On life expectancy, cf. *Luther's Works,* 13, p. 122, n. 71.

Today sexagenarians are generally useless for all government. To such an extent have their bodily strength and competency over all matters decreased. There are also the additional factors of intemperate living, drunkenness, and unrestrained luxury by which we assail our bodies as though with battering rams.

Let us now turn to the story which contains a very sad calamity that befell the patriarch Jacob. Not for him only was this a sorrowful burden, but it was a terrible disgrace also for his whole household and his sons. For the defilement inflicted on a girl who is almost still an infant is a very great disgrace. Moses does not call her a בְּתוּלָה or עַלְמָה but a יַלְדָּה, an infant. Shechem was also still a boy. But he says that Dinah went out to see the daughters of the land, that is, the women of that region, free from care and without any fear of any injury and much less of defilement, since, indeed, she was not yet marriageable. But this is her downfall. The fact that Shechem rapes a little girl and defiles her when she is under age and not yet mature for marriage increases the disgrace. The brothers had a just cause for indignation and wrath. But they will be too cruel in exacting vengeance, as we shall hear.

The grief of the father himself was undoubtedly very great and especially pitiable. For he lives in the land of Canaan for eight years after leaving Mesopotamia, and during these years he builds a house and sets up a tent for the cattle. He is no longer a stranger or a guest but an inhabitant of the land. There he sets up a church, erects an altar to the Lord, and preaches the promise and the commandments of God for propagation to his whole posterity. He has peace and tranquillity, that is, the common and customary kind such as commonwealths and households usually have in this life, mixed with difficulties and disadvantages of a political and domestic nature. He also discharges his household duties, multiplies his flocks, amasses wealth, provides food for his household, and endures the troubles which usually befall men, the hatred of neighbors, thefts, plunderings, and plots. These are common and daily evils which cannot be corrected or avoided and must be borne together with other evils, while in the meantime thanks must be given to God that public peace and tranquillity remains. But it is such a rest as cannot exist without the sweat of the face, without thorns, and without thistles (cf. Gen. 3:18-19). This Jacob certainly had during these eight years.

But now an unusual and frightful trial returns, one that cannot be numbered among the daily thorns and thistles. Let anyone guess for himself how great is the grief of the father who has an only daughter and what a cross it is to see her dishonored and defiled in a most shameful manner. It is not a spiritual trial concerning faith, hope, and patience such as the former ones were. But among the domestic temptations it was nevertheless a most atrocious and intolerable trial that his only daughter, not yet of marriageable age, should be violently defiled and that this should happen in a quiet and secure place, not at the hands of enemies but at the hands of a neighbor, a friend, a prince who was the defender and father of his country, in the hospitality and good faith of which he had hitherto found satisfaction together with the greatest safety. From this man, contrary to all expectation, he is compelled to endure such an outstanding disgrace. Accordingly, this is the very worst and most unworthy trial. But this is how the greatest and saintliest of men are described, namely, that they were subject not only to the sweat of the face and daily thistles and thorns in their households but also to the very worst of bitter vexations at the hands of heathen and ungodly men.

It is assuredly unworthy and wretched that such a great patriarch should experience such disgrace when he was protected by so many promises that he would be under God's keeping and the protection and custody of the angels. Where are now those hosts of angels and מַחֲנָיִם ? Where is the glorious victory by which he conquered God and man? Where is that glorious acclamation: "You have prevailed against God and man"? Who is on guard here? Who is keeping watch? God and the angels close their eyes and pretend not to see. God ignores the matter and acts just as if He did not know or see the daughter being dragged away to be defiled. For He permits this to be done while the angels rest and do nothing. It is certainly a great and deplorable disaster, which should not befall godly men but the enemies of GOD, the heathen and the ungodly. And so we must learn patience if ever these sad and unusual experiences are our lot, things which it seems cannot be endured by any method or patience, such as this temptation certainly was, exceeding all human endurance and patience, as the cruel vengeance of the brothers will testify later. In this way the saintliest men have been subjected to tragic calamities, and to our reason it seems that the kingdom of God is administered in such a way that the grief of the godly and ungodly is equal, indeed, that the happiness of the latter is by far greater than that of the godly.

Why, then, does God permit the holy patriarch to be burdened with this cross just as if he were not a saint, acceptable and welcome in God's sight? It was done for our sake, that we may learn patience and consolation in adversity and may stop our mouth if similar calamities befall us too. For we are not better than such great men, and so we should not ask for a special good fortune but should accustom ourselves to this disciplining and testing of faith, consolation, and patience since, indeed, it seemed good to God to permit those unaccustomed and unheard-of monstrous calamities beyond that sweat of one's face and common spiritual tribulations.

Undoubtedly, the thought occurred to the excellent patriarch: "What sin have I committed, wretched man that I am? Perhaps I have been smug and have not prayed seriously and ardently, or some sin has been committed in my household and church without my knowledge. O Lord God, have mercy on me and cleanse me from my faults" (cf. Ps. 19:12). With such thoughts the godly are tormented so that they are afraid and alarmed just as if they were flung into such great troubles on account of some extraordinary fault. This concern and grief grew with his love for his daughter, the only one he had, and one who was not yet marriageable. Then also he was a stranger, who could not avenge this wrong, and perhaps he thought that he would have to fear even greater wrongs.

Furthermore, people also debate what this going out and visiting the daughters of the land was.[6] For Scripture does not explain it, and one man suggests this, another that. The Jews say that she went out to inspect the customs and celebrations of that people and city, impelled by a kind of curiosity. It is also likely that there were some games, dances, or weddings there. Dinah wanted to see the daughters of this region, how they were decked out and adorned and how beautiful they were. The text seems to indicate the same, namely, that she was curious, since, indeed, she went out without the permission of her father and mother, on her own without a companion. She is too secure and confident, for she was still a child and did not fear any danger to her modesty. It seems, then, that she sinned out of curiosity, because she went out to the daughters of the land and their associates

---

[6] Lyra *ad* Gen. 34:1, p. 97 verso, note "k," citing Josephus, *Antiquities of the Jews,* I, 21.

without consulting her parents. By nature girls find pleasure in the society of other maidens of equal age in their neighborhood. Meanwhile, the brothers are away from home in the field. Leah is at home with her little daughter Dinah, who goes out without consulting her mother. Accordingly, it is an example which should be carefully noted and inculcated in girls. They should not form the habit of strolling about and looking out of the window (cf. 2 Sam. 6:16) and lounging around the door, but should learn to stay at home and never to go anywhere without the permission of their parents or without companions. For the devil is laying snares against the modesty of this sex, which by nature is weak, irresponsible, and foolish and hence exposed to the snares of Satan. Dinah wanted to establish contact with the neighboring girls and imitate their customs and adornment. For her father lived outside the city. But the maidens had come forth for some marriage procession, and Dinah ran up to look at it. She was seen by Shechem, who was in that procession or dance with the daughters of the land. When he had seen her, he seized her and humbled her, for this is the way the Hebrews speak of defilement. This is an unworthy thing to do. He could have loved her whom he had seen and could have sought her for a wife. But he indulges his lust and passion. After he sees that she is endowed with singular beauty surpassing the daughters of the land, he is inflamed with love and seizes her by violence. He does not ask for her; he does not seek the consent of parents or of the girl but defiles her by violence. In such a case murder and misery usually follow. Murders and very serious calamities usually follow this wrong, as all the histories testify. Rape and the defilement of virgins have never passed by without bloody slaughter, and this deed is an example. For God does not connive at this license and madness of lusts and does not leave the deed unavenged when anyone indulges the fires of passion and lust; for He wants us to offer resistance to the flesh when it fights against us, so that if the rein is relaxed, it may not drag us headlong into outrageous sins of every kind.

Moses says significantly here: "He seized her." It is acting too roughly to seize another man's daughter, a man who was almost a sojourner or guest in that city, who lived securely and peacefully under the shadow of prince Hamor's protection. That this man should have such a disgraceful wrong inflicted on him is certainly something unworthy. But the disobedience and curiosity of the girl is punished quite severely, for she is overwhelmed and defiled by violence.

3. *And his soul was drawn to Dinah the daughter of Jacob; and he spoke tenderly to her.*

Shechem sees that he has sinned, for he feels that the maiden is suffering this great disgrace unwillingly; he sees her wailing and complaining. However, inflamed by his love for her, he is drawn to her and coaxes her to incite her to reciprocal love. This young puppy Shechem must have been brought up in a wanton manner. It appears that he was brought up with too much license, without the rod and discipline. Such youths are ruined by the indulgence of parents, and they grow in vices and lusts, in which they indulge without fear and shame. Solomon says in Prov. 29:15: "The rod and reproof give wisdom, but a child left to himself brings shame to his mother," that is, if one allows a child to do as it pleases, saying: "What our little daughter does is good, she is a plucky little hussy." Later, it comes to pass that the father is caught in confusion, and the mother in disgrace. This is the punishment for neglect of training. God wants the youth to be controlled and restrained by discipline, for this age is very weak and inexperienced and its thoughts are only of foolish, juvenile, and ruinous things. Therefore they cannot control themselves nor see what is good for them. God has ordained parents and teachers to keep an eye on them and control their drives and morals so that they remain within certain limits of duty.

Shechem, accordingly, is drawn to the girl with juvenile love. He does not yet repent and grieve about his deed, but he thinks that as the prince of the land he can sin with impunity. There are extant quite a number of sayings on this point like: "Holiness, godliness, faith are blessings for people in a private station: kings may go wherever they please." "It is behaving like a peasant for a prince to obey the laws of godliness and righteousness." "Lords must have an advantage." "Princes are exempt from the laws, they have their own privileges." So whatever pleases the prince is permitted. Thunder and lightning! Even less is permitted to magistrates than to those in a private station. Both their lust and their license should be punished more severely because they are the governors and guardians of discipline and should be examples of all virtues to others. But they cry: "I am a prince and lord of the land; why should I not be able to indulge myself?" No, the greater you are, the more you must humble yourself so that you may be able to lead the way for others in virtue and good examples, according to the common saying: "The whole world arranges itself according to the example of the king." [7] The evil examples of the magnates and princes are the most pestilential of all and have a very wide influence, for they corrupt many and draw them to license in sinning. The examples of people in a private station are less harmful and more easily corrected. The sins of princes are plainly diabolical. So they are punished in a severe manner, as Shechem was. For he thought that anything was permitted him as a prince, and he paid a horrible penalty. It cost him his neck. He himself and his parents and the whole city perish in a wretched manner. These are ethical matters.

Moreover, it is added in the text: "He spoke tenderly to her," that is, he soothed her with coaxing, kind, and comforting words which usually gladden a sorrowful heart. They were words of love, to which he added promises and gifts that he might comfort and soothe the sorrowful, violated girl. But it is in vain, for she remains in her grief and sorrow.

4. *So Shechem spoke to his father Hamor, saying: Get me this maiden for my wife.*

5. *Now Jacob heard that he had defiled his daughter Dinah; but his sons were with his cattle in the field, so Jacob held his peace until they came.*

יַלְדָּה, that is, a daughter, girl, little girl, in German: *Kindlein, die noch jung sind.* "Get me this pure girl," if I may speak like him, "who is still almost an infant and stays among the children." Now he makes a late request to his father that she be obtained for him as his wife. Why did you not seek the consent of the maiden, of her parents, and of your father earlier? The Phrygians become wise too late! Nevertheless, he does not repent yet but still increases his sin, which otherwise vanishes and is blotted out through repentance. For repentance removes sin; impenitence, on the other hand, magnifies, enlarges, and aggravates sin. He does not say: "I have sinned and I acknowledge that I have given grievous offense by defiling the daughter of an excellent man." No confession is heard, no repentance.

[7] Claudius Claudianus, *De quarto consulatu Honorii,* 300.

No, he thinks that he has acted rightly or that it is a small sin to rape a maiden and defile her. By the same sin he involves his father Hamor, who loves his son and treats him delicately as the future prince and his heir. As will be stated below, he was more highly honored than all who were in his father's house. So he does not reprove and chastise his son but becomes a partaker of another man's sins and agrees with him. This is the worst aspect of the matter.

At length, however, the report of the unworthy crime seeps through to the aged father Isaac [8] and to the sons Simeon, Levi, etc. For this rumor could not long be concealed because both persons were noble. Then, without a doubt, Jacob's house was filled with grief, sorrow, and the tears of the parents and the whole household. The two wives were still alive and suffered great grief upon hearing the news, and Leah especially was deeply grieved. The servants, maids, and shepherds all took it very badly. Some attested their grief with tears and wailing. Jacob himself, smitten with great sorrow, kept silent. For he found no remedy or consolation. He is not even able to think of avenging the injury inflicted by a very powerful lord. Accordingly, he does nothing. He does not make complaints to the perpetrator of the crime, nor does he approve the deed. But he is silent and patiently enduring, waiting for counsel and a remedy from the Lord. For what was he to do, being a stranger and a foreigner and much inferior in forces and power? Hamor undoubtedly despised him in comparison with himself, and Shechem thought: "What does it matter that I have defiled his daughter? Come, I shall marry her as my wife!"

6. *And Hamor the father of Shechem went out to Jacob to speak with him.*

7. *The sons of Jacob came in from the field when they heard of it; and the men were indignant and very angry because he had wrought folly in Israel by lying with Jacob's daughter, for such a thing ought not to be done.*

The rumor is spread from the house to the field and the brothers of Dinah in the same hour in which the crime was perpetrated and announced in Jacob's house. Some servant rushing to the sons said: "Alas! What evil has befallen the house of your father! Shechem has raped and defiled Dinah, your sister, etc." The text says: "Having heard what had happened, they left the flocks and came, very sad and

---

[8] This is how the original reads, but perhaps Jacob is meant.

disturbed." Here that word is also used which Moses employed in chapter 6:6: "He was touched by grief in his heart," and which is likewise found in 3:16: "In pain you shall bring forth children." For it signifies the anxiety of an uncertain heart which is destitute of all plan and thought, to be troubled, fearful, and afraid to such an extent that you cannot summon up courage even to think. In this manner, the sons of Jacob were perplexed and astonished and so crushed that they lost the power to think and were unable to find what they should advise or do.

To this confusion and anxiety anger was added, and this was even more burning in proportion as remedy and counsel were offered in less degree. By far the most grievous aspect of the matter was that an uncircumcised man had perpetrated the violence and did not acknowledge the crime or manifest any sign of repentance. Prince Shechem is keeping their sister captive at his house, and they cannot demand her back by force. Since a judge is lacking, they have no one before whom they can lay complaint about the wrong inflicted. Hamor, however, is coming to settle the matter with Jacob and his sons. But he will not heal this wound, and the brothers will not be mitigated until they avenge their wrong.

"To work folly" is a proverbial idiom among the Hebrews. By this proverbial way of speaking they indicate something very reprehensible and abominable, a great shame, disgrace, and infamy, which turns up in song and story. It is as though some one said: "What great disgrace, what great evil has befallen this man in his family!" So it is added: "Which thing ought not to be done at all!" The Jews deviate from this interpretation because they do not understand the Bible. But the true meaning is this: "This should not be done; this is no way to act; it is going too far and laying it on too thickly!" For I think that rape was forbidden and a capital offense not only in Jacob's house but also in that whole area. Therefore the meaning is that besides Jacob's household the rest of the neighbors and inhabitants of this land were also disturbed and very much offended by this affront to so saintly a guest. The indignity of this crime stirred up compassion and won over to Jacob's household even the hearts of strangers who were lovers of justice, equity, and discipline, just as we heard above that King Abimelech was strongly opposed to adultery and took precautions by a special edict that no one should touch Rebecca.[9] We shall

---

[9] The original reads "Rebecca," but from Gen. 20 it would seem that Sarah is meant.

not think that they were absolute barbarians and strangers to all discipline, honorable customs, and laws. For it is impossible for peace to be kept in a state without justice and some measure of discipline. So this deed displeased the inhabitants of this land. The favor, goodwill, and compassion of all men inclined to the house of Jacob, but the hatred of good men and their detestation of the crime descended on the house of Shechem. For they all judged that this should not have been done, that is, that a sin had been committed against good morals and the laws.

8. *But Hamor spoke with them, saying: The soul of my son Shechem longs for your daughter; I pray you, give her to him in marriage.*

9. *Make marriages with us, give your daughters to us, and take our daughters for yourselves.*

10. *You shall dwell with us; and the land shall be open to you; dwell and trade in it, and get property in it.*

Hamor addresses them without a preface, and he forgets about making an appeal to their goodwill. He acknowledges no guilt; he does not confess the sin, and much less does he plead an excuse. He is too proud, and for this reaon the sin is aggravated. The sons of Jacob, offended by the bitter and heavy disgrace, are not appeased but even more irritated. For he is detaining Dinah, and he only says: "Give her to my son as a wife," when before all else he should have begged pardon on behalf of his son, saying: "Excellent men and dearest brothers, forgive us this offense! I shall chastise my son Shechem, throw him into prison, and place him in fetters that he may learn after this to live honorably and peacefully with our guests." He does nothing of the kind but seems to support and defend the deed, and thus he makes himself a partaker of the whole evil and calls a severe punishment upon himself.

Therefore parents are to learn that they should not be too indulgent towards their children but that they should restrain them even as they were restrained by the discipline of their fathers and grandfathers. For Hamor [10] here completely forgets all honor and duty and as if on the basis of a good deed he seeks Dinah as a wife for his son and regards it as satisfaction for such a great crime, for rape and defilement, if the defiled maiden is married to his son. הִתְחַתְּנוּ means to conclude mar-

---

[10] The original reads "Shechem," but it is obvious that Hamor is meant.

riage relationships, as though he meant to say: "Establish marriage relationships," that is, "Become husbands and brides with us." חָתָן, properly speaking, signifies a husband and likewise a relative by marriage. From the noun the word is brought into the Hithpael: "Conclude marriages with us, become our friends and relatives-in-law; we want to become mutually linked in marriage and merge into one people." But where is the acknowledgment of the sin? "He did not commit any evil," he thinks. "Surely it is no sin to court a maiden for a wife? Indeed, it is a laudable virtue!"

He adds further: "You shall dwell with us, and the land shall be open to you; dwell and trade in it, etc." If he says this seriously, he is making a fairly liberal promise, and I really believe that he did speak this seriously, for he understands that a great crime has been committed by his son, but with a kind of pride he does not want to repent or to humble himself. This is the way such proud hypocrites are accustomed to act. They can cause the loss of all their property before they can acknowledge a sin, for they think that nothing is more disgraceful than to admit a mistake. Yet it is honorable to acknowledge a sin, but it is horrible and impious to defend it, to pretend not to see it, and to adorn it. Hence he offers his whole land, the marriage of his son, and all his goods, but in the meantime he maintains silence on the sin and covers it.

11. *Shechem also said to her father and to her brothers: Let me find favor in your eyes, and whatever you say to me I will give.*

12. *Ask of me ever so much as marriage present and gift, and I will give according as you say to me; only give me the maiden to be my wife.*

The son also offers a dowry and other great gifts provided only that they give him the daughter. But there is no confession or mention of sin. As Sirach 17:26 says: "From the dead, as from one that is not, confession ceases." But God should be placated first of all and afterwards the father and the brothers, and unless God has been placated by a humble acknowledgment of sin and the men have been reconciled by expressing regrets for guilt, no steadfast union of hearts can be made, neither in respect to treaty arrangements nor in marriage. For defending sins, or at least hiding them, does not gain favor but estranges or exasperates hearts even more, and before God a sin which in other respects is very light is aggravated by impenitence. Accordingly, no serious reconciliation is sought, but there is only hypocrisy and pretense, by which the crime of Shechem grows, for impenitence which makes a small sin great is death and the devil itself. On the other hand, the most atrocious sins are forgiven and taken away if true repentance takes place. All men are sympathetic in the case of killings that have happened by accident and readily pardon the one responsible for the killing if he acknowledges it and is troubled about his sin and if he complains that he was deceived and overcome by Satan; but if the deed is excused and defended, as, for example, the Centaurs [11] and the nobility think that they are permitted to rage against the pitiable throng of peasants with violence and slaughter, both God and men detest that cruelty, and they find no room for forgiveness at all. So also here, the proud and ungodly Hamor, the despiser of God and men, steps forth with his son. His words and ample promises are mere pretenses, which he would perhaps not have kept if possession of the girl had been given to him.

13. *The sons of Jacob answered Shechem and his father Hamor deceitfully, because he had defiled their sister Dinah.*

14. *They said to them: We cannot do this thing, to give our sister to one who is uncircumcised, for that would be a disgrace to us.*

15. *Only on this condition will we consent to you: that you will become as we are and every male of you be circumcised.*

16. *Then we will give our daughters to you, and we will take your daughters to ourselves, and we will dwell with you and become one people.*

17. *But if you will not listen to us and be circumcised, then we will take our daughter, and will be gone.*

So far we have heard of the fictitious and pretended humility of Shechem and his father. Shechem's love for the maiden had extorted from him the promise that he would give what they demanded for his betrothal to her. But it is love that makes promises, and it is madness that does not acknowledge sin. The son and the father do nothing by which the sin could be expiated and pardon obtained. Accordingly, the sin, which is most heinous in itself, is increased by impenitence

---

[11] From Luther's use of this title elsewhere (W, *Briefe*, VIII, 401) it is clear that he is referring to members of the court.

and by not confessing it and making satisfaction. For he nevertheless retains the girl who has been carried off in a most unjust manner, and she is the daughter of such a great man, a patriarch, prophet, and priest of God. This circumstance greatly enlarges this sin. If the matter were brought before a court for settlement, its atrocious nature would be truly perceived. But we shall treat the matter theologically; we shall not involve it in the many inextricable questions by which the lawyers today make all matters of law perplexing and difficult.

The rape of a virgin is a capital crime of itself by all law, divine and civil, as the rape of Helen, for example, was the cause of the destruction of Troy, and in all ages this crime has been punished in a fearful manner. But a greater and more difficult question arises, namely, whether the sons of Jacob are right in replying deceitfully, without the knowledge of their father Jacob, who keeps quiet. There is no doubt that Shechem and Hamor are unjust men, since they do not acknowledge their sin and do not repent, confess, and make satisfaction. Therefore let sin be opposed to sin, wrong to wrong, insult to insult, and reason to reason. Neither side follows what is just and right.

Concerning the slaughter of the Shechemites the lawyers and the opinion of Holy Scripture are in agreement. "Vengeance is Mine, I will repay," says the voice of God (Heb. 10:30). Likewise, it is said: "What is just you should carry out in a just manner." For no one should assume for himself the power either of judging or avenging a wrong that has been inflicted. The Germans say: "He who retaliates is in the wrong." But many explaining this question have engaged in painstaking toil, and Lyra and Burgensis have had a very keen contest between themselves as to what side is in the right.[12] But below (v. 30) Jacob himself will censure this deed when he says: "You have brought trouble on me by making me odious to the inhabitants of the land, the Canaanites and the Perizzites, etc." There he seems to condemn the slaughter committed by his sons. In chapter 49, when he is about to bless Simeon and Levi, he does not forget or excuse the deed but says: "Simeon and Levi are brothers; weapons of violence are their swords. O my soul, come not into their council; for in their anger they slay men, and in their wantonness they undermine a wall" (vv. 4-5). According to all the teachers, he is there referring to this slaughter committed against Shechem, and so he curses them before his death

---

[12] Lyra *ad* Gen. 34:13-17, p. 98 recto, "Additio."

and condemns them, although they have a very just cause for the slaughter.

Again, however, when he comes to the blessing of Joseph, he says (Gen. 48:22): "I have given to you rather than to your brothers one mountain slope which I took from the hand of the Amorites with my sword and with my bow." He says that he has acquired it with his sword and he hands it to Joseph as a blessing that has been well acquired; mention is also made of this in John 4:5: "near the field that Jacob gave to his son Joseph." But now in this place Moses says that the sons of Jacob spoke deceitfully, and below they receive a curse for this deed. And yet Joseph receives the possession of this land as though it were justly acquired. How do we bring these matters into concord?

We shall take a reply both from the text and words of Moses and follow these words as far as possible in the explanation of this question. They replied, says Moses, with guile to the petition of Hamor, which was quite just, as it seemed; that is, they made pretense and lied in word and deed, not jokingly, not courteously, but destructively, for the destruction and ruin of the Shechemites. This assuredly was a mortal sin, and it cannot be understood otherwise. It is not without purpose therefore that Moses says: "They replied fallaciously and deceitfully," that is, their feelings were contrary to what their words sounded forth. They pretended that they wanted to attach themselves to them and to preserve them safe and unharmed, and yet they were thinking of killing them. This their actual deed will show!

It is added: "And they spoke because he had defiled their sister Dinah," that is, they disputed, wrangled, and expostulated; they quarreled with each other. They said: "You have raped and defiled the daughter of a priest and very holy prophet whom God appointed as a teacher and father of the church in this land." By all the circumstances they could, they exaggerated the atrocity of the injuries. For it is a far more serious offense to violate the daughter of a king than the daughter of a peasant. Simeon and Levi were sons of a prophet who had [13] the promise of that land. So they had received the certain hope from their father's sermons that they would be the lords and priests of the promised land. For there is no doubt that Jacob taught the promise with great care and propagated it to his posterity. And together with the promises, he at the same time handed down the

13 The Weimar text has *habentes,* but we have read *habentis.*

commandments of God concerning the godly direction of life and morals. This doctrine and confidence the sons had drawn from the teaching of their father, and from it they concluded: "We are the lords of this land; although we are strangers, nevertheless, the promise of it is due us by divine right. Surely, then, we should not suffer such an outstanding and notorious wrong at your hands, should we? You are now holding a land that is not yours." These boasts they made with great insolence and pride resulting from the promise made to their father. "We are the ones," they think, as we will hear them below making a very proud reply to their father when he reproves them for the slaughter which was committed, saying: "Surely he should not abuse our sister as a harlot," should he? Such pride there was continually among the Jewish people, prompting them to say: "We are the people of God, we are a royal priesthood, etc."

Accordingly, they talked and engaged in proud discussions about the violation and pollution of their sister, the daughter of such a great man, who in lineage, beauty, and piety excelled all the maidens of this locality. For in this way they intensified this injury, which in kind and individuality is in many ways different from the common variety of deed. For she was not the daughter of a burgher or peasant but of the highest prophet in this land, nor was it only a private person that was violated, but the public ministry was despised. Moreover, if anyone dares to take a daughter from such a great patriarch and ravish her by force and keep her against his will, what will he not dare against others? What else remains but that sometime later they will also rob them of life and all goods? So they say: "Come, then, since we have the promise of dominion over this land, let us also dare something! We also will undertake a little deed!"

But why do they attack them treacherously and not openly? For even if it seems that they can be excused on the grounds that it is permissible to deceive an enemy, according to the proverbial statement: "Guile or virtue, who asks about that in the case of an enemy?" [14] nevertheless, it is not right for them to use pretense in a familiar and friendly conference and discussion. They had not yet declared themselves to be their enemies. Therefore I do not think that they were without sin, even as their father himself will condemn them. It is strange, however, that Jacob retains possession of the land. For he seized it after the slaughter of the citizens and had pasture for his

---

[14] Vergil, *Aeneid*, II, 390.

flocks there when he lived with his father Isaac in Hebron, and he will say below that it was not bought with money but acquired by his sword and bow. This really provides the jurists with ample material for questions and discussions.

Moses, however, indicates that the sons of Jacob did not do what is right in speaking deceitfully with Hamor and Shechem and in tricking them into utter destruction. For although it seems that their guilt is on a par with the punishment, there is, nevertheless, a difference between justice and the execution of justice, the sin and the punishment which is inflicted on account of the sin. For it is written: "Vengeance is Mine, I will repay" (Rom. 12:19; Heb. 10:30; cf. Deut. 32:35). It is likewise stated: "What is just you should execute with justice." Shechem is not punished unjustly, even as the Trojans are not attacked and overthrown unjustly, because of the rape of Helen. But it is not yet agreed whether they execute justice in a true or just manner. For no judge is present, and they simply repay evil for evil and revenge one wrong with another, measure for measure.

At first, however, they speak quite openly and sincerely. "We cannot do this," they say, "to give our daughter to one who is uncircumcised." From this it appears that they were not accustomed to marry their daughters to any men but to those who received circumcision. But they are devising tricks with this innocent front, and they employ this pretext to have a situation and opportunity for attacking them. Accordingly, they add: "Only on this condition will we consent to you: that you will become as we are, etc." This is the beginning of their treachery, in which they sin, and it is this that their father condemns. It would have been right and frank if they had said: "Return our sister, or we will take her by force; for it is not permissible to marry her to a man with a foreskin." But it is trickery for them to say: "If every male among you is circumcised, we will give our daughters to you."

But it is still strange that Jacob's sons had such boldness that they dared to make this demand or could bring themselves to think of such an atrocious vengeance. For look at their ages! Jacob [15] is 108 years old. Reuben, who is the oldest, is about 19; Simeon is a year younger, and so they come one after the other. They are young puppies! These youths presume to undertake such an act of violence against a whole city when they have no experience or knowledge of military matters or of any other matters. It is a strange boldness! At that time, how-

[15] The original reads "Isaac," but it is obvious that Jacob is meant.

ever, human nature had more vigor, for a youth of 14 was fit for marriage. In our age a boy of 18 is not fit for affairs of state, not to mention the endurance of military service.

Why then were they so proud? The magnitude of the wrong must
be added to the magnitude of their confidence, by which they knew
that they had a father to whom promises about the possession of the
land had been made. Nor did they dare such a deed on their own,
but they had their servants and shepherds as helpers, and perhaps
also some of their neighbors whom they summoned to their aid. It is
likely that Jacob [16] had about a hundred men in his household. For
so many flocks there is need of a large number of shepherds, whom
they had as friends and allies. Moreover, a hundred armed men who
are courageous (it is stated that they entered the city confidently),
making a sudden attack, can easily slaughter six hundred others, especially if God allows it because of the sins which He wants to punish
in this manner.

Therefore, since it does not seem that they have enough strength
to overwhelm them, they employ fraud and demand that all the males
should be circumcised and so be weakened that they might not be
ready to offer resistance. That is acting with fraud and guile. For
although this pretext is quite honorable in appearance, it is nevertheless vain and unnecessary, because afterwards it was still necessary
to marry their daughters to men who were not circumcised.

18. *Their words pleased Hamor and Hamor's son Shechem.*

19. *And the young man did not delay to do the thing, because he
had delight in Jacob's daughter. Now he was the most honored
of all his family.*

The young man, madly in love with the girl, eagerly accepts the
condition and so is deceitfully enticed into the trick of receiving
circumcision. To be sure, the father and son also involve the whole
tribe in the same sin and danger. For if Shechem and Hamor had
been blessed with any discernment on that occasion, they would
have refused such a hard and difficult condition even for this reason,
that it was not expedient for the state to change the religion and
customs of their ancestors and fatherland. "We shall restore your
sister to you," they should have said, "we will confess our sin and

----

[16] Here again the original reads "Isaac," but Jacob is meant.

beg your pardon." In this way they would not have brought themselves and the whole people into this crisis.

But this is how matters usually turn out. When punishments for sins are threatening a city or a district, the rulers and subjects first become fools so that they are entangled and caught in common sins and punishments. All the histories of all the nations testify this. For example, when the kingdom of Israel and Judah was to be laid waste by the king of the Babylonians, the prophets were slaughtered at Jerusalem and elsewhere, innocent blood was shed, and the whole land was filled with avarice, slaughters, sins, and acts of madness of every kind. When the final act in the devastation of Jerusalem and the whole Jewish nation was impending, it was first necessary for God's Son to be crucified. Today also, when the Turkish armies are about to devastate Germany, all places must first be filled with usury, treachery, malice, treason, and persecution so that the iniquities of the Amorites are filled up; in short, we must act in such a way that our sins become ripe.

So also in this example, punishments were threatening the citizens for various outrageous acts. Therefore the whole tribe is involved in the folly, sin, and horrible punishments of its prince. As is stated in the heathen poet: "The Greeks suffer punishment for whatever folly their kings commit," [17] that is, the land must bear it when its rulers are fools. Thus the people of Israel are stricken because of David's sin in numbering the people (cf. 2 Sam. 24:15). The insanity of our rulers also calls down punishments upon us which we have merited for a long time so that our princes become insane and mad and let the Turk come into the land. So that both subjects and rulers should be punished, it is necessary for them to increase and multiply their sins by a kind of final act of folly, just as Shechem here is the initial author and beginner of this stupid plan. For he himself is circumcised, and he persuades the whole people to do the same.

20. *So Hamor and his son Shechem came to the gate of their city and spoke to the men of their city, saying:*

21. *These men are friendly with us; let them dwell in the land and trade in it, for behold, the land is large enough for them; let us take their daughters in marriage, and let us give them our daughters.*

[17] Horace, *Epistles,* I, 2, 14.

22. Only on this condition will the men agree to dwell with us, to become one people: that every male among us be circumcised as they are circumcised.

A very fine orator! But he says nothing about restoring the maiden and about placating the wrath and mitigating the grief of the father. He still persists in despising God and men. Therefore wrath comes upon them. At the same time, however, the stupid people are led into error so that they agree with and approve of the rape and defilement of Dinah. This is what a stupid and unwise prince brings to pass on account of the sins of the people, which are punished by the acts of madness of the kings, as all the histories and works of all the poets demonstrate. For this is the course of the world from the beginning right up to the end.

Similarly today, with so many crimes being committed with impunity among the people because of their smugness and contempt of God and men, it will at length come to pass that punishments and disasters by which we will be overwhelmed and perish will be brought on as by the folly of some ruler. Because the people are so bent on mischief, a ruler will commit some act of folly and cause some misfortune which will drag us all into ruin. Because we do not listen and are not corrected by God's voice and threats, punishment will at length come.

It was a horrible sin on the part of Hamor and Shechem to keep silent about their sin and not to acknowledge it and, indeed, to despise a very holy man in their smugness. What about Jacob? What about his daughter? He who is not terrified over against such a great crime and is not moved by the judgment of God or men will certainly be bold enough to plot against the life of the parent just as he previously plotted against the chastity of the daughter. Blindness and madness follow this smugness so that men do not consider or understand the plots and dangers hanging over them. Shechem is mad with lust and love for the girl; the father is indulgent to him, and so also the whole tribe. There is no one who thinks about the expiation of the sin. They are foolish and mad, and no one opens eyes and ears so that at least one might have said: "Come, let us act gently! Let us return the girl and assuage the wrath of her father and brothers!" Among the Trojans, for example, some advised that Helen should be given back and that the interests of their fatherland should be considered and that it should by no means be endangered on account of one man's lust. Others, however, were not in favor of this and indulged their lust and madness. Therefore overthrow and devastation followed. So also this people agrees with its ruler, and for that reason they suffer and perish together, and justly too.

23. *Will not their cattle, their property, and all their beasts be ours? Only let us agree with them, and they will dwell with us.*

This is too much! Lyra and Burgensis discuss the question whether also Shechem and Hamor acted with trickery.[18] It appears that they act fraudulently, or, at least, that they deceive their fellow citizens, because it was not in the agreement that all the property which the sons of Jacob had would be their common property in the future. Therefore, if they said this seriously, it is a case of manifest fraud and ill will, by which they not only omit to acknowledge the rape of the girl and the insult previously offered, but they are also thinking of getting the best of Jacob and plundering his goods. In this way the sin would be truly increased and grow. But if they are only indulging in rhetoric and not speaking from the heart, then they wanted to deceive the people the more easily to persuade them with the hope of acquiring the flocks and property of Jacob. Nevertheless, these matters seemed to look forward to establishing a tyranny over their neighbors and oppressing them. For what is the point in saying: "Will not their flocks be ours?" if they only sought social ties with their neighbors and did not think of seizing their goods? Therefore they act deceitfully, whether it is in deceiving the sons of Jacob or in telling lies to their own fellow citizens.

Perhaps this was also the conclusion or suspicion of the sons of Jacob. "If they were bold enough to rape and violate a daughter not yet of marriageable age, what will they not do to us or our father?" For reason argues that he who dares the greater crime also dares the lesser one. It is a lesser crime to seize goods and reduce men to slavery than it is to rape a girl. It seems that they expostulated and disputed with them along these lines above. But paying no attention to all these matters, those asses, Hamor and Shechem (for חֲמוֹר means ass), harangue the people and promise that they will be lords not only of the girl but also of her brothers and of all their goods.

So their sin grows and immediately draws another sin with it since it is not removed by repentance. Thus when a fornicator or adulterer remains in his raging lust and meets one by whom he fears that he

18 Lyra *ad* Gen. 34:20-22, p. 98 recto, note "h."

will be hindered or betrayed, he will not easily keep his hands off him but will kill him so that he may be able to give free rein to his lust in safety. There is an excellent statement of Gregory that wherever the serpent inserts his head, there he will easily insert his tail and whole body.[19] If the devil succeeds in getting his head into the hole, the snake soon slithers after it with his tail.

24. *And all who went out of the gate of his city hearkened to Hamor and his son Shechem; and every male was circumcised, all who went out of the gate of the city.*

Here the Greeks "suffer punishment," as is stated in the well-known verse,[20] on account of the folly of the king. It would have been more in keeping with what is right if they had said: "This wrong is too severe; the girl should rather be restored to her father. Our religion and paternal rites should be maintained, and another more suitable method should be possible by which this crime may be expiated. Let us not seek their goods, for there will never be a firm union between us if we scheme to get their goods." But they are all deaf, dumb, and blind, and they rush into the nets of the devil and the snares of death (cf. Ps. 18:5). For all who went out of the gate of the city, that is, who lived in the city, were circumcised. For it is a Hebrew idiom which signifies that a citizen of a state and its city is one who is accustomed to enter it and to go out into the field.

Accordingly, the wretched citizens obey their stupid ruler who involves the whole people in his impenitence so that all become guilty of this sin, for the doer and the one who consents are punished with the same punishment, as is stated in Rom. 1:32, namely, that "those who do such things are worthy of death, and not only those who do them but also those who consent to those who do them." Thieves and fences, criminals and informers belong under the same punishment. Kings become fools and sin against God and men. Nor are they troubled about the sin, but they are smug as though they had done well. They do not think that they have been deceived but rather that they have cheated strangers and guests. Here a horrible punishment follows.

25. *On the third day, when they were sore, two of the sons of Jacob, Simeon and Levi, Dinah's brothers, took their swords and came upon the city confidently, and killed all the males.*

[19] Gregory, *Moralia in Job*, I, 53, *Patrologia, Series Latina*, LXXV, 552.
[20] See p. 206.

26. *They slew Hamor and his son Shechem with the sword, and took Dinah out of Shechem's house, and went away.*

It is strange from where these youths obtained such confidence or where they learned to use the sword and the bow against the enemy, being shepherds and men of the land. The Jews entertain many foolish notions about the third day.[21] But experience teaches that in all diseases the pain is most violent on the third day. Women, for example, feel the greatest weakness and pain on the third day after childbirth and after nature's struggle in childbirth. So also when nature toils in forcing out a stone, the weakness is not felt in the struggle itself, but after the stone has been forced out, all members and the whole body are fatigued.[22] Whether the same thing happens in circumcision will have to be ascertained from the Jews. But because Scripture attests the same, we shall have no doubts that there is a corresponding experience.

Therefore Simeon and Levi seize this opportunity. When the Shechemites were lying down and no one was prepared for battle but all had need of attention and rest, they attacked the unarmed and weakened men. Nor were these two youths, Simeon and Levi, alone, but they had shepherds, servants, and also some of their neighbors with them. Moses says that they entered confidently and proudly, not only because of that occasion and opportunity to overwhelm unarmed men but also because they trusted in their rank and reputation, namely, that they were sons of a patriarch and lords of the world. Nor did they only fight for the recovery of their sister, but they also attacked them as enemies of the promise and people of God.

They killed every male, slaughtering not only the ruler Hamor or his son but all the men and even the infants crying in their cradles. This is too atrocious and cruel! But this is how these matters are done in human affairs when enemy rages against enemy, as we see also in the case of the cruelty of the Turk, who either slaughters or drags off men and women into captivity. It is also the secret judgment and wrath of God, by which He permits all the citizens to be slaughtered. Perhaps they learned this from their ancestors, who were accustomed to kill all the citizens in captured towns. In Num. 31:17-18

---

[21] Lyra *ad* Gen. 34:25, p. 98 verso, note "a."

[22] Luther is referring to a disease from which he himself suffered.

Joshua is ordered to kill all the males and women of the Midianites and to spare the virgins only. Saul is instructed to extirpate the whole people of the Amalekites, adults together with the little ones (cf. 1 Sam. 15:3). It is said that the same custom is characteristic of the Persians today.

In this way the wretched Greeks are punished for the folly and sin of their king; their princes have committed folly, and the people must suffer. But the people had deserved this punishment because they had been partakers of other men's sins and had summoned destruction upon themselves by reason of their own smugness and ill will. So we today teach and charge our fellow citizens to hear and embrace the Word of God with grateful hearts and to cease provoking God's wrath with their cheating, plunderings, and usury. But there is no limit or end to their greed, rapacity, and cheating in their contracts and their whole life. Therefore we make no progress in our teaching and censuring, but sins are heaped up and go about with impunity. Therefore, when a prince comes and imposes a garrison on a city and when the soldiers wildly vent their madness on those whom they should have protected and defended, then we cry out that we are being oppressed unjustly, and we complain about the tyranny of princes. But such things should have been thought of long before, and the Lord God should have been heeded when He gave warning of these things and invited us to repentance by His Word. So also at that time the iniquities of the Shechemites were filled up. Therefore the punishments came through the folly of the princes, and they were involved in this folly so that they became partakers in their sins, in the rape and defilement of the girl, and perished with them.

Because we impose no limit on usury, thefts, and crimes of every kind and because we do not hear the Word and pay no attention to the testimony of our conscience when it cries out against our lusts, we also shall not escape with impunity but shall be held fast in punishments by the just judgment of God, and our complaints about unjust oppression will come late and in vain. On the other hand, Simeon and Levi sin in the opposite direction. For although the Shechemites are punished justly and although Simeon and Levi have a very just cause and are grieving as a result of the rape of Dinah, nevertheless, they act unjustly, because their father did not wish or approve this slaughter. But they carry out the slaughter under their own rashness and daring without orders from their father.

27. *And the sons of Jacob came upon the slain, and plundered the city, because their sister had been defiled;*

28. *they took their flocks and their herds, their asses, and whatever was in the city and in the field;*

29. *all their wealth, all their little ones and their wives, all that was in the houses, they captured and made their prey.*

After the citizens have been killed, the city is open to plunder together with the women, children, and their whole substance. All is done without the knowledge and consent of the father. For if he had known it, he would undoubtedly have forbidden it. I think, moreover, that the rest of the sons of Jacob joined in the plundering, especially those born from Leah, except Joseph and Judah, although some of them were still youths. But the older ones joined by their households and the neighboring shepherds plundered the city. Simeon and Levi were the leaders, and so their father in his last blessing calls them "vessels of destruction" and condemns them as murderers (49:5). He also threatens to divide them among Israel, and this also happened later. Levi was deprived of his inheritance, in place of which the priesthood was given to him, the beggar's staff. For the Levites did not live from their own incomes but from the sacrifices and the tithes. Simeon was also afflicted with perpetual poverty. They paid a fairly heavy penalty for this sin throughout their generations.

The Jews extenuate this deed in whatever manner they can, and they are immoderate and effusive in the praise of their race.[23] They arrogate to themselves a reputation for righteousness but take all commendation away from the Gentiles. They permit themselves so much indulgence that they explain the passage from chapter 49:5, "Simeon's and Levi's swords are weapons of violence," as referring to Joseph, saying that he cursed these two brothers because they had sold him into Egypt. They do this to cover the disgrace of their own nation and to adorn it with praises of sanctity and righteousness. Indeed, Burgensis even testifies that the Jews set up this law, that it is permitted, yes, even an act of piety and pleasing to God, to destroy and kill a Gentile on whatever occasion or in whatever manner that can be done by a Jew.[24] In such a manner they rave in their desire for

---

23 See *Luther's Works*, 8, pp. 215—219.

24 During these years Luther was much preoccupied with such reports, which he had "read in the histories"; cf. *On the Jews and Their Lies* (W, LIII, 482, 530).

honor and in their hatred against us. Josephus, who in other respects was a great man, in his zeal for his nation, nevertheless, tells the most disgraceful lies in his histories contrary to Holy Scripture, as, for example, when he makes a hero and a holy man out of Saul.[25]

It seems, however, that the sons of Jacob have some excuse, as this example terrified the cities of the Gentiles so that they might not persecute Jacob. Jacob likewise will only say that they have caused him trouble and made his name stink before the inhabitants of the land. But below, when he is on the point of death, he curses them, and so he openly testifies that they did wrong.

Only after the deed has been committed, does a discussion about the ethics of it follow, as is stated in the German proverb: "The justification lagged behind." Among certain nations there was also the custom that they first hanged a thief and later conducted inquiries about the legality of the act. The jurists likewise say that many things are done in actual fact which are not done legally. If this were abolished, the profession of the jurists would be superfluous, because there is no need of their profession before a deed has been committed, but after it has been committed, the question is asked whether it was done legally or not. In this case it is their office to give advice by which a man can defend what is his right. Therefore the question is asked whether the sons of Jacob can be excused inasmuch as they committed their act not on the basis of the law but with trickery, lies, and violence. Frankly, we conclude that they sinned, for they did not demand a judicial decision concerning this deed. It would have been possible for this to be given among the neighboring cities. Jacob also condemns them, and God imposed very hard punishments on their whole posterity.

But from this question another much more difficult one arises, namely: "Why did not Jacob order everything which they plundered to be restored, especially those things which could have been restored — wives, maidens, servants, cattle, and the rest of the substance of the city?" What is more, Jacob later assigns this part of the Shechemites to Joseph, and it is said that Joseph was buried here so that even in death he might occupy this inheritance. Accordingly, if they acted unjustly, why do they not restore what has been taken by force? Here it is right for us to reply that many things are permitted to the saints with impunity which are not permitted to others.

[25] Josephus, *Antiquities of the Jews,* VI, 43 ff.

Hence, the judgment of God is mingled here with the injustices of men. The inheritance and property of the Shechemites becomes vacant, the owners being killed on account of their sin. Therefore God justly assigns this to those who have suffered wrong, and this is the reason why the sons of Jacob, with God's permission and concession, invade their property and keep what they have seized. So also the children of Israel were not permitted to plunder the Egyptians of their own accord, but the Egyptians were plundered because they deserved this punishment and owed the people of Israel wages for many years of slavery. Finally, the command of God was added, which wanted to punish the Egyptians and remunerate the Hebrews.

In the same manner the sons of Jacob and their father were the victims of unusual disgrace and injury. A girl was defiled and forcibly raped, and this was the filling up of the sins of the Amorites, concerning which mention was made above in chapter 15:16: "The iniquity of the Amorites is not yet complete." But what will be paid to Jacob in recompense for such a disgraceful wrong? God replies: "Receive this booty in compensation for the disgrace which you and your children have borne." In this way Jacob by divine authority becomes the owner of these possessions, and there is no discussion about the legal rights of the owner.

For God conducts Himself towards us as we are accustomed to conduct ourselves towards Him. We take action first as it pleases us, and after taking action we make inquiries about legality and want our action to be approved by Him. So He punishes us before He asks about legality, just as is stated in Ps. 18:26: "With the crooked Thou dost show Thyself perverse." But later He allows us to shout and complain about the wrong and injustice which we suffer at the hands of those who afflict us with the just judgment of God. Why are we killed? Why are our goods plundered? I reply that God can do this and invert the regular order because we put action before legality.

Therefore, although the sons of Jacob act unjustly, nevertheless, God is not unjust when He punishes the Shechemites, whom He warned previously not to do anything contrary to law and His commandments, namely, that they should not defile, rape, or retain the daughter of another man. Because they did not obey Him, they were punished. Jacob, who understood God's judgment and vengeance on the adversaries who had harmed him, by divine authority retains the booty, although not without groaning and tears. This his own words, by which he expostulated with his sons, testify.

30. *Then Jacob said to Simeon and Levi: You have brought trouble on me by making me odious to the inhabitants of the land, the Canaanites and the Perizzites; my numbers are few, and if they gather themselves against me and attack me, I shall be destroyed, both I and my household.*

From this it is clear in what manner the deed of his sons pleased Jacob. The Jews try to avoid these words and invent the glosses that they are words of fear and not of reproof, and they therefore contend that he did not condemn his sons.[26] But below he will call Simeon and Levi vessels of violence and wrong by whom violence and injury was inflicted on the Shechemites, and he will curse them and their whole posterity. Accordingly, it is certain that he did not say "You have troubled me, etc.," out of a kind of trepidation but that this violence and cruelty displeased him. Therefore he calls them violent murderers and plunderers, and he really magnifies this crime because it was such an act of folly that it pointed to the greatest danger and disgrace for him. "The madness is twofold," he says, "being first of all unjust towards the Shechemites and, secondly, dangerous to me."

This is a new temptation. In the first place his daughter was defiled after he had lived eight years in this area, and this caused him the heaviest grief. Now, when he had overcome this grief and trouble in some manner and reflected how he might be able to remedy this evil, his sons cause a different and far more severe disturbance, and, to the best of their ability, they become responsible for the destruction of their parents and of the whole household. For the excellent patriarch raised the complaint: "I have lost my daughter, and now you have brought it about that my life is endangered and all of you are destroyed together with me." It is therefore a very sharp reproach and accusation; they are not words which fear and trepidation wrung from him. "You have inflicted violence not only on others," he goes on to say, "but also on me and my wives, the whole household, and our whole substance. Indeed, this violence will prove to be your destruction! What am I to do? I have very dear wives in Rachel and Leah, from whom you were born to me; I have a household and a domestic church. If the neighboring cities should combine their strength and attack us as the perpetrators of this tragedy and most cruel slaughter, how shall we resist such large numbers, we who are

[26] Lyra *ad* Gen. 34:30, p. 98 recto, note "e."

small in number? You should not have exacted such vengeance which will prove to be the destruction of us and our belongings. They will kill me," he says, "and I will be destroyed together with my whole house."

Therefore he does not extenuate but horribly magnifies the crime of his sons. In his final agony he reproaches them with it and could not forget it, and he calls them vessels of violence and wrong. For it certainly involved them in great danger. However, that God averted this danger from Jacob's house by His wonderful goodness is clearly a special blessing of God. Thus citizens can often cause a disturbance in the state which brings destruction to a whole city. But when the danger declines with even some gain and advantage, another Master is present, who is a Helper at the right time, as God also shows Himself here to Jacob. Often a man is thrown into danger by the folly and rashness of another, just as Jacob's life and his whole household is brought into a critical situation by the madness of his sons. But God's is the work and blessing, for He draws good from evil and turns evil into good and brings a happy conclusion from an evil beginning.

These things do not come to pass by the wisdom of Jacob, Levi, and Simeon, but by the goodness of God alone. For he whom God loves will find peaceful and favorable outcomes in the greatest of dangers. For the sake of one good man the best interests of a whole district are often taken into consideration, as the history of the three kings of Judah, Israel, and Edom testifies (cf. 2 Kings 3:9, etc.). They were leading their armies through the desert of Edom against the king of Moab and after being without water for seven days were brought into an extreme crisis. At this point the king of Israel in despair raised the complaint: "Alas! The Lord has assembled us three kings to give us into the hand of Moab" (cf. 2 Kings 3:10). They would all have perished of thirst in wretched fashion, but Jehoshaphat was a good surety then. To the king of Israel Elisha said: "What have I to do with you? Go to the prophets of your father, etc. The Lord of hosts lives, in whose presence I stand, but if I did not have respect for the countenance of Jehoshaphat the king of Judah, I would not have paid attention to you or have had regard to you" (cf. 2 Kings 3:13). Under those circumstances the presence of King Jehoshaphat was salutary for the three armies so that for his sake help and victory was granted by God and such a supply of water that not only were the men and animals refreshed but they also gained a very illustrious victory over the enemy. By whose merit did that come to pass? Surely not by the merit of the king of Israel or Edom? By no means, but because godly King Jehoshaphat had been brought there by the rashness of the two kings, and for his sake God grants them rescue and victory. So also Egypt was preserved for Joseph's sake and Syria on account of Naaman. In the same manner all was regarded as lost here so that Jacob simply despairs of himself and his whole household. But he has the promise, and so help follows of necessity, and it is necessary that he with his household should be rescued from the midst of the teeth of the neighboring peoples and cities.

But they should not have tempted God in reliance on this help and promise. Jacob's sons, for example, proudly boasted that they had a patriarch as their father, who had the promise, and so they thought they were permitted to undertake anything and to revenge the wrong that had been inflicted. For that is tempting God by rashness and a kind of presumption. However certain Jacob was of God's protection, he would nevertheless have forbidden this deed. But that the danger which was threatening from the neighboring peoples was warded off came to pass not by the merit of the sons but by the merit of the father.

This is an illustrious example which reminds us that good and saintly men sometimes run into the greatest of misfortunes and dangers not through their own but by someone else's fault. To the others, indeed, who are involved in the same danger no way of salvation or liberation appears, but they think that all is lost. But because there are some godly men, or only one godly man, in the same ship, the ship must reach port safe and sound, however much it has been tossed about by a heavy storm, even though a thousand devils have been fighting in opposition and causing tumult in the same ship. So also for the sake of Paul alone, a ship is saved and 276 men who were with him in the ship, as we read in Acts 27:37. In the same manner, the world continues for the sake of the church in the world. Otherwise heaven and earth would be burned up in one moment, for the world is not worthy of one grain of wheat since it is full of blasphemies and godlessness. But because the church is in the midst of the ungodly, God for its sake permits also the ungodly to enjoy the common blessings of this life. Whatever the world has it has by the blessing of the church, as the angel says in Acts (27:24) to Paul: "Lo, God has granted you all those who sail with you," and they were certainly idolaters and ungodly men.

The pope and the Turk, etc., also do not deserve the fruitfulness of the earth and the annual produce of all the things growing from the earth, for they are ungodly men. But because God has this tiny and beloved flock in the world, He bestows all the blessings and benefits of this life on its account. With this assembly removed, the world would be reduced to nothing and become like Sodom and Gomorrah, as is stated in Is. 1:9.

Therefore we should learn from this example that God helps also the ungodly for the sake of the saints and often by His kindness corrects the rashness of very foolish men, by which they stir up troubles and dangers, and turns it to something better. For in this way He honors His saints. Syria, for example, is preserved on account of the one man, Naaman, Egypt on account of Joseph, and Israel on account of Jehoshaphat. Nevertheless, the ungodly will have their punishments, even as punishment will be in store for the sons of Jacob, Simeon and Levi, when their father curses them and their posterity.

Secondly, these words demonstrate that the holy man Jacob is again wrestling with a very great trial of the spirit and faith which is nearly extinguished. The flax is smoking, and the reed is bruised and nearly broken (cf. Is. 42:3). For they are not words of faith but simply words of the murmuring flesh and struggling faith, and weak faith at that. He has almost lost those glorious promises: "I will surely bless you, etc." Those suns and stars of the Word and promises were obscured and covered by the black clouds of this alarm, doubt, and near despair. For he says: "I shall be killed; I and my house shall be laid waste!" He is full of fear and distrust, and yet it is not despair.

But this is the nature of faith. When the sun is shining and the sky is clear, we find satisfaction in the consolations set before us and sing "We Praise Thee, O God, etc.," [27] and "I will bless the Lord at all times" (Ps. 34:1). Again, Ps. 30:7-9 says: "Thou didst hide Thy face, I was dismayed. To Thee, O Lord, I cried; and to the Lord I made supplication: 'What profit is there in my blood, if I go down to corruption?'" These seem to be the words of those who despair, for the psalm says: "Lord, Thou hast brought up my soul from Sheol, Thou hast saved me from those who go down into the Pit. I was already done for."

[27] Luther is quoting the Latin hymn *Te Deum laudamus*, traditionally (but incorrectly) ascribed to St. Ambrose and St. Augustine.

In this manner faith struggles with weakness when the devil and the flesh exercise dominion, and it appears to the one struggling that faith is no longer present. Thus Jacob complains here: "I have become abominable to all my neighbors, I have been thrown into extreme danger, and I think of nothing but destruction." Where is faith here and the remembrance of the promises? Why does he not induce his heart to say: "You have prevailed against God. How much more, then, will you prevail against neighboring nations?" All this has slipped away from him. Trial devours the splendid promises and most glorious victories of faith. But he does not yet despair, although he is very similar to one in despair. He does not fall into misbelief and is not an unbeliever, although it appears so. This is trial, just as Paul says of himself: "So that we might not rely on ourselves, we had the sentence of death in ourselves" (cf. 2 Cor. 1:8-9). It is necessary for the saints to be disciplined in this way, to descend into hell and the abyss, and to be recalled from there into heaven.

For so far Jacob retains a smoking flax in his heart. When it was announced that Simeon and Levi had smitten and plundered the whole city, it was impossible for him not to be deeply moved on account of so many murders. So there was undoubtedly very great weakness here, complaining, wailing, and crying out to God, and in his chamber he prayed alone with tears: "O Lord God, help me, Thou who hast given me the promise; I am involved in very great danger!" This prayer was heard according to the promise, for he had the spirit of faith or of grace and prayers. Lucifer and the dawn again arise in him, faith is stirred up and conquers all dangers. For the sin of the sons is covered, and the excellent father is defended from his neighbors, nor was there anyone who dared to oppose him, as we shall hear in the following chapter. The two brothers Simeon and Levi did not deserve this defense. But old father Jacob received forgiveness for all the sins of the sons together with the booty of the Shechemites, but in such a way that both parties were punished, the latter by destruction, the former by the curse of the father.

31. *But they said: Should he treat our sister as a harlot?*

Hear how the sons reply to their father, the high and mighty rascals! They do not acknowledge their sin; they are not sorry for the unjust slaughter and violence but defend it. It is as though they meant to say: "We have acted justly by killing the Shechemites because their atrocious sins deserve severe punishments." Accordingly, they amplify the rape of Dinah in a dramatic manner, even though Shechem wished to have her as his wife and not as a harlot. Nor do they console the venerable old man or display grief on account of the slaughter which has been perpetrated or alleviate it by an acknowledgment of their guilt and an expression of regret. They do not do penance or seek pardon for having provoked their neighbors by slaughters and plunderings and for seriously disturbing their father's heart.

The old man himself had to endure this proud response and the defense of their crime, and this brought even more affliction and sadness to the heart that was sorrowful and faint by reason of his former trepidation. Jacob has to bear the sin of his sons, and for his sake the punishment is postponed, and the proud and violent sons are tolerated until their time.

However, the wonderful goodness and mercy of God shines forth in this example, for He helps and rescues the godly even when it seems that all is lost. If only the flax remains smoking and a man is not turned to folly and blasphemy, but sighs, groans, and cries out, that cry fills heaven and earth. All the affairs of this patriarch of ours were in such a hopeless state that it seemed that they could not be restored to a healthy condition. But God does not desert the man to whom He has so often promised help and protection. It was wretched for him to be thrown into such great danger and distress and in his danger to be laughed at by his sons, as it were, and for grief to be added to grief. But he endures all this with wonderful patience, and he is freed by divine intervention. Our Lord God takes a hand, and so it all turns out to be good, as follows.

CHAPTER THIRTY-FIVE

1. *God said to Jacob: Arise, go up to Bethel, and dwell there; and make there an altar to the God who appeared to you when you fled from your brother Esau.*

S O FAR the patriarch Jacob has been in the greatest of grief and distress, one temptation rushing upon another. His only daughter had been defiled, and the Shechemites were slain. From this slaughter a great danger arose by which he himself and his whole house might have perished if God had not protected and rescued him when he was in danger. For all human help and protection was lacking, nor was there anyone to comfort the wretched and afflicted father. The sons replied proudly to his reproof and justified their very bad case. In this way, then, he hangs between heaven and earth, sick with cares and cruel griefs. To this is added weakness of faith, with which he is afflicted so severely that he forgets all the promises, which were truly splendid, and even his former rescues, in which he had experienced the hand and the help of the Lord.

Furthermore, these examples of the fathers are set forth for the churches to be read and learned so that the godly may see that they are disciplined in a wonderful manner through weakness and strength, through triumph and dejection, through good fortune and bad fortune so that by being tossed to and fro in various ways they might at length become martyrs, a very sweet odor and a "column of smoke," as is stated in the Song of Solomon (3:6), and that their flesh might be completely destroyed in them. Secondly, these examples teach us that our sufferings are trivial and light over against such troubles. Therefore let us seek consolation from here and prepare our hearts for patience. For we have not yet been smitten by such great difficulties and troubles as this one patriarch endured in his life.

But now in extreme necessity and despair, as it were, God comes to the help of His patriarch, as is stated in Ps. 9:9-10, and He is really a helper in need. For He does not forsake His saints who hope in Him, although they seem to be forsaken and cast off. For this is what it means not to forsake those who are nearly forsaken. But God makes an affirmative out of a negative. When the godly say: "There is no help in God: I am lost," God replies: "You are not lost, and you will not be lost as you conclude, but I shall give you a mouth and wisdom even in the extremity of the greatest dangers so that you are not forsaken." It certainly appears to be a forsaking, but in reality it is not. Therefore God again sends forth His Word and comforts the troubled old man. We have often stated that in the legends of the saintly fathers it should be especially noted when God speaks with them.[1] Therefore the stories of the Holy Bible excel the stories of all other nations. For they are holy and useful because God is speaking there. They should not be scanned in a superficial manner like the legends of dumb saints, where God is not speaking, but the worth and treasure of these stories should be recognized and unfolded, namely, the Word of God, which He is speaking to the saintly fathers. But this is what makes them golden legends,[2] in comparison with which the examples of the Eremites are obviously obscured. Their men, indeed, lived according to the precepts of God and in faith, and therefore they deserve to be judged to have been great men. But in no way are they like the fathers whom God met in tribulation and for whom He caused a new sun to rise. Other legends cause an uproar by reason of their great and unusual miracles, but the stories of the fathers are not to be estimated from such works but rather by this holiness which is the Word of God.

Therefore after God sees that Jacob is forsaken and despised and ridiculed by his own sons and that they are not very much distressed for having brought their father into a very critical situation and for having made him very sad, He is present in season and comforts him. For his groaning filled heaven and earth. "Your prayer and tears," He wants to say, "compel Me to come to your aid. The things which seemed to threaten you with destruction will not harm you at all. I am the Lord your God! The Shechemites were killed by My permission, and this whole tragedy was enacted that I might prove you, discipline you, and make you approved and chosen. But be of good courage! I will restrain and check all the fury and raging of the people and change your grief and lamentation into joy. You will be a lord in Shechem, for so it has been ordained by Me."

---

[1] See, for example, Luther's Works, 3, pp. 1—12.

[2] Cf. Luther's Works, 29, p. 79, n. 14.

When Rehoboam wanted to bring back the Ten Tribes, he was forbidden to do it, and the Lord says to Shemaiah (2 Chron. 11:4): "You shall not go up or fight against your brethren, the children of Israel. Return every man to his home, for this thing is from Me," namely, "that I might punish the father Solomon and his son Rehoboam." God also at times allows the Turk and the pope to go on a rampage, and again, when it is His will, He represses both. For He who has set a limit for the sea has also appointed definite boundaries for the ragings of the devil and the world, just as Christ says in the garden (Luke 22:51): "Let them have their way for now."

But God permits all these things to be done that He may teach us to pray, cry out, and groan. For this is the column of smoke ascending from the desert. In this manner a very great storm is calmed here, and Jacob receives very welcome consolation and peace of heart. "The citizens of neighboring cities will not overwhelm you," He says. "Disregard this storm and the raging of the people. Go on, preach, read, conduct public services, pray, and let Me take care how the storm and oncoming billows are to be calmed!"

Furthermore, Bethel is not far from Shechem, and we have had a discussion about its name above.[3] Jerusalem has 10 names, and many think that Bethel is Jerusalem or that it is Mount Moriah, on which the temple was built and which still retains the old name among the Turks today. David bought this hill from Araunah and built an altar there because Abraham had offered Isaac in the same place, and it has its name out of respect for God and His worship because Adam, Eve, Cain, and Abel made offerings on that mountain and it was always a holy place to the following patriarchs and set apart for the usages and exercises of divine worship. Later it was occupied by the Jebusites, but David recovered it and restored it.

But that Moriah is not Bethel is clear from the fact that Bethel was a place in the vicinity of Ai and Shechem. It was not in the tribe of Judah nor in the tribe of Benjamin. From this quarter idolaters arose with whom Hosea and the other prophets were in continual conflict. For they boasted that in this place God had spoken to the fathers and that it was more important and more reputable than the temple at Jerusalem. Lyra is of the opinion that Bethel is Moriah.[4] This does not seem likely to me, or, if they are one and the same place,

3 Cf. *Luther's Works*, 5, pp. 251—252.
4 Lyra *ad* Gen. 35:1, p. 98 verso, note "b."

[W, XLIV, 165, 166]

the name must have been changed later. According to the geographers, Bethel is not Moriah nor Jerusalem, or it was so called by paronomasia because it was the house of God.

The Lord orders the patriarch to build an altar at Bethel, and He reminds him of his former tribulation and comforts him with the examples of preceding temptations and rescues, as though He meant to say: "Recall the promises made to you before this time and reflect what happened to you previously when you fled from your brother Esau and what you suffered and in what a kindly manner I rescued and defended you." Furthermore, it was about 30 years from the flight of Jacob up to this time. For he was in Mesopotamia for 20 years, lived for eight years in Shechem, and was on his journey for two years, and almost all of that time he was harassed by the hatred of his brother. "Remember, therefore," the Lord went on to say, "that you also had a promise of protection previously in Bethel and how I rescued you like a father from many great temptations and kept My promises faithfully." At this statement Jacob breathed again and recovered his courage. The wound inflicted by his sons was suddenly healed, because the Word of God makes alive and gives comfort.

However, it is not expressed in the text how God spoke with Jacob, whether it was through a dream or a clear vision or even through the person of a prophet. For God is accustomed to employ these three methods. But at that time there was no prophet or patriarch present because they were all dead, unless his father Isaac perhaps sent a messenger to his son Jacob or a letter by which he ordered him to return and to go up to Bethel. But in whatever way that was done, it is enough that we have heard that God spoke with him. In whatever manner He spoke, it is certain that this is the Word of God. But such is the perversity of human nature that we do not believe that we are hearing the Word of God whenever He speaks through a man. For we weigh the Word according to the authority and weight of the speaker. We hear a man speaking as a man, and we think that it is a man's word and so neglect it and scorn it. We should, however, give thanks to God for placing the authority of the Word in a man's mouth, or that of a minister who is like us in all respects, and who can speak with us, console, and encourage us by means of the Word.

But we do not recognize the greatness of this blessing, and we are not thankful. Therefore the legends of the fathers are more preeminent also in this respect, not only because of the Word but also because of the faith of the patriarchs, by which they gave firm and certain assent to the Word. When we hear the minister teaching and pronouncing the absolution, we cannot come to the conclusion that we have been taught and absolved and have received consolation through the Divine Majesty. We say, of course, that it is the word which we have heard in the church, but the word of a pastor. But it is the Word not of a pastor, or Peter, or any minister but that of the Divine Majesty. Our stories, accordingly, are colder on account of colder faith, but in the fathers faith was much more ardent, even as it shone forth in a wonderful manner in their whole life. Therefore they deserve to be called the sacred stories of the fathers, and they are such.

But if we believed that God is speaking to us through parents, pastors, and ministers of the Word, we should feel our hearts inflamed by a wonderful joy. For we should glory as follows, saying: "I am baptized." By whom? Was it not by a pastor? By no means, but by the Holy Spirit. I have been absolved by the Holy Spirit, by God Himself. Why, then, should I be afraid? Before whom should I be alarmed? Why should I be troubled about my sin? Accordingly, in comparison with the fathers, we are hardly little children, and still on the breast. For they saw many scandals of idolatry among the neighboring nations, and yet they firmly embraced the Word of God. We have numberless examples of faith, both from our own and former ages, set before our eyes, and still we do not believe.

First, then, it is very necessary to observe God's words carefully when He is speaking, and then the faith of the believers. Then you will see true miracles in the stories of the saints, who by faith in the Word overcame all evils of the world and the devils. This victory they obtained not by means of their own wisdom, which was consumed, according to the well-known statement in Ps. 107:27, but because the Word came to comfort them, and by means of faith by which they clung to the Word, for "our faith is the victory which overcomes the world" (cf. 1 John 5:4). God causes us to triumph and conquer through His Word, by which He raises us up and confirms us. This, therefore, is a glorious consolation which God shows to Jacob. For it is just as if He were saying: "I have death and life and all times in My hand. Only believe, and you will be saved!"

But He adds the command about raising an altar, that is, about instituting worship, and there this rule is to be noted, that without the Holy Spirit no method or means of worshiping God is to be taken up. Jacob, for example, does not on the basis of his own judgment fabricate the idea that the house of God is in this place, but he has it from revelation. When he slept here formerly and saw the angels of God ascending and descending, he added: "This is none other than the house of God" (cf. Gen. 28:17). Altars are not to be raised and acts of worship are not to be invented by one's own rashness, but respect must be paid to the commandment of God. In later times Jeroboam erected a calf in Bethel that the people might sacrifice and worship there. In order to obscure the commandment of God about building the temple at Jerusalem, which Solomon had had, he heaped high praise on this commandment given to the patriarch Jacob about raising an altar and instituting worship in Bethel. For this, he contended, was much more ancient and therefore more distinguished than that old commandment about building the temple at Jerusalem.

Before the present time also, although God was to be sought and recognized in His Word and sacraments, the pope, casting these aside, invented relics and memorials of the saints, and by these he imposed on the wretched people the idea that they should believe that the worship of God was bound to these matters. Such a stage of madness was reached that in some places men displayed the shoes of Joseph, the milk of the Virgin Mary, and the breeches of St. Francis as relics. To these were added the fictitious and prodigious works of the saints like Francis, Dominic, and others, whose holiness they estimated by their life and works. For men alienated from the truth have to be deceived and infatuated in this way. But if you carefully unfold Holy Scripture, you will see that nothing pleases God without the Word.

2. *So Jacob said to his household and to all who were with him: Put away the foreign gods that are among you and purify yourselves and change your garments.*

Jacob is satisfied with the consolation which he hears in the Word of God. So the storm becomes silent, and a great calm ensues on the sea; winter passes away; the flowers appear, and the nightingale sings. Therefore he gives thanks to God with joy, saying: "Blessed be the Lord God!" His sorrow and trouble cease, for the light of the sun which has risen disperses the darkness of tribulation. He also repeats the very words which he heard God speaking and the temptations of about 30 years. But he is not yet done with all troubles, for there still remains the horrible temptation in the case of his son

Joseph. However, he gives thanks for his former victories and makes preparation for the journey to Bethel, where the Lord had first comforted him.

Moses, moreover, says that Jacob spoke to his household and all who were with him. Here he distinguishes between members of the household and outsiders. The members of the household were his wives, children, servants, and maids. By others "who were with him" he means those whose hearts God had touched so that they joined themselves to Jacob's house, either because of the hope of intermarriage or because they were added from the booty and spoils of the Shechemites. For I have often stated that it is quite credible that when the patriarchs were teaching, many of the heathen flocked to them, for they saw that the patriarchs were godly and holy men and that God was with them, and therefore they heard and embraced their doctrine.

For when ambassadors and preachers were sent by God into the world, we must not think that their ministry passed away without fruit. Not only were those joined to them who were of the blood of the patriarchs but also outsiders such as those who were confederates of Abraham above, Eshcol and Aner, who all undoubtedly heard the Word, and likewise Abimelech.[5] Later on, Joseph in Egypt, Daniel in Babylon, and Jonah in Nineveh taught the doctrine of God. Therefore God gathered a church in the world not only from the one family of the patriarchs but from all nations to which the Word made its way.

In this manner many of the Canaanites attached themselves to Jacob and believed his word, and these were rescued by God from impending evils and idolatry. Thus when Rahab the harlot in Joshua 2 saw that the whole city was in danger, she attached herself to the spies and begged that they might save her and her family. For the hearts of some to whom the godly come in the world are always touched, and such I think were those whom Jacob brought with him. For the Word is not taught without fruit, but it gathers a congregation in the world not only from those who hear it by word of mouth and who are in the church of the patriarchs, but it also brings in outsiders and strangers who have been preordained.

An additional factor was the connection with the Canaanites because of the marriages of the 12 patriarchs who married heathen women. Judah married Tamar, a Canaanite woman, and Joseph mar-

[5] Cf. *Luther's Works*, 2, pp. 372, 398.

ried the daughter of an Egyptian priest. This was a union of Gentile and Israelite blood, so that Ruth the Moabitess also became the mother of Christ. For God is not only the God of the Jews but also the God of the Gentiles, although He has published His grace and Word in the world through the Jews. Finally, there were also commercial ties between the patriarchs and the heathen, and from this there often arose the opportunity to speak about God and religion. For they were not dumb pieces of wood and stones, but in their conversation with men they invited strangers to themselves with special friendliness so that they might become associates of their doctrine and religion.

It was a very beautiful sermon of the patriarch Jacob to his household and church gathered from members of his house and strangers and by which he exhorted them to the correction of faults which were clinging to the church. The first sin which he reproved was in conflict with the First Commandment, namely, idolatry. This he wanted corrected and purged away. "Put away the foreign gods that are among you," he said. For this is the head and fountain from whence all other faults flow, and all reformation is useless if the doctrine is not purged first. For behold the folly of the pope and of all subsequent councils! They first ordain certain ceremonies; they order the priests to wear long attire and to read the canonical hours and Masses carefully; they forbid dicing and harlotry. They call this the reformation of the church. Some such course will be decided on in a council, if ever there is one.[6] For the cardinals and bishops are stupid bunglers who think nothing of the Word and doctrine and do not understand or care about it.

It is necessary then for the ax to be laid to the root of the tree (cf. Matt. 3:10) and for the head of the serpent to be attacked, for it can withstand without danger the blows to its body, however heavy they may be. But if you strike its head even with the smallest of rods, it is immediately killed. Moreover, the special might of Satan is set on attacking and destroying the Word and doctrine which is contained in the First Commandment. This he attacks very keenly. Accordingly, before all things we must make an effort to have the true and certain doctrine regarding God. Then a true reformation and establishment of churches can be instituted on this basis. When Ferdinand was preparing the defense against the incursions of the Turks, he proclaimed fasts, processions, and supplications to the

---

[6] See Introduction, p. x.

saints.[7] Of what use are these except that they provide sport for Satan? An effort should rather have been made that sincere faith and pure doctrine concerning the worship of God should be taught. But they invert the order and defend manifest errors in doctrine and establish the madness of idolatry. Later, they are eager to placate God's wrath with external rites and supplications. So God is provoked and mocked in a twofold manner.

Let us therefore remember the command of Jacob, who says: "Put away the foreign gods," that is, remove the scandals of doctrine and the scandals of ungodliness, and let the people truly learn to fear God and to trust God. Then at length there will be a place for long garments, tonsures, and the like.

Furthermore, the two words for "foreign gods" are not set forth in the same number in the Hebrew. "Gods" is put in the plural, but "strange" in the singular, in the genitive case. "Gods of a stranger or of a strange matter!" Moreover, there is an antiphrasis in the word נֵכָר, for it means both unknown, or strange, and known. Below, both meanings occur in one verse. Joseph knew his brothers and made himself unknown to his brothers, that is, he did not want to be recognized; he made himself unknown. This figure is used in all languages. The Latins, for example, call a war, which is not good at all, *bellum,* and a wood *lucus,* which does not shine at all.[8] The Germans have many such expressions, for example: *Halt, ich will dir rathen, will dir helfen* ("Come! I will advise you, I will help you"). This is spoken by antiphrasis, and the meaning is that I would like to punish or destroy another man. Likewise we say: *Der Henker kann dem Dieb wohl raten,* etc. ("The executioner will manage to give the thief good advice!"). The meaning of this word is the same, "gods of a known or unknown thing." But the proper meaning must be sought from idiomatic usage. In this passage נֵכָר must mean "unknown." War *(bellum)* has its name from a word meaning beautiful *(bellus),* and indeed, to the inexperienced it seems very beautiful *(bellum)* and sweet, just as vengeance, too, is sweet, but we learn from experience that it is a very bitter and sad thing because it is *bellum* by antiphrasis — honey is sown, and mustard comes up. So also at the outset a new form of worship has a wonderful effect, and it seems most certain and the truth itself and appears to be pure

[7] Apparently a reference to the battles between Ferdinand I (1503—1564) and the Turks at Vienna in 1529 and again in 1532 and 1541.

[8] Quintilian, *Institutiones oratoriae,* I, 6, 34.

nectar (for the sectarians are accustomed to promise and boast that there is nothing more certain, nothing better or more outstanding), yet in the end we experience that it was pure darkness, errors, and ignorance. Therefore it is called נֵכָר, that is, "known," as though you meant to say "not known at all."

Such idioms remind students of theology that a knowledge of the Hebrew language is very necessary. Therefore I exhort them to put some effort into the learning of this language. As for the rest, when the human mind has once wandered from the true and only God, it becomes necessary to follow an infinite multitude and confusion of gods. He who has once forsaken God finds it impossible to abide by one definite deity, that is, in one religion or definite worship of God, just as there is an infinite succession of sins through unbelief, or the loss of faith.

It is possible to see this in all the histories. Israel, after departing from God, worships Baal, Chemosh, Astaroth, etc. After we fell away from Christ, the Son of God, our Savior, there followed Dominic, Francis, Vincentius, Christopher, Clara, etc., and innumerable other new cults which the crowd of priests and monks devised daily without measure because man's lust could not be satisfied in any manner. Accordingly, to turn aside from the oneness of God is to be plunged into a multitude of unknown gods. For this reason Jacob called them "gods of a strange matter," that is, of an unknown and foolish worship which nevertheless seems very well known and very holy. Let us therefore apply our hearts and all our efforts to the one God, who is Father, Son, and Holy Spirit, and let us remain in the Mediator Christ. This is the first part of the reformation.

The Jews understand the strange gods here as statues or images of idols,[9] with which they, indeed, have always abounded, and they had as many gods as there are demons in hell. This we find to be the case also under the papacy. But Jacob does not only understand them to be golden or silver images but what is attached to them or the state of mind produced by them, which is the head, so to say, of a silver or golden statue, namely, the worship. For otherwise there is nothing sinful in a statue, but I can make use of it, just as Rachel above used the idols of her father Laban when she put them under her bottom. But the sin that condemns is the trust of the heart which is offered to a statue, although the image itself is

9 Lyra *ad* Gen. 35:2, p. 99 recto.

the occasion for evil. But there is an affection and an idol in the heart previously, just as the people before our own time and kings even now run to statues and worship the images of Mary of Ratisbon [10] and other saints, and this is really worshiping wood and stone. For faith which is owed to God the Creator alone is transferred and offered to a silver statue, not the Creator. What can be said or done that is more foolish? For why, by the same reasoning, do you not worship the talers and money in your purse? Therefore Jacob is not only paying regard to external images, but before all things he wants God to be worshiped sincerely and the doctrine to be pure, and so he begins his reformation from the First Commandment.

The second part, "purify yourselves," includes the sins of the Second Table. He wants them also to be corrected. "In the first place," he says, "the gods who, you think, are known gods are quite unknown. Accordingly, put them away and then do penance for your sins against your neighbor. Let there not be among you thieves, whoremongers, and adulterers, so that body and heart may be whole, chaste, and innocent of offense against your neighbor." This is external righteousness.

The third part, the matter concerning the changing of garments, is quite external and ceremonial. "Lay aside your rather dirty garments," he means to say, "that we may celebrate the Sabbath; adorn yourselves also with an external act of worship." For such ceremonies are nevertheless necessary, even though they do not justify. For a certain respect is also owed to external ceremonies, gestures, and customs so that there may be honorable and orderly gatherings in that place where the Word is taught and where invocation is made and other sacred acts are performed. But before all things the heart should be well ordered by true faith towards God and reconciliation and then by love towards one's neighbor which is perfect and without any offense. Thirdly, there should be external discipline in assemblies, that all things may be done decently and in order, according to 1 Cor. 14:40. But those who neglect these matters indicate that they believe nothing and despise God and the church. For in an ecclesiastical assembly we should not conduct ourselves as if we were in a tavern. Some dignity is required here.

This is a beautiful reformation by which the doctrine is first purged and then the sins are purged — usury, thefts, plunderings, and

[10] Luther may be referring to the shrine of Mariahilf, near Amberg at Ratisbon (or Regensburg).

lusts. Finally, a reminder is given that the people and priests should dress in an honorable manner in the temple. Our reformers overthrow the order. For they begin with shoes and clothing and neglect what is superior and more important. It should rather have come to pass that the heart is pure inwardly through faith and that the body and its members should also be pure outwardly by means of love and ceremonies in clothing and customs.

Finally, in the command which is given to Jacob the idiom should be noted. For in the reading of the Bible we should pay attention to this point, that we seek from the Hebrew text defense and testimonies for our doctrine concerning the plurality of Persons in God. For the words are: "Gods (plural) spoke (singular): make an altar for God (singular)." This idiom must be carefully observed, since God speaks concerning God. For although the Jews circumvent it and say that the change of persons is customary in Holy Scripture — a fact which we, to be sure, also acknowledge — we nevertheless do not entertain the Jewish sophistries. We cannot convert them, just as we cannot convert other stubborn men. Because it agrees with the New Testament, we retain τὸ ῥητόν ("the literal wording") in this passage.

Accordingly, where God (or Gods) is speaking about God, there the three Persons are expressed and the one God. But the God for whom the altar is to be made we understand as the Son of God, who is one true God with the Father and the Holy Spirit, as we have stated above concerning the man wrestling with Jacob.[11] These matters instruct us and strengthen us in an excellent manner. For Moses was not inebriated when he transmitted these matters, nor was the Holy Spirit, who spoke through him. Whether it is an angel or Moses speaking with us, it is God's Word. This, then, is what God wants to say: "If you honor that God who appeared to you in Bethel, you will honor the Father and the Son and the Holy Spirit." For when it is stated that אֱלֹהִים, "Gods," spoke, the plurality of Persons in the deity is expressed.

3. *Then let us arise and go up to Bethel, that we may make there an altar to the God who answered me in the day of my distress and has been with me wherever I have gone.*

It must be carefully observed that in the story of so many patriarchs no slaughterings of sacrificial animals are described or cele-

[11] See p. 125.

brated, although Holy Scripture above often says of Abraham, and Isaac, and Jacob that they built altars. Concerning Noah, Adam, Cain, and Abel we read that they made sacrifices and, indeed, offered burnt sacrifices which the fathers undoubtedly made according to the ritual which Moses describes later, so that they slaughtered and roasted lambs, oxen, and goats and burnt a part as a burnt offering to the Lord and ate a part themselves. What other use would there have been for altars? Therefore, wherever Scripture mentions them, there without a doubt there were sacrifices of burnt offerings and offerings of cake, flour, incense, and the other things which are described in Leviticus. But this is worthy of note, that these patriarchs also raised altars and that Moses nevertheless does not make mention of sacrifices and offerings. But he leaves it to the reader to draw the rational consequence that there were sacrifices, burnt offerings, and libations, etc. where altars were established.

Again, however, when Moses deals with the sacrifices and burnt offerings of the Levites, he relates these slayings so carefully that he does not even pass over the hair, the skins, or the excrement. You will find there nothing but offerings of incense and slayings, etc. He does not say what God said and what those suffered and did who made the sacrifices. On the other hand, in the stories of the fathers nothing at all is said about the slaying of oxen or sheep, etc., and what part they kept and what they burnt. But the chief thing is added, namely, the sermons which were held by the fathers at the altars. Moses cooks, roasts, and seethes; in these legends nothing but an altar is set up without any mention of incense, wine, or any offering.

Jacob, accordingly, wants to build an altar. For what use? "To the God who answered me in the day of my distress, etc.," he says. These are true altars, in comparison with which the sacrifices of bulls and goats are only shadows, so to say, and external signs. But to preach, to hear the Word, to give thanks, and to pray, these are the true sacrifices. These Moses describes in the fathers. Those external sacrifices he hardly touches with a word. "I will proclaim there," says Jacob, "how God was with me wherever I went and how He heard me." Therefore to make offerings and sacrifices is really nothing else but to confess and praise God, namely, that He is our God who wants to hear us according to His promise and to be with us in every tribulation and to rescue us from death. For this is the meaning of His being our God and of our giving Him thanks — that He has hitherto cared for us and preserved us and that He will also care for us hereafter, even though He allows us to be tempted almost beyond our strength.

In this manner and to this end it is right for churches to be built. But when these sacrifices are missing, it is more correct for them to be called stables for beasts and pigsties than altars and churches. For church assemblies have been ordained for this purpose, that we may learn concerning God that He is our God, who permits us to be afflicted for our salvation. This is what it means to preach about faith, our patience, and God's mercy and government. You should not conclude that there is a church and an altar where this does not sound forth, even as under the papacy the churches were only theaters of the devil, who mocks and kills souls in a most wretched manner.

However, in time God ordained the Levitical slayings and sacrifices for an external sign so that the rude people might be drawn by some outward show to the true worship and knowledge of God, just as He has given us Baptism, the Keys, Absolution, and the Lord's Supper not on account of the work itself that has been performed, as the papists dream, but that we may recall the blessings of Christ, who says: "This do in remembrance of Me, so that the heavenly message may sound forth in your midst, so that you may call upon Me, so that you may give thanks, so that you may hope in Me and be patient in bearing the cross until I come and rescue you from all evils." This we teach carefully and practice publicly in the congregation and privately among the sick. We do not slaughter bullocks, sheep, etc., but we praise God. For similarly Jacob does not say here that he will raise an altar to make sacrifices, although that also is included, but that he may celebrate and praise God, who heard him in the day of his distress, namely, when he fled from the face of Esau, his brother.

He acknowledges that God heard him. Accordingly, he was constant in prayer, seeking, knocking, and making invocation. Esau and Satan were his taskmasters, who urged and compelled him to cry to God and implore His assistance. For God wants us to call upon Him, and He wants to hear us and be our God. Above we have often heard that Jacob was involved in very great difficulties and that in his state of alarm he had lost God in some measure. In his flight to Mesopotamia, for example, he was as wretched as he could be, and later, in Laban's house, he was afflicted by infinite ills of which he was unworthy. At length, on his return from Mesopotamia, he had to struggle with the Son of God.

His whole life, accordingly, has been beset by disasters, and this is what he means when he says: "the days of my distress." For a period of almost 30 years it was necessary to endure one evil after the other. Surely God does not seem to be merciful and kind here, does He? He certainly is, for it is added that He hears prayer. Psalm 66:16-20 proclaims the same fact concerning Him: "Come and hear, all you who fear God, and I will tell what He has done for me. I cried aloud to Him, and He was extolled with my tongue, etc. . . . Truly God has listened; He has given heed to the voice of my prayer. Blessed be God, because He has not rejected my prayer or removed His steadfast love from me!" He Himself is very ready to hear; let us only be ready to cry out to Him. That He hears is a matter of certainty, for He Himself has spoken, and He Himself has given the instruction (John 16:24, 23): "Ask, and you will receive." "Truly, truly, I say to you, if you ask anything of the Father, He will give it to you in My name." Likewise He says (John 15:7): "If you abide in Me, and My words abide in you, ask whatever you will, and it shall be done for you." Therefore, we should be censured for not asking, not crying out, and not pressing on. Jacob's example, however, should be an invitation to us, for he praises God not in regard to his own works or sacrifices, which were also performed to declare his gratitude for God's deliverance. But he does so because he has a God who makes promises, hears him, defends him, and rescues him from all evils which at times seemed quite irremediable.

We should carefully learn this and take note of it. The example of our first parents teaches the same thing. When, after the Fall, they were summoned by God in the words "Adam, where are you?" (Gen. 3:9), they found themselves in the struggle with eternal death. But when God says later that the Seed of the woman will crush the serpent's head and testifies that their generation will remain and that He will preserve the human race and that the Seed to crush the serpent's head must be born (Gen. 3:15), they are raised up again and made happy. Nor are they terrified at the statement (Gen. 3:19, 16): "In the sweat of your face, etc." "In pain you shall bring forth children." "I will gladly bear the pain of childbirth and death," said Eve, "only let there be an end to God's judgment and wrath which we have incurred by biting into the apple and by the transgression of His commandment. If a bodily punishment takes the place of the eternal one, I shall bear it with a calm heart." Thus our whole life is most wretched and a truly bitter apple, but it is still vital and vivifying. Eve's other apple was very sweet and very delectable to the sight, but it brought on eternal death. Therefore it is better to endure troubles with the hope of eternal deliverance than to avoid them and rush into eternal ruin. We see that the prophets and patriarchs suffered exactly the same things and gloried in afflictions, as the Psalms and many statements of the apostles in Rom. 5 and elsewhere testify. Let us therefore persuade our hearts that we do not abandon the worship or invocation of God because of any fear of evil. For since I am safe and saved from eternal death and damnation, let the Turks and Tartars, the pope and plagues of every kind assail us without measure; I shall not be broken in spirit, for I have that compensation and blessed exchange by which I know that death has been changed into life, destruction into eternal salvation, and sin into righteousness. For I know that for the godly all things work together for good (cf. Rom. 8:28).

Our ingratitude, however, is to be deplored. Because of it we do not acknowledge God or give Him thanks that the Son of God has changed eternal death into temporal punishment. For we want to live agreeably and in ease in this life, and we shudder at and avoid even a small cross. But there is need of the mortification of the flesh, and this obedience must be shown under the cross with a calm mind so that we are grateful because we know that Christ died for our sins. He Himself testifies that His yoke is easy and His burden light (cf. Matt. 11:30). Finally, since Jacob praises God with such great joy as his Liberator from bodily temptations, how much more appropriate will it be for us to confess and give thanks for eternal and temporal blessings!

To the fact of being heard he adds that God "has been with me wherever I have gone." He was truly with Jacob and attested it by His actual work of liberation. But this was quite hidden and not apparent. It was as Jeremiah says (Lam. 3:22): "It is of the Lord's mercies that we are not consumed." For as far as appearances and outward sight was concerned, the devil, Laban, and despair were with him, but Jacob says: "During all of these 30 years the Lord has been with me."

This is the true method of making sacrifices which was employed by the fathers and prevailed also at the time when the pomp of the Levitical sacrifices reigned supreme. For Moses did not pay any special regard to the temple, altars, sheep, and oxen which David and

Solomon offered. For they are only offscourings and shells or peels of the true acts of worship which God requires for a time and uses as external marks for our sakes in order to stir up our senses from a state of dullness. But the true worship is expressed in the New Testament with its "This do in remembrance of Me; baptize in My name, etc." It is horrible, however, that the pope makes a sacrifice and an *opus operatum* [12] out of the Mass and abandons the real kernel of worship, which is to give thanks, pray, hope, and confess even under the cross and in disaster. He retains the peel, namely, the work and the sacrifice of our hands, although we do not eat or drink our flesh and blood here.

But the true acts of worship are described in Ps. 50:14 in the words: "Offer to God a sacrifice of thanksgiving and pay your vows to the Most High." External rites serve these and stir you up to praise Him who hears, rescues, governs, and saves so that you trust Him, endure His hand, learn to be mortified and die, and in all these respects show forth a patience worthy of godly men. This is the sacrifice of our body and a reasonable sacrifice (cf. Rom. 12:1).

4. *So they gave to Jacob all the foreign gods that they had, and the rings that were in their ears; and Jacob hid them under the oak which was near Shechem.*

You see that the patriarch had an obedient church and one that believed the Word of God, because they immediately abandon the foreign gods and accept reformation from their teacher. Accordingly, the whole body of the church is purged and beautifully established. Later also Moses, like a rhapsodist, gathered together many things from the rites and ceremonies of the fathers. Among other images, however, there were the תְּרָפִים which Rachel had stolen above from her father. They called the idols or statues gods not because they were mad enough to regard and worship wood, gold, and silver as a god, but they bound to that place the god who hears and has regard for that worship, thought out by human rashness. Of such silver, golden, wooden, and stone images the papacy was full. For although we knew that all these were carved and formed by the hands of craftsmen, we nevertheless fell down before the statues and worshiped them on the supposition that God has regard for this or that image. We also

[12] That is, a work that avails through the sheer performance, regardless of the attitude of the recipient.

set up the fiction that Saints Barbara, Anne, and Christopher individually had regard for their statues and heard our prayers. This was Egyptian darkness and exactly the same raving madness which was formerly among the heathen in the invention of an infinite number of deities. For this is the way they worshiped Juno, Bacchus, Ceres, Priapus, etc.

But I do not think that there were golden images in the individual houses but wooden ones such as our people had in their homes before our time. It was a kind of wooden image adorned with silver and golden jewels. Dionysius, for example, plundered the statue of Jupiter by taking the golden and silver ornaments from it, such as the golden braided work, clasps, coral rosaries, etc., that are in use among us. Such, I think, were also the earrings, so that they had reference to the statues and not to the worshipers of the statues. Lyra, however, inclines to the view that Moses understands the ornaments either as miters or priestly garments which those used who were about to worship or offer sacrifices, either priests or others.[13] For such ornamentation was employed in all worship forms, true and false. To me, however, the more correct meaning seems to be that the earrings were the ornaments of the idols.

The word נֶזֶם itself signifies a little moon or semicircle of gold like a new moon, by which they adorned the brow from one ear to the other as though with a diadem. Today we call it *Perlin*, or golden braid or fillet. Aaron also had a נֶזֶם among his priestly ornaments. Later, kings used the same and made their diadems from them. It was therefore customary at that time to adorn the heads of statues with such little moons out of reverence for the deity so that they might have some appearance of sanctity. However, according to Lyra's view, it could also happen that priests used them.

Jacob, however, heaped all these into one pile and buried them. The honesty and obedience of these people was truly outstanding. They promptly and readily handed over what they regarded as very precious. The greatest part was plundered as booty from the Shechemites, who were idolaters. Moreover, he persuaded those of his household and the strangers by his excellent sermon to remove these things so that he himself might go down to Bethel with a church purged from idolatry. But why did he bury the idols, whether of gold and silver or wooden ones decorated with gold, under the oak? Why did

---

[13] Lyra *ad* Gen. 35:4, p. 99 recto, note "a."

he not rather melt them down and give the money in alms to the poor or put it to other uses? What was the use of gold and silver buried in the earth? My reply is that he did it because of the abuse of these things, which, he knew, God utterly rejected. He himself wanted to despise ill-gotten gains utterly since he had other resources derived from the blessing of God to expend on the poor.

In Deuteronomy (7:25) Moses orders all the graven articles of the heathen to be burned, and he does not want them to be sought by the people of Israel or kept in their homes so that they themselves might not become abominable to God as the graven articles were. From this it is clear that they were some kind of wooden images adorned with clasps and little caps and mantles made of gold and silver. For gold is not burned. But the kings perhaps had gold and silver idols. Moses had this commandment from the fathers that idols were to be simply cast away and burned as something ungodly and abominable, although there could be some use for the gold and silver. At this time God wanted the First Table to be so pure that He did not want even the gold and silver from which the idols had been cast to serve the uses of the saints, although in themselves they are good creations of God, because they had been contaminated by idolatrous acts of worship by which God is offended. Jacob buries the idols in the ground in this manner to testify that he is uncontaminated by the plague which is called idolatry. The same is preserved in the Law of Moses to terrify an uncultured people so that it may learn to flee and execrate this abomination.

We in the New Testament know that an idol is nothing in the world, as Paul testifies in 1 Cor. 8:4. Hence the holy martyrs and bishops melted down the images and converted them to godly uses, for the support of the church's ministers or of other godly and poor people. They did right, because the ceremonial laws of an uncultured people had ceased. It had need of this severity when it did not have the Spirit but was simply ruled by law and coerced by external discipline that it might not fall into idolatry. We are also accustomed to use certain terrifying objects to scare children from vices or other things that are not permitted, as we do when we exhibit painted dragons or misshapen monsters and compare shameful things to them so that the children may learn to shudder even at the mention or sight of these things. This people also received such a pedagogy, for Moses forbade idols to be sought or brought into homes so that they might learn that they were very hateful to God and an abomination to Him.

Adults, however, do not need these things, and so we do not observe this law, and there is no need for it. For what do we now have in the churches that was not produced by the most disgraceful idolatry of the popes? There is not a prince or state that supports its church servants or schoolteachers with its own new stipends, although some of the ecclesiastical properties were acquired in an honest manner and donated to the church for the preservation of studies and schools. But what was contributed for Masses, vigils, and the worship of saints is nothing else but the wages of a harlot and the most disgraceful idolatry. This silver and gold is all עם, that is, they are earrings, they are clasps of idols contributed for the retention of superstition and idolatry. But we use evangelical freedom so that we do not throw away or bury gold but take pains that it should be transferred to a godly and legitimate use and that what has been given hitherto to idolatrous Mass priests should in turn be distributed to godly teachers and ministers of the Gospel. Would that we might be able to obtain this from those harpies who unjustly divert the ecclesiastical revenues to themselves and leave to the pastors or scholars hardly enough to keep away hunger!

In the duchy of the elector of Saxony parishes and schools are supported from this source. We concede that the prince should retain what is left or distribute it to poor scholars. Therefore when it is asked why we do not also throw away the ill-gotten gains of the Babylonian whore, we reply that it is being spent for godly purposes and that we have succeeded in bringing it about that the money which formerly served the devil is henceforth serving God. Among a people under the Law a severer discipline was required because of dangers from the neighboring nations, since the light of the Gospel was not yet as great as it is now nor did they have this time of grace which by God's blessing has shined upon us today. Therefore the ceremonial laws do not bind us.

5. *And as they journeyed, a terror from God fell upon the cities that were round about them, so that they did not pursue the sons of Jacob.*

This was a fortunate and safe journey under such a Leader and Commander as Jacob had. It is an illustrious and memorable example which testifies that believers and those who cling to the Word of God have the protection of God, the Creator of all things, against all the gates of hell (cf. Matt. 16:18). What was spoken by the prophet is true: "Those who are with us are more than those who are with them" (2 Kings 6:16), provided only that we can determine this firmly enough and believe it. For this weakness of faith and unbelief really enfeebles and crushes the hearts of the godly. Nevertheless, there are always some who in one way or another retain this consolation. In the midst of these dangers Jacob himself was weaker in faith than any of the members of his household, as we have heard on several occasions. Nevertheless, the ineffable groanings in his heart filled heaven and earth and aroused God to show forth consolation and help.

These matters are intended for our learning and consolation (cf. Rom. 15:4), so that we conclude for certain that we cannot be forsaken, whether we believe firmly or weakly. For even the weak are defended. Thus Paul orders the weak in faith to be received (Rom. 14:1), although that weakness of faith is in neophytes who are still being trained in the perception of the rudiments of Christian doctrine. But the weakness of great men, like Jacob and other saints, consists not in the Word or doctrine but in temptation when they seem to have nearly lost faith. This is a faith in difficulties, not weakness of the untrained, and yet these also GOD receives and protects, as this example and countless others testify. But He tempers the life of the saints in this manner so that we do not become proud and do not "rely on ourselves but on God who raises the dead," as 2 Cor. 1:9 says. It is the work of the Creator to enrich the poor, to raise from the dead, to encourage the afflicted, and to cast down the proud. First, then, He strengthened Jacob with the Word when He ordered him to go up to Bethel, and He added the sign of protection and divine help, the commandment about raising an altar. For since it was necessary for him to build an altar and to bring an offering, it was necessary that he remain alive. It was as though He meant to say: "You will not be destroyed by the neighboring nations, but you will go up and bring an offering in Bethel." Third, there is the additional deed itself and the experience. For He struck terror into the neighbors who were grumbling and indignant that they could not pursue the sons of Jacob and the old father with his wretched and unwarlike company because of the slaughter perpetrated by the strangers in their neighborhood and in their very sight. For the

Lord is the General and Commander of this army which Jacob led, and He comforts him with this word: "Be brave and joyful in heart. I shall fight for you without arms and without violence. I shall only terrify their hearts so that they do not dare to attack you or pursue you."

Who, I ask, would dare to engage with this General, who first conquers and lays low the strength of the heart, so that when this has been laid low, all strength and members of the whole body must totter and be crushed? Those who have experience in warfare are accustomed to watch for this and to make a prediction about the outcome of the battle. When the opposing armies have been drawn up, they immediately see which of the two armies will conquer. For in this army, they say, there shines forth a special alertness both in the men and in the horses. On the other hand, in the one which is to be conquered all appears to be sluggish and dead, as it were. Soldiers with experience affirm this, and it agrees with the Holy Scriptures, for victory is from heaven according to Ps. 144:10: "Who givest victory to kings." Likewise in Ps. 33:17 we read: "The war horse is a vain hope for victory and by its great might it cannot save." When God wants to grant a victory, He at the same time also adds alacrity and strength to hearts; if God gives, it is given. But when He takes away courage from the enemy and crushes them, then also their weapons fall from their hands. It is stated in Ps. 76:6 (cf. v. 5): "At Thy rebuke, O God of Jacob, both rider and horse lay stunned. They have slept their sleep, and all the men have found no riches in their hands."

In this manner God comforts Jacob with word and work in his great temptation. For as they were setting forth, the neighbors were so overwhelmed by terror that no one dared even to make a sound, to say nothing of drawing a sword. For He shattered the power of their bows, as well as shields, swords, and warfare so that they were not ready and brave enough to fight, although they were otherwise very powerful and warlike. Nor did this happen through the services or stratagems of Simeon or Levi but by the power of the promise and the faith of the patriarch and his own, however weak it may have been.

The Holy Spirit reminds us by this example that we should learn the doctrine of creation correctly, namely, that all things are in God's hand, and that we should accustom and encourage ourselves to confident trust in our Creator, which, to be sure, is still very small and weak in us. For if we firmly concluded that God is our Creator, we would certainly believe that He has heaven and earth in His hands and all things which are contained by these. To be sure, if we saw the world shattered and falling into ruin with all the elements and hanging over our necks, we would nevertheless say: "Even in falling you will not fall unless God wills it." Even if it were hanging over our head, we would say: "You will do no harm and not overwhelm me. And even if it seems good to God that I should be overwhelmed by your huge mass, let what is good in the Lord's eyes be done. My times are in His hands (cf. Ps. 31:15). But if it seems otherwise, I shall scoff at you, O heaven and earth, together with the Turks and papists and all other ragings of the whole world."

In this way sure and final devastation was hanging over the house of Jacob. Nor were the Canaanites lacking in strength and will, plans, arms, and manpower. But what hindered them? The Lord said: "No! Here shall your proud waves be stayed," as He says in Job (38:11) and as Ps. 65:7 says: "Who dost still the roaring of the seas, the roaring of their waves, the tumult of the peoples. The nations are in turmoil, and those who dwell at earth's farthest bounds are afraid of Thy signs." We live in the midst of the sea itself, and as the waters of the Flood were 15 cubits higher than the loftiest mountains, so also now the ocean is three ells higher than the earth. But why does it not overwhelm us? Because God has set a limit for the sea (cf. Prov. 8:29). Its waves, indeed, are billowing and crashing against the shores just as if they were about to rush out onto the land, but that attack is checked and restrained by God.

The same can be seen in all the threats of the world in raising a tumult against the church. The Turk is like an ocean swelling and turgid with billows, and if he had to be repressed by our strength, it would have long since been all over with us. For we Germans are snoring, buried in sleep and wine, and we are destitute of leaders who could measure up in wisdom, strategy, and strength of heart to manage such great undertakings. If the Turk had moved forward, he would long ago have occupied all of Germany. For there is no one who could protect us, neither the emperor, nor kings, nor princes: God alone fights for us. Nor will an assault be launched on Germany unless it is in accordance with God's distinct decision and will. Otherwise the Turk would have overwhelmed us in our laziness long ago without any trouble. For both the princes and nobles have been completely ruined by luxury and pleasures. But that we are saved comes to pass by the power and goodness of God, and the prayer and faith of the church also obtains this defense. Accordingly, the emperor will make no progress in Belgium [14] and will vent his rage no further than God has previously appointed. These matters, then, are handed down to us for our consolation and to arouse our faith so that we may make invocation and believe with more fervor.

The providence and government of God shines forth also in the histories of the heathen. Hannibal could have gained possession of Rome without any trouble and difficulty after slaying the warlike leaders and armies of the Romans. But he was checked by God, and when the others did not understand this, they cried out: "Hannibal, you know how to conquer, but you do not know how to exploit victory." [15] But he was not destined to get any further. Charles captured the king of France after he had been defeated in a great battle near the river Ticinus in the year 1525. In the next year he took Rome by storm and his army plundered it, and so he had two very powerful monarchs in his power. Nor did he lack opportunity and strength to carry out an illustrious campaign against the Turkish tyrant in the year 1532 after gathering together a very select army from the farthest limits of the Roman Empire. But he did not make use of this opportunity, and he will seek to obtain it in vain in the future.[16] For it is God who takes away the spirit of princes and is terrible to the kings of the earth. With a single word or nod He shatters the spirits of the great warriors Pyrrhus, Hannibal, etc.

This is the true knowledge and faith regarding creation, and this lesson should be carefully meditated and practiced so that we stir ourselves up to pray and to believe. For it is ungodly and useless to place confidence in fortifications, ramparts, and guns. If ever it seems good to God that the Turk should fall upon Germany, those mounds piled up at great expense and toil will not protect us, and in that case I would certainly not like to stay in this town; I would rather crawl out. But when we bend our knees and cry out to our Creator, He will be able to surround us with walls of fire, as is testified in Ps. 125:2: "As the mountains are round about Jerusalem, so

---

[14] See Introduction, p. x.

[15] Livy, *History of Rome*, XXII, 51, 4; see p. 157.

[16] Charles V (1500—1558) had captured Francis I of France at the battle of Pavia on Feb. 24, 1525; his army sacked Rome in May 1527; and in 1532 he led an army to resist the Turks.

the Lord is round about His people, from this time forth and for-evermore." Likewise we read in Ps. 34:7: "The angel of the Lord encamps around those who fear Him." I hate that mass of ramparts and fortifications, for it is nothing else but a waste of money and a display of extreme folly.[17] We should rather aim to make it our firm determination that we are in the hand of the Creator, and not only we but also our enemies and the devils with all the gates of hell (cf. Matt. 16:18). For if the devil had free power to fall upon us, none of us would remain alive for one moment.

We should learn to place our trust in God our Creator and Pro-tector, not in fortifications, guns, wisdom, and power. To do the latter is pure folly. The Turk and the devils break through without any trouble and lay everything waste, because God does not want His people to trust in anything else but Himself. This is the reason why men have acknowledged this confidence in the Creator through the Son, through whom He has received us into favor and made a covenant with us, and this covenant is to have the confidence that our life depends on God alone, against all the snares and might of Satan and the world. If He wants me destroyed, He has no need to send soldiers, but if not, defiance to all the Turks, death, and the devil in hell!

Therefore let those who have God's promise remember that they should have the confidence that God wants to be our Keeper, De-fender, Shepherd, and Father on account of the Son, as Christ testifies (John 16:27, 23; 15:18): "The Father Himself loves you, because you have loved Me." "In the world you have tribulation; but be of good cheer, I have overcome the world." "If the world hates you, know that it has hated Me before it hated you." "And yet," He means to say, "your life in this sinful body is in My hand." Why, then, are we alarmed and terrified at the threats and power of the enemy? To be sure, we rather rejoice in the Lord, who has called us with His holy calling and taught us to trust and to conquer in Himself.

This is the lesson of this passage which Moses wrote down with special care, stating that terror fell upon these powerful peoples. Many of these undoubtedly grumbled and said: "Shall we leave this outstanding insult from our neighbors unavenged? Surely this band of thieves and beggars is not going to commit acts of violence in

---

[17] For Luther's views on defense against the Turks, see *On War Against the Turks* (W, XXX-2, 145—146).

our neighborhood with impunity?" But the leader of Jacob's camp is the Lord of hosts and of the whole of the heavenly militia, just as Elisha's servant saw the mountain full of horses and chariots of fire round about Elisha (2 Kings 6:17) and the sweet voice of the psalm declares: "He will give His angels charge of you to guard you in all your ways" (91:11). We know that these things are true; they are repeated so often in Holy Scripture, and yet we do not believe them. Such a great and deplorable state of wretchedness is unbelief. The matter is most certain, the words are trustworthy, and yet the heart does not believe.

6. *And Jacob came to Luz (that is, Bethel), which is in the land of Canaan, he and all the people who were with him,*

7. *and there he built an altar and called the place El-bethel, because there God had revealed Himself to him when he fled from his brother.*

Jacob reaches Luz safe and sound with his whole company. For the protection of God and the hosts of angels round about shelters them so that they do not lose even a hoof. The neighbors are very much offended; booty consisting of women and children was driven off, but the bravest and most warlike giants do not dare to make a sound. Why? Because this is how it pleases God.

On the way, however, the widows of the slaughtered Shechemites undoubtedly indicated their bereavement and grief with tears and wailing. Then Jacob alleviated their sadness and grief with whatever words he could, and later some of the women were joined to the patriarchs in marriage. Jacob did not marry a wife from the Canaanites, but his sons and the members of his household attached some of the women to themselves. But Simeon, Levi, Judah, and Reuben were then married men. Jacob in a friendly manner consoled the widows with the hope that he wanted to give them in marriage to members of his household and others. In the kings of Israel who were to originate from Jacob there was a similar friendliness to outsiders. For later Salmon married Rahab, Boaz Ruth, and so those widows came into the possession and fellowship of the church, which was a very beautiful compensation for their bereavement and bodily ills.

This kindness by which Jacob and the patriarchs treated this sex honorably and lovingly so that they had consolation in their exile and captivity is to be praised. This is how he comforted them: "My dear daughters, you should bear this loss patiently and with equanimity. For this is pleasing to God, and whatever bodily loss you have suffered, that will be made good in fine fashion by other spiritual blessings that are far greater." For he was not a barbarian and a monstrous enemy such as the Turks and Spaniards are, but he wanted to take thought for the interests of all and to show them a way of salvation. He was full of faith, patience, and kindness. The same virtues also shone forth in his wives Leah and Rachel, who embraced the widows lovingly and with all dutiful piety made an effort to soothe their grief and to attach them to themselves as associates in all their blessings and eternal life.

Luz is a city having this name from ancient times, as is evident from chapter 28:19. Jacob was the first one to change its name, and he called it Bethel. Above, he prophesied that the house of God was there. But now this name receives confirmation from God, just as the angel also called Jacob Israel, but this name did not stick to him. So it is repeated by God that it may be firm and constant. In the books of Judges and Joshua the story is told how the sons of Ephraim expelled the inhabitants of Luz. Later it kept the name Bethel. On the question whether Luz and Jerusalem were one and the same city I have spoken above.[18] All the stories of the kings testify that they were separate places. But under Abraham and Joshua, Bethel, Ai, and Hai were neighboring cities. But Luz is Bethel, and throughout Scripture it is placed in the neighborhood of Ai. It was 12 milestones distant from Jericho according to the testimony of Jerome and was on the way down to Jericho.[19] Jacob reached this place in safety, laden with gold, silver, and the booty of the Shechemites, and he retained possession of this area because the statement follows below that Joseph was sent to his brothers, who were pasturing the flocks of their father in Shechem (cf. Gen. 37:12).

The details mentioned above about the building of the altar are repeated in this passage. For Moses, omitting the other ceremonies and sacrifices which he describes fully in Leviticus, only recounts this one thing, namely, that it is necessary to praise God, console the weak, correct the erring, teach the ignorant, and practice the Word in simplicity. Then sin and death are destroyed, and righteousness and

---

[18] See *Luther's Works*, 5, pp. 251—252.

[19] Jerome, *Liber de situ et nominibus locorum Hebraicorum, Patrologia, Series Latina*, XXIII, 878; the Weimar text has "et Hiericho," but we have read "ad Hiericho."

eternal life are recovered; the devil is trampled underfoot, and God is exalted. This worship is very pleasing to God. Afterwards invocation is added and the prayer of the church, by which we seek to be confirmed and preserved in this doctrine and faith and to be defended by God in every tribulation. These are the two true and highest acts of worship — teaching and praying, and mortification of the flesh and the purging out of the old leaven in our flesh will follow them. Moses pays special regard to the Word and the salvation of souls. It is likely that not only the members of Jacob's household but also their neighbors came to the altar that was built. For God is not only the God of the Jews but also the God of the Gentiles.

The name of the place, אֵל בֵּית־אֵל, is new and singular. For the אֵל is placed in front, and this also occurs in the composition of the name בֵּית־אֵל itself. Moreover, we have not retained the Hebrew proper names everywhere, but at times we have made them common nouns in the German translation.[20] In this place, for example, the Latin translator renders it "house of God." But we retain this word because it is very noteworthy on account of the addition אֵל. Although the place was previously called Bethel, he here calls it "God-Bethel." It is very common in the Hebrew language for proper names to be joined with the name of God, names like Isaiah, Gabriel, Daniel, Ezekiel, and Jeremiah, "the exaltation of God." In the German language we have few of these.[21] In Greek there are more, like Theodosius, Theodorus, etc.

Now this place Bethel cannot be God, and yet it is called El-Bethel. Accordingly, we have a dispute with the Jews concerning names of this kind because of the passage in Jer. 23:6 and 33:16: "And this is the name by which He will be called: 'The Lord our Righteousness.' " [22] From this passage we are eager to prove and demonstrate that it is necessary that the Branch of David, or the Messiah, to whom all concede this passage must be understood to refer, is true God. For he says: "This is His name, by which men call Him, 'Lord,' " and the tetragrammaton יהוה is used here, which belongs to God alone. Therefore we contend that Christ is true God who justifies us because He has a name which is assigned to God alone.

[20] In the very next verse, for example, Luther translates *Klageiche*.

[21] Luther is referring to such names as Gottfried, Gotthardt, and the like.

[22] In 1526 Luther had devoted a special exposition to Jer. 23:5-8 (W, XX, 549—580).

For this passage is very firm and strong. But we cannot meet the slippery slanders of the Jews so that they may not slip out of our hands. For they bring up other similar cases in which the name of God is assigned also to other things, as this place is called El-Bethel, where אֵל is the proper name of God. Above also, in chapter 33:20, it is stated that Jacob erected an altar and called it "God of the gods of Israel." But it does not follow, they say, that because a thing has the name of God, it is therefore God. It is one thing to have God's name and another thing to be God. In Exodus (17:15) Moses calls an altar "the Lord is my banner," that is, "my triumph, victory, and exaltation," even though an altar is not the Lord, exaltation, or a triumph. Such examples they bring up against us and attack the passage in Jeremiah.

Lyra really raises a sweat and replies: "Christ is called Righteousness and our Lord in His own person. But other things or places are not a person and are not capable of having this name, but they only signify a certain divine effect which is brought about through that name." But the Jews are not moved, and indeed, they contend that Christ is mere man. I must admit that I have not yet determined how these slippery eels can be caught and held. For us it is indeed enough that this testimony agrees with the New Testament, in which it is clearly stated that Christ is our Righteousness and true God, until we can convince them from other passages. But it is impossible to block up all ways for the sects to prevent them from slipping from our hands, just as Christ Himself could not convince the Pharisees and Sadducees even when they were overcome.

We will nevertheless reply that this name for Christ should be preached and proclaimed, even though He is not called by the proper name Jehovah according to Jewish slander. For His name was Jesus of Nazareth, the son of Mary. But this is how we Christians interpret it. "This will be His name," that is, it will be preached, made known, and published concerning Christ that He is "the Lord our Righteousness." The Jews only cling to the syllables, namely, that He is not called thus. But the situation with this name is different from the other names, as in the case of Bethel and the altar, in the fact that He is our God. For that is not the common name which is published of the altar, but it is only the literal, or historical, or memorial name. For it is never said or proclaimed of the altar that it is our Lord.

In this way the rest of the names which are assigned to Christ by

Isaiah are predicative. Men will call Him "Wonderful, Counselor, Everlasting Father, etc." (cf. Is. 9:6). If the Jews do not accept these, let them go with their scoffings! Nevertheless, it is certain that a true proper name such as the one given to Christians in Baptism is one thing and that a name of praise and virtue by which one is celebrated is another thing.

But why does Jacob raise an altar? Because God reveals Himself there. He wants to thank God for making His Word known and to celebrate the memory and confession of God who has been revealed. אֵל בֵּית-אֵל signifies "God dwells here," whether it is a house of wood or stone. When the confession of God and the ministry of the Word sounds forth there, or God is praised and invoked, then it is a temple and a church, even though it is under the open sky, or a tree, or under that oak under which Jacob buried the idols. The idolaters and ungodly priests later followed this custom. They chose very pleasant spots on the mountains or in the valleys, or near rivers and trees, to which they lured the people to make sacrifice under the open sky according to the ritual of the fathers.

In the Hebrew, however, it is expressly stated: "Because there God (plural) had revealed Himself." When Scripture speaks of God in the plural, such passages should be carefully noted. Above, in chapter 1:26, it is stated: "Let Us make man in Our image, after Our likeness." It is likewise stated (Gen. 3:22): "Behold, the man has become like one of Us," and (Gen. 11:7): "Come, let Us go down, and there confuse their language." In chapter 18:2-3 we read that Abraham saw three men and said to them: "My Lord, if I have found favor in Thy sight, do not pass by Thy servant, etc." These passages are truly noteworthy. For they signify that the fathers had the same knowledge and faith concerning the Deity which we teach today. It is foolish to object that the doctrine of the Trinity was nowhere promulgated in the Old Testament, when it is manifest from so many passages that the godly men at that time also concluded that there was a plurality of Persons in the Godhead. But this mystery was not expressed by means of individual letters. This was reserved for the New Testament, where there are very clear testimonies.

But it was not unusual for the fathers to teach that there were several Persons in unity of Essence. But the majority of men did not agree, just as the Turks and Jews do not agree today. To be sure, most of those who hear us pay no heed and do not believe. Their fate is what Isaiah says of his hearers: "Their heart has been blinded, their ears have been made heavy, and their eyes have been closed; lest they see with their eyes, etc." (cf. Is. 6:10). For men who are deluded by their lusts or opinions do not see or hear even in seeing and hearing, and they live among living men like senseless tree trunks and stocks of wood.

Many now hear us teaching and read our writings, but with their hearts they are wandering about in the kitchen or elsewhere. So it comes to pass that although they stand with ears erect, they nevertheless understand nothing. This is a kind of insensibility which is not natural but voluntary, by which man withdraws his heart from things present and observes and desires strange and lofty things. Hearts of this kind Isaiah calls hearts that have been made fat, as though they have been covered with slime, and eyes that have been made heavy, such as the disciples had in the garden who did not pay attention to what Christ was saying (cf. Matt. 26:36 ff.). Of this kind are the majority among Jews and Christians alike. There are very few who have any regard for the doctrine of the fathers or who imitate their faith.

Let us, however, remember that it is here clearly stated: "There were revealed אֱלֹהִים," in the plural number. The verb is also noteworthy: Gods "were revealed" *(Dii detecti),* for it signifies "to be laid open," "to be revealed and to appear what one is," "to uncover what was hidden." In Lev. 18:7 we read: "You shall not uncover the nakedness of your father, etc." God has become uncovered to Jacob and has been revealed and has appeared to him as Father, Son, and Holy Spirit in the incarnation of the Son, just as Jacob above saw three Persons on the ladder and that God would become man of his seed as the One who was about to bless all the families of the earth. Thus Gods are said to be revealed, and yet there is one God. To what end would Moses have been compelled to write this when he could have used other words had he not wanted to describe that this great mystery had been revealed to the fathers?

Jacob, however, celebrated this revelation in many illustrious sermons. For this reason the altar was erected in memory of this excellent gift, namely, that the Trinity had been revealed to him and the incarnation of Christ and spiritual and bodily promises had been handed down at one and the same time. Nor were those wanting who heard these things listlessly and with heavy ears. But the patriarch received great light and consolation from this source, and since he escaped the danger into which he had been thrown by his sons, he now spent his days without worry in peace and found repose in the promises and divine revelations. But another disaster will soon follow; there is nothing permanent in the life of the saints, and everything is full of varied conflicts, although not without interspersed releases.

8. *And Deborah, Rebekah's nurse, died, and she was buried under an oak below Bethel; so the name of it was called Oak of Weeping.*

This temptation is somewhat lighter and more tolerable than the one which follows as a result of Rachel's death. But what point was there in writing about the death of this old woman and giving it prominence? That we might know that the life and all doings of the saints were very much like ours. They were, indeed, men full of faith, but at times they still showed themselves to be very weak in temptations for our consolation, so that we may not despair in our weakness, for they were clothed with the same flesh which we carry about with us today. They excelled us in gifts, but in the fellowship of grace and salvation and likewise in the protection of God there is equality. Deborah the nurse is introduced as a saintly woman and as very dear to the patriarch Jacob, perhaps because by age and her outstanding piety she was very well fitted to strengthen him in his very grave temptations. Hence Jacob laments her death, and he names the oak under which she is buried after the weeping.

This was also the reason why the death of Deborah was commemorated, namely, that Holy Scripture might show the patriarchs to have been not senseless tree trunks and stocks of wood or ἀστόργους ("without natural affection"), such as the monks were. For these men regarded it as praiseworthy for themselves to despise parents, brothers, and sisters, and they abused the saying of Christ (cf. Luke 14:26): "He who does not hate or leave father and mother, etc." From this source they invented special evangelical sanctity, if they hated and despised their parents. But what else was this but hating one's own flesh and the whole human race? Somewhere the story is told of a certain person who could not bear the sight of any man at all.

They taught that anyone who loves associating with men cannot enjoy the company of the angels. For this solitary life they called angelic. But it was really Satanic, for they took away from men the emotions created by God in human nature. God does not want us to despise or abandon father and mother by means of our own wisdom and rashness without the urging of a call, as Jerome exhorts those to do who are about to enter monasteries,[23] for this is a self-chosen work. But if any tyrant wanted to compel you to abandon the confession of sound doctrine or parents were to drive you to this course, then He orders you to risk your life and goods and to leave your parents rather than to abandon the confession of the Word. This is where the saying of Christ applies. When denying God or abandoning one's father are necessary alternatives, one should say to father and mother: "I do not know you; I do not have a father or mother." And this must not be done by one's own choice but under the urging of God's call.

This I say for the sake of the histories, or as men call them, *The Lives of the Fathers* [24] of former times, in which many such raving heresies are found. Holy Scripture describes the saints as men prepared for dangers of every kind and for the forsaking of all their goods. But when necessity does not demand this, they are full of στοργαῖς ("natural affections") and the emotions which God has implanted in nature, such as love of one's spouse, children, and relatives and mercy towards those who have suffered misfortune, etc. For Moses has depicted the patriarch Jacob as being very closely attached to his wives and children, and nothing is more carnal than this. He writes that he wept and grieved because of the death of this saintly woman Deborah. But in these affections there was a heart subject to God's will and prepared to render obedience in its vocation. Other men are also deeply moved by the death of friends and relatives and even much more by that of wives and children. This is not sin, but these are good emotions and στοργαὶ φυσικαί ("affections belonging to nature") when a father weeps for the death of a son and mourns the loss of a wife. This should not be censured, and indeed, the opposite of this is condemned by Paul (cf. Rom. 1:31) as a vice, namely, ἀστοργία ("lack of natural affection"). He wants us to weep with those who weep and to rejoice with those who rejoice, that is, to be affected by the adversities and good fortunes of others (cf. Rom. 12:15).

When I hear that the Turks are venting their rage on Christian blood in a most cruel manner, that they are impaling little children

[23] See p. 28, n. 13.

[24] The *Vitae Patrum* appear in *Patrologia, Series Latina,* LXXIII—LXXIV.

on stakes, that they are abusing women for purposes of unmentionable disgrace, it certainly becomes me to groan, and the human heart cannot help being deeply moved at such monstrous behavior. But some Stoic will object: "You are a delicate martyr! You weep and lament like a woman. It becomes men to despise such things! Of what concern is it to us that virgins and women are dragged off to be defiled and slaughtered?" This is raving madness, not fortitude! For what can be mentioned or thought of that is more foreign to all humanity than not to be affected by the disasters that fall on others, and such atrocious ones too? It is not godly or Christian to laugh in the midst of the dangers of others, when, for example, we see people being led into error or the emperor and the Turk attacking in rather cruel fashion and the pope plunging so many thousands of souls into eternal ruin. In this case it becomes me to be a man and to think that nothing human is foreign to me, as the man says in the comedy.[25] But the Christian should be moved much more by common evils and the destruction of so many bodies and souls. Christ Himself enjoins φιλοστοργίαν ("tender affection") when He says (Luke 6:36): "Be merciful, even as your Father is merciful," and Paul in Rom. 12:13 says: "Contribute to the needs of the saints."

Therefore this class of monks, lacking natural affection (ἄστοργον) and quite removed from all godliness and all association with the human race, is to be detested. For if all men want to imitate them and withdraw into corners away from the sight of men, who will eventually preside over the church, state, and household? God has called us into this world and put us into this world, not outside of the world. John the Baptist and CHRIST are called from the desert to teach and preach in the world. The same point is made by the description of the holy fathers, which testifies that they were φιλοστόργους ("men with tender affections"), fond of common society, and endowed with tender feelings towards their own people and others. For it is ungodly and inhuman not to condole with others and weep with them in their miseries or to be affected with longing for those who depart from this life when they have been very dear to us in life. We see how sad and bitter the death of this excellent woman was to the patriarch Jacob. I think that he was sometimes refreshed by her words and consolations in the greatest troubles. For women have their gifts, and God has often used this sex to show forth great

[25] Terence, *Heautontimorumenos*, I, 1, 25 (line 77); see also p. 351.

miracles. Thus Agatha, Anastasia, Agnes, and Lucia overshadow the legends of even great men by their faith and steadfastness in confession and martyrdom. The Holy Spirit roused and strengthened their hearts so that they laughed at the most atrocious torments and sufferings.

Accordingly, I think that this Deborah was a wise and godly matron whose service and counsels Jacob used to rule his household, and in great dangers and difficulties he often found support in her word and consolations. For there is usually a certain special grace in women who are lovers of godliness to comfort, to encourage, and to alleviate grief, and the discourses of women have almost more influence than those of men. Therefore God in Paradise added Eve to Adam not only for discharging household duties but also to comfort him in the common troubles.

Deborah, moreover, was very old, and she was regarded in the household as a grandmother. For she was Rebecca's nurse and on that account was very dear to Jacob himself and also to the grandchildren. She nursed them and attended to them in all kindness; and the στοργή ("natural affection") of grandmothers towards grandchildren is usually greater than that of mothers, because in their affection love gets down to the children's level and in so doing becomes extraordinarily ardent. Her age can easily be gathered from the reckoning of the years [26] since she was Rebecca's nurse. For in this year Jacob is at least 106 years old. His mother Rebecca was given in marriage in her 30th year to Isaac, who was 40. The latter begat Esau and Jacob in his 60th year, when Rebecca was 50. If 106 years are added to this time from their birth, the sum would be 156 years for Rebecca, and the nurse exceeded these by about 40 years. Therefore at that time she was 186 or 190 years old. On account of her age and other gifts she was held in reverence by the whole church and household. For she had seen and heard the greatest of the patriarchs for a long time, Shem for more than 100 years, with whom Jacob lived for 50 years, Rebecca 100 years, but the nurse 130 years. Such a woman was instructed in doctrine and experience in very many matters, and so they justly regarded her as a grandmother.

It is likely that Rebecca died at this time or a short time before, being overcome perhaps by heartache and worries, although there is no mention of her death. It appears, however, that after the years of

[26] Cf. *Computation of the Years of the World* (W, LIII, 58—59).

Jacob's servitude were completed, Deborah was sent to recall Jacob
from Mesopotamia, as Rebecca had promised above, saying (Gen.
27:45): "Then I will send and fetch you from there, etc." For she
had her origin in Syria and was attached as a companion to Rebecca
by her father and mother when she was to be married to Isaac. (See
chapter 24 above.) Accordingly, she remained for a time with Jacob
that she might be a source of comfort and refreshment to him and
his household. But she dies on the journey as they return home. The
grave at the oak, which Jacob names from the weeping, testifies that
Jacob and his household were smitten with great grief, attesting their
grief by tears. The Holy Spirit recounts this that we may know these
people to have been φιλοστόργους ("tenderhearted") and that it is
ungodly not to be affected by the disasters of others, not to grieve
and not to weep. For not even the beasts lack this feeling. Therefore,
as a sign of their respect, love, and longing for their excellent nurse,
he calls the burial place "Oak of Weeping" to signify that he with
his whole family attended the funeral of the kind nurse with tears
and grief. It would have pleased them more to bring her back home
to Father Isaac, but it pleased God otherwise. Therefore, let us
learn to rejoice with those who rejoice and to weep with those who
weep that we may not become senseless tree trunks and wooden
stocks like the many examples extant in *The Lives of the Fathers.*
These men, going beyond their calling, withdrew into desert places
away from association with human affairs and from interest in them.

9. *God appeared to Jacob again, when he came from Mesopotamia
in Syria, and blessed him.*

10. *And God said to him: Your name is Jacob; no longer shall your
name be called Jacob, but Israel shall be your name.*

It has often been said that God repeatedly raises and consoles the
saints and does not allow them to be tempted beyond their strength.
So He now repeats and confirms the promise made above in chapter
28:13, where He appeared to him in dreams, on the ladder. This He
did to soothe his grief and sorrow by which he had been smitten
as a result of Deborah's death. For the life of the saints is nothing
else but a descent into hell and an ascent, since indeed light and
darkness and temptation and consolation succeed each other in turn.
Not yet, however, has the patriarch finished with all evils; there still
remain far more serious evils to be endured. Accordingly, he is

strengthened by God to bear with greater courage both present and future disasters.

Moreover, it is expressly stated here that "God appeared to Jacob," but at the beginning of this chapter He only said: "Arise, go up, etc." These two statements seem to differ. God was able to speak through his father Isaac or through the nurse Deborah, whom Holy Scripture does not celebrate in vain because the patriarch Jacob wept for her. It is likely that she was a very wise matron and a prophetess full of the Holy Spirit who reminded Jacob about many things. However, those things which the saints speak should be regarded as being spoken by God Himself. When, for example, we teach the Gospel, baptize, call men to the ministry of the Word, and ordain ministers, we ourselves do not preach, we do not baptize, we do not ordain, but God is speaking through us. So it is called God's Word, God's sacrament, God's ministry, and it is rightly said: "God is speaking, God is baptizing" when He does it through ministers, since indeed all things are attributed to God which holy men have spoken.

For example, these are words of Adam: "This is bone of my bones" and likewise: "A man will leave his father and his mother and cleave to his wife" (cf. Gen. 2:23, 24). Yet Christ says that God spoke this (cf. Matt. 19:5). Therefore when we speak the Word of God, it should not be taken as the word of man. In this manner it is likely that Jacob was ordered to go up without an appearance and only by a prophetic spirit, either through his father Isaac or through Deborah, who, being full of the Holy Spirit, advised him to flee from Shechem. In this place, however, Holy Scripture says: "God appeared to Jacob," namely, Christ Himself in the form of an angel. It was a manifest appearance and far different from His speaking through a man.

When Deborah, the excellent counselor and comforter, was dead and the organ of prophecy was extinct, God took her place and did not forsake Jacob but Himself appeared, after Deborah had disappeared, to add a new appearance to those which he had above, especially on the ladder. For he saw Jacob weeping and lamenting because of the loss of the excellent prophetess, and He addresses him in a loving manner. But the blessing is to be understood as having to do with the spiritual, the future, seed, for the bodily blessing is only given for the sake of the spiritual one, just as this whole life is lived with this end in view, that we should be baptized, believe, be sanctified, and be saved. This is God's ordinance in parents, teachers, and ministers. To this end He has created the ministry of the whole creation and also of the angels, that the kingdom of God may come, that the name of God may be hallowed (cf. Matt. 6:10, 9), and that we might be saved and obtain the inheritance of eternal life.

Accordingly, a spiritual blessing is especially included here, for God wants him to press forward in the expectation of it and in faith in it. It is as though He were saying: "Be of good courage! For even though all died, yet I am alive and I repeat My promise to you as you grieve and weep so that you may conclude for certain that a posterity and blessed seed will come from your flesh, as I promised to Abraham and Isaac." That he might have a sure pledge and testimony of the divine will, He changes Jacob's name and calls him Israel. This change of name shows that God is dealing with him not concerning common matters but concerning special matters of the greatest importance. His usual name is the one he obtained by carnal birth through his parents. But this is significant and full of consolation, that He gives a new name to Jacob.

We are born into this life as sons and daughters of carnal parents and, as Paul says (Eph. 2:3), as "children of wrath," bringing with us the name of sinful and corrupt nature because of original sin. But when we are baptized, we receive a new name. He who is baptized is no longer called the son of John, or Peter, etc., although among men there is need of these names in the associations of civil life. But before God his name is changed and abolished, and he is called by a new name as a result of Baptism and faith, namely, he is called a Christian. This name reminds us of Baptism, which should be practiced in daily tribulations and produce its effects so that we grow into a new and perfect man (cf. Eph. 4:13-15) and in this way the name of Christian be perfected until our name and Old Adam are abolished.

Therefore it should be noted that GOD Himself gives a name to the patriarch Jacob, and by this new name a difference is made between the flesh and the spirit. For Israel is a divine name, and God has a different reason for giving a name from that which is customary with parents, relatives, neighbors, the fatherland, and the condition in life. But the name by which God calls and recognizes us is a special one, as He says to Moses in Ex. 33:12: "I know you by name." Paul also had regard to this when he said: "Not all who are descended from Israel belong to Israel" (Rom. 9:6). Not all are Israelites who are descendants from the flesh and bear the name of Israel. But the true Israelites are spiritual and have a spiritual name given by God. This is explained fully and learnedly in Rom. 9.

God, however, wants to say: "Hitherto I have not revealed your name to you by which you are named in My presence, but I allowed you to be called by your paternal name and according to the flesh. But now I am giving a name to you in accordance with what I have done with you, even as I have not exalted you as a son of the flesh. But I have led, governed, afflicted, purged, and sanctified you by many vexations that I might make you a new man and a new creature, and now I give a new name to you not of the flesh but of the spirit."

The etymology of the word has been explained above.[27] שָׂרָה signifies to fight, or rather, to conquer, to overcome. The word Jacob does not differ much from it, for that also means supplanter, that is, victor. But here He says that he conquers God: "You will be a conqueror of God." This is a common name for all Christians. For not only are we conquerors of the devil, sin, death, men, and this life but also of God. For He Himself has promised that He will help us; indeed, He has given Himself to us. If it were not for that, we would not be conquerors of God. For He is ours through the promise, and He has said: "I will be your God; trust Me, etc.," and from this it comes to pass that we come forth as conquerors of God.

After having given us the promise He pretends that He is quite alienated from us; He allows us to be tempted and simply hides His face as though He had forgotten all promises. Then it is necessary to beg, ask, knock. And when it seems to us that we are still being neglected and are succumbing, it is necessary to persevere and to press on in faith, prayer, and patience. In this manner we overcome God, not abandoning the promise of God who promises. In this perseverance in prayer and faith God becomes a visible God from a hidden God, comforting us and doing what we wish, as it is written (Ps. 145:19): "He fulfills the desire of all who fear Him," and likewise (John 15:7): "If you abide in Me, and My words abide in you, ask whatever you will, and it shall be done for you." These are true Israelitic words which conquer God and by which God is overcome. But what Christ adds is necessary: "If you abide in Me, and My words abide in you," and likewise (John 14:23): "If a man

[27] See p. 141.

loves Me, he will keep My Word, etc., and We will come to him and make Our abode with him." For God is conquered and makes and pronounces us Israelites when on account of faith in the promises He hears and preserves us.

But the Israelites according to the flesh are not such people. For these could not perform what is required for an Israelite who is a victor because he is, so to say, one who abides in the Word and perseveres in beseeching, seeking, knocking, and pressing on. God therefore assigns this constancy and victory to Jacob and speaks to him as follows: "You have been subjected to discipline long enough and frequently enough, and I have often hidden My face from you. But because you have clung to the promise so firmly, I have been compelled to yield to you, to hear you, and to help you, and now I pronounce and declare you Israelite and conqueror of God." Not that he was not such a long time before, but He now manifests this honor of Jacob for his consolation. Above, it was stated prophetically (Gen. 32:28): "Your name shall no more be called Jacob, etc." But here this is fulfilled and made public with the appearance of God Himself. "Such you were hitherto," He says, "but now you will also be called by this name."

But now the question arises why the Lord should say that he will no more be called Jacob when he is still called Jacob and Israel indiscriminately by Moses, in this chapter, for example, and also in all the prophets? Without any grounds Lyra enters on a discussion about the active and contemplative life and says that he is called Jacob on account of the active life, because he tramples underfoot the passions of the flesh, but is called Israel on account of the specu-lative life, for he now sees God.[28] He does not, however, adduce the etymology for the word which Eusebius and the grammarians have, namely, "Israel," that is, "a man seeing God," but he interprets Israel as one directed to God, that is, going about with God in pleasant speculations and the contemplation of the future life, concerning which matter he also cites Gregory.[29] But I omit these views, for I think that not even the fathers themselves understood what they taught concerning the twofold life. For the monks called that the active life which consisted in curbing lusts and controlling external morals

28 Lyra *ad* Gen. 35:9-10, p. 99 recto, note "1."

29 Gregory, *In Primum Regum expositiones*, IV, 29, *Patrologia, Series Latina*, LXXIX, 255.

by fastings and mortifications of the flesh, by filthy dress and similar devices, which the fanatical Münzer called *entgroben,* that is, the correction of the coarser vices.[30] The heathen called it external discipline which is useful and necessary in this life, especially in the early years, which have need of training and doctrine lest men become utterly barbarous and uncivilized and unfitted for any of the duties of common life.

But theologically the active and speculative life should be defined in a much different manner. For this is such, especially at the present time, that one's eyes brim with tears. For it does not consist of pleasant speculations and consolations, such as those of the monks; but he who wants to be an Israel and conquer God must be engaged in those exercises of which we spoke previously, namely, begging, seeking, knocking, and retaining the Word and the promise. This is the true speculative life of the godly, where reason and imagination fail, where the senses and understanding are mortified with all their powers, and where a man lives solely by the Word of God. It is written in Deut. 8:3: "He humbled you and let you hunger and fed you with manna, which you did not know, nor did your fathers know; that He might make you know that man does not live by bread alone, but that man lives by everything that proceeds out of the mouth of the Lord."

Other speculations of the monks are imaginings, cold, dead, and dangerous because they proceed from their own will and reason, without the Word and the promise. Therefore they are to be avoided. He who wants to speculate about GOD successfully in a godly manner should not do it without the Word but should apprehend the incarnate Son and begin from the manger and the swaddling clothes in which He was wrapped until he comes to the ascent into heaven. In this way he will receive in faith and remain in the Word and the promise which has been given. I have known some who boasted about their speculations that they were so captivated by the pleasant nature of these speculations that it seemed to them that they were caught up and lifted up to heaven, as it were. I do not approve of such experiences and do not desire them for myself, because they are without the Word and those who follow after them are men ignorant of the Law and the Gospel.

[30] Thomas Müntzer, "Deutsch-Evangelische Messe," *Schriften und Briefe,* ed. Günther Franz (Gütersloh, 1968), p. 162.

But the true speculation which makes an Israelite is the mortification of all the powers which belong to our senses and reason and clinging in faith alone and in the expectation of the promise. The true use of these speculations is seen in the agony of death, for then we are conscious of no advice and no help. Therefore speculation is necessary, that is, the apprehension of the pure and only Word, an apprehension independent of the senses, according to the statement (John 8:51): "If anyone keeps My Word, he will never see death."

The Law of God sets up and ordains the active life; it does not ordain monastic traditions but those things which belong to our vocation in external life. Let men individually consider in which kind of life they are engaged, and in that let them serve their vocation and carefully practice the duties commanded in the Decalog. Afterwards, in trials you will become an Israelite by retaining and practicing faith in the promise. As you were a Jacob in the Decalog, so you will be an Israel in the promises, which urge you on to prayer. The outstanding example of this is the Canaanite woman in Matt. 15:22-28, who is very well exercised in the speculative life and who presses on in such a manner that she does not allow herself to be repelled by any words, however harsh. She knocks at and pounds the door so long until Christ is compelled to yield and listen to her and to praise her faith and perseverance.

The doctrine of the speculative life is rightly taught if the speculative and active life are distinguished according to the Decalog and the promises, and this the monks did not understand. For the Decalog shows the works of each one's own calling. But temptations do not teach us to understand the Decalog but to apprehend God by faith, not to boast of merits and promises, as the Pharisee does in Luke 18:11-12 and as we read in Isaiah (58:3): "Why have we fasted, and Thou seest it not?" For this boasting is condemned by God. Outside the promises I can recall those things which I either did or suffered in persecutions but not after the example of the monks, who imagine that the merit of eternal life is in works. I thought that these matters should be repeated from the fathers that we may not seem to have rejected their writings completely, for they should not be neglected but be read with judgment. Lyra and Gregory do not seem to have understood what the active or contemplative life is, for they place both in monastic ceremonies and traditions. But let action remain in the Decalog and contemplation in the promise.

Jacob becomes one who tramples on the Law and is an Israel in the promises.

But I return to the question why Moses or the following histories did not retain the name Israel everywhere. I reply that God is speaking about the chief name, concerning the promises, in which Jacob was exercised and had to be exercised. He has to be Israel and be called Israel especially and properly on account of these promises. But he was also called Jacob according to the common custom of men on account of his works. That is not the chief name, just as the works which godly men do according to the Law are not their principal works, but they are Jacobitic, even though they are required by this life. God demands both, that we believe and do works, so that we are both Israelites and Jacobites. But from faith and the promise we are above all named Israelites. By our own works, however, that we obey our magistrates and parents, that we live honest and chaste lives, etc., we are Jacobites. Since this obedience is imperfect, it does not justify, but it is necessary as a fruit. But faith apprehends the immaculate and irreprehensible righteousness of the Son of God, which makes Israelites.

So much concerning the spiritual blessing, which gives a name to Jacob from the faith by which he apprehends this blessing. What follows pertains to bodily blessing.

11. *And God said to him: I am God Almighty: be fruitful and multiply; a nation and a company of nations shall come from you, and kings shall spring from your loins.*

12. *The land which I gave to Abraham and Isaac I will give to you, and I will give the land to your descendants after you.*

This is a repetition of the preceding promises for Jacob's consolation. The individual points and words almost agree with the former story, when circumcision is given to Abraham, where Abram's and Sarai's names are also changed. God also employed the same name שַׁדָּי which He used here; you can also look up its explanation in the remarks made above.[31] But the question why He says that kings are to be born from his loins, and yet later, when the people request that they be given kings, they are severely reproached by God (cf. 1 Sam. 8:7), this does not belong to the discussion of this passage. He adds "and to your descendants after you" that no one

[31] Cf. *Luther's Works,* 3, pp. 80—83.

may have doubts about the certainty of the promise, since it is established that Abraham and Jacob were strangers in this land and did not even have a footprint of land in it except the portion of Shechem, of which Jacob had gained possession with his bow and sword, as he will say below. Therefore He explains the promise that He will give this land to the posterity of Jacob. For the father also rightly claims for himself what is given to the son. In the meantime, however, he is content with the far better promise relating to the name Israel. For God was his land and possession, and so the grief which resulted from Dinah's defilement and Deborah's death was mitigated. But more serious matters remain.

13. *Then God went up from him in the place where He had spoken with him.*

The saintly patriarchs were constant and diligent in teaching and praying, and to these exercises they daily assigned the morning hours. But especially on the Sabbath the people came together for preaching and the common prayer of the church. After dismissing the congregation, Jacob prayed alone with eyes raised to heaven and meditated on the Word. Then God appeared and did not speak through his father Isaac or Deborah but was present in person as above, when he said: "I have seen the Lord face to face" (cf. Gen. 32:30). It was a vision like the one in his previous struggle, except that he understood that it was God Himself who was speaking, which he did not immediately perceive in his struggle. Moses himself testifies that it was a divine revelation when he says: "God went up from him."

14. *And Jacob set up a pillar in the place where He had spoken with him, a pillar of stone; and he poured out a drink offering on it, and poured oil on it.*

15. *So Jacob called the name of the place where God had spoken with him, Bethel.*

The special fame of this place above others is to be noted. For now it is called Bethel a third time. But would this not produce false prophets and idolatry? Jeroboam, to be sure, abused this fame and shifted all the divine worship of religion to that place (1 Kings 12:29). For this reason Hosea and the prophets of his day had such great conflicts and difficulty in condemning and abolishing idolatry at Bethel. They removed the august name of the place and called it בֵּית־אָוֶן (Hos. 4:15), that is, "house of grief and affliction," and yet they made little enough progress. For the false prophets made objections to the godly priests and prophets, saying: "Why is it that you glory in the temple at Jerusalem? Read Genesis, and there you will find that God appeared to Jacob in this place and that therefore it was called בֵּית־אֵל and אֵל בֵּית־אֵל." What more certain and more reliable argument could be advanced? It also seems an irrefutable argument. "Why do you bring in Moses against us or the new command of Solomon?" they say. "Or do you think that they could have transferred worship from so holy a place to Jerusalem or would have wanted to do so? For the patriarchs Abraham, Isaac, and Jacob offered sacrifices here, and the piety of King Jeroboam is to be praised, for he was a very religious king and brought the people back to the same place which the patriarchs honored, to which God Himself descended, which He approved, and where He spoke to the fathers."

This, then, was the occasion and cause for persecuting and slaughtering the godly teachers and prophets, as Amaziah reproaches Amos bitterly, saying (Amos 7:12-13): "Flee away to the land of Judah and eat bread there and prophesy there; but never again prophesy at Bethel, for it is the king's sanctuary, and it is a temple of the kingdom," that is, it is the house of God which King Jeroboam founded.

But the true answer to these specious objections of the false prophets was this: "God spoke with the prophets at His own time and in His own places, but later He clearly said through Moses (Ex. 20:24): 'In every place where I cause My name to be remembered I will come to you and bless you,' not in any place you please — mountain, meadow, or river, but you should have regard for that place which the Lord has chosen." Therefore He gave them a tabernacle, altar, and Levitical priesthood that He might bind the hearts of men to these; and the prophets carefully inculcated the same, but in vain because of the very great outward show which the idolaters had as a result of the worship of the fathers and the fame of this place. Indeed, they came to more conclusions, namely: "If Bethel is a holy place, then by the same reason Gilgal, Mizpah, Shiloh, and Tabor are holy places, where the fathers performed illustrious deeds." This was the source of an infinite multitude of idols, as was the case with pilgrimages among us, because they refused to have regard for the Law of Moses, who had ordained the tabernacle and other ceremonies by divine command and for this reason called the tabernacle

מוֹעֵד, that is, "sure," "established," and "fixed," so that he might lead erring hearts to a definite method of divine worship.

Moreover, after Jacob has set up the stone, he observes the same rite which he employed above, for he pours oil on it, and perhaps he took the same stone. But a libation consists of liquids, especially wine and oil. It was the rite for initiating and anointing and was also taken up later by Moses, for he anoints the priests and their clothing, etc., just as Jacob anoints the stone that the place may be consecrated and dedicated to God and that the church might come together in this place to hear the Word of God, to pray, and to give thanks. I omit the hidden meaning. This is a bodily blessing and the constitution of a church, and I believe that the patriarch Jacob did more in this place than Moses wrote. For above, he made a vow that he would offer tithes if he returned safely, and so I think that he gave tithes to the sons of Eber for the preservation of the church.

16. *Then they journeyed from Bethel; and when they were still some distance from Ephrath, Rachel travailed, and she had hard labor.*

17. *And when she was in her hard labor, the midwife said to her: Fear not; for now you will have another son.*

The word כִּבְרַת (cf. Gen. 48:7; 2 Kings 5:19) is one of those which neither the Jews nor we understand. The whole language would be much more obscure if we Christians had not shed light upon it by the Latin and German translation of the Bible. For when the Jews have doubts about a word, they resort to equivocation and multiply meanings and make it more obscure by their glosses. Therefore the grammarians are still quarreling about this word, and the case is still before the judge. Jerome is quite long-winded although he offers a bad interpretation.[32] He says that the Septuagint translators rendered it as "hippodrome," that is, a place where there were horse-racing contests, although the etymology supplies no reason for this. I do not know what they wanted to express unless perhaps this, that the distance to Bethel from the place where Rachel travailed was the space of a hippodrome, the distance of a horse race.

One rabbi offers one view, another rabbi a different view. One makes it a composite word; another one makes it a simple word.

---

[32] Jerome, *Liber Hebraicarum quaestionum in Genesim, Patrologia, Series Latina*, XXIII, 991; at least in current editions, the Septuagint does not have ἱππόδρομος here, but it does in Gen. 48:7.

Those who want it to be a composite word derive it from כְּ, the adverb which signifies likeness, and בְּרַת, like a בְּרַת of land, that is, the space of land for coming to Ephratah, but it is not yet expressed how far it is. Others derive it from בִּרְיָה, a word which is used in 2 Sam. 13:5, in the story of Tamar and Amnon, and signifies food, or a morsel, as though he wanted to say the space of ground for one breakfast, over which anyone would walk in the morning up to the time of his morning morsel, that is, a quarter mile or thereabouts. If one or the other etymology is to be approved, this one pleases me most. Others explain it simply as a measure, but they do not define its distance. Jerome derives it from בָּחוּר, "chosen." He says that it signifies a chosen time of the year, namely, spring, "when the year is the most beautiful," as the poet says,[33] and men passing along the way pick the little flowers from the neighboring plains and fields. But this has nothing to do with the measure of distance which Moses wants to indicate. Therefore I shall follow those who give the explanation that the distance to Bethlehem was as far as one has to go to breakfast, a short distance, so that one might gain an appetite for the breakfast morsel.

Now let us look at the trial that follows the peace and security of conscience which Jacob obtained from the divine appearance and promise. But we cannot yet completely explain this passage until we come to chapter 48, where Jacob indicates that at this time he did not understand the words of promise, although they were full of consolation.[34] The reasons for this obscurity are the following trials. For he is promised a blessing and posterity: "Be fruitful and multiply," and yet to outward appearance the opposite and something different from what is promised takes place. Therefore we shall postpone this discussion to chapter 48, where Jacob for the first time will learn from experience how the promise had to be understood. Now he is content with the fact that God descends to him and promises him consolation and help; but how he is to understand this he will experience below.

After the appearance he makes preparations to return to his father with tranquil heart, and he had already come close to Hebron. For Bethel was situated between Jerusalem and Hebron, which are about six German miles distant from each other. Jacob is a distance of three or four miles from Hebron. It is likely that he left his flocks and the whole family and hurried on ahead to his father, taking a few com-

---

[33] Vergil, *Eclogues*, III, 57.

[34] Cf. *Luther's Works*, 8, pp. 151—152, et passim.

panions with him. Accordingly, while they were making their way from the north and Bethel toward Hebron, this unexpected disaster directly contrary to the promise happened when he was almost on the threshold of his father's house. He was bringing joys and consolation with him as a result of the promise and was transported at the thought of bringing his dearest wife, who was heavy with child, to his father and making her rejoice at the sight of his father. On this journey she travailed and died, overcome by the labors of childbirth.

Surely this is not consolation or blessing or multiplication, to take away his chief and best-loved wife, who had been very excellently trained and was very well-mannered and most expert in household administration. For at home with her father Laban she had been inured to domestic duties and the care of the cattle, and by means of her own toil she had acquired the means of sustenance with her husband, living a thrifty and austere life. Jacob, accordingly, is deprived of his most faithful comrade, whom he hoped to set up in his father's house, in the bosom of his aged father Isaac, especially since she was pregnant, that she might gladden the old age of his father with beautiful offspring. She also had a heartfelt longing to see her father-in-law. But suddenly all hopes and joys fall to the ground, and most of the sweetest desires and expectations go wrong in Jacob, Isaac, and Rachel.

Is this the meaning of increasing and being blessed by God? To be sure, it is the worst of curses! But our Lord God has a Hebrew language, by which the last comes first, and what at first are sufferings are later glories. The cross and suffering must precede, according to the statement of 1 Peter 1:11, which speaks of the Spirit of Christ "predicting the sufferings of Christ and the subsequent glory." And the Lord says to Moses: "At last you will understand My counsel," [35] even as Jacob below in Egypt understands the last things when Joseph comes to life again, whom he thought to be lost and dead. In the meantime, however, he is robbed of all comfort, and the whole house is filled with grief and sorrow, and very gloomy darkness rushes on after the setting of the sun, when his very dear wife dies, who had been sterile for the first six years and for 10 years after the birth of Joseph. Because of his continuous expectation and desire for offspring, the love of her husband for this woman had been increased after she had become pregnant. Then she was the very dear mistress of the whole

---

[35] Apparently an allusion to Deut. 32:29.

household, the hope and consolation of the house. But she is summoned from this life contrary to all hope and expectation and dies in an inconvenient and unfortunate place. For if she had met her end before this time in Syria, it would have been somewhat more tolerable. Now the grief increases, for she succumbs on the very threshold of the paternal home.

I forbear mentioning the grief and sorrow because his godly wife was torn away from him, which of itself is by far the most bitter grief. For there is nothing more excellent and sweeter in this life than mutual concord and goodwill between husband and wife. Sirach 25:1 says: "My spirit is pleased with three things, the concord of brethren, love of neighbors, and a woman and her husband who walk together in agreement." There is no grief at all as a result of the departure of a peevish and wicked wife, but among these spouses there was the greatest of warm goodwill and the kindliest στοργή ("affection"). She had been modest, saintly, industrious, popular among neighbors and her household, in love with her husband, and obedient in all things. Accordingly, it meant great sorrow and grief for the patriarch Jacob. Now Jacob loses all hope and his greatest joy, and he thinks: "What point is there in God's saying that my family will be increased and multiplied when He takes away the mother through whom I was to increase and be multiplied?"

He did not understand the promise, nor could he reconcile these two aspects, which are really very different, with each other, to promise seed and posterity and to take away the mother of the household from whom Jacob himself and the whole household with Grandfather Isaac awaited offspring. Because of the consolation recently shown him, it was impossible for Jacob to fear any danger to his wife. Indeed, all with one accord praised Rachel's good fortune because she was destined to be the mother of many children, since, indeed, God had said that Jacob would be multiplied. No one thought that this would come about in any other way than through Rachel. Jacob often said to her: "My dear Rachel, let us thank God, who has once more promised me offspring. Now at last you will be fertile." For this reason, much as he loved her otherwise, he now loved her especially. But the most beautiful hope of the spouses and family proved deceptive, as happened to Eve when Cain was born, for she said (Gen. 4:1): "I have acquired the man of the Lord." She thought: "The Lord Himself has come, who will bruise the serpent's head." But not only was she mistaken in her hope; another great evil also threatened from him.

So God says here to Jacob: "You will increase, but I will take your wife from you." These statements are directly contrary. She was the mother of her firstborn Joseph and the mother of the household, and now Benjamin and others were awaited from her. Accordingly, she gives birth on the way as they were traveling to Grandfather Isaac, but she does so with great difficulty and danger to her life, nor is she able to fulfill her fondest desire, to place a little infant on the lap of the grandfather, but she dies from the labors of childbirth, and with her both joy itself and the most beautiful hopes are extinguished. The midwife sees that she is in travail and disturbed by the fear of death. Therefore she comforts her and says: "You will also have this son." But in vain, for Rachel feels that her strength is failing and that she is gradually being seized by death. Therefore she calls the name of the son בֶּן־אוֹנִי, from "grief." This end of Rachel is assuredly wretched and sad both for her husband and the rest of the household. She fell asleep in childbirth, in her calling and the station into which she had been placed by God, and she met death under the cross which has been imposed on women by God in the words: "I will multiply your sorrows and conceptions, etc." (cf. Gen. 3:16). She is not exempted from the dangers and calamities that befall ungodly women. This also must be regarded as a wretched experience, that the same difficulties which usually confront ungodly women are placed in the way of such a saintly woman, who was the pride and joy of this house and the whole church.

Careful consideration should be given to this example, and the grief and sorrow of the excellent patriarch should be kept in mind. All the circumstances of this story increase and emphasize this grief, nor is it yet the end of his troubles. For after the loss of the mother, soon and almost in the same year, he loses the firstborn of this mother, Joseph. In a third calamity, Bilhah, Rachel's maid, is defiled by Reuben, the firstborn of the other wife. Surely that is not the meaning of blessing, is it? "Surely it is not God but the devil who has spoken to me," Jacob could well have thought. An impatient man could easily have broken out in these words. Jacob did not reach his father without these two great disasters first befalling him, the death of Rachel and Reuben's incest with Bilhah, who had succeeded Rachel. This was too much, to be overwhelmed by three severe storms in such a short interval of time, one of which would have sufficed to kill an impatient and carnal man.

We, indeed, are tender martyrs, for we do not understand, and much less would we be able to withstand, the magnitude of these evils. Christ's passion is more sublime than all other afflictions, and it does not affect us so much because He is God. But the fathers were like us and experienced all human emotions, even as Jacob loves Rachel for the excellent virtues with which she was endowed. She hopes that a great posterity is to be born from her, but she dies in childbirth in the midst of that hope itself. Accordingly, the grief of others should be more moderate, if any are deprived either of wife or children, for we see that the fathers suffered the same things. For we are much inferior to them, nor do we have promises of a kingdom, posterity, and the priesthood as they did, all of which Jacob lost at that time.

Such temptations, moreover, become more severe when terror of conscience becomes an additional factor in them and Satan adds oil to the fire. For when the devil sees hearts tried and terrified, he is not slow to hurl his fiery and poisonous darts (cf. Eph. 6:16) against them so that they think God is angry with them and opposed to them. Therefore in all temptations it affords great comfort to be able to conclude that God is present and favoring us. But the human heart finds it difficult to embrace this comfort when our Lord presses a person to His bosom in such a way that his soul wants to depart. But the love of God is really such as He exhibited in His own Son, even as Christ says (John 15:9): "As the Father has loved Me, so have I loved you," that is, according to the Hebrew idiom mentioned above, by affliction before glorification. This idiom the world does not understand because He fills the stomachs of the ungodly, whom He does not love, with bodily gifts. But He adds (cf. Luke 6:24-25): "But woe to you who are rich. Woe to you who laugh now, and you who are full."

In this manner the troubles of the holy fathers are set before us for an example, that we may see how they were disciplined and note their illustrious faith in the midst of disasters and learn not to lose the sight of God smiling, blessing, and promising if ever He takes from us those things which are sweetest and have been established by His promise. To be sure, faith should come to this conclusion: "Although this disaster is very bitter for me, nevertheless, I believe that God is true." But in such unexpected cases faith is smitten very hard and is shining forth with difficulty like a smoking flax (cf. Is. 42:3). So it must be stirred up by such examples.

18. *And as her soul was departing (for she died), she called his name Benoni; but his father called his name Benjamin.*

Moses narrates everything briefly. Without doubt, however, many words, groans, and tears intervened before he was called Benjamin. Rachel herself commended her soul to God and found rest in the consolations offered by Jacob in her last agony and in the travail of childbirth itself. For she was full of faith and had been trained in quite a hard school previously in the common troubles of her husband in Laban's house. In these she had been his companion. So Sarah and Abraham used to endure common dangers. For godly wives are affected by the trials of their husbands; they grieve with them and weep with them. Such στοργή ("natural affection") was also outstanding in Rachel. Therefore her death was a very sad event to her husband, her household, and her neighbors, to whom her virtues and godliness were known.

But it is necessary to learn the consolation by which we sustain ourselves at the death of wives, children, and friends. For although our death and that of our relatives is very sad, it is nevertheless a sure fact that we will live forever. It was certainly better for Rachel to die in this way while praying to God and believing in Him than if she had been permitted to enjoy all the joys of this life, even those which God had promised. For after death we will be happier in infinite ways and the possessors of more blessings than we left behind in this life. For the latter are momentary and perishable, and in place of them we obtain eternal things. But the flesh cannot refrain from wailing and grieving, as this example testifies when they give the son a name derived from grief. Moreover, I think that he was so named for a time; then, when the grief had been somewhat alleviated, Jacob changed his name and said: "I do not want to have a mournful reminder in my house any longer which continually reminds me of the last word and the grief of my wife whom I have lost and renews the grief," but he calls him בִּנְיָמִין, that is, "son of my right hand."

There are also discussions about the reasons for this name.[36] I think that it can be understood from the household arrangements. Leah was the left-hand wife and Rachel the right-hand one, that is, the chief, special wife. Therefore the son of the right hand is the son of his dearest wife, so to say. By means of this name he wanted to set

---

[36] Jerome, *Liber Hebraicarum quaestionum in Genesim, Patrologia, Series Latina*, XXIII, 992.

forth a memorial of his love towards his favorite wife rather than of
his grief and sorrow for her. So he changes the sadder name into a joyful one. Another reason is political or ecclesiastical. This son who
was born from his dearest wife will enter upon the promised inheritance due the son of his chief wife; he will be the heir of the kingdom
and the priesthood. For Jacob is of the opinion that the promise and
blessing belong to Joseph, even as he himself had obtained it in preference to his brother Esau, and if Joseph were to die, he thinks that
Benjamin would succeed him. He does not yet understand that Judah
will be the father of Christ. He will learn it for the first time in Egypt
at the suggestion of the Holy Spirit. He is more confirmed in this
view because he does not hope for another son. So he loves Joseph
in a special way, which was the source of the hatred of the brothers
for Joseph. When this broke out and Joseph was sold by his brothers,
the father was smitten with incredible grief.

19. *So Rachel died, and she was buried on the way to Ephrath (that
is, Bethlehem).*

Rachel departed in faith while she was praying to God. She was
taken to heaven into the bosom of Abraham, her father. But she was
buried not far from Bethlehem, about a quarter of a German mile
away. There she died and was buried in a neighboring field or on
the road just as if the wife of a shepherd died in the field in the midst
of the flocks. There was no house nor any lodging house except Jacob's
tent. This is the way of the saints to heaven.

אֶפְרָתָה and בֵּית לֶחֶם are different words but they mean nearly the
same thing. Ephrathah is "fruitful, fertile." Bethlehem has the same
meaning, namely, "house of bread, food," "where there are good
tidbits."

20. *And Jacob set up a pillar upon her grave; it is the pillar of Rachel's
tomb, which is there to this day.*

The fathers decorated sepulchers magnificently. They did not
throw away the dead like the bodies of beasts, but they set up memorials of them for a perpetual and immortal reminder so that they might
be testimonies of the future resurrection, which they believed and
expected. Therefore funeral ceremonies and the funeral procession
are to be retained, and likewise the weeping and sympathy, not that

there should be prayers for the dead, as Lyra wishes,[37] or that we should fear death, but rather that in death itself we should learn to exercise faith as it struggles against the terrors of death and think that we indeed die and are buried in dishonor but that we will rise again in glory. Jacob, for example, retained this consolation: "You have been disappointed in your hope of joys in this life, my Rachel, but what a happy disappointment, because you have exchanged bodily or perishable blessings for eternal blessings." The pillars were erected to this end, that by the example of the fathers we may learn to neglect and despise the present life for the sake of the other better life which remains. Then, too, in reliance on the promises, we should endure God's will with equanimity. For what can the devil or the Turk do, even if they take away our life? If we believe that Jesus died and rose again, so also God will bring with Him those who have fallen asleep through Jesus, as 1 Thess. 4:14 says.

21. *Israel journeyed on and pitched his tent beyond the tower of Eder.*

The Latin translator has made עֵדֶר a common noun, but it is the proper name of a citadel, or tower, which was a lookout in the territory of Bethlehem, which, it is certain, has always been pasture land. Jerome writes that עֵדֶר was later changed into a temple which in his day was called *Angelus ad pastores* because the angels appeared there to the shepherds on the night when Jesus was born. There was always a crowd of shepherds and flocks there because of the sheep pastures, and so it had its name from pasturing flocks. The citadel was situated beyond Bethlehem towards the south. Lyra says the same and follows Jerome.[38]

Others assign an ambiguous meaning to the word עֵדֶר and interpret it as the city of Jerusalem itself because it is stated in Micah 4:8: "And you, O tower of the flock, hill of the daughter of Zion, etc." This error arose from the obscure and faulty translation and the neglect of grammar. For Micah is speaking about the tower of the flock as a common noun by metonymy, which is clear from what follows: "You tower of the flock, עֹפֶל," that is, "fortification," or "citadel," of a city. It is therefore a proper name of a place in a field near Bethlehem, where the temple which is called *Angelus ad pastores* is today.

37 Lyra *ad* Gen. 35:20, p. 99 verso, note "1."

38 Jerome, *Liber Hebraicarum quaestionum in Genesim, Patrologia, Series Latina,* XXIII, 992; Lyra *ad* Gen. 35:21, p. 99 verso, note "i."

22. *While Israel dwelt in that land, Reuben went out and lay with Bilhah, his father's concubine; and Israel heard of it.*

After the death of Deborah and Rachel, there follows another striking and foul disaster for the most saintly patriarch, the horror of which I cannot adequately express in words. I commend it to the rhetoricians and orators for amplification. For it is a horrible crime! The firstborn Reuben, who had been destined for the kingdom and the priesthood, destroys himself with his whole posterity. It is a cruel deed, but worst for the perpetrator himself. Nevertheless, we shall mitigate it somewhat and say that he sinned in folly and lust. Bilhah, I think, was beautiful and not very steadfast, for she easily yielded to the stupid young man. If she had rebuked him more severely and threatened to tell his father, she would have been able to repel him. But it sounds bad enough! Therefore Bilhah is to be blamed no less than Reuben.

Moses calls her a concubine, or mistress, but she was nevertheless a true wife and the mother of two sons, Dan and Naphtali, which were two of the largest tribes, from whom Samson and Barak originated. But they suffered striking and perpetual disgrace at the hands of their father Reuben himself. Deborah and Rachel were scarcely dead and buried and their bones were still warm, so to say, when this crime is perpetrated. For they were the mistresses of the household morals and discipline, and when they were removed, Bilhah, Rachel's maid, remained in charge. Then there was a sudden change and confusion of discipline in Rachel's tent which she herself could easily have averted by her care. She would not have allowed her maid to behave in such a wanton manner. The devil was the author of this great disgrace to vex the saintly man who had the promise that peoples and kings would be born from him. But what is the beginning of this blessing? The wife on whom the whole hope of posterity depended dies. Now the tent of his chief wife is most foully polluted. For Jacob thereafter did not have intercourse with this concubine, and it would not have been strange had he been overwhelmed by the magnitude of his grief. I, to be sure, could not have held out and conquered, for it was too hard and altogether intolerable!

At that time his wound and grief as a result of the death of Rachel and Deborah was still fresh. At this point, when his grief was not yet over, but while his tears were still flowing, his firstborn Reuben inflicts a new wound. Bilhah, moreover, did not act unwillingly or under compulsion but willingly. Nor was it a case of fornication, or adultery, or defilement, but it was an act of most disgraceful incest to sleep with one's father's own wife while he was still alive.

But these things are written to comfort us so that we may know that our afflictions and disasters are not extreme and not even comparable with the troubles of the patriarchs. Secondly, we should know that sins are remitted, but not without punishment. For this tribe later on was weak and quite forsaken, the dregs of the whole people of Israel, and the birthright was taken away from it, that is, the kingdom and the priesthood. So it would have been much better for Reuben to die seven times, for this story is being published to all eternity to the end of the world; all churches and schools reecho with the recounting of this disgraceful act at which all descendants and posterity had to blush. Nor is there any story extant which celebrates the fact that something of outstanding importance was performed by God in this tribe. Accordingly, Reuben survives, and so does the tribe which originated from him, but in perpetual disgrace. This indeed is punishment enough, that his whole posterity had to hear the father's disgrace resounding from all the pulpits.

But where are those brave sons of Jacob now when it comes to avenging wrongs and crimes? Why do they not slay their incestuous brother? Shechem was slain because he had defiled their sister Dinah. But that was a deed that could have been glossed over, covered, and healed by an honorable marriage. For it was not incest or a prohibited degree. Here there was need of special severity against an incestuous man. Dan and Naphtali had quite a just cause, for it could always have been thrown into their teeth that their mother had been involved in incest. Although they were not born from incest, their mother committed incest later. With this stain she had been tarnished by Reuben. Therefore Reuben was a seedbed of very great hatred and perpetual animosity.

The Jews try to excuse this crime according to their custom of being very effusive in praise of their own. In former times the Greeks, and today the Italians also, despised all other nations in comparison with themselves and called them barbarians. So also the Jews are eager to extenuate, cover, and gloss over the faults of their nation, even when they are manifest. Accordingly, they say that Reuben was not incestuous but that it was a wrong against his father. For after Rachel's death, they claim, Jacob transferred Bilhah's bed into Leah's bedroom. For this reason his son Reuben became angry and took

Bilhah's bed away; he did not sleep with her, etc. In this way [39] they distort Holy Scripture with their senseless and vain tomfooleries. But in the Hebrew the text clearly states: "He slept with Bilhah, he lay with her," even as the woman says to Joseph below, in chapter 39:7:[40] "Lie with me." Similarly, it is stated in chapter 49:4: "Unstable as water, you shall not have preeminence because you went up to your father's bed; then you defiled it — you polluted his couch!" In 1 Chron. 5:1 we also read: "He was the firstborn; but because he polluted his father's couch, his birthright was given to the sons of Joseph, the son of Israel, so that he is not enrolled in the genealogy according to the birthright."

Such a great sin cannot be covered, and what great grief came upon the excellent patriarch as a result of this disgrace of the son and wife we can more easily imagine than express in words. It is certainly a wonderful thing that these tragic misfortunes also happen to saintly men, in whom the Holy Spirit dwells, speaks, and rules, and where the true, pure, and holy church is. Yet the devil has so much power there that he stirs up such atrocious disturbances. At that time there was no other woman in Jacob's house who might succeed Rachel, who had died, and from whom the posterity promised by God might be expected. There was only this woman, and she is defiled and polluted by his son. What sadder and more horrible thing could happen to a man in life?

So far he has been called Jacob. Here for the first time in the story he is called Israel when Moses says: "Israel journeyed on, and pitched his tent," and likewise: "While Israel dwelt, etc." This name Scripture emphasizes with special care to give due emphasis to the most disgraceful act of incest. For it wants to indicate that Reuben committed this crime after his father had been honored, after his name had been changed and the promise had been given that he had to increase and beget kings. After such great honor, Reuben goes off and defiles Bilhah and pollutes the foremost tent, which had been Rachel's. It is not without a special purpose, then, that he is called Israel in this place, for the Holy Spirit takes it with ill grace that a father exalted in this manner [41] by God should be most disgracefully dishonored by a son in the wife who had succeeded the deceased Rachel.

[39] The Weimar text has *Si*, but we have read *Sic*.
[40] The original has "chapter 36."
[41] The Weimar text has *si*, but we have read *sic*.

It is certainly wonderful that he could live so long. But he lived in the Word of promise, otherwise it would have been impossible to endure and overcome so many serious calamities. Now he learns what increasing and being multiplied is, namely, that he himself is not able to beget any more children. For Rachel, from whom he expected a numerous offspring, is dead, and Bilhah is polluted. After this he therefore lived alone without a partner for his couch. He had no further intercourse with the polluted Bilhah nor with any other woman. Therefore the Holy Spirit at once attaches a catalog of the sons of Jacob to indicate that there were not more than 12, that this is to be their total. David also, on account of Absalom's incest, lived as a celibate to the end of his life, and Jacob, moved not so much by age as by grief and indignation, was also continent.

22. *Now the sons of Jacob were twelve.*

23. *The sons of Leah: Reuben (Jacob's firstborn), Simeon, Levi, Judah, Issachar, and Zebulun.*

24. *The sons of Rachel: Joseph and Benjamin.*

25. *The sons of Bilhah, Rachel's maid: Dan and Naphtali.*

26. *The sons of Zilpah, Leah's maid: Gad and Asher. These were the sons of Jacob who were born to him in Mesopotamia.*

In the Hebrew it reads: "The sons of Jacob who was born," the singular number being used for the plural. Previously he is called Israel because of the horror of the crime. Now he is again called Jacob. Moses wants to say: "In this way ended the begetting of children on the part of the patriarch Jacob, who had the promise about the multiplication of offspring and the coming forth of kings from his loins; nothing follows for him." How, then, is Holy Scripture fulfilled? After Benjamin's birth and his mother's death in childbirth, Jacob ceased begetting children, and he has only 12 sons. How, then, does he increase? Here you see how Jacob took the true understanding of the promise from this disaster. For after losing Rachel and seeing her tent defiled by incest, he understood it to mean that those were already born from whom kings were to come forth, namely, Joseph and Judah, the latter of whom is the father of the kings of Judah and the former the father of the kings of Israel. These were descended from the loins of Jacob, and those who were born from them are understood to have originated from Jacob. In this way Jacob was taught by the disaster that he should abstain from marriage in the future, and so he also had no intercourse with Leah. So far, then, the outstanding example of great misfortune in Jacob and of sin in Reuben.

These are the 12 patriarchs, whose sanctity is celebrated in Scripture and who were the fathers of the saintly people of Israel. But in what enormous and outrageous sins the devil involved them! For he makes Reuben a son such as will not easily be found in the histories of the heathen, for even the heathen abominated this crime, as Paul says in 1 Cor. 5:1: "It is actually reported that there is immorality among you, and of a kind that is not found even among pagans; for a man is living with his father's wife." This, moreover, happened in the church of the holy patriarch Jacob. Later there followed murders and horrible lies, for all the rest of the sons except Joseph and Benjamin, and especially the sons of Leah, were matricides and parricides. To the best of their ability they kill their father with such dire crimes that he was more disturbed and saddened by them than by all the other disasters. They also slaughter their brother Joseph and send his coat to their father as if he has really been killed, and they not only bring him no comfort but even laugh at their excellent father.

But these matters are set forth that the infinite forbearance and inestimable mercy of God may be commended so that no one, terrified by the magnitude and multitude of his sins, may lose heart or cast aside his faith in God. For even patriarchs were the worst scoundrels. Nor were they without the Word, a teacher, discipline, or a father's examples. They had Deborah as a teacher; they witnessed the demonstration of so many instances of God's help and wonderful acts; they heard so many promises made to the fathers. But what did Reuben and the others learn after hearing so many beautiful sermons? They were a pack of scoundrels and had to pay a very heavy penalty, a bitter penalty indeed.

These matters then serve for our instruction and reproof so that we should fear the wrath and punishment of God. Then, too, they also serve for our consolation in case any of us have wayward and disobedient sons. They should bear this misfortune with moderation since, indeed, we are not better than the patriarchs. For individually contaminated by atrocious crimes were Asher, Dan, and the Benjamites, as the second last and last chapters of Judges testify, and this applies even much more to the Ephraimites. For the devil attacks the church far more violently than outsiders.

27. *And Jacob came to his father Isaac at Mamre, or Kirjath-arba (that is, Hebron), where Abraham and Isaac had sojourned.*

28. *Now the days of Isaac were a hundred and eighty years.*

29. *And Isaac breathed his last; and he died and was gathered to his people, old and full of days; and his sons Esau and Jacob buried him.*

Here again the name Jacob occurs, but above, the name Israel was set over against the crime of Reuben. It also appears that the patriarch proceeded rather slowly with his cattle and baggage or that he himself went on ahead either on foot or riding on a camel and visited his father on several occasions before he brought up the whole household. Mamre is the proper name of a man, of one of three brothers who were in league with Abraham. See chapter 14:13 above. For this Mamre, a firstborn, the city has its name, for either he himself exercised dominion in Hebron or some of his posterity. Isaac, moreover, was now very old and blind and did not see Jacob and his grandsons. He only heard the series of trials and misfortunes which he had endured up to this time, namely that Deborah and Rachel had died, etc. He deplored the magnitude of his son's troubles and comforted him, saying that these were infernal and diabolical evils but that God is more powerful than the devil and does not permit us to be tempted beyond our strength (cf. 1 Cor. 10:13). For "greater is He who is in us than he who is in the world" (1 John 4:4), and the father himself who had been afflicted with similar difficulties throughout his whole life was able to console his son with special earnestness and effect.

After Jacob has found contentment in the kindly words and association of his father for several years, his father dies. Now Jacob is the sole survivor, and all other fathers from the Flood right up to this time are dead. Accordingly, the whole burden of government presses upon Jacob alone, who still lives on in the midst of such great ill will caused by his sons, and he holds out against the assaults of the devil by praying, teaching, exhorting, and warning. He undergoes great difficulties in extreme old age, nor does he still have Isaac or any other patriarch as his associate. Isaac dies in a tranquil and quiet old age, full of days, not like the voluptuaries but sick of this life and exhausted by difficulties and troubles. "I am tired of life;

I want no more of it," he would have said. So he prayed that God might set him free and bring him at length into port and a better life.

This manner of speaking, "he was gathered to his fathers," bears witness to the future resurrection of the dead since, indeed, it is a people to whom we are gathered. For on dying we do not disappear into the air. Therefore the Holy Spirit does not say: "He disappeared after he ceased living" but "he was gathered." He was not scattered, tossed this way and that, or afflicted as he was in a wretched and disastrous life but freed from all evils and gathered to his people like the other fathers who sleep in peace and whom God gathers into His bosom, where they enjoy pleasant rest. This is the force of these words which are used quite significantly. There is a people of the dead, among whom are Adam, Seth, Abraham, Deborah, etc. These people have been gathered into the bosom and arms of God. There they enjoy pleasant rest and they will be resurrected in their time. By this figure, then, Holy Scripture shows that the fathers died not as the heathen die, but that they have been gathered together and are preserved under the hands of God. In Is. 57:2, for example, we read: "Let peace come; may he rest in his bed who has walked in his uprightness." And the hour will come in which they will appear again and come forth from their graves more beautiful than the sun and the stars, namely, those who walked uprightly. Reuben did not come to this hope of a future resurrection unless he was purged by penitence, even as Paul was a persecutor and enemy of Christ who shed much innocent blood, but he removed this sin by the blood of Christ.

Such passages should therefore be carefully noted together with the words which the Holy Spirit employs. God does not cast off or scatter the saints but gathers them, and in such a way that not even one of their bones or hairs perishes. Moreover, the brothers Esau and Jacob came together for the burial. In the text Esau is placed before Jacob. There is no doubt that Esau also visited his father previously and that his father often reproved him in a loving manner and admonished him to lay aside his hatred and desire for vengeance. So he came to the funeral to indicate his obedience and respect toward his father. This is a sure sign that he returned into favor with his brother and attached himself to the true church so that he might become a partaker of the spiritual promise from grace, if not from the promise. Similarly, we heathen are received into favor not as a result of a promise but from mercy.

CHAPTER THIRTY-SIX

IN THIS chapter the historical sequence should be studied. For Moses makes use of anticipation, which is called ὕστερον πρότερον.[1] For the events which follow this chapter right up to chapter 40 should have been set forth in an earlier section before those words: "Now the days of Isaac were a hundred and eighty years" (Gen. 35:28). All the events which are described in the following three chapters happened before Isaac's death. He lived to see Dinah defiled, the Shechemites slain, and the deadly victory of the sons of Jacob, as well as the death of Deborah and Rachel, and, in addition, the selling of Joseph into Egypt and Judah's incest with Tamar.

All these facts can be gathered from chronology.[2] Otherwise it appears as if Isaac died immediately after Jacob came to him, and this is false. For he lived at the very least 13 years after the return from Mesopotamia to Hebron. Then, too, it is certain that Isaac was 180 years old when he died. But Esau and Jacob were born when Isaac was 60 years old, and if these years are taken from the 180 years, 120 years are left. This is the age of Esau and Jacob when Isaac dies. Joseph was 30, and Isaac died 13 years after Joseph was sold, in the year before his liberation from prison. But the life of the old man was a wretched one, deprived as he was of his eyesight from the time that he blessed Jacob, that is, from his 87th year. For then his eyes became weak, as we heard above. Accordingly, let us remember that the three following chapters are to be placed between these words: "Jacob came to his father Isaac" and "the days of Isaac were a hundred and eighty years" (Gen. 35:27-28). For chronology gives us many useful reminders and explains history and often offers opportunity for many very beautiful thoughts. For the excellent patriarchs and prophets were true saintly martyrs who bore many troubles, the endurance of which is quite beyond us.

It was necessary for these matters concerning hysterology to be said first. For because Moses had stated in the preceding chapter that

---

[1] Cf. *Luther's Works*, 4, p. 300, n. 1.

[2] Cf. *Computation of the Years of the World* (W, LIII, 61).

Esau and Jacob had come together for the burial of their father, he thought that this was a very suitable place to speak about Esau, of whom he takes leave in this chapter and whom he will not mention hereafter.

1. *These are the descendants of Esau (that is, Edom).*

The name Edom has always stuck to this region. The Latins and Greeks call it Idumea, and Vergil speaks of "Idumean palms." [3] But the envenomed and pestilential Jews, in all their commentaries, call the Christian empire of Rome Edom, although they themselves are truly that cursed and condemned people. In their prayers they pray against Edom and make petition that their Messiah may slaughter us, and they have very foolish opinions about the origin of the Roman Empire. Moses, moreover, did not want to forget Esau, for he is Abraham's grandson, and Esau and Jacob were equal in birth and in the glory of the blood which both of them had. Esau had his origin from the very noble blood of Sarah and Rebecca, Abraham and Isaac. Therefore Moses did not want to set him aside, but he enumerates his sons and grandsons and recalls his bodily blessing, concerning which mention was made above: "By your sword you shall live, and the time will come when you will break his yoke from your neck, etc." (cf. Gen. 27:40).

At the beginning of Genesis mention was made also of the generation of Cain. Although he was a reprobate, excommunicated and cursed in the land, God nevertheless left him an opportunity for repentance so that he himself and his posterity could obtain the blessings of the spiritual promise. Likewise in Esau there is commended the example of divine patience also in the reprobate. For there is no doubt that Esau and Ishmael took the instruction of Abraham, Isaac, and Jacob with them, and likewise the sacrificial rites and especially those connected with circumcision. Many illustrious men, therefore, were born from Esau's blood. But they differed in this, that they did not have the promise of the Messiah. They were not promised mercy and the blessed Seed, the Virgin's Son and the Savior of the world, but for all that they were still not cast off, neither themselves nor their posterity, like the other heathen.

Many Ethiopians, Ammonites, and Edomites attached themselves to the confession and worship of the God of Israel in accordance with

[3] Vergil, *Georgics,* III, 12.

God's call. Many of the Ninevites and Babylonians were saved by accidental mercy, although Christ was not promised to the heathen as He was promised to the seed of Abraham, and the oracles of God were not entrusted to them. For we must concede this honor to the seed of Abraham which Ps. 147:20 praises: "He has not dealt thus with any other nation." This people of Israel has patriarchs, prophets, and the sayings of God, and Paul says in Rom. 15:8-9: "For I tell you that Christ became a servant to the circumcised to show God's truthfulness, in order to confirm the promises given to the patriarchs, and in order that the Gentiles might glorify God for His mercy. As it is written, 'Therefore I will praise Thee among the Gentiles, and sing to Thy name'" (Ps. 18:50), but Christ did not come from Gentile seed.

It is necessary to distinguish between the promise and truth and accidental mercy. We have mercy without the promise; the Jews have mercy with the promise. Salvation is of the Jews, John 4:22 tells us. From the tribe of Judah comes the Conqueror of death and the devil. Esau and Ishmael lacked this promise, but they were not excluded from mercy, for the histories testify the opposite. Nor did all who had the promise attach themselves to the church. For not the sons of the flesh are the sons of God, but the sons of the promise. Indeed, among the former division of the people many foul and shocking crimes arose such as are not even read in the histories of the heathen. David, for example, is cast out of his realm by his son. His whole house was full of calamities and more unfortunate than that of Tantalus and the sons of Pelops in Greece.

Therefore to say "We have the promise, and therefore we shall all be its heirs" does not follow; neither does "We do not have the promise, and therefore we have been rejected." From all peoples God has taken some, so that we should not boast. But he who boasts, let him boast in the Lord (cf. 2 Cor. 10:17), both he who has the promise and he who does not have it, so that He Himself may be righteous and may make righteous those who are of faith.

Accordingly, Moses tells the story of Esau not only because of respect for Abraham, Isaac, and Jacob, whose grandson and son he was, but much more for this reason, that we may know that he became a partaker of the blessing which Jacob had. For an approach to fellowship with the true church was always open to him, provided only that he humbled himself and said earnestly: "May God only have pity on me and make me a participant of the crumbs which fall from the table of the church (cf. Matt. 15:27), which is in the house of God." This humility and obedience are pleasing to God, even though you do not have the promise.

On the other hand, the sons of the promise lose the blessing when they are proud. For this is what GOD means when Peter says: "Humble yourselves therefore under the mighty hand of GOD" (1 Peter 5:6), and for this reason He humbles and disciplines His saints so that they should not be proud. So I think that there were many excellent men full of the Holy Spirit among the posterity of EDOM, although there was no shortage of those who were aflame with an inordinate and bitter hatred against ISRAEL. So the papists today are very hostile to us and regard us as an abomination and accursed refuse. But there are many of them who embrace and love us and our doctrine. This I think was the reason why Moses inserted the generation of Esau in the number of the saints and joined him and some of his posterity with the holy church: they became participants not in the promise but in the mercy which the promise shows forth.

In the Latin translation this chapter is very obscure and confused. Moses first describes the posterity of Esau the way it stood during his lifetime; secondly, the relationship, or genealogy, of his wives; and thirdly, the dukes and kings. Among these, he indicates, there were some good men, who were converted after long experience in hearing the Word. For it was not a long way from Seir to Hebron, therefore there was easy access to Father Isaac and to his church; and when the Word is revealed at one place, it scatters abroad its rays and is everywhere spread abroad to neighbors. Therefore Moses intimates that not all who were to originate from Edom were damned, although he had been rejected from the promise and had lost his birthright.

It is assuredly an amazing thing that nearly all the firstborn in all of sacred history were unfortunate. In Egypt all the firstborn were slain by God. This seems to be the reason why the Law is conditional and those who have the Law generally become worse. They are proud on account of the Law, as though it has been given to nourish pride in the right of the firstborn, whereas it has been given to humble that pride. Therefore the arrogance and insolence of the firstborn was checked by God when they abused their honor and dignity. For all that was done and said looks to the unique firstborn Son of God, Jesus Christ, and His alone is all glory, might, and power. Now let us turn to the generation of Esau.

2. *Esau took his wives from the Canaanites; Adah the daughter of Elon the Hittite, Oholibamah the daughter of Anah the daughter of Zibeon the Hivite,*

3. *and Basemath, Ishmael's daughter, the sister of Nebaioth.*

The same has been said above in chapter 26:34, but with other words and changed names. For Esau's first wife is there called Judith, and her father is called Beeri the Hittite. Here he is called Elon, for a change of names is quite common in all languages. Several useful rules have therefore been handed down by others with which many obscure passages are explained.[4] The first is that all men generally have two names, like Martin Luther and Philip Melanchthon. The second rule is that fathers and mothers, sons and daughters are such by nature or by law. The third rule is that names are often given and changed by some stroke of fortune, as Jacob was called Israel from an event, and others have obtained names from their offices, whether it be pastor, judge, or burgomaster. Often also changes are made as a result of age. We are accustomed to give a different name to maidens in infancy than in adolescence, and at times men invent names from clothing, at other times from color and form, and at other times from some association or other. Eusebius, for example, was called Pamphili on account of his associate, the martyr Pamphilus.

We also have reason to think that the same thing frequently happened among this people. Judith is here called Adah, and it is possible that she was transferred from her natural father to a legal father and that thereupon her name was changed. Indeed, look at the examples belonging to our time under the papacy! How great was the stupidity of those who in changing their names took oaths on the laws of the pope! In Baptism I was called Martin, but later in the monastery Augustine. What could be more disgraceful or more sacrilegious than to reject one's baptismal name because of the donning of a cowl? The popes are ashamed to be called by their own name which they obtained in Baptism and, to be sure, they are not worthy of retaining it, and so they adopt new names. Julius II, for example, was previously called Julianus.[5] By these changes they testify that they have defected from Christ and Baptism, and this same thing has become a firmly established custom in all the monasteries.

4 See p. 179, n. 13.

5 Julius II (1443—1513) became pope in 1503; his name was Giuliano della Rovere.

Esau's first wife, then, was called Judith, that is, a "Judaean," "a grateful singer of praise." So Leah calls her son Judah because she acknowledged God's blessing and wanted to show forth her gratitude. It was a beautiful name, but it seems that Judith degenerated and that therefore a change of name ensued, but not for the better. For Adah means "necklace," "ornament"; she was delighted by elegance and splendor in clothing and womanish ornamentation. After she became the mistress, she wanted to be Adah, the adorned woman, the woman in velvet, the woman with the necklace. So she lost her very beautiful name and was no longer called Judith but Adah, one who presumably sat in front of the mirror frequently, combing her hair and adorning herself.

The second name is Oholibamah. אֹהֶל means "tent," as when Moses stated a little while ago (Gen. 35:21) that Jacob pitched his tent beyond the tower of Eder. In Ezek. 23:4 אָהֳלָה occurs, that is, "her tent," namely, that of the woman, for God is speaking there with indignation against a harlot who has her own church, having cast aside the Law and the priesthood of the Lord. Moses furthermore signifies that this woman was a lady and a queen. Above she was called Basemath, as though you were to say, "An aromatic, sweet-smelling woman," for she had a good odor and a good name. "A splendid young lady," "a fragrant flower," "a real carnation." Now she is called Oholibamah, "the woman of the palace," "she of the lofty tent," "the gracious lady from the castle above!"

The third woman is called Basemath and was called Mahalath above (28:9). It seems that Moses purposely changed the names of the three women. This one was Ishmael's daughter, of the blood of Abraham, whose granddaughter she was, and she was related to Jacob and Esau in the third degree. The name itself means "sick," "weak." Moses signifies that the girl was of tender health, and so they said she would not survive and live, and they called her "the sick one," "weakling." This woman alone changes her name for the better, for she is now named Basemath, that is, "the sweet-smelling one," "the aromatic one," "the flower," "the fragrant rose." For even as the two former women degenerated and lost their excellent names, so this third one bettered herself and regulated her morals in a godly manner, but not without the cross and wretchedness. Above in chapter 26:35 it was stated that the two wives were מֹרַת to Isaac and Rebecca, that is, they tormented the holy people and the whole household. From this Judith could easily be changed into Adah, and the household said: "She is not a Judith, for her ways do not agree with her name." Adah is a real showpiece, and the second one has an evil reputation and is tyrannical. The third one came into the house later and was more welcome and dear to all. Now follow the sons of these women.

4. *And Adah bore to Esau Eliphaz; Basemath bore Reuel;*

5. *and Oholibamah bore Jeush, Jalam, and Korah. These are the sons of Esau who were born to him in the land of Canaan.*

Adah is the mother of the famous Eliphaz, who is Abraham's great-grandson and Isaac's grandson and Esau's son. Many think that he was one of the three friends of Job, and if this is true, it would be necessary for Job to have lived a long time before the children of Israel left Egypt, for the computation of the years shows that Eliphaz was 70 or 80 years old when Isaac died. When Esau had the meeting with his brother Jacob, Eliphaz was at least 60 or 55 years old, for Esau married a wife at the age of 40. From that time to Isaac's death is 80 years. But I leave this opinion about Job undecided because there is no evidence of this in Scripture. It is likely that he was one of the grandsons or great-grandsons who retained his father's name. Adah bore only one son, and Basemath likewise bore one son. From these two women Esau has two sons. But the mistress and queen, Oholibamah, bears three sons. This woman, then, excelled the rest, for she was the mother of three sons, and it is quite likely that she in particular was מָרַת in Isaac's household.

All these are born in the land of Canaan in his father's house, for Esau married his first two Hittite wives at the age of 40. Accordingly, these five sons were born while he was still at the house of his father. Jacob proceeded to Mesopotamia when he was 77, and therefore 37 years intervened from Esau's nuptials up to the stealing of the blessing. So long did Isaac put this off. And Eliphaz and the rest of Esau's sons were with their grandfather for so many years and heard him preach. They did not see Shem, but Eber and Deborah. So also Esau's wives heard Isaac in his old age and Rebecca, and they reached the hundred mark if they lived after the death of their father-in-law. In such a long time it is likely that they forgot their hatred and bitterness. I think that Moses wrote these things to show that after the reconciliation of the brothers their hearts were at length mitigated and that Eliphaz was a good man since, indeed, there is nothing evil extant against him.

6. *Then Esau took his wives, his sons, his daughters, and all the members of his household, his cattle, all his beasts, and all his property which he had acquired in the land of Canaan; and he went into a land away from his brother Jacob.*

7. *For their possessions were too great for them to dwell together; the land of their sojournings could not support them because of their cattle.*

8. *So Esau dwelt in the hill country of Seir; Esau is Edom.*

Here begins the discord between the brothers and the hatred of Esau towards Jacob and his parents after he had lost the blessing. Being angry and moved by the size of his flocks, which he saw this land could not support, he gave way and migrated to Seir, from where he had married Oholibamah. He follows her to her fatherland. I think, however, that this migration took place two or three years after Jacob's departure into Mesopotamia. For so long he remained with his father. At that time also Isaac's home was in great confusion, for he was plotting his brother's destruction and brought great grief on his parents because of his hatred toward his brother. He also divided the paternal substance with Jacob, even though the latter was absent. But his parents claimed a double portion for Jacob by the right of the firstborn. Then Moses indicates the bodily blessing, which falls to Esau's lot, when he makes mention of the size of his flocks. For he originated from the blood of a great patriarch and did not lose anything but the promise of the Seed. So it is certain that he increased greatly and became very rich. Indeed, I do not doubt that many of Esau's offspring were converted to the GOD of Abraham and Isaac, as the Books of Kings testify. Esau also retained circumcision and the doctrine of the fathers and of the promise.

9. *These are the descendants of Esau the father of the Edomites in the hill country of Seir.*

10. *These are the names of Esau's sons: Eliphaz the son of Adah the wife of Esau, Reuel the son of Basemath the wife of Esau.*

Moses repeats the beginning of this chapter, which he is accustomed to do also in other places. When he wants to add something, he repeats what precedes. When, for example, he reviews his own genealogy in Ex. 6:16, he subjoins what he had said at the beginning, "These are the names of the sons of Levi according to their generations," that it might not seem that he has his origin from another tribe than Levi. Here he does the same thing, since he wants to add something to the matters mentioned above and to explain them more fully. Five sons were born to Esau in Canaan, of whom Reuel seems to have been an infant and to have been born only after Jacob's departure for Mesopotamia. Eliphaz, however, the firstborn at that time, was 36 and already old enough for marriage. For so long a time, moreover, the Hittite wives reigned in the house of Isaac and Rebecca and lived on their resources. Moses relates these matters to remind us of the cross and trouble which the saintly parents endured on account of the pride and haughtiness of their daughters-in-law, which he takes note of above, although it is likely that they became milder in time. Otherwise, mothers-in-law by nature are accustomed to hate daughters-in-law, but Rebecca must be excused because she loved her son Esau and for his sake her daughters-in-law and grandsons. Nor did she deserve to be harassed by the Hittite women, those proud mistresses who imitated the customs of their homeland. For the Hittite nation was very powerful and the worst among the Canaanites. In Ezek. 16:3 it is stated: "Your mother a Hittite, etc." They had their name from terror, for they were tyrants and hateful to all men. They sorely afflicted the saintly mother Rebecca for about 40 years. Basemath was scorned and despised by the two and regarded as a waiting woman but is nevertheless placed before Oholibamah so that Moses may indicate his hatred and that of the Holy Spirit for the Hittites. Edom is the name of a region of which Esau is called the father, not the name of a person. From Esau, who is called Edom, this nation obtained its name Seir.

11. *The sons of Eliphaz were Teman, Omar, Zepho, Gatam, and Kenaz.*

12. *(Timna was a concubine of Eliphaz, Esau's son; she bore Amalek to Eliphaz.) These are the sons of Adah, Esau's wife.*

13. *These are the sons of Reuel: Nahath, Zerah, Shammah, and Mizzah. These are the sons of Basemath, Esau's wife.*

On the return of Jacob, Eliphaz was 56, and these sons were

already born to him, and I think that they were great lords and men of violence, with whom Esau went out to meet and terrify Jacob, and although they became reconciled to him, they nevertheless displayed their glory and power by that expedition. Teman is well known in the Holy Scriptures, and I think that the region of Teman was named after him, of which mention is made in Jer. 49:7, where we read: "Is wisdom no more in Teman?" that is, in Idumea, for it is a part of it.

Timna was the sister of one of the leaders of the Horites in Seir, and both Adah and Timna were Hittites, and so they found it easier to agree with each other. Timna's son Amalek was adopted by the first wife Adah, and for this reason Amalek is numbered among the sons of Adah. From him there arose a very famous nation in sacred history, concerning which it is stated in Num. 24:20: "Amalek was the first of the nations, but in the end he shall come to destruction." But it has a very distinguished origin. Esau is its grandfather, Isaac its great-grandfather, and Abraham its great-great-grandfather. This was an outstanding nobility as far as paternal blood was concerned, and so the pride of the Amalekites was great. It was Hittite by maternal origin.

14. *These are the sons of Oholibamah the daughter of Anah the daughter of Zibeon, Esau's wife: she bore to Esau Jeush, Jalam, and Korah.*

Moses enumerates the sons and grandsons of Esau to show what kind of host Esau had when he came to meet Jacob. But here the question occurs why Oholibamah is called a daughter of Anah and a daughter of Zibeon. For how can she be daughter of two men? The Jews enact strange tragedies and hold two quite disgraceful opinions.[6] The first is that Zibeon was an ungodly man who despised marriage, that therefore he slept with the wife of his father Seir and begat Anah, so that Anah is the natural son of Zibeon and also his putative brother with respect to Seir. The second opinion is that Zibeon defiled his daughter-in-law, the wife of his son Anah, and so committed incest both with his mother and daughter-in-law. They regard Oholibamah as a most incestuous woman, whose father was born through incest from his father.

But I detest the Jews and the comments of the rabbis with my whole heart because this is their custom, indeed, their manifest mad-

[6] Lyra *ad* Gen. 36:14, p. 100 recto, note "d."

ness, that from wherever they can they gather together whatever redounds to their own praise and the disgrace of the heathen. They are a most accursed people and are held captive and possessed by Satan, and Christ's picture about the mote and the beam (cf. Matt. 7:3-5) truly applies to them, and likewise the one about straining out a gnat and swallowing a camel (cf. Matt. 23:24). For all the Jews most impudently make the same boast that one of the Pharisees makes of himself: "I am not as other men are" (Luke 18:11). "We are the people of God," they say, "the holy nation, adorned by God with great gifts." And one of their rabbis said that it is a strange thing if one wise man is found from among all nations but that among the people of Israel all excel in wisdom. To be sure, it is a most pestilential nation, and it was so already under the fathers, under Jacob and under David. For look at their illustrious deeds! Reuben mounts the couch of Bilhah, his father's wife, and Judah commits incest with his daughter-in-law. The same stains, moreover, these hypocrites fasten upon Anah, the father of Oholibamah. But why do they not first see the beam in their own eyes? For what is more outrageous than Absalom's revolt against his father, by which he ejected him from his kingdom and did his best to kill him and defiled his concubines? Now let the rabbis go and boast of their Jewish wisdom! Then, too, the Jews were always a rebellious people against the prophets and kings, and they murmured against God and killed the prophets in a most cruel manner. Therefore I violently hate the comments of the rabbis, in which they wickedly corrupt Holy Scripture by their lies.

Because it is said that Oholibamah was the daughter of Anah, the daughter of Zibeon, they conclude from this passage that she had two fathers and that Anah defiled his mother, etc. This is a real Jewish conclusion, that is, an asinine one, which is also rejected by Lyra and by Santes Pagninus. No one doubts that there were such crimes among the heathen, but concerning Anah there is no clear text or testimony of Scripture which accuses and convicts him, as there are plain histories extant concerning Reuben and Judah and likewise also concerning the rest of the brothers, who sold Joseph and killed their aged father with grief. For he bewails the loss of his son in these words: "I shall go down to Sheol to my son, mourning" (Gen. 37:35), that is, "I shall die of heartache." Similarly, he says: "You will bring down my grey hairs with sorrow to Sheol" (Gen.

42:38). Therefore the ancestors and patriarchs of the Jews were parricides. For it is always a case of the worst coming from the best. Angels become devils, the people of God become crucifiers of God's Son, the prophets become false prophets, and our hearers and disciples become authors of sects and heretics. Nor is what Christ said to the Jews without any point (John 8:44): "You are of your father the devil." From this it follows that the Jews are a mad people and given over to a base mind (cf. Rom. 1:28), just as they outdid themselves in doing evil in David's time and in the time of the prophets. Therefore I make it a practice to refute and condemn their glosses with whatever reasons I can.

For us also it would not be difficult to devise several opinions, if it were permitted. We could say that Anah also slept with his mother and that from this incest Oholibamah was born and many similar things. But nothing is to be imagined in Holy Scripture without clear testimonies of the Word. Below (v. 24) we shall hear that Anah was a notorious rascal and the author of an abominable act of copulation, namely, of asses with horses. But if he had no respect for the order and sight of God and nature but dared to mingle animals of a different genus, which is contrary to nature and the ordinance of God in the creation and concerning which Holy Scripture says in Gen. 1:25: "God made the beasts of the earth according to their kinds and the cattle according to their kinds, and everything that creeps upon the ground according to its kind," it could also come to pass that he slept with his mother.

Nor, to be sure, do I exonerate the heathen of such outrageous crimes, since Paul also preaches of their promiscuous and incestuous lusts in the first chapter of Romans. But because the idiom which Moses uses concerning Oholibamah is also employed of honorable daughters, as in the case of Mehetabel below, who was the daughter of Matred, the daughter of Mezahab, I do not twist the words maliciously into a foreign sense, but I shall interpret them honorably. For it is customary in Holy Scripture for daughters to be called the daughters of fathers and grandfathers. In Ex. 6:20 Moses says: "Amram took to wife Jochebed his father's sister," who is the mother of Moses and a daughter, that is, granddaughter, of Levi, his grandfather. Amram took her as his wife since she was an orphan. Therefore there is no reason for inventing disgrace and crimes when Scrip-

294

ture or historical necessity does not compel us, as was previously stated in regard to the examples of the patriarchs of the Jewish people.

Then also it belongs to the honor of Esau that we should think that he would by no means suffer such a disgrace and would never have married Oholibamah had he known that she was born from incest. Therefore I think that both of them were honorable Hittite women, although they later began to be proud and puffed up by the nobility of their race. Perhaps also they brought idols into Isaac's house and invited others to the worship of these, and perhaps the holy parents were gravely offended by this and much afflicted by the idolatry in regard to the First Table and the arrogance and pride in regard to the Second Table. But their origin was honorable. Oholibamah was Anah's daughter, who was her natural father, and Zibeon's daughter, who was her grandfather.

15. *These are the chiefs of the sons of Esau. The sons of Eliphaz the firstborn of Esau: the chiefs Teman, Omar, Zepho, Kenaz.*

16. *Korah, Gatam, and Amalek; these are the chiefs of Eliphaz in the land of Edom; they are the sons of Adah.*

17. *These are the sons of Reuel, Esau's son: the chiefs Nahath, Zerah, Shammah, and Mizzah; these are the chiefs of Reuel in the land of Edom; they are the sons of Basemath, Esau's wife.*

18. *These are the sons of Oholibamah, Esau's wife: the chiefs Jeush, Jalam, and Korah; these are the chiefs born of Oholibamah the daughter of Anah, Esau's wife.*

19. *These are the sons of Esau (that is, Edom), and these are their chiefs.*

First Moses recounted the genealogy and family of Esau, and now he describes their dignity, power, and rule. Above in chapter 14:6 we heard that the Horites dwelt in Seir; these the sons of Esau drove out and destroyed. Accordingly, the whole region of Seir went over into the possession of the Edomites, as is clear from Deut. 2:4, where it says: "Command the people, You are about to pass through the territory of your brethren the sons of Esau, who live in Seir; and they will be afraid of you, etc." Likewise we read in Deut. 2:5: "I have given Mount Seir to Esau as a possession." This was a bodily blessing, which God bestowed the more readily because Eliphaz and others retained circumcision and the doctrine about God which they had received from the fathers. For Isaac preached illustrious sermons to his grandsons, and Esau even functioned as a priest in his father's place while Jacob was absent. Therefore one should not regard all of them as having been rejected. For although they lost the promise of the coming Seed, they nevertheless obtained accidental mercy.

Accordingly, he enumerates the chiefs who drove out the Horites, for they married wives from the Horites. Later, however, discord arose between the relations and grandchildren, and Esau's sons gained the victory against the inhabitants of Seir, and they did not succeed to the rule. From these 12 chiefs they later chose a king, and, joining their forces, they drove the Horites from their boundaries and possessions. The Lord gave them the victory, as was stated above in the blessing (Gen. 27:40): "You will live by the sword." I think that they gained possession of the land of Seir at about the beginning of the descent into Egypt, when they began to exercise dominion there and thought that Jacob was forgetting and forsaking his blessing. "Let him go," they said, "and farewell to him! We have been appointed as chiefs and lords of this land. Now it will appear which of the two families is blessed." In this way a bodily blessing always precedes the spiritual blessing.

Six chiefs sprang from Eliphaz, Esau's firstborn, but he himself was not a chief. Amalek also belongs to this number. By what method Korah is included in the number, I really do not know. For only the grandsons, not the sons of Esau, are enumerated under this title of chiefs. Perhaps it came about by a change of names or through adoption, which is very frequent in Holy Scripture, just as Joseph adopts Ephraim as his legitimate son. For the Hebrews, however, אַלּוּף signifies chief, from אֶלֶף, that is, "a thousand." For this reason Matthew adduces Micah 5:1, which reads: "And you, O Bethlehem, in the land of Judah, are by no means least among the rulers of Judah," whereas the prophet says "among the thousands of Judah." The words are similar. If anyone had several villages and a thousand men under his power, he was a chief.

20. *These are the sons of Seir the Horite, the inhabitants of the land: Lotan, Shobal, Zibeon, Anah.*

21. *Dishon, Ezer, and Dishan; these are the chiefs of the Horites, the sons of Seir in the land of Edom.*

22. *The sons of Lotan were Hori and Heman; and Lotan's sister was Timna.*

23. *These are the sons of Shobal: Alvan, Manahath, Ebal, Shepho, and Onam.*

24. *These are the sons of Zibeon: Aiah and Anah; he is the Anah who found the mules in the wilderness as he pastured the asses of Zibeon his father.*

25. *These are the children of Anah: Dishon and Oholibamah the daughter of Anah.*

26. *These are the sons of Dishon: Hemdan, Eshban, Ithran, and Cheran.*

27. *These are the sons of Ezer: Bilhan, Zaavan, and Akan.*

28. *These are the sons of Dishan: Uz and Aran.*

29. *These are the chiefs of the Horites: the chiefs of Lotan, Shobal, Zibeon, Anah,*

30. *Dishon, Ezer, and Dishan; these are the chiefs of the Horites, according to their clans in the land of Seir.*

The word שָׂעִיר signifies the same as faun, or satyr, *Feldteufel*, "field demon." Cf. Is. 13:21.[7] They are accustomed to appear in the woods and fields, shaggy and hairy. The heathen call them *lares* ("household gods") and *genii* ("guardian deities"), but they are devils, even though they pretend that they do men good. Because Edom was born hairy, he was called Seir, and so the word Seir remains, whether derived from the present or former inhabitants. Esau, however, had married a wife from the daughters of Seir, or of the Horites, and so mention is made of the relationship in honor of Isaac and Abraham, whose grandson and son Seir was. For although he was deprived of the blessing in particular, there still remained στοργή ("natural affection") and fondness on the part of the parents towards their son so that they did not cast him aside completely, even as Cain was not driven out by his parents for Abel's murder in such a way that they did not retain any love or concern for their son. For στοργαί

---

[7] Luther translates the word *Feldgeister* in Is. 13:21 and *Feldteufel* in Is. 34:24.

("natural affections") are not hindered or removed except in those matters which are in conflict with God's commandment. Therefore God honors even Esau's relationship for Isaac's sake. For what point was there in mention being made of Seir and the Horites, who were crushed and expelled by the new possessors of Seir? They are mentioned for the sake of secular sanctity,[8] as men say, or for the sake of the dignity of the political order.

The second reason is that there might be a testimony of the origin of the Edomites so that they might not be regarded as illegitimate and spurious. And this is, so to say, the fourth section in which the relationship of Esau is enumerated.

The Horites derive their name from the concept of whiteness, for חוּר means white, bright, large. In the East magnates use linen just as the Turk today uses a linen hat. Purple and the toga was a mark of distinction for the Romans; for the Orientals it is linen. Accordingly, it is stated of the rich voluptuary in the Gospel that he was clothed in purple and linen (Luke 16:19). Hence the Horites are mentioned from the clothing, like Roman Torquati ("men adorned with neck-chains"), etc.

Eliphaz married Timna, the sister of the Horite chief Lotan, and from her he begat Amalek. These people should not be completely condemned because they could be improved and recover their senses through the sermons of Esau. Mention was made of Anah previously, and the Jewish lies were refuted in which they find delight so that they may dishonor the Edomites and heathen and bring disgrace upon them just as they are also rejected by others.

For the public testimony of history is one thing, and nothing of this kind is extant concerning Anah to the effect that he committed incest with his daughter-in-law. A hidden deed is another thing and should not be brought forth into the light of day. It is said, for example, that "the church does not judge concerning hidden matters, but they are to remain among the secrets of confession." For this reason private confession should be retained in the church, for in it consciences afflicted and crushed by the terrors of sin lay themselves bare and receive consolation which they could not acquire in public preaching. We want to open up confession as a port and refuge for those whose consciences the devil holds enmeshed in his snares and whom he completely bewitches and torments in such a way that they

8 See p. 166.

cannot free or extricate themselves and feel and see nothing else but that they must perish. For there is no other greater misery in this life than the pains and perplexities of a heart that is destitute of guidance and solace.

To such, then, an approach to confession should be opened up so that they may seek and find consolation among the ministers of the church. Or, if the matter is so unbecoming that they are ashamed to make it known before a minister, let them pour it out upon the bosom of another Christian and godly man, whoever it may be, whose reliability is proven, and in his presence let them make their complaint concerning those matters which are pressing and pricking their conscience and let them seek advice, saying: "My dear brother, help my disturbed and afflicted conscience that I may not die in my sins or cut my life off with a rope or a sword. Advise me, dear brother! I am going to hang myself, drown myself, or do myself some harm and die in my sins, etc." In this case, when he hears the Word of God concerning the remission of sins, either from a minister or from someone else, he will be encouraged and receive the consolation by which his heart, wounded by the darts of the devil, will be healed. We do not ask here what or what kind of sins should be recited, but the special importance and usefulness of confession consists in the fact that salutary remedies are brought forward from the Word of God to those who are groaning and struggling with despair so that they do not succumb to the burden of sins and the terrors of the devil, which he is accustomed to increase to infinity. But it is especially important in special and unusual cases, such as sometimes occur when the devil is driving human nature on and deforming it with loathsome sins. Such a case happened formerly at Erfurt when I was a confessor there, a case which one of my colleagues heard in private confession. I shall, moreover, recount this instance for the sake of those who will be future pastors and teachers of the church.[9]

At Erfurt a virtuous young girl from an honorable family worked for a rich woman who was a widow. Her son, a youth, overcome by the girl's beauty and captivated by love for her, made advances on her to sleep with her. The young girl, feeling an aversion for the unworthy deed, as becomes an honorable woman, on several occasions repelled the passionate youth. Finally, when he became

---

[9] This anecdote is also recounted in Luther's *Table Talk* (W, *Tischreden*, III, 501—502).

more and more insistent daily and persevered in his illicit plan, the young girl, impelled by the indignity of the affair and in the interests of her good name and to protect her modesty from such great infamy, told his mother the whole story and urged her to curb her son, who was setting snares for her. The mother, after deliberating on the matter, entered upon a plan with the young girl and told her to agree to her son's love and to appoint a definite time when it seemed quite safe to come together and consummate the matter. At that very time she would occupy the girl's bed and at this opportunity she would prevent her son from making such unworthy attempts. The young girl approved the plan and entered upon the agreement. At the time of night previously fixed, the son put in an appearance, seeking to sleep with the girl according to the agreement. The mother who had previously determined to check and curb her son's passions in this way, overcome by lust and at the inspiration of the devil, prostituted her body to her son. From the unseemly and incestuous intercourse a little girl was born. She was exposed and brought up by others, but at last the mother, moved by natural affection, took the girl to herself.

The same son, ignorant of all these happenings, began to love this girl also and demanded her to be given to him as his wife. The mother, finding herself in the greatest of straits, dissuaded her son and opposed his illicit passion to the best of her ability. He, despite the unwillingness and opposition of his mother, made a pledge to the girl and made her his wife. At that time clandestine betrothals were customary and valid. After the nuptials the mother, in doubt and despair, wanted to lay violent hands on herself. For she was troubled about the incest which was committed by the married couple every night, but she could not dissolve the marriage. But since she alone knew of this and could no longer endure the grief and anxiety in her heart alone, she went to a confessor, explained the business, and sought advice and consolation from him. He was uncertain what advice he should give, being astonished by the atrocious nature of the matter. Accordingly, the same case was set before the jurists. They also had their doubts about the legality of the matter, since it was an unprecedented case, and offered the opinion that the matter should be committed to the goodness of God. But that was not satisfactory, and her conscience was not yet freed from doubt and despair. At length, this matter was referred to a committee of theologians, and they delivered an excellent opinion. First they asked whether the son knew that his wife was his mother's daughter conceived from his own blood. The mother said that he did not know it. "God alone and I know of it," she said, "nor does the girl who is my son's wife know that she is her husband's sister." Then they asked whether it was a good marriage and how they agreed with each other. "Excellently," she said. Accordingly, they decided that it was necessary to have regard for the afflicted conscience of the mother by absolving her but that the marriage already confirmed for a long time by means of betrothal and marriage rites and by bodily copulation should be conceded to the son. For the mother was only one person, and she was not able to prove the matter, and great evils would follow the separation of the married couple.

This sentence and decision of the theologians before whom the matter was transacted in secret was very laudable. For it is necessary for the law to exercise dominion in the public forum, not in a matter of conscience, and the gate of absolution, so to say, should never be closed to sinners, no matter how far the sinner falls. I have recounted this story for the sake of the younger theologians who are either already discharging the ministry of the Word or are about to do so, so that they may act cautiously with disturbed consciences and not put a snare upon those confessing their sins or add affliction to those afflicted. Judgments are difficult in hidden cases, and so learned and prudent pastors are required who do not burden or involve consciences but liberate, encourage, and heal the consciences which the devil has driven mad and enmeshed in his snares.

Another case is reported of an adulteress who had conceived a bastard from an adulterer and passed him off as legitimate to her husband and other sons. But when she became troubled in heart because of the adultery which had been committed and because the legitimate sons were being unjustly deprived of that part of the inheritance which was about to fall to the lot of the bastard, the question arose how she was to be advised. Should she confess the sin to her husband and sons and seek to have the bastard admitted to a share in the property? That is what some were advising. But since it seemed that this could not be done without danger, others advised another course. At last, however, the Holy Spirit suggested the best advice to the woman. For when she was lying on her bed sick and no hope of life was left, she summoned her seven sons to her and said to them: "My dear sons, I beg you to pardon me. I confess that by reason of human weakness I slipped into the very grave sin of adultery, from which an illegitimate son was born. He is in your midst, but I will not say who it is. But I pray that you may be willing to regard him as legitimate and that you refuse to exclude him from your inheritance." All agreed with complete equanimity and individually congratulated themselves that the bastard was not mentioned by name, for no one wanted to bear that stain. After that the brothers found it easy to come to an agreement. But the mother, having heard the comfort of the forgiveness of sins, found peace in the agony of death and was saved by true faith in God and the knowledge of His mercy. Therefore secret matters should not be blabbed forth rashly, as the Jews do it falsely in regard to Anah. Then, too, assistance should be given to afflicted consciences in such cases so that they may be freed and snatched from Satan's jaws, lest Christ's blood be shed in vain and be lost on him.

Chief Anah, however, is credited with the discovery of mules. For when he was pasturing the flocks of his father in the desert, he mated asses with mares, from whom mules were born. In his eighth book, chapter 44, Pliny gives a full description of the variety of these mixtures among the heathen.[10] They are in conflict with nature and the creation. Therefore it is a disgraceful and abominable discovery, and Pliny adds that the third genus which is born from different species is sterile because God does not want it to be propagated.

However, I have my doubts about the word יֵמִם, and I am not able to say anything definite about its meaning. For the Jews in their hatred of the Gentiles are very bold in inventing crimes to bespatter them with some blemish. Moreover, the vowel points used in the Hebrew language are a recent invention on which we cannot rely safely everywhere. Therefore it is possible that he discovered the pools and ponds of which there is frequent mention in Luke (cf. Luke 5:1-2; 8:22-23). Jerome has the same view,[11] and the text itself is not at variance with it, although it is added that he pastured asses. However, I make no firm pronouncement, though I have followed the rabbis in the German translation. But it seems very fitting because of the scarcity of water in the desert that the discovery of pools should be attributed to this man or someone else. The Hebrew letters agree

---

[10] Pliny, *Natural History,* VIII, 44—45, 105—107.

[11] Jerome, *Liber Hebraicarum quaestionum in Genesim, Patrologia, Series Latina,* XXIII, 993—994.

and the points too, if correctly written יַמִּם, which means pools. There is a great blessing and usefulness in pools, especially in dry, desert places. But if he meant mules, then he should also have made mention of mares, and this was not done by Moses.

31. *These are the kings who reigned in the land of Edom, before any king reigned over the Israelites.*

32. *Bela the son of Beor reigned in Edom, the name of his city being Dinhabah.*

33. *Bela died, and Jobab the son of Zerah of Bozrah reigned in his stead.*

34. *Jobab died, and Husham of the land of the Temanites reigned in his stead.*

35. *Husham died, and Hadad the son of Bedad, who defeated Midian in the country of Moab, reigned in his stead; the name of his city being Avith.*

36. *Hadad died, and Samlah of Masrekah reigned in his stead.*

37. *Samlah died, and Shaul of Rehoboth on the Euphrates reigned in his stead.*

38. *Shaul died, and Baal-hanan the son of Achbor reigned in his stead.*

39. *Baal-hanan the son of Achbor died, and Hadar reigned in his stead, the name of his city being Pau; his wife's name was Mehetabel, the daughter of Matred, daughter of Mezahab.*

So far Moses has described the chiefs from the line of Esau, or Edom, and then the chiefs of Seir and the Horites who were joined by marriage to Esau and his sons. The sons of Edom destroyed these heroic men and seized their land, which was later called Edom, or Idumea. Today it has lost this name, and from the time of Jerome it has been called Gabalena.[12] For just as kingdoms are changed, so also names vary. Now he also recounts the kings of Edom. For we stated previously that God honored the patriarch Isaac and Rebecca in these men, even as He bestows this honor on Abraham

---

[12] Jerome, *Liber de situ et nominibus locorum Hebraicorum, Patrologia, Series Latina,* XXIII, 903.

and Sarah above, that He blesses Ishmael and promises him a great posterity for their sakes. For He says to Abraham in chapter 17:20: "As for Ishmael, I have heard you; behold, I will bless him and make him fruitful and multiply him exceedingly; he shall be the father of twelve princes, and I will make him a great nation." These gifts God gave to the Ishmaelites as a favor to Abraham, and the Ishmaelites undoubtedly retained circumcision and the rest of the ceremonies, and perhaps also the doctrine and faith of the promised seed, and so were joined to the church of Abraham, just as, on the other hand, many from the family of Abraham fell away from the house and family of Abraham and became heathen.

In this manner, God bestowed Mount Seir, or the land of the Horites, on the Edomites by whom the former were destroyed. It also seems that they remained in the faith and religion of their fathers Abraham and Isaac; but the Horites, seeing that they refused to correct and change their idolatrous worship, were destroyed. In this place, then, the bodily blessing of Esau is described, and from this an approach has also been made to the spiritual blessing. Although Christ was not to be expected from the seed of Esau, yet he and his sons were not denied the enjoyment of the common blessings of the promise along with the people of Israel. In the Books of Kings, for example, we see that at one time the Edomites were friends and subjects of the kings of Judah, as in the times of David, who subjugated Idumea; at other times they again revolted, as under Joram.

All these matters are mentioned in honor of the fathers Abraham, Isaac, and Jacob and as a favor to them so that no one should think that the way to grace and the blessing of the promised Seed was shut off for the Edomites.

It is asked, however, whether these chiefs and kings were before or after Moses. If they were after Moses, then he himself could not have written these things but the addition was made by another man, such as is also the case with the last part in Deuteronomy. For he did not say of himself: "There has not arisen another after Moses with whom God spoke face to face in this way" (cf. Deut. 34:10). It is the same with the other matters related there about the sepulcher of Moses, etc., unless you were to say that he foresaw these matters and foretold them under the prophetic spirit.[13] But because the Holy

[13] Cf. *Luther's Works,* 9, p. 283, where Luther states that "Moses cannot have written chapter 34."

Spirit mentions these kings and chiefs, we also hold them in remembrance.

The chiefs, moreover, were mentioned above before the kings. They did not reign successively but all together in such a way that each ruled over his cities, families, and subjects in his own place, and the land was usually divided into 12 or more provinces. Among these there were many illustrious men like the grandsons of Isaac and Rebecca, although their mothers were descended from the ungodly family of the Horites. But the kings who are enumerated in this passage succeeded the chiefs. For they saw that a monarchy was necessary so that the whole region might be brought under one head into one body and the defense against the neighboring Philistines, Arabians, and Egyptians whom they had as hostile foes might be firmer. This, then, is the monarchy of the kings of Edom.

But this catalog of kings and chiefs of Esau reminds us that the spiritual promises were fulfilled very slowly. For Paul says in 1 Cor. 15:46: "It is not the spiritual which is first but the physical, and then the spiritual." God endowed the offspring of Esau with many great bodily gifts; He gave them sons and grandsons, and all these were chiefs and kings. Jacob had a spiritual blessing and a promise, namely: "Be lord over your brothers, etc." (27:29), concerning which mention was made above.[14] But he is a most wretched shepherd, wandering with his sons as a stranger and an exile. Therefore how is God true when He does not fulfill the promise made to Jacob but blesses Esau and multiplies him after He has taken away the blessing from him? Here, then, Esau's posterity boasted that the birthright was in their possession but that Jacob was rejected because they were the rulers of the land. The flesh thinks that this by no means agrees with the truth of God and is greatly offended at the pride of those who abound in bodily gifts.

But a reply must be given from Ps. 2:4: "He who sits in the heavens laughs; the Lord has them in derision," and the heathen poet said: "They are lifted on high that they may tumble with a greater fall," [15] and this agrees with the statement in Ps. 73:18: "Truly Thou didst set them in slippery places; Thou didst make them fall to ruin, etc." This, indeed, is the fortune of the ungodly. They are lifted on high by the success and glory of the flesh, even as the Edom-

14 Cf. *Luther's Works,* 5, pp. 137—141.

15 Claudian, *De raptu Proserpinae,* III, 387.

ites boasted, saying: "We have the kingdom; we hold the land of Seir and the Horites. Jacob is a beggar and a vagabond who is spent by troubles, disasters, cold, and heat, and he is unfortunate on every count. He has disobedient children who are rascals. Reuben has gone up to the maternal couch; Dinah has been defiled by Shechem; therefore he does not have the blessing by any means." But God allows these things to happen so that faith may be exercised and that we may learn to depend on the Word alone and not to have regard for visible things and those things that are perceptible to the senses but for the things that do not appear and that we may retain this consolation against all understanding and judgment of reason. This consolation Paul gives us in 2 Cor. 4:9, when he says that we are "persecuted, but not forsaken; struck down, but not destroyed, etc."

For the things which are discerned by the eyes are deceiving and transient, but the things which are promised and not seen are sure and steadfast. But delay and postponement are to be awaited in faith and borne with equanimity, for the invisible things will appear at the right time. Of whatever kind the glory of the kings and chiefs of the Edomites was, the dignity of the promise of the Seed, of the prophets, of the wonderful liberations from Egypt and from other enemies, and likewise of the most illustrious victories which the people of Israel had was much greater and more excellent, so that the blessing of the Edomites should not even be compared with these gifts. Jacob, however, is still a rotten dried tree trunk, so to say, buried in the earth, but he will germinate at the right time. That which blooms immediately and is attractive by its outward appearance is not steadfast and lasting. Here, too, the verse of the poet is in place: "O beautiful boy, trust not too much to color," [16] that is, "Be on your guard against that which is imposing, but regard and admire those who have the promise." For the Divine Majesty is accustomed to raise the proud so that they seem to flourish and increase, but added is what was quoted from the Psalm before (73:18): "Thou didst make them fall to ruin." In this way God deceives and deludes the devil and the world.

Therefore those who have the promise and faith are cold and hungry, despised and undistinguished, just as a certain man said that he took no great pains to cultivate or to understand the doctrine of religion but that it was perfectly plain to him that the most wretched

16 Vergil, *Eclogues,* II, 17.

of men are those who serve God and Caesar. But the ungodly boast about their scepter and rule, and they have reason to do so, for God fills their belly with good things, He gives them the kingdoms and riches of the world according to Ps. 17:14: "May their children have more than enough; may they leave something over to their babes." He also gives bodily blessings to the saints, but slowly and in the midst of many tribulations so that their faith may be exercised and that they may learn to know the gifts of God and to use them in a godly manner.

Let us therefore remain in that assembly which has the Word, even though it is despised and abject. The ungodly, proud, and greedy grow and are increased excellently in this world. They keep on growing so that everyone thinks they will continue to have success. The godly even begin to murmur and to feel displeasure, saying in the words of Ps. 73:13: "All in vain have I kept my heart clean and washed my hands in innocence." But the Psalm replies: "Truly Thou didst set them in slippery places" (v. 18). In the end confusion follows. These matters therefore belong to our doctrine that we may not be offended by the scandals that are customary and always present in the world. Then, too, those of the Edomites and Ishmaelites who realized that this honor and these blessings were given by God out of respect for the blood of the patriarchs and who were grateful at the same time, for them an approach to grace and eternal salvation was opened. But the greater part were ungodly and proud and therefore perished.

Furthermore, I am of the opinion that these kings belonged to the time of Moses, because chiefs were born to Esau before the death of Isaac and exercised dominion in the land of Seir while Jacob was still living in Mesopotamia. On his return from there, they met him under arms with their father, and their government lasted for 20 or 30 years, up to Isaac's death. Then the flowering of the flesh and the bodily blessing began, but the kings ruled for more than 200 years. Later other chiefs followed. Therefore it can be seen how the glory of the flesh increased among those who lacked the promise of the Seed.

In the meantime Jacob, with whom was the flower of the blessing, is an exile in a foreign land, but there appears in him absolute aridity and sterility, and on seeing this, the Edomites taunted him saying: "That, to be sure, is the blessing which Jacob seized by fraud from our father Esau." They declared that it was a just judgment of the Lord, who did not leave this wrong unavenged. "Behold, we have princes and kings," they said. "The Israelites are slaves and captives exposed to all injuries and disasters." The priests and jurists also preached the same, even as the Turks and papal priests boast of the success of their side today. Very few of the godly were fortified against this great scandal and looked to the promise and concluded that God could not forget His promise and that it would subsequently come to pass that a shoot would sprout forth from the dry trunk who would at length blossom and bring forth fruit.

I think, moreover, that these kings were good men on the civil plane and that some of them were saints since, indeed, the Holy Spirit did not disdain to enumerate and honor them. Their histories and achievements, as well as the descriptions of their kingdom and towns, are unknown to us, although there is no doubt that some memorials of them existed among the Jews. The sons of Esau wrote up the illustrious deeds and the status and administration of the whole kingdom.

The first king is Beor, and when he dies, Jobab of Bozrah succeeds him. Bozrah is a celebrated city in Idumea, and mention is made of it in Isaiah and Jeremiah (48:24; 49:13, 22), although Isaiah uses the word improperly by means of the figure called catachresis and understands it as Jerusalem (Is. 63:1). There is also another Bozrah in Arabia Petraea. Augustine and Ambrose [17] think that this Jobab is of the family of Esau and that he is Job, and there are many conjectures linked with this opinion. For the letters agree and also the names of his friends, and of these Eliphaz the Temanite seems to have had his origin from Teman in the land of Edom, and likewise Bildad and Zophar. If this is true, it agrees well with history, for Job was very wise in God's Law and embraced the doctrine and circumcision of his father Esau.

Lyra argues in opposition because there is a difference in the initial letters.[18] Jobab is written with י, Job with א. But I reply that it is not unusual in Holy Scripture for א to be inserted and י to be omitted, and vice versa, as well at the beginning as at the end and in the middle of a word. Therefore it is a weak argument. In our nobility this name Jof has also maintained itself, that is, Job, Jobst, etc. But be that as it may, the Hebrews say that Job was descended from Nahor, the brother of Abraham, of the family of Bethuel and Laban

[17] Ambrose (?), *Commentaria in epistolam ad Romanos, Patrologia, Series Latina*, XVII, 131.

[18] Lyra *ad* Gen. 31:33, p. 101 recto, note "f."

in Syria. From here they think that Balaam also had his origin, and this is quite likely and in agreement with Holy Scripture. Therefore, if it is permitted to make a conjecture, it appears that the city of Haran was an outstanding church and school in Mesopotamia where Job and his like came together, and likewise Balaam, for the Word was spread abroad through that family.

Accordingly, just as Abraham and Isaac established and ruled their church, so also Nahor, and the doctrine was transmitted from those patriarchs and governors of the churches to posterity. From these churches and schools came forth prophets, teachers, and patriarchs, among whom was Job. But I make no decision as to whether he was descended from Esau or Nahor. This, however, is agreed upon, that his origin is connected with Shem, and this is the holy line of Christ laterally. For the doctrine remained with Shem, and from there it was propagated to Idumea, Mesopotamia, Arabia, Syria, and later through Joseph to Egypt.

In this way God gathered and preserved His church from the beginning, just as under the papacy Baptism, the Keys, the Eucharist, and other pure articles of faith were retained, while the pope in the meantime established others concerning relics, the invocation of saints, and purgatory, by which he corrupted and weakened sound doctrine. So Jerusalem was full of altars and idols. And yet God always preserves His church in the world in the midst of hypocrites and idolaters. Therefore we leave the discussion concerning Job's origin undecided. The friends of whom mention is made in his history were undoubtedly wise and learned men. Balaam also was a good prophet until it came to gold. When that comes, he is corrupted.

Because of the epithet Temanite, however, I rather incline to this view, that Job was descended from Esau, because Arabia is closer to Judea and better known there, although Mesopotamia is also close by. But the Arabians extended almost over the whole East, and Job complains that he had suffered this disaster from Sheba, that is, the Chaldaeans. But we cannot make a definite statement on the matter because there is great obscurity and confusion in the proper names of the Hebrew language because of the change of letters, even the consonants, as with Hadad and Hadar. Likewise, Moses calls his son Gershom, as though you were to say, "a stranger there," "a guest here" (Ex. 2:22); and yet throughout the whole of Scripture he is called Gershon.

Hadad smote the Midianites. This victory was granted to him by God in honor of Isaac, although Midian was also a son of Abraham. But I think that the former was a good man, whereas the latter was proud and joined idolatrous worship with the doctrine of Abraham. Therefore he was conquered on the plain of Moab, where they engaged in battle after having proceeded through another area from their own lands that they might join in battle. These are stories close in time to the descent into Egypt.

Shaul was from Rehoboth, that is, from a broad river, on the water, from the nearby river Nahar, or the Euphrates, just as we say on the Elbe or on the Rhine. There was, moreover, a union or association among the blood relations of the Idumeans, and they also concluded relationship ties with their neighbors in Mesopotamia.

Baalhannan, Hannibal by changing the word around, is the Latin *vir gratiosus* ("a gracious man"), John. Of the eight kings, however, only three have cities, Bela, Hadad, and Hadar. They seem to have been good householders, who increased and adorned their state in peace, built cities, and established them by means of laws and judgments.

Mehetabel was a distinguished and famous woman, since she is honored by Moses in preference to all the others. The name means as much as "benefactress of God," one who has done well before God or is doing well through God, like Theodosia. Her lineage is also mentioned, namely, that she was born in an illustrious family from honorable parents, and the description is like the previous one concerning the origin of Oholibamah, where we said that the poisonous lies of the Jews must be rejected. For she can be called a daughter of her father and a daughter of her grandfather, who on the death of her father took his place as her guardian, a custom which is usually kept up also now under the sanction of civil law.

Moreover, I think that this Hadar was the last king of the Edomites and that Jephthah speaks of him in Judges 11, saying that on the ascent from Egypt the king of Edom was asked to let the children of Israel pass through his land but they could not obtain permission from him. I think that God exacted punishment for this pride and that the monarchy of Edom was again split into provinces. Two years after leaving Egypt, the people of Israel were on the approach to the Holy Land, but when they sinned against the Lord, they were compelled to go back again and to travel around the land of Edom.

They completed that journey in 38 years; for so long they retraced their steps about the mountains of Edom. Therefore in my opinion this Hadar was the last king, and on his death the chiefs followed who are enumerated in the last place.

40. *These are the names of the chiefs of Esau, according to their families and their dwelling places, by their names: the chiefs Timna, Alvah, Jetheth,*

41. *Oholibamah, Elah, Pinon,*

42. *Kenaz, Teman, Mibzar,*

43. *Magdiel, and Iram, these are the chiefs of Edom (that is, Esau, the father of Edom), according to their dwelling places in the land of their possession.*

After the kings and the destruction of the monarchy because of the sin of king Hadar, who did not offer the children of Israel a crossing through Idumea, these chiefs follow, each one in his place and according to his name and family, just as Moses says, and he indicates that there was not a succession such as there was among the kings. But the historical order of events is quite consistent. The kingdom of Edom lasted for the 200 years that Jacob spent with his posterity in Egypt. But after they came out of Egypt, Idumea was again divided into provinces, by which it was governed until the time of David, who subjected Idumea. But although the rest were descendants of royal stock, they are not enumerated. Later, under Joram, a second mention will be made of the king of Edom, when the Idumeans revolt from the king of Judah.

The genealogy of Esau, then, is fittingly added to the history of the two patriarchs Isaac and Jacob. For in this we see the glory and flourishing of the flesh and of ungodly men in this life. They abound in rank, resources, and successes; they gain possession of the empires and kingdoms of the world and either disregard or oppress the godly, just as the Edomites in proud fashion looked down on Jacob together with his posterity. On the other hand, Jacob, who has the promise and is the highest patriarch in the whole world and the governor of the true church, is oppressed in a wretched manner and afflicted by domestic and other troubles, so that it seems that he has been deprived of the spiritual blessing and grace. Yet in the end finally follows what is stated in Mary's song: "He puts down the mighty and exalts the lowly" (cf. Luke 1:52). This is the conclusion, this is the end of the ungodly and the godly, as Christ says (Luke 6:24-25): "Woe to you that are rich, for you have received your consolation. Woe to you that are full now, for you shall hunger," and again (Matt. 5:4): "Blessed are those who mourn, for they shall be comforted."

Let us then make efforts to attach ourselves to the poor and to the mourners who have the promise rather than to the ungodly who, even though they flourish for a time, are finally overthrown and destroyed. But the godly, who are oppressed for a time, have certain protection and consolation in GOD, who is present and sustains the afflicted, mitigates their troubles, and gives eternal life and glory to the little flock when it again emerges from troubles. Nor should we be shattered in spirit, even though great toils and adversities must be endured, but we should conclude that God's Son, our Lord Jesus Christ, the guardian and leader of all who labor and are oppressed in the world, is at our side even as He has promised (Matt. 28:20): "I am with you always, to the close of the age," to whom with the eternal Father and Holy Spirit be praise and glory forever! Amen.[19]

[19] In the first edition of the Lectures on Genesis, this was the end of the third volume.

CHAPTER THIRTY-SEVEN

1. *Jacob dwelt in the land of his father's sojournings, in the land of Canaan.*

THIS last story is the story of the last of the patriarchs, Joseph, with which Moses concludes the Book of Genesis, a very beautiful and happy climax, as it were, of everything and especially of the life and troubles of Jacob. For when his home and household was in a most disturbed condition and full of great disasters and the worries by which we have heard that the saintly patriarch was afflicted, not so much on account of the enmity of his brother and injuries from his father-in-law, which he overcame with great courage, unconquerable faith, and wonderful patience, as on account of his domestic afflictions, Dinah's defilement, and the deaths of his nurse Deborah and his wife Rachel, and finally on account of the unspeakable incest of his son, who polluted the paternal couch — in these great difficulties, his one hope and comfort in old age and in troubles remained in the firstborn son of his deceased wife, Joseph, who with his piety and saintly life in one way or another healed and encouraged the sick heart of his father. Suddenly and unexpectedly he is also removed, so that the unhappy father after the loss of his dearest wife is also deprived of the son who was especially beloved. For Joseph is sold and removed far from the sight of his father into Egypt by the hatred and malice not of strangers or enemies but of brothers. When they fraudulently concealed their crime and displayed the bloody coat to their father as though he had been torn to pieces by a beast, the father's only conviction was that the son had perished in a wretched manner, and he was so dismayed at heart that he refused to admit any comfort from the rest of his sons and daughters.

Into these troubles and into hell itself the aged Jacob is hurled by the wickedness and criminality of his sons. As a result of this, his faith was undoubtedly so severely tried and shaken that it was not without great conflict that he was able to retain the promise given to him. His heart was smitten not only στοργῇ ("by natural affection") towards his son but also by doubt and unbelief as to whether God wanted to keep His promise or whether He had cast him off completely on account of certain sins, since, indeed, he had to be deprived of that son who he hoped would be the heir of the promised blessing and of all good things.

This story, then, is the last trouble of the saintly man and by far the most serious one of all, and it is a very horrible one. The very beginning and the whole exposition contains a sharp and very vehement struggle. For it is full of shameful and wretched grief which all but kills the saintly old man, who is exhausted by so many troubles and hardships. There is also the additional crime of his son Judah perpetrating incest with his daughter-in-law Tamar, which also increased the grief and sorrow of the father. But he nevertheless retains hope and confidence with wonderful constancy, and by reason of the numerous examples of illustrious rescues which he experienced throughout his whole life he encourages and sustains himself until new light and consolation shine forth. For there follows the wonderful and peaceful outcome by which his great and unexpected grief is changed into the greatest unexpected joy. For Joseph, whose destruction the father had mourned, is recalled from darkness to light, from death to life, after being preserved by God and rewarded with great honor and dignity by the king of Egypt after he himself had also emerged from many difficulties.

This is the end of the first book of Moses and the sixth and last book according to that division of our exposition which we set out above.[1] But just as there is nothing more beautiful in Holy Scripture than Genesis as a whole, so also this example is outstanding and memorable among the rest of the stories of the patriarchs and plainly of such a kind that I am not able to do it justice in words and thoughts. Therefore I could wish to leave its exposition to others who far excel me in learning and eloquence. But because the order of the exposition[2] begun requires that we should at least say something, we shall read through the story itself, admirable and lofty as it truly is, even though we cannot treat and explain it according to its worth.

But first of all the thread of the narrative must be taken up again from the foregoing events. For at the end of chapter 35:29 Moses

---

[1] Cf. *Luther's Works*, 2, p. 3.

[2] The Weimar text has *enarrationes*, but we have read *enarrationis*.

related that the patriarch Isaac died old and full of days and was gathered to his fathers and buried by his two sons Esau and Jacob in the land of Canaan. From this point he digressed to a description of the genealogy of Esau, taking opportunity from the fact that Esau had been present at his father's burial and with him in all probability all his sons and relatives, who then had returned into favor with Jacob, a reconciliation having been made between the brothers. Therefore all that follows right up to chapter 40 was done while the patriarch Isaac was still alive. Accordingly, we called attention to the fact that following the true historical order these things should be inserted in chapter 35, before the last section beginning with the words: "Now the days of Isaac were, etc." (v. 28).

This reminder is very necessary so that the reader may the more easily find his way through this description, which is somewhat confused, and get rid of the difficulties. For all the other interpreters, and especially Lyra and Augustine, involve themselves in no little difficulty with this passage, and so much so that Augustine nearly begins to have troubles and doubts about the authority of Holy Scripture.[3] The same thing usually befalls those who concern themselves with contradictions, who try hard to shake the reliability of sacred history. If ever they fall on passages of this kind, they stick to them very closely and cry out that the holy sermons and histories hang together poorly and that all is confused and uncertain. Therefore they never reach the true light and knowledge of sacred things.

Among the Cabalists there is a rule which says: "In the Law there is no former or latter." But this is not universally true, nor can it be applied to this narrative. For Isaac is still alive when Joseph is sold into Egypt and also 12 years later, when he is again brought forth from prison and elevated to the rule and government of all of Egypt. Accordingly, the following story about the defilement of Tamar is to be referred to the same time. For this crime was perpetrated by Judah while his grandfather Isaac was still alive. Later, however, we shall review the reckoning of the years and the catalog of persons. For if anyone gathers together the years from Jacob's marriage until the descent into Egypt, he will find that many great and wonderful things were done in these 46 years. And although the story seems quite confused to the inexperienced and to those who are eager to find contradictions, nevertheless, godly readers, being

---

[3] Cf. Augustine, *Quaestiones in Heptateuchum*, I, 122, *Patrologia, Series Latina*, XXXIV, 580—581.

reminded of the historical order, will easily unfold and clearly see the true order of the narrative.

Moses now proceeds with the history of the patriarch Jacob and writes that he dwelt in the land in which his father had been a stranger. For he had come to Isaac while he lived in Hebron in the land of Canaan, and there he also settled his own family. Furthermore, it is called a land of sojourning because although it was promised to Abraham, Isaac, and Jacob, they nevertheless did not possess anything in it that was their own for certain except the right of burial bought by Abraham, as we heard above. Accordingly, Jacob also journeyed from place to place in the manner of his fathers and as herdsmen are accustomed to do, wandering here and there as the convenience of his flocks and pastures determined. But in that sojourning he did not leave his father Isaac since he brought Dinah to him after she had been defiled and his very dear son Joseph, whom old Isaac also undoubtedly saw and embraced with great joy and pleasure.

2. *These are the generations of Jacob. Joseph, being seventeen years old, was shepherding the flock with his brothers; he was a lad with the sons of Bilhah and Zilpah, his father's wives; and Joseph brought an ill report of them to their father.*

Holy Scripture is accustomed to set forth a description of the generations even when it counts only one son, as Joseph alone is named in this place, the other sons of Jacob being omitted as though all the rest were outside of the number and as though this one were the only true son since, indeed, he is numbered in the genealogy before the rest. To be sure, he is the only one who has a right to be preferred to all the others, for he was born from the chief wife and was anxiously awaited a long time by his parents and to him belonged by marriage law the whole dignity and honor of the distinction of being the firstborn, although he did not yet hold that honor, as we shall hear.

What then is the offspring, or family, of Jacob? He has a son who is called Joseph. Yet what is his condition, what is his fortune? Listen to Moses! "Joseph, being seventeen years old, was shepherding the flock with his brothers." This is how Joseph was situated as a youth of 17, old and strong enough to be able to be a husband on the example of the rest of the brothers. For Judah, Reuben, and the others at that time had wives and sons, but he is still living as a celi-

bate in his youth, without a wife and a household. He alone is loved
by his old father and is an object of delight to him, because he was
born from his sweetest wife, who had died, and the whole life and
interests and morals of this paragon of innocence commended him
in a wonderful manner.

But to whom does he join himself as a companion? He does not
associate with the chief sons of Leah, with Judah, Simeon, Reuben,
and Levi. For these men very proudly despise this son of Rachel.
The young man of excellent character also sees that the sons of the
maidservants are cast off and despised and regarded by the four
sons of Leah as the vilest of slaves. Therefore he finds delight
especially in associating with them. For the insolence and ferocity
of the rest was great. Reuben, indeed, had been humiliated in some
degree because of the disgraceful stain of incest by which he had
polluted his father's couch. I also think that Judah was rather modest.
But Levi and Simeon were the proud warriors and murderers who
had slaughtered the Shechemites. They were very coarse, uppish,
and proud peasants and ruffians!

It is assuredly a remarkable factor that they sat at the feet of the
saintly parents, Isaac, Jacob, Rebecca, and the nurse Deborah for
such a long time without any progress and improvement in morals
and life. For they are described by Moses in such a way that it
seems that their outrageous sins nearly equaled the disgraceful examples of the heathen. Therefore let us not be surprised if such
a large multitude departs from true godliness in this last evil time
and hears so many illustrious sermons in vain, and let us be content
when even a few retain an interest for the Word and are improved.
For we see that the holy patriarch Jacob had the same experience,
for in his home and household the chief sons were the authors of
such great misery, such bitter grief and pain for their fathers!

But in the youth Joseph a singular modesty shines forth. He
bears this senseless and boorish insolence and contempt for himself
and the brothers born from the maids with due moderation. Indeed,
it would be more fitting for him to be proud as the firstborn than
for Simeon and Levi. Accordingly, we shall treat this story in this
manner: we shall exaggerate their arrogance in a hateful manner that
the grace and mercy of God, who knows how to bring good from
evil, may be more clearly perceived. We shall not cover their foul
disgrace and outrageous sins but amplify them as much as we can.

For it is unworthy and a cause for grief that an excellent parent should be treated and mocked by his sons in such unworthy ways. They grieved their pious father Jacob too deeply altogether and played with the poor old man in a pitiable manner!

Joseph also had the same reason for avoiding association with them and for staying with the despised sons of the maidservants, although he himself was born from a nobler mother. He lets the murderers of Shechem alone. From this the excellent character and good sense of the youth is evident, and this Moses wants to commend. For he had a good nature, a mild, humble, and modest disposition, to which piety was added and honorable and gentle ways by which he won over to himself the hearts not only of his parents but also of his neighbors. So it is not strange that his father loved him especially, not only because he was his son but also because of his disposition and the beautiful virtues with which he was endowed. Joseph is like a shining morning star in Jacob's house with whom those stupid and gross peasants could not even stand comparison. Therefore he abandons them and attaches himself to the despised brothers; he pastures the flocks along with them in accordance with the wishes and good pleasure of his father, although he was his chief son and the future king of Egypt. The great king in Egypt has to mind the sheep in his youth!

But Joseph is also worthy of commendation on this account, that he reported the evil doings of the brothers to his father. For he was a lover of justice and honesty and full of love and obedience towards his father, and so he could not conceal from him anything that was done by the brothers by which others were harmed and ill repute came upon his father's house. Accordingly, when he heard that some disgraceful report was being circulated about the brothers, he reported it to Jacob as to a judge whose duty it was [4] to take precautions so that his home and church, adorned with so many magnificent promises, might not be deformed by evil examples and that the name and worship of God which Jacob and those of his household professed might not be blasphemed by outsiders. Joseph wanted this profession to be unimpaired and unharmed and uncontaminated by any scandal. The impudence of the brothers undoubtedly brought great grief upon him when he saw disgrace heaped upon themselves and the whole church of Jacob among the heathen.

[4] The Weimar text has *doceret* but we have read *deceret*.

Accordingly, he complained to his father on several occasions about their arrogance and the wrongs which they inflicted in turn either on himself or on their neighbors. "Reuben, Simeon, and Levi," he said, "are restless, turbulent men who frequently stir up tumults and quarrels by which they offend the heathen living round about us who are watching our life and ways very carefully. These scandals should be removed from our home and church so that we may not be reproached on their account among those who are without."

Today also we are surrounded by papists who have very sharp eyes and ears and very keen noses with which they keep watch on us in hostile fashion to see if anything disgraceful can be smelled concerning us or if even our honorable deeds and words can be slandered. Paul therefore is careful to remind us: "See to it, brethren, that you walk carefully that you may give no occasion to an adversary to speak evil" (cf. Eph. 5:15), and likewise: "Conduct yourselves wisely toward outsiders" (Col. 4:5). Our adversaries are very eager to hunt up even all the most fickle of idle talk about us. They do not see our good deeds or care about them but despise them. But they are delighted with evil things and an adverse report.

Therefore the patriarch Jacob had to be concerned about a blameless report and a good name in his household as a bishop and teacher of the church. For it does not become a pastor to live in a dishonorable manner or to administer his household and home in a disgraceful manner. It is far better to bear the contempt and hatred of adversaries than to fall into reproach and into the snare of the devil, as Paul says in 1 Tim. 3:7.

The same concern and desire for avoiding offenses of every kind which tended to bring contempt on Jacob's house, the church, and the promise was to be found in the youth Joseph. There is no doubt that he was much hated by his brothers and that they took their father's admonitions very badly. They were therefore also very indignant if they found out that their atrocious sins had been brought to light by Joseph. "A curse upon that traitor," they said, "who immediately reports to our father whatever he hears has been done or said by us." For they assumed for themselves unrestrained license in perpetrating anything at all, unknown to their father, and they interpreted the godly and friendly chastisement of others in their family as a betrayal. Indeed, in their hatred of them they became worse and daily augmented their malice and sins, quite unconcerned whether they were ill spoken of or well spoken of among the heathen.

Lyra and Burgensis make anxious inquiries in this passage as to what disgraceful crime it was of which Joseph accused his brothers.[5] For this is how it reads in the old translation. But it is a superfluous question, for the simplest meaning can be derived from the Hebrew text. The word דִּבַּת itself means rumor, report, opinion scattered among the people, as in Num. 13:32, when Moses sent spies into Cannaan and when they returned, they all made a דִּבַּת of the land go out, that is, they published a bad report, an unfavorable opinion or rumor concerning the land. Moses says the same thing here of Joseph: "Joseph brought an ill report of them to their father." He used to attach himself to the four sons of the maidservants, Gad, Naphtali, Asher, and Dan since they were more modest than the remaining four brothers, who prided themselves immoderately because of their birthright from their mother Leah and by their life and morals won ill repute for themselves. Nor did they respect their father but thought that everything was permitted to them because they were sons of a patriarch and had promises. But Joseph, being a lover of discipline, peace, and honor, was troubled about the wickedness of his brothers and fairly often made a report of their sins to his father and urged him to enforce the principles of discipline in his home and church more strictly. This was one cause for hatred, namely, that Joseph was a careful guardian of his father's house and wanted its reputation and good report for doctrine to be preserved unimpaired. He is a good man and promotes what is good. But he wants scandals to be removed, and so he experiences the fortune which is the common lot of good men and incurs the hatred and persecution of his brothers. Now the second cause is added.

3. *Now Israel loved Joseph more than any other of his children, because he was the son of his old age; and he made him a long robe with many threads.*

This really was a hard and intolerable matter for these great princes in their pride. They were not able to bear this love towards Joseph, for he was still a boy and the youngest of them. "We are the masters," they said, "born from mother Leah, the chief wife, before Joseph was conceived. I, Reuben, was born in the first year

[5] Lyra *ad* Gen. 37:2, p. 101 verso, note "d," and p. 103 verso, "Replica."

after the marriage, Simeon in the second, Levi in the third, etc. Joseph is the issue of the latest birth. Therefore we are the substance and special ornament of this home. Rachel with her offspring is a kind of addition and accession. Accordingly, the honor and goodwill of our father and the whole family is owing to us."

For these reasons there flared up in them that hostile and cruel hatred toward their brother because they did not have a sound mind but were full of ill will and possessed by the devil. Reason and common sense dictate that Joseph is rightly and naturally loved by his father in preference to the others because Rachel was his chief wife and from her the firstborn Joseph was awaited with such great longing on the part of his parents for seven years and at length born in Jacob's old age, and then, too, he was endowed with an excellent character and every kind of virtue. I also would have loved such a son more than the rest, even if he had not been the firstborn, inasmuch as he showed himself obedient and compliant in all things. Accordingly, even by nature it was the most just and fair love, a love which they, burning with criminal and ungodly hatred, were not able to bear because they wished rather to be esteemed and honored by Joseph and to hear from him the words: "You are the masters and leaders of our father's house; whatever pleases you pleases me." This is the probity and modesty they looked for in their brother. But when Joseph respects his father and shows him due honor and finally also is a faithful and careful guardian of his father's house and discipline, they sadly afflict and torment the excellent old man and by fraud and violence drive the boy Joseph from their home. For they do not endure a curb being put on their desires and license and want their outrageous crimes to be praised rather than censured.

The same perversity is also today running through all ranks in the church, state, and home. For all men are grumbling against those who remind them of what is right, and they are indignant with those who reprove faults and sins, even enormous public sins. One must not oppose anyone but allow everyone to do what he likes! One man makes his rank a pretext for his impudence, another his wealth, another his country or parents, and for these reasons one is supposed to connive at their sins and disgraceful conduct. "I occupy a magistracy," they say, "therefore my rank is to be treated with consideration. I am a citizen of Wittenberg or Nürnberg, and therefore I rightly claim more for myself than a guest or a stranger." On the other hand, those who are modest and remain within the limits of duty and the laws are regarded with hatred by all. The very same thing happened to excellent Joseph in the household of Jacob.

That he was loved by his father in a special way over and above the other brothers increased their envy. Jacob, to be sure, also loved them as his own true sons, but for just reasons he is more ardent στοργῇ ("with natural affection") towards Joseph, and because they could not endure this, they are worthy of hatred. I am surprised that there was a place for them in the holy church of Jacob for so long. I would have killed all of them or driven them out of the house. For what madness and malice is it to be angry with a father who loves an upright and godly son who has been born from a very dear wife! Above, therefore, we stated that this wickedness should be amplified and exaggerated as much as possible.[6] For they really go too far!

But a discussion arises here among the grammarians why Moses sets forth the fact that Joseph was born in Jacob's old age as a reason for his love. For the contrary can be proved by many arguments, and history shows the opposite. Burgensis has noted that the Chaldean translation reads: "He loved him because he was for him a son with the wisdom of old men," that is, he was such a son and there was such wisdom in him that he could vie with any old man in wisdom. The statement of Isaiah 65:20 could also be applied here: "The child shall die a hundred years old," that is, all will be wise beyond their years; boys will be just as wise as if they were 100 years old. Lyra contends against this, arguing that he is called a son of old age because his father begat him in old age.[7] But I do not see how this view agrees with what is also stated below about Benjamin, who was born about 13 years after Joseph and is similarly called a son of old age by his brother Judah in the presence of Joseph (cf. Gen. 44:20).

But although I am accustomed to leave discussions of this kind to the Hebrews, nevertheless, the reason which Lyra follows seems to be too weak since, indeed, Benjamin was 13 years younger. Joseph is the seventh son, after Dan and Naphtali. Gad and Asher were born either after Joseph or at the same time with him. Finally Gad, Asher, Issachar, Zebulon, and Dinah were born, and they were all younger than Joseph. How, then, will this text stand that Joseph was born in old age? Historical consideration also demonstrates that the

----

6 See p. 316.

7 Lyra *ad* Gen. 37:3, p. 103 recto, "Additio i."

same can be said of all the sons. Jacob only began to produce children when he was 74. Accordingly, I leave this question for elucidation to the Hebrews, for I know that many colloquial phrases and idioms of the Hebrew language have been lost to us whose force and proper meaning we shall not easily wholly restore.

Burgensis' view is allegorical and quite appropriate, namely, that Joseph was the son of old age, that is, wise. But I would rather say — and the words themselves and the whole story seem quite clear in wanting to say — that the patriarch Jacob did not think that he was a father except of these two, Joseph and Benjamin from Rachel, as he will say below: "You have made me childless: Joseph is no more, and Simeon is held in chains, and you will take away Benjamin, etc." The words of the text should be read and considered in such a way that they are applied to the feeling of the father who thinks: "Rachel was promised and given to me by God and for this reason is the true mother, and those are regarded by me as my sweetest and true sons whom she has born. Moreover, she bore Joseph and Benjamin to me in my old age, and so I love them especially." This was the viewpoint of Jacob so that if a choice had been given him between the offspring of Rachel and Leah, which of the two he could do without or was willing to do without, there is no doubt that he would have preferred the sons of his old age to the others.

I for my part, then, interpret this text in accordance with the feelings of the father's heart. After so many troubles and crosses he had found rest in this son, who had been born from his legitimate and chief wife, who to his great grief had died in childbirth. Therefore this son was his only comfort and delight; he alone mitigated the worries and troubles of the old father while the rest of the brothers were crucifying him and daily heaping up new worries. The singular piety and virtue of the youth increased the father's goodwill and love. For he was wise, modest, honest, and godly and equipped with excellent gifts of intellect. Therefore he is his pride and joy. For it is common among parents that even if a man is the father of 20 sons and among these has only one good and obedient son, he feels just as if he had no other offspring besides this one. For he would like to disinherit the ungodly, disobedient sons or lay aside all concern and worry for them.

There remains, however, the other grammatical difficulty concerning the robe with many threads. I readily acknowledge that I do not know what sort it was. In the German translation we have translated "a coat of many colors," following the usual interpretation. Lyra says that it was a silk garment;[8] Burgensis passes over this passage in silence. Others think that it was a garment woven together from many threads, that is, of diverse colors, where the warp is red and the woof is purple, an iridescence when two kinds of colors appear to be mixed. But their opinion does not seem a likely one to me, although I have nothing to offer against it. In the Hebrew it says: "He made for him פַּסִּים," that is, a coat of threads, or a linen coat, which the Greek version has translated πολύμιτον, that is, having many threads. But whether it is a garment of many colors cannot be gathered from the text. This word, moreover, is found nowhere else in Holy Scripture except in 2 Sam. 13, about Tamar, whom her brother Amnon defiled. For in that place the text says: "She put ashes on her head and rent her *polymitam* robe, her פַּסִּים." "For with such cloaks (מְעִילִים) the virgin daughters of the king were clad of old" (cf. 2 Sam. 13:18, 19). I would like to interpret it as a beautiful white smock, a white garment such as was in use in oriental regions, in which the most beautiful and most distinguished garment was white and made of linen. Western people, by contrast, are delighted with purple.

Therefore, let me be permitted to draw a conclusion and to hazard a guess, namely, that Jacob made the cloak for his very dear son as the future heir and priest and by this he honored him above the others and in this way distinguished him from his brothers. For it was a priestly robe of the kind that Hannah in 1 Sam. 2:19 [9] brought to Samuel, a short shirt, a מְעִיל like the one Tamar had on. I would be prepared to say that Joseph's robe was such a מְעִיל. In this way the clothing of the angels is also depicted as being very white and made up of many linen threads. I believe also that Christ's cloak was similar, the one without seam, which his mother Mary wove, a cloak made by weaving. In all of Scripture מְעִיל is a very celebrated word in the appearances of angels and likewise at the transfiguration of Christ. His face shone like the sun and His garments became white as snow (Matt. 17:2; Mark 9:3); and likewise the raiment of the angel at Christ's tomb was white as snow (Matt. 28:3). Solomon, moreover, says: "Let your garments be always white as snow" (cf.

[8] Lyra *ad* Gen. 37:3, p. 102 recto, note "a."

[9] The original has "2 Sam. 2."

Eccles. 9:8). In Moses the magistrates are called Horim, that is, those clad in white, from their white garments, just as the nobility could be called *torquata* ("adorned with neck-chains") from the golden chains with which it is adorned. In the same manner, accordingly, Jacob seems to have adorned Joseph with a special white, priestly garment that he might signify his special love towards his son and his future dignity as a result of the priesthood. But if anyone wishes to retain the former interpretation, that it is a garment of different colors, I shall not quarrel with him.

It appears, however, that Tamar's robe, in whose story alone this word פַּסִּים occurs, was white. She must have worn a beautiful white smock. Then also I am influenced by the description of priestly attire in Moses, who first assigns to them an undergarment reaching to the thigh, and then a shirt, a "cowl." Moreover, it was a linen shirt, a tight close-fitting garment, an undergarment covering all members of the body right down to the heels, not with flowing sleeves but tight ones without folds, so that the priests might be free for the duties connected with sacrifices and for slaughtering animals, like our butchers. Thirdly, there is added the priestly or pontifical robe. The high priest also had a מְעִיל that was completely hyacinthine, the beautiful pure yellow silken gown! The robe of the high priest alone was tawny, or the color of gold. Samuel's garment which was brought to him by his mother was like this, although it was a different color, a choir gown. For מְעִיל was white or silver-colored, and it was also permissible for others to use it. But the high priest alone was adorned with the hyacinthine or gold color. Job, for example, tore his מְעִיל (Job 1:20). David also cut a piece from Saul's מְעִיל in the cave (1 Sam. 24:4), and from this we conclude that it was a royal adornment and belonging to the nobles who among the Orientals did not wear chains and purple garments but linen ones. The Jews did not use silk but skins, in this matter imitating Adam and Eve. Today also we first clothe boys in skins and then, too, adults are accustomed to use them. But the type of split clothes that have become customary today do not deserve the name of garments, but they are mere monstrosities and portents of this last unhappy age. Finally, we must add here that Moses prevents the people from using garments made from different threads, or made from wool and linen, just as he does not want seeds and animals to be mixed (Deut. 22:9-11). Therefore my view of the matter is simply this, that the cloak was woven of threads of one kind and white, not sewn, worked, or woven together.

So much about Joseph's cloak, by which Jacob wanted to attest his love for his son who had been brought up in the hope of entering the priesthood. Therefore, by a special adornment he separated him from the rest of the rustic group of brothers so that they might know [10] that he would be the future ruler and heir in the house. This, however, was the source of the monstrous hatred in their hearts. The devil inflamed them with horrible ill will and fury against their own brother without any cause. They neglected and despised the many warnings and exhortations which they had often heard from their father and other godly men in the church of Jacob. In short, they took no account of the many blessings with which they were endowed daily by their dear father as his sons, and by which they were nourished along with the wives, children, and numerous household. For all these blessings, they think they will render satisfaction if they push their brother out of the home or kill him along with their father.

This example, moreover, is set before us for our consolation, that we may not be broken in spirit if ever we have similar experiences, but we should individually do our duty, each one according to his calling, in teaching, reproving, and rebuking both in the church and state and home. Our labor will not be in vain in the Lord (1 Cor. 15:58). But if any refuse to heed and to obey godly admonitions, they will have to learn wisdom in the end to their peril and disadvantage.

4. *But when his brothers saw that their father loved him more than all his brothers, they hated him and could not speak peaceably to him.*

What beautiful, fraternal love there was in the household church of Jacob together with the excellent discipline of the patriarchs when the older patriarch Isaac was still living with Jacob! They hated their innocent brother so much that they could not exchange a single word with him in a friendly and kindly manner; they snapped at him and criticized his every word and deed. Therefore, just as he was the most loved son of his father, so he was most despised in the eyes of his brothers. They hated him very bitterly out of sheer malice, but especially was this the case with Simeon and Levi. For I do not think that all felt alike originally and in the beginning. For Reuben had been humbled because of the consciousness of the sin he had committed, and I think that the rest were also milder. This hatred

---

[10] The Weimar text has *sciret,* but we have read *scirent.*

of the brothers therefore will have to be understood like the murmuring of the apostles against Mary Magdalene, who anointed Christ (Matt. 26:8-9). For the other disciples had been persuaded and incited by Judas. And to make this incidental addition, Jerome thinks that Judas Iscariot had his origin from the tribe of Simeon.[11]

However, we do not extenuate this sin or excuse any of them. But we have stated that their malice should be amplified by all means, not only out of hatred of outrageous sin and the devil but also for our consolation, since God endured such pestilential men in the church and the home of the saintly patriarchs, and these He later pardoned in His mercy. But even if they repented, it is impossible to close one's eyes to the fact that at this time they were aflame with ill will and spite against a man who was absolutely innocent. God, moreover, permits this unjust and sinful hatred and closes His eyes to it; indeed, He provides them with ample opportunity to envy their brother to their own undoing. They acted just like the Jews who persecuted Christ the Savior with a monstrous hatred and seized opportunities for slandering Him and speaking evil of Him in each of His words and deeds, even though He filled the whole people with infinite goodness and welldoing and many kinds of miracles and blessings! Still everything had to be wrong! They were satisfied with none of this until at last God provided them with the opportunity to glut their hatred in accordance with their liking by delivering His only-begotten Son into their hands that they might crucify Him and so satiate their wicked cruelty and impious hatred.

But how unhappy and wretched men are when God leaves them to themselves and does not resist their raging lusts, although we are all constituted by nature in such a way that we find it hard to allow a curb to be put on us. But woe to those at whose sins God closes His eyes! For at length what is stated in the common saying follows: "He who says what he wants will hear what he does not want." So also, he who does what he wants will experience what he does not want, for we do not control ourselves, nor do we check our desires by the precept of others. Therefore if God is indulgent to us, we fall into such madness and wretchedness that we are involved in horrible sins and punishments together with the Jews, and in the end we experience regrets and are ashamed too late. The Sodomites, for example, could not be checked by any means from venting their madness

---

[11] Cf. *Luther's Works*, 8, p. 50, n. 28.

against good and saintly Lot according to their liking, but suddenly they pay the most bitter punishments and perish. Things had to go as they wanted, and in the morning the hellish fire came from the sky and did what they did not want. Before the Flood Noah was not heeded, but men took the wives they wanted. Therefore the Flood came and did what they did not want. That is how people want it! Our fellowmen will at some time experience the same, inasmuch as they want all bonds of discipline and morals dissolved and abolished.

This, then, is a holy, blessed, and safe kind of life, when God does not close His eyes to our faults and forbidden pursuits but immediately corrects and chastises us with His rods, troubles, and crosses of every kind or through men who by their admonitions lead us back to the right path so that our foolish lusts are curbed. On the other hand, it is a very bad sign when all things succeed according to his heart's desire for a scoundrel who is plotting evil. Jeremiah says of the false prophets (Jer. 12:2): "Thou art near in their mouth and far from their heart," that is, whatever they purpose, teach, and do is approved by all in such a way and received with such enthusiasm as if it had been sanctioned by God. "Thou dost not check or curb their hearts, that is, their ungodly purposes and desires," the prophet means to say. But to what end? "Thou hast fattened them for sacrifice and the day of killing."

In this manner, the sons of Jacob rage and indulge in hatred and envy, but they are compelled at last to experience what they do not want. Therefore nothing is more pleasing and acceptable to God than to endure the discipline and chastisement of the Lord with equanimity. But if we do not endure having a curb placed upon us, we will at length be held fast in far more atrocious punishments, for it is said: "Even if you escape Me, you will not escape the hangman or the devil!" At times some return to the right way and are converted, but not without severe punishments by which they are brought back to repentance. It seems, then, that Simeon, the forefather of Judas Iscariot, and Levi were the leaders and authors of this crime and that they also involved the others born from the maidservants with them, who would not have dared to attempt any such deed of their own accord. Nor did their wicked plan lack an occasion and success. God closed His eyes and permitted them to capture and sell their brother, and, indeed, Joseph himself adds oil to the flame and now of himself supplies the third cause for hatred.

5. *Now Joseph had a dream, and when he told it to his brothers, they only hated him the more.*

6. *He said to them: Hear this dream which I have dreamed:*

7. *behold, we were binding sheaves in the field, and lo, my sheaf arose and stood upright, and behold, your sheaves gathered round it, and bowed down to my sheaf.*

This, at length, is the chief reason of their envy. It seems that Joseph purposely disclosed this dream to his brothers to offer outright opposition to their arrogance and envy. For Simeon and Levi especially arrogated the rule and dominion to themselves because, although Reuben was humbled, they themselves were still innocent. Therefore both of them thought: "I am the master of my brothers; I shall assume the right and rank of being the firstborn for myself; my brothers will bend their knees to me, and the sons of my mother will bow down before me." This is what we heard above in the blessing of Jacob (Gen. 27:29), and below it will be said of Judah: "Judah, your brothers shall praise you; your hand shall be on the neck of your enemies; your father's sons shall bow down before you" (49:8). This dominion Simeon arrogates to himself, and he promises it to himself full of confidence and hope. Accordingly, Joseph sets this dream over against that stupid arrogance. It is as if he were saying: "I shall not allow you to be led along any longer by a doubtful and vain hope. For I, who am despised and rejected by you, will be your lord, not that I am arrogating dominion over you to myself, but I am reporting my dream which I have dreamed to you." So he speaks in a familiar and friendly manner with his brothers as though he were somewhat foolish and a boy, saying: "Listen to this dream, etc. I thought that we were binding sheaves, etc." The boy relates this strange and unexpected dream in a very boyish manner, without any hatred and evil lust, in pure simplicity and innocence. But God encumbers their hearts and increases the reasons for hatred so that they are incited and inflamed, but to their own great disadvantage. Now the fire really starts to burn!

8. *His brothers said to him: Are you indeed to reign over us? Or are you indeed to have dominion over us? So they hated him yet more for his dreams and for his words.*

The telling of the dream gives these princes grave offense. He should have kept quiet and applauded the brothers, agreeing with them and saying: "Simeon and Levi will reign, etc.," so as to confirm such holy desires on their parts. But this is the hand of God, who puts a piece of bacon into the trap for Simeon and Levi. Because they set a snare for an innocent man, the Lord in turn hates them, and He permits them to press on, keenly impelled by their own wishes, and to pollute themselves with a most disgraceful murder.

9. *Then he dreamed another dream, and told it to his brothers, and said: Behold, I have dreamed another dream; and behold, the sun, the moon, and eleven stars were bowing down to me.*

To bow down to the earth signifies a gesture of adoration and a movement to a place. For to adore means to be bent or to be prostrated on the earth, or to fall forward to the earth and by this external rite to show respect for another. We are accustomed to bend the knee either before princes or before God. But first something must be said in general about dreams. This matter, I know, is very extensive and wide-reaching, and so I must explain it briefly. For I am not qualified to have dreams or to explain them, nor do I seek this ability or knowledge for myself, and I have concluded a pact with my Lord God that He should not send me visions or dreams or even angels. For I am content with this gift which I have, Holy Scripture, which abundantly teaches and supplies all things necessary both for this life and also for the life to come. This I believe, and I give it my assent, and I am certain that I cannot be deceived. However, I do not detract from the gifts of others, if God by chance reveals something to someone beyond Scripture through dreams, through visions, and through angels. They may be gifts, to be sure, but I am not concerned about them and do not desire them. For I am influenced by that infinite multitude of illusions, deceptions, and impostures by which the world was horribly deceived for a long time through Satan under the papacy. I am also influenced by the sufficiency of Scripture, and if I do not put my faith in this, I shall not easily believe an angel, a vision, or a dream. But, as I said, this reason is peculiar to me, and I would not dare to prescribe anything for others. For I have enough and more than enough revelations when I know what is to be believed, and what is to be hoped for, and what consideration is to be paid to others, and in what way one should pass this life in a godly and honest manner. And this, in accordance with my slender gifts, I communicate to others so that they may also know and understand the Decalog, the Creed, the Lord's Prayer, etc.

Nevertheless, we shall say something about the doctrine and meaning of Holy Scripture concerning dreams, for it sometimes approves of dreams and at other times disapproves of them. Sirach 34:7 says: "Dreams have led many astray: and they have failed by putting their hope in them." Solomon likewise says (Eccles. 5:7): "When dreams increase, empty words grow many: but do you fear God." Again, sacred history testifies that the holy patriarchs and prophets had dreams, like Jacob, Joseph, Daniel, and Pharaoh and ungodly men likewise, which nevertheless were revealed to them by God. In Num. 12:6-8 the Lord says to Aaron: "If there is a prophet among you, I the Lord make Myself known to him in a vision, I speak with him in a dream. Not so with My servant Moses; he is entrusted with all My house. With him I speak mouth to mouth." Here God confirms dreams and visions, and it is a remarkable passage which required an accurate and more copious explanation. "Moses," says God, "saw something greater and has other greater revelations besides those which you who are his disciples and who have visions and dreams have heard from him. I know what Moses and I are accustomed to confer and converse about together. Moses saw the sufferings of Christ."

Moreover, from this passage there have arisen the customary forms of speech found in the prophets concerning dreams and visions. Concerning the sending of the Holy Spirit Joel declares: "Your young men shall see visions and your old men shall dream dreams" (cf. Joel 2:28). Therefore we cannot deny that God employed these means of revelation from the beginning in the church of the fathers and prophets. The first mode is the chief one, prophecy or inspiration, as in the case of David and the prophets, who have transmitted doctrine and promises with clear words and a manifest meaning through the illumination of the Holy Spirit. Then there are visions or certain images and appearances. Thirdly, there are dreams. Thus in the New Testament the first type is doctrine; to this are added the sacraments as external ceremonies, and they could be called visions. Our Baptism, the Lord's Supper, and Absolution are visions, so to say, because they are external ceremonies.

But since Holy Scripture both approves these three types of revelation and also condemns them, it seems that the same rule and judgment should be followed in regard to dreams which we are accustomed to follow in visions and prophecies, namely, the analogy of faith. For these, too, are sometimes true and at other times false just like dreams. For they do not always arise only from God but also from the devil, who is God's ape, and just as he is accustomed to awaken prophets, so he also stirs up visions and dreams, God permitting this in His wonderful counsel. But even when he speaks the truth through dreams, he is looking to something different from God's intent in this connection. God shows forth His Word and signs for the salvation and redemption of men, but Satan seeks the destruction and ruin of souls and the darkening of God's truth, and therefore he lies even in telling the truth. Hence dreams are also related in the histories of the heathen, such as those of Brutus, Caesar, Sulla, and Hannibal were.

Livy writes that Hannibal in a dream saw a young man with the form of a god who said that he had been sent from Jupiter to act as Hannibal's guide into Italy and to say that Hannibal should follow him and never again take his eyes off him.[12] But looking back, Hannibal is reported as seeing a serpent of wonderful size behind him, moving along with great destruction of the trees and bushes. This was truly a dream foreshadowing the future, and it made a definite impression, for the devil had an excellent knowledge of the status of the whole world, and it was easy to guess the future from what preceded and to show it by means of a dream to Hannibal. Such also were the predictions of Lichtenberger and of Arnold in *De villa Dei*.[13] These men had a prophetic spirit which men elsewhere call a Pythian spirit. The outcomes at times agreed with them, at other times not. When it came true, it came true; when it failed, it failed.

Moreover, in the dream of Hannibal Livy and all the Italians think that the serpent signifies Hannibal, who was about to devastate Italy. But the truer interpretation is that the devil or God through the devil wanted to indicate that Hannibal had a beautiful youth, that is, a prosperous good fortune before him, as though he meant to say: "So far you have been fortunate, Hannibal, and have achieved great things. But this success will not be continuous. For a horrible beast will follow you, namely, the Roman Empire, which will envelop and lay waste the whole world." In this way a lying dream which originated from Satan nevertheless foretold the truth. But Hannibal himself did

[12] Livy, *History of Rome*, XXI, 22, 6—9.

[13] "Lichtenberger" or "the Lichtenberger" was an astrologer and prophet of the late 15th century, also called *Claromontanus*, whose *Pronosticatio* enjoyed wide circulation.

not understand this, and the Italians, rather greedy for honor, were not keen on hearing that the Roman Empire was represented by such a disgraceful and monstrous beast. But we turn our eyes to the images in the visions of Daniel (Dan. 7:1-8), where the kingdoms of the world are not compared to men or angels but to monstrous beasts. Therefore the serpent by no means signifies Hannibal but the future devastation through the beast of the Roman Empire, and Satan wants to say this: "Your success and fortune will not be constant; you will not accomplish what you have begun; you will not carry it out." Nor was there need of the Holy Spirit for this revelation, for Satan saw the strength, the plans, the wishes, the purposes, and the whole condition of both the Roman and the Carthaginian states. God permitted this to be indicated to Hannibal in a dream, but without an interpretation.

Many such certain and uncertain dreams are extant in the histories of the heathen. For as God governs the world through good and evil rulers, so He also uses the ministry of good and evil angels alike. God sometimes implants true dreams in the ungodly and at other times false ones, and the devil also has his prophets, whose predictions, however, are uncertain.

Another type of dreams is natural, and from them doctors at times make a conjecture about certain humors and feelings and likewise bodily temperaments. These are general and common to all men, and in regard to these Cato's precept is to be observed: "Pay no attention to dreams!" [14] However certain ones do at times have a meaning. But I offer no discussion on these but refer the reader to Macrobius, by whom the same are treated more copiously. [15]

The third class is prophetic and true. This class Holy Scripture commends, and it has a bearing on the government of the church or on revelations necessary for this life or the life to come. Some are prophecies, so to say, which are not to be despised.

But the question is how they can be separated or distinguished. As far as I am concerned, I am not a dreamer or an interpreter of dreams, as I stated previously. Therefore I do not want to judge excepting *a posteriori* and from other circumstances pertaining to the church and the salvation of souls according to the norm and rule of

[14] Cato, *Disticha*, II, 31; cf. *Luther's Works*, 5, p. 237, n. 45.

[15] Macrobius, *Commentaria in somnium Scipionis*, I, 3, 1—20, ed. F. Eyssenhardt (Leipzig, 1893), pp. 484—489.

the Word of God. For all dreams that are inspired by God are most certainly fulfilled, and in such a way that they are salutary to the world and the human race. Accordingly, they are quite correctly estimated from their effect. Nor am I speaking only of those which are offered to saints like Daniel and Joseph, but also of those which are revealed to ungodly men like Pharaoh, Nebuchadnezzar, and others. For the outcome agrees with them, and they have an interpretation attached; these are two infallible signs of the certain dreams, when God, who implants dreams in the mind, at the same time adds an interpretation and execution. In the third place, the same dreams strongly influence the dreamer; they make very keen impressions, as was the case with Pharaoh, in whom there was such great consternation of heart and ἔκστασις ("distraction") that he felt that it was an admonition from God. Here God does not permit an ungodly or false prophet to interpret a dream which has been sent to an ungodly man, but He provides a true prophet, Joseph or Daniel, who teach its significance under the illumination of the Holy Spirit.

But when the Spirit Himself is the interpreter of those things which He suggests, then there can be no doubt about outcome and certitude. You will find nothing like this in the dreams of the heathen except that keen disturbance of the heart. But because they have Satan as their author, who can and is accustomed to give reminders of future events, they are generally ambiguous and deceptive, and no interpreter is provided, as is the case in dreams from God which the prophets report with certainty and faithfully, with the Holy Spirit as their teacher. From the dreams sent to them, Daniel, Jacob, and Joseph gather the doctrine and meaning of Holy Scripture concerning very important matters, not only concerning the empires which they taught were established and preserved by God but also concerning the kingdom of Christ and the chief articles of Christian doctrine. Therefore it depends on a good interpreter! A good interpreter is required, as we say in the German proverb.

Therefore the Holy Spirit is first accustomed to suggest dreams, then to show an explanation, and thirdly, to carry them out, and this can be beautifully applied to the Trinity of Persons. The Father gives the dreams, the Son interprets them, and the Holy Spirit carries them out. I call these true and prophetic dreams which do not deceive. But concerning these I do not assume the power of judgment for myself, except *a posteriori;* the rest of the throng of dreams I completely despise. I do, indeed, have dreams from time to time, which move me somewhat, but I think little of them and I have made a pact with my Lord that I want to believe Moses and the prophets. I do not desire dreams for this life and have no need of them for the life to come.

In the meantime, however, I leave to others their gifts. For I know that God has often set various revelations before rulers and kings through the medium of dreams, but let those who wish to act as interpreters see to it what kind of spirit is in them and whence they proceed. The Turks also have both dreams and prophecies telling what will be the status and end of the Turkish kingdom. But I do not believe that these arise from the Holy Spirit, because neither the Turk nor the pope has prophets, otherwise they would be manifested by the confession of true doctrine and faith. Therefore, whatever they may be, we do not care about dreams of this kind nor their author because they do not have an interpretation added, even though the outcome and execution is, at times, in agreement. For the devil is trained and equipped with an infinite number of examples of God's government, and he likewise knows the wishes, purposes, and plans of men and even governs them. Therefore he easily perceives the fortune and outcome of their deliberations and empires. He sees that what has been thought up succeeds in one way or another, and that up till now no indication at all is apparent that God wants to place some impediment in the way of some resolution that has been taken up; and so predictions about the future are easy for him. In this way Lichtenberger predicted the Bavarian War because the devil saw the counsels of Maximilian, the Count Palatine, and other princes. He does the same at other times, and if God does not offer opposition with His special counsel, the outcome foreseen corresponds. But the devil is not concerned about whether the dream is salutary for human affairs or not. It is no concern of his if everything falls into ruin at once.

However, this whole life which we live is sheer dreaming and dark night. For no light shines in the world except this earthly and bodily light. The light of the sun is a cause of error for us so that we believe that we are in the light. But we are really wandering as though we were in a black night. Therefore our life is truly sleep and night spiritually, just as in Joseph's dream his parents are compared to the sun and moon but his brothers are compared to the stars shining in the darkness of this life. Moses attests the same thing in Ps. 90:5, saying: "Thou dost sweep men away; they are like a dream," that is, our life is fleeting, flying, and transient, just as the Elbe is always flowing or any river is borne along by its swift current; "as water rushes past, so Thou hast made men a raging stream and a passing torrent." Job also says (14:1-2): "Man that is born of a woman is of few days and full of trouble. He comes forth like a flower and withers; he flees like a shadow and continues not." What is more, Moses adds: "They are a dream" (Ps. 90:5), that is, our life is a dream by comparison with eternal life.

Therefore we are truly held fast in the midst of night and the thickest darkness unless that Morning Star shines forth concerning whom it is stated (Ps. 119:105): "Thy Word is a lamp to my feet." If we do not have Holy Scripture lighting and governing our actions, this whole life and the universal light of reason, all wisdom, and, in short, all plans are darkness and confusion. Augustus, Alexander, and Caesar are held fast in the thickest darkness; they do not know what they are doing. It is so also with Nebuchadnezzar, Pharaoh, and all other kings and monarchs except that they seem to themselves to be doing many things excellently and exercising outstanding wisdom. But they are mere dreams, as is stated in Isaiah: "The multitude of all the nations that fight against Ariel . . . shall be like a dream, a vision of the night" (cf. 29:7). So also the achievements of the heroes celebrated in the poems and histories of the heathen, of Hector and Achilles, for example, are like dreams. "As when a hungry man dreams he is eating and awakes with his hunger not satisfied, or as when a thirsty man dreams he is drinking and awakes faint, with his thirst not quenched, so shall the multitude of all the nations be that fight against Mount Zion" (Is. 29:8). In this way it usually comes to pass that a dreamer seems to himself to find a sack full of gold or to be playing with a beautiful girl, but on waking he discovers that he has been deceived. In the same manner this whole life is night and sleep.

But it is a happy dream when God bestows His Word and Holy Scripture during this night, even as in natural life or sleep He gives a revelation such as this one is in Joseph's dream. But as I pointed out previously, the interpretation and execution of the Holy Spirit should be added to this. For so much I understand about dreams *a posteriori* and no more. Therefore I cannot judge when faith should be placed in them if God does not interpret them.

Then also it should be noted that the impure spirit also gives dreams, for by his manifold knowledge and varied experience he is by far better equipped than we are. We do not know the plans and purposes of princes and others; indeed, I hardly know my own. But the devil is very cunning and has an exact grasp of all the deliberations of kings, wise men, jurists, and theologians, with this one exception, namely, what my faith and hope in God is, how I stand with God; for faith and God's Word is a dark cloud to him into which he cannot penetrate with his light. This he himself reveals through the crystal and mirror of mercury,[16] in which he shows a city or some person obscurely and covered with a cloud or rain, by which it comes to pass that it cannot be recognized or clearly perceived what will come to pass there. Thus he mocks men and at the same time acknowledges that he cannot look into man's heart. Here he burns his mouth and nose!

In this sense the angel says to Mary (Luke 1:35, 31) "The Holy Spirit will come upon you, and the power of the Most High will overshadow you." "You will be pregnant and conceive a son," but in this manner, that there is a concealment and overshadowing of such a kind that neither angels nor demons are able to perceive or understand it. Therefore the beam of diabolical light does not penetrate into the Word and the believing heart, and for that reason I am more delighted with the Word and faith than with a dream, and I have prayed the Lord that He should not give me dreams, because they are deceptive. But the Word is a sure shade and darkness, which the evil spirits, however lofty they may be, cannot look into. Therefore even though the prophets and dreamers are not to be despised if their prophecies and dreams are analogous to the Word of God and faith, this should be urged most of all, that first Moses and the prophets should be learned, that is, that before all things we have the pure Word and its true understanding. From that we will be able to interpret all visions, all dreams, and prophecies and, indeed, also to judge the good and evil angels alike.

But let us return to the dreams of Joseph. There are two dreams, of which the first has a bearing on the land and is rustic, for he only dreams about his own sheaf and those of his brothers. His own sheaf stands erect from the earth, and the rest bow down and do homage to it. Jacob is not at all moved by this dream. Therefore he

[16] An amalgam of tin and mercury was used to coat mirrors in Luther's day.

does not speak against it but is silent, for it agrees with his own opinion, according to which he concludes that Joseph, being born from his chief wife, would be his chief heir, to whom the birthright, the kingdom, and the priesthood was owed and a double portion of the inheritance. Therefore it still agrees with the thoughts of Jacob and confirms them; it is the protasis, or prelude, to the true dream. For no mention has yet been made of the parents, that they would have to do him homage, but only of the brothers. But it was sanctioned by nature and law that the firstborn should exercise dominion over the brothers, as other examples above testify.

But Simeon and Levi had claimed the right of the firstborn for themselves much earlier, and so they are inflamed with hatred and jealousy towards Joseph. However, they have no other right but time, for they were brought to the light of day before Joseph from their mother Leah, who was given first in marriage to their father, wretched Jacob, who was deceived in unworthy ways by Laban. For the birthright is not to be estimated according to the prerogative of time, but they still assumed this dignity for themselves. Levi hoped for the succession after Simeon's death, and they had also brought the rest of the household over to their side to obey their authority; therefore also the rest of the brothers come to an agreement and with one accord oppose Joseph, just as the apostles, persuaded by the one Judas, murmured against the Magdalene (cf. Matt. 26:8; Mark 14:4-5; John 12: 4-5). These two, however, are deeply moved, over and above the rest. The dream also makes its fairly sharp impressions and cannot be numbered among common dreams. Then also, their father is not offended by it but confirms it by his judgment and authority. Thus also the father's interpretation is added, which is divine and a very firm argument for its certitude.

The second dream is not lowly or plebeian but heroic and, as it were, heavenly. For it has images of the sun, moon, and stars, not sheaves which signify the labors of rustics and the works of men. Yet in it are included also his father and mother with his brothers, of whom no mention had been made in the former dream. Therefore the father is also moved by it and reproves him as follows.

10. *But when he told it to his father and to his brothers, his father rebuked him and said to him: What is this dream that you have dreamed? Shall I and your mother and your brothers indeed come to bow ourselves to the ground before you?*

11. *And his brothers were jealous of him, but his father kept the saying in mind.*

Above, the hatred of the brothers is recounted; here they really begin to rave. For neither nature nor the customs of any nations whatsoever nor God Himself endures it that parents do homage to sons. Therefore it is an absurd dream conflicting with reason and common sense. But it still makes a strong impression, for the sun, moon, and 11 stars are distinctly expressed, which the number of the father, mother, and brothers. He does not use another number. Lyra says that Jacob despised and completely rejected it as manifestly absurd and by his paternal authority convicted the youth of stupidity for dreaming with a kind of boyish levity that homage would have to be paid to him by his parents and brothers.[17] But the text shows the opposite: not only did the father refrain from despising this dream, but he kept all the words. This idiom is also used in Luke (2:51) concerning Mary who "kept all these things in her heart." Jacob, indeed, chastises his son, for at first sight the matter seemed quite absurd, but the impression is so strong that the father cannot altogether disregard it, although at first he speaks against it; for he is of the opinion that Joseph is his firstborn from Rachel, who was betrothed to him first and whom he had loved very ardently and for whom he had likewise endured the hardest toils and troublesome servitude for seven years. But the son long expected was born at last in extreme old age. Whom would these and similar weighty arguments not move, unless something different were revealed by God?

Finally, Jacob has the promise about the future Seed in whom all the nations are to be blessed. All the patriarchs valued this very highly, and Jacob undoubtedly hoped that the Seed would come from Joseph and thought that He would be such a Lord that all his brothers and the mothers and fathers in his whole family would do Him homage. Accordingly, he weighed the whole matter very carefully. "Who knows what the dream may still signify?" he thought. "Who knows what that homage will be, whether in the present or the future? If the blessed Seed is born from Joseph, not only I and his mother, but also our posterity will do It homage." This was fulfilled later in Christ. David also, who was a father, adored a Son not yet born, as Ps. 110:1 tells us. Adam and Eve and all the fathers from the beginning of the world who adore this Son in eternity did the same.

---

[17] Lyra *ad* Gen. 37:9-11, p. 102 recto, note "c."

Such thoughts undoubtedly also suggested themselves to the patriarch Jacob. Therefore it is a wonderful dream in which the father and mother are indicated by the sun and moon, but the brothers and rulers about to follow by the stars. Then he made the further conclusion: "The most distinguished and highest creatures are symbols of us; the thing itself is not represented. We are the thing itself, and we are certainly distinguished to the degree that a thing is superior to its symbol. Accordingly, if God considers father, mother, and brothers worthy of such great honor that the most beautiful creatures are compelled to be symbols of them, human nature must be regarded highly by God. The sun is a symbol representing a father. Therefore the household and the state, and much more the church, are very highly valued and honored before God." These and many other conclusions Jacob made as a result of his son's dream.

Therefore it was a very beautiful explanation which first of all reminded him of the coming Seed because of the promise given to him and the fathers. "My seed," he thought, "will adore the future Christ. The sun, the moon, and the stars, that is, whatever princes, kings, fathers, and mothers there are in the kingdom and administration of any kind, all these will be subject to His rule." Therefore he does not reprove his son as a false prophet or some vain dreamer, but he calls to remembrance the promise of the coming Seed and reflects how great His majesty and glory will be. He himself, to be sure, is the father of the Seed as Abraham was, and yet it will be necessary for him to be prostrated before the Seed and to adore it. This is also a true thought, although he is still in error in regard to the person, for he thinks that it must be born from Joseph. But later on, without changing the name or meaning, God changes the person and assigns this honor to the kingdom of Judah. This Jacob will at length learn below.

Then also, the historical explanation of the dream is remarkable. For it means the greatest adornment for the state and home that God bestows greater honor on father, mother, brothers, and household than on the sun, moon, and stars. This meaning has a bearing on the household, and it pleases me very much. The Fourth Commandment could certainly not be explained and adorned with greater dignity. Finally, in the church the true and lofty stars are the ministers and teachers, who are nevertheless under Christ, so that He Himself is the Ruler and King of the whole earth.

So far we have explained historical matters, but now the grammarians also make trouble for us. For the question is asked in what way there is to be a fulfillment of what is stated in the dream under the prompting of the Holy Spirit Himself, that the father, mother, and brothers will adore Joseph, even though the mother is dead. All lose sweat on this passage, wondering how Rachel adored her son when she was dead for two years before Joseph had his dream. In fact, I am of the opinion that the space of two years was not yet completed. Before we reply, therefore, we shall number the years of Jacob's life in order, especially from his marriage to the descent into Egypt. For during that whole time he was tossed about by many wonderful events, the magnitude of which cannot be expressed by any powers of speech.

Joseph is already 17, born seven years after the marriage. But after he was born, Jacob remained in Mesopotamia for six years. Then for eight years he dwelt in Shechem, as is clear from our *Chronology*.[18] After that time he set out for Bethel, and Benjamin was born. Deborah now died, and the mother passed away in childbirth round about Joseph's 16th year. Hence the wound resulting from Rachel's death is still fresh, for I do not think that more than one and a half years intervened. However, God again comforted the saintly man by giving him this hope in connection with the birthright of his son, even though a little while ago the mistress of the house, Deborah, a very saintly matron, had died. Dinah had likewise been defiled round about the same time, a girl of 11 or 12 years of age. For at that time the nature of men was stronger and more vigorous, even as we shall hear later that Judah married a wife [19] in his 12th year.

Therefore after so many and such great calamities, the destruction of the Shechemites, the defilement of Dinah, and the deaths of his wife and the nurse Deborah, who had been a pillar and ornament of the whole family, and likewise after the incest of his son Reuben, God bestows new consolation on the patriarch Jacob through his son Joseph, whom he considered to be his firstborn. For Benjamin is still a boy one or two years old, and in these dreams Joseph is clearly promised the chief place and the Seed which will bless all nations, as he himself interprets under the illumination of the Holy Spirit. Therefore Jacob again comes to life as though he were raised from

18 See p. 188, n. 1.

19 The Weimar text has *uxorum*, but we have read *uxorem*.

death and hell. He is in heaven again! He thought: "God wants my beloved son to be the firstborn and the heir of the blessing." So he rejoices and is in high spirits and gives thanks to God with his whole heart. Soon he again falls into the abyss of hell because of a quite unexpected and unforeseen misfortune.

After the excellent consolation by which Joseph was declared to be greater and loftier than the sun, moon, stars, heaven, and earth since, indeed, from him there would come the One whom sun and moon, patriarchs and kings, and even angels would adore, he begins to think: "Now I will also have peace for once." Then his delightful hope and all his thoughts suddenly fall to the ground in a pitiable manner when Joseph is removed by the criminal wickedness of the brothers. For they explain Joseph's dream in another manner and come to the following conclusion: "Rachel is dead and cannot adore her son; therefore the dream is vain and a Satanic illusion." Under this pretext they laugh loudly at the folly of their brother, who invented dreams about his mother for himself. In this way their pride and presumption concerning the sovereignty grew. For such thoughts are accustomed to occur to men's minds when God wants to punish sins; they regard God's Word and absolute truth as something quite absurd. That is how matters must have their course!

These brothers, on the example of their father, should have weighed the dream of Joseph more carefully and curbed their illicit desires. But they madly rush into the most atrocious sins and become the worst parricides, fratricides, and matricides; for, to the best of their ability, they really kill their old father, who is in high spirits and experiencing very pleasant satisfaction in his son Joseph. They could not have done more to him if they had plunged a sword or a spear through him; they could not have tortured him more cruelly with another instrument of torture. They are, indeed, admonished through the dream repeated by their brother, nor are other very weighty arguments lacking — nature, laws, the matter itself and the innocence of the excellent youth, and finally, the chastisement of their father, who from time to time exhorted them to brotherly kindness. By all these things they should have been influenced and prevailed upon if their hearts had not been made of iron. But when God sees that Pharaoh wants to be hardened, He loosens the curb for the devil and puts occasions in his way to become hardened.

In this way, then, these brothers smugly despise all admonitions and think: "Joseph is a fool, and our father is an old man in his dotage. They are stupid and sluggish men, destitute of all counsel and thought. We are the rulers whose privilege it is to give orders in the home and church of our father. Therefore we will pay no attention to this foolish dreamer."

But what shall we say to this manifest absurdity concerning Rachel's death? Lyra says that the father first despised the dream. But he does not satisfy me. For even though at the first impulse he seems to neglect and indeed to find fault with the dream, he nevertheless later pays attention to it and keeps it in mind. Augustine [20] really sweats and adduces the theological opinion that these matters are to be understood and fulfilled in the future Christ, whom Adam, Eve, and all that is living or dead, and finally hell itself, adore according to the statement of Paul in Phil. 2:10: "At the name of Jesus every knee should bow, in heaven and on earth and under the earth." These are theological views and true ones.

But what shall we reply as far as Joseph's home was concerned? How does dead Rachel adore him? I follow the solution customary in Holy Scripture, namely, the solution by synecdoche. For although Rachel is not alive so that she may adore in her own person, she nevertheless adores in her sons and husband and the whole household. So, for example, we say by synecdoche that all the brothers hated Joseph, although Judah, as I think, did not hate him and others only agreed to the crime and were not leaders in the matter with Simeon and Levi.

So the meaning of the dream is this: "The sun, and moon, and stars will adore me, that is, the whole family, parents, brothers, older and younger." Below, moreover, we will hear that Jacob in the end adored his son Joseph when he said (Gen. 47:29): "If now I have found favor in your sight, put your hand under my thigh, and promise to deal loyally and truly with me. Do not bury me in Egypt, etc." There he speaks with his son in the manner of a subject who is pleading as with a prince, although with paternal feeling. He does not issue instructions to him but entreats him as a superior. In the Epistle to the Hebrews, too, it is written (Heb. 11:21): "By faith Jacob, when dying, blessed each of the sons of Joseph, bowing in worship over the head of his staff." Although this passage can be

[20] Augustine, *Liber quaestionum in Heptateuchum*, I, 123, *Patrologia, Series Latina*, XXXIV, 581—582.

translated differently, it nevertheless seems that Jacob adored and worshiped his son. As he was lying on his bed, on Joseph's approach, he raised himself just as if some prince were coming, and he did this not only for the sake of the government exercised by Joseph over Egypt but also because of the blessed Seed which he hoped for from him and concerning which he had previously received a revelation. This is the simple solution of this objection by means of the synecdoche common in Holy Scripture.

The other knotty point which engages Augustine is in the account of the death of Isaac, of which we made mention above. But there is an easy explanation by means of the figure ὕστερον πρότερον, which men commonly call anticipation or recapitulation and of which there is frequent use in Holy Scripture. The historians of the heathen also often use the same figure. When Livy, for example, describes the history of one month or year, he cannot relate all things at once which happened at the same time, in one moment and in different places. So Moses first brings Isaac's life to an end and later Joseph's, and yet certain things happened at the same time which cannot be described at the same time, just as two can sing together but not speak together; to be sure, a whole choir sings together, but it cannot preach at the same time.

Accordingly, Lyra and Augustine make a correct reckoning that Joseph was sold 12 years before Isaac's death, but they forget the historical figure of anticipation. For above, Isaac's death has been added to the same historical order and outline of events of his life, and with this narrative those things which happened about the same time cannot be related. Augustine could have easily extricated himself if he had understood that the death of Isaac was related before the selling of Joseph by means of ὕστερον πρότερον. For the authority and certitude of Holy Scripture is not on that account to be called into doubt, but let the reader remember that it is accustomed to narrate events in a historical manner, as I have often given a reminder elsewhere.

So far, then, Moses has related the two dreams of Joseph with which the Holy Spirit plays a prelude to the illustrious history about Joseph's future dominion in Egypt, or, as Scripture explains it elsewhere, concerning the man sent ahead of Israel that it might be preserved in a time of famine (cf. Ps. 105:17). From this we should learn to know God's providence and solicitude for us, inasmuch as He indi-

cates and foretells a long time before what the future will be and
He regulates and controls it by His goodness in such a way that it
may have a tolerable outcome. This is how Joseph himself will interpret it below, saying (Gen. 50:20): "You meant evil against me; but
God meant it for good," and likewise (Gen. 45:7): "God sent me before
you to preserve for you a remnant on earth, and to keep alive for you
many survivors."

Therefore it is certain that God exercises faithful and diligent
care for us before we even think about our successes. To be sure,
the folly of men is also reproved by such examples. We are so im-
petuously foolish and evil that we often sin against our own advantage
and are our own worst enemies, except that God in His boundless
goodness upsets our plans and governs matters in a different manner
from what we had thought. These brothers, for example, are insanely
intent on their brother's destruction when he was about to be their
own salvation and that of the whole land of Canaan, and if he had
been destroyed, they themselves would have been compelled to die
of hunger. But God in a wonderful manner turns all the evils they
are meditating into good even contrary to their deliberations and
before they had formed them. This is somehow prefigured and prepared for by these dreams.

But now let us proceed to the remaining matters and first of all
consider the wonderful example of God's government in Jacob, namely,
how God brings His saints down to hell and leads them back again,
comforts and saddens them, that we may become accustomed to trust
His Word alone and cling to it. For the affairs of the godly must
be brought to the point that they feel nothing, understand nothing
else, and see nothing on which to rely, especially in death, but the
Word. Accordingly, let us learn to die according to the flesh and
to depend on the Word so that even if the world were to be shattered
and totter,[21] we may nevertheless confidently say: "I believe in God
the Father, etc., and in Jesus Christ, His Son, etc." But Jacob now
lives in Hebron and has a son of 17 who is the hope and comfort
of his old age. He thinks that his troubles are over, and now he
finds himself in a worse plight than he had experienced in his whole
life.

12. *Now his brothers went to pasture their father's flock near Shechem.*

---

21 Horace, *Carmina*, III, 3, 7; see p. 9.

13. *And Israel said to Joseph: Are not your brothers pasturing the flock at Shechem? Come, I will send you to them. And he said to him: Here I am.*

14. *So he said to him: Go now, see if it is well with your brothers, and with the flock; and bring me word again. So he sent him from the valley of Hebron, and he came to Shechem.*

From this it appears that the pastures hitherto were around Hebron, where Isaac and Jacob lived with their household. There is no doubt that there were good and honest men who rented fields to Jacob and his sons, since they had nothing of their own in this land and yet there is mention of pastures and sheaves of hay and of fields which they cultivated. It seems, moreover, that the inhabitants were descendents of the three brothers Aner, Eschol, and Mamre, who were godly men and diligently heard the Word and attached themselves to the church of Abraham and Isaac. It appears also that at that time the pastures were consumed in the fields and meadows of Hebron and that this was the reason for their migration to Shechem. Or perhaps they changed their place because they were no longer able to endure the presence and conversation of Joseph, against whom they burned with such great ill will and hatred that they could not speak with him in a familiar or friendly manner or endure the sight of him. For it is possible for one to flee out of hatred and envy of another, as is said of Cain (Gen. 4:5): "Cain was very angry, and his countenance fell"; he was not able to look on his brother with a friendly face and kindly eyes. But at the first sight of him, he became hot and by the sternness of his countenance showed that his heart was inflamed by anger. The same reason could also have prompted these brothers to change their pasture. Joseph, however, stays at home with his father while the rest withdraw and avoid familial association with him.

Secondly, we see that his family still held Shechem since they go there to pasture. For when the citizens were killed, Joseph and his brothers took their place, and there is no doubt that the widows of the Shechemites and any who were left of that people remained with Jacob in their fatherland. I think also that the neighboring Canaanites became completely reconciled to them through the marriage relation concluded with Judah, as will follow in chapter 38. As a result of this, they also loved the rest of the brothers who were good and honest men, but they undoubtedly detested those debased scoundrels Simeon and Levi, the murderers at Shechem. But Joseph with his posterity later gained possession of this locality in which he was nearly killed by his brothers. For below the possession of this land will be given to him by his father, and this Jacob would not have been able to do if he had not held it as his own. Therefore they pass from rented lands to their own pastures in Shechem. Again, when the pasture on these fields is consumed, they return to Hebron, for they cannot and will not stay any longer with that worthless traitor who wants to be adored by the rest.

Furthermore, the kingdom of Israel and Ephraim, as well as the kingdom of Joseph, is named from this land of Shechem, and the first king Jeroboam had his origin from this tribe. For they had regard to the prophecy by which the dominion over this place is conferred on Joseph below; and although he was overwhelmed by the monstrous cruelty of his sons, Jacob retained this place, God Himself presenting it to him and changing a heinous crime into good. For polities of this kind that do not have divine traditions and precepts are merely fortuitous, and God dispenses them to whom He wills; he who has one has it! Jacob did not have a promise or command about the slaughter of the Shechemites, but after Hamor was killed with his son, he obtained jurisdiction over their land with the consent of the neighboring people. In this way many things befall many men by chance and by the fortune of events, God so permitting it without any divine bestowal or promise.

The matters which remain concerning the text contain no difficulty, neither in regard to the history nor the grammar. Moses describes the anxious care which Jacob as a father bestowed on household matters. Although he was advanced in age and years and absent from his flocks, he was nevertheless concerned about his sons and flocks. These matters are set forth by the Holy Spirit to fashion our manners so that we do not cast off all concern for temporal matters like the monks, who subsist on the toil and worries of others. It is an example dealing with household matters and a beautiful description of paternal concern, by which Jacob takes account of his flocks and sons, how each single thing is administered. So he sends Joseph off to them, saying: "Go and see what is being done!" Above, it was stated that Joseph brought the evil report spread abroad about his brothers to his father, and he reported the evil deeds not only of his brothers but

also of the servants and maids and also whatever harm the cattle
and whole household suffered.

One should certainly not overlook this care in those who have
been placed over the administration of the church, the state, and the
home and who are at the same time true bishops of their home and
keep an eye on the fields, cattle, etc., as Jacob does. The pope made
a distinction between secular, or carnal, and spiritual matters and
taught that the domestic sphere should be avoided as though it were
disregarded and disapproved of by God and He wanted all concern
for this to be removed from His followers. For they said: "We are
serving God in heavenly and spiritual matters; let us abandon those
heathen and profane matters, etc. Well, what is to be done? Let us
read the canonical and matutinal hours," they said, "and in place of
these things devour the wealth of the world and rule over kings,
princes, etc."

Therefore let godly householders know that all their actions are
pleasing to God, whether they care for the flocks or the fields, or even
for stinking dunghills. Moreover, let the wife milk the goats and cows,
etc. All these matters are not to be regarded as profane and forbidden
if they are done by saintly people. From where do we all have our
origin if it is not from marriage and domestic arrangements? It is as
though the papists were born from tree trunks and stones! If mothers
did not bear, suckle, clean infants and keep them warm, the whole
human race would have to perish. But since God Himself is the
Author of these offices, there are no grounds at all for thinking that
the worship of God is hindered by these matters, but they are the
most excellent and most pleasing exercises of godliness toward God
and men. For God wants the fetus to be borne in the womb and
to be suckled and kept warm by the earnest care of mothers that it
may be nourished and grow, and so He has placed milk in the breasts.
If anyone nevertheless happens to have the gift of chastity so that
he can do without domestic troubles, let him enjoy his gift. But it
is one thing to be immune from certain burdens of this life and
another thing to condemn the life itself as though it were profane
and heathen.

But if we estimate the matter more correctly, we shall certainly
find that there is nothing more profane and secular, as they themselves say, than the whole order of bishops, however much they may
befog the inexperienced by the title of spiritual persons. Indeed, they

themselves are rather to be condemned because of the perverse and ungodly judgment by which they condemn the ordinance of God as full of dangers and troubles.

Careful attention must be paid to the Author, because it is God who sets up, praises, remunerates, and adorns domestic works. For in the histories of the fathers Holy Scripture always mingles these seemingly trifling, foolish, and mundane matters with the sublime works of faith and the cross and also with other spiritual exercises to testify that God tends to the greatest and least matters alike. For the Lord of the greatest and least, of kings and slaves, of men and women, etc., is the same. We all have one and the same God, and we are one in the unified worship of God, even if our works and vocations are different. But each one should do his duty in his station, even as Jacob is a saintly and spiritual man meditating on God's Law, praying, administering and governing the church. In the meantime, however, he does not overlook lowly domestic duties connected with the fields and the flocks, and this is set before us as an example that we may know that all our actions in domestic life are pleasing to God and that they are necessary for this life in which it becomes each one to serve the one God and Lord of all according to one's ability and vocation.

These matters should be dealt with often and inculcated especially in the youthful age that it may learn to form a more correct judgment about these matters than the corrupters of law and the papists are accustomed to do, who do not cease to prefer the orders and rules of monks and nuns to domestic and civil offices, however much they are commended and adorned by God. Let them know that a woman suckling an infant or a maid sweeping a threshing floor with a broom is just as pleasing to God as an idle nun or a lazy Carthusian. This they should know over against the papal abomination which was introduced into the church in former ages when they said that all other estates were secular [22] and useless and they honored only their tonsures and cowls. "We are spiritual," they used to say, "we pray for others; you citizens, peasants, princes, nobles, and all seculars cannot serve God! Therefore give us your gold, silver, castles, towns, and lands, and we will pray for you day and night while you plow your fields, and rule your household and subjects, etc!" For so I my-

---

[22] The Weimar text has *seculatores,* but we have read *seculares.*

self taught while I was still a monk. But God in His boundless mercy forgave me my sins.

We must often reflect how horribly demented and infatuated the whole world was through the papists, canonists, and sophists, who limited the invocation and worship of God to the monasteries only, as though God could not be worshiped and invoked in common life. This incorrigible race of men, jurists and monks, do not cease even now to move every stone so that this horrible abomination of the monasteries should be restored and so that the works demanded by God and performed in the home by women and also state duties which are really works of God may be obscured. For a woman, a citizen, a prince, a noble, etc., is a creature of God, and we are all individually created for certain duties so that those who attend to these duties carefully in their station should know that they are pleasing to God, provided only that they abstain from sins.

This light was removed from the church of God through the popes so that no more knowledge either of the Creator or His creatures remained among men, and the bishops and monks will again try to extinguish this knowledge unless their ungodly counsels and endeavors are impeded in the Imperial Diet which is being held at present. [23] For with their whole strength they will strive that the papacy and the monasteries be restored with all the decrees of the pope, even though they themselves despise and deride them. For they do not pray or fast but live in gluttony and reveling day and night. Nevertheless, they will try to deceive the emperor with their commendation of the divine acts of worship which are to be restored in the monasteries, just as though the filthy monks alone were performing the office and worship pleasing to God with their howling and shouting in the churches.

Against these monstrous observances passages of this kind concerning the life and actions of the patriarchs should be carefully noted. Sometimes God led them through lofty heights. When Jacob, for example, struggled with an angel, it was one of the highest works when there was no place or time for milking goats but for struggling against sin and death and conquering through faith and hope. At other times, He leads them outside of those lofty heights, just as the same Jacob was at the head of a state and of a household and took care of his flocks, servants, family, etc. For the godly are not

[23] See Introduction, p. x.

appointed to one work only, as the monks bind themselves to certain works, but at one time they devote themselves to spiritual exercises, at other times to domestic or political concerns.

Moreover, in this passage the obedience of Joseph is also commended inasmuch as he waits upon the call of his father immediately. For the Holy Spirit relates this at length not so much for the sake of the story that follows but that He may honor in the youth Joseph those boyish virtues which are bodily and foolish matters in the eyes of the papists, as though there were nothing infirm or human in their lives; yet those very things are most precious and excellent before God.

15. *And a man found him wandering in the fields; and the man asked him: What are you seeking?*

16. *I am seeking my brothers, he said, tell me, I pray you, where they are pasturing the flock.*

17. *And the man said: They have gone away, for I heard them say: Let us go to Dothan. So Joseph went after his brothers, and found them at Dothan.*

Joseph sets out for his brothers with ready heart; and when he had wandered for some time in the field, he is shown the way by a certain man who meets him on the road. But he does not know what great danger is threatening him and how very close to him destruction is. For he is not warned by anyone, and God Himself permits him to fall into the hands of his cruel brothers. He disregards both of them, the father Jacob, and son Joseph, and He pretends not to notice those things which the brothers were planning openly for a long time and allows the son to be sent by his father and to be cast headlong into destruction. Where now are those angels, the מַחֲנַיִם, which are celebrated above because they fought for Jacob against Esau? No angel appears here to warn Jacob and say: "Take care not to send Joseph to the rest of your sons; they will kill him, and you will be deprived of the sweetest delight of your heart!" All the angels and God Himself are silent! This is assuredly something remarkable and unheard-of, which I am unable to fathom or express in words. For God permits the father Jacob and his son to fall into very present destruction.

But it is great and noteworthy consolation for us that we see

God governing the saintly patriarchs exactly as He governs us. For He does not lead the patriarch Jacob only by miracles and lofty exercises of the Spirit exceeding the common grasp of godly men, but He confronts him also with the daily dangers, misfortunes, and accidents that can befall anyone of us. The excellent Joseph, a model of innocence, is 17, has the Holy Spirit, and is full of the grace of God and His goodwill. He has also lived a very saintly life in the church of Jacob, but he is overwhelmed by a wretched misfortune, not unusual for us, perhaps, but quite unworthy of such a saintly man.

Therefore it is an example that belongs to our consolation and reminds us to remember that we are men and think nothing human foreign to us.[24] For if such experiences befell the patriarchs, who were full of the Holy Spirit, why are we surprised or why do we murmur when we suffer similar trials? Indeed, let us rather rejoice and give thanks to God when we feel ourselves being tossed about by the same misfortunes with which God exercised the saintliest of men from the beginning.

In such danger we see the deepest silence of God and the angels. They allow Joseph to rush headlong into the most sorrowful disaster and death itself; they see that the father will be very wretched and afflicted on account of the death of his son, yet they do not hinder the endeavors of the brothers. Let us therefore mutually exhort one another to endurance by the examples of these men, who were like us in the bearing of the cross, for these examples are nearer and more familiar to us and therefore move us more than the example of the Son of God. For the latter is inclined to be too sublime and without comparison, even though He also says of Himself (Matt. 26:24): "The Son of man goes as it is written of Him," as though neither His heavenly Father nor the angels are mindful of Him since, indeed, He is given over to the cruel Jews to be tortured and crucified. In the same manner these two go into death, while God and the angels keep silent and even rejoice, for this does not take place for the destruction of Joseph and Jacob but for the salvation of many. But this plan of God is still secret, although it is an excellent one and very useful. For by means of this trial and vexation God will take care that Jacob does not perish of hunger together with his sons, and He will bring it to pass that Egypt is converted to the true knowledge of God and many are gained and won over.

[24] See p. 254, n. 25.

This is truly a very salutary plan, but it is hidden before their eyes. For God thinks: "I will first mortify both of them because I will benefit not only them but I will also have regard for all of Egypt through them." This was God's purpose and good pleasure at that time, however sad and troublesome the outward appearance of being disregarded by God was. Let us therefore look at this example as often as we are afflicted and tempted, and let us stoutly resist the flesh when it rages and is angry. Let us say: "Why God neglects me in this way, I do not know, but I have no doubts about the excellent, wise, and most useful plan of the Father, although the flesh does not see but murmurs and struggles against the Spirit. Nevertheless, the cross must be borne and overcome by faith and patience, for in the saintly fathers I see the wonderful plans of God by which they are ruled." For in this way these three all die together, the grandfather Isaac, the father Jacob, and the son Joseph. But behold how much good God draws forth from this and how wonderfully He handles this misfortune and ill will of the devil so that they make this wretched shepherd who is as good as dead, Joseph, the king of Egypt and the lord of many peoples, and, what is the chief thing, the doctrine of God is propagated throughout the whole kingdom. All this comes out of the small trial! Therefore we also should conclude: "Well! God has loaded me down with this or that cross! So what? I shall bear it with equanimity." The flesh is indeed weak; it groans, howls, and complains, but God says: "You know nothing; you are a fool! Wisdom belongs to Me, and from this cross of yours I will bring forth the greatest good."

Christ says of His saints in the New Testament: "Will not God vindicate His elect, who cry to Him day and night? I tell you, He will vindicate them speedily" (Luke 18:7-8). O that we could believe this! If we could firmly assent to this voice of God's Son and have this spirit which could say with joy, "Let life, body, and goods be taken away and all things be lost, I am sure that God does and permits this by His excellent wisdom," then we would be true Christians and conquerors of the whole world, and that would truly be giving oneself over to the obedience of God and His will, as Paul says in Rom. 12:2: "Be transformed by the renewal of your mind." But this transformation hurts! Why? Paul goes on to say: "That you may prove what is the will of God, good and acceptable and perfect." Here you will learn by enduring, grieving, and groaning what God has decided concerning you.

Therefore I do not doubt that the groaning which reigns today in our hearts and the hearts of all the godly against the pope and the Turk, and the horrible blasphemies which we hear with great grief of heart, sighing and shouting "COME, O LORD!" will hasten the liberation of the godly! What if the groaning tears the world apart? God will not have patience, says Christ, but in a short time will execute vengeance. He will come; He will not stay away! And when He begins to judge, He will find a way by which the enemies are completely destroyed and the church is preserved. By means of the Flood He destroyed the whole human race when they were very smug and certain that no evil was impending because there were still many saints and wise men in outward appearance among them. In this way the kingdom of Babylon perished as well as Sodom, Jerusalem, and Rome. Who destroyed them? Those groanings and tears in the hearts of the saints! Moses cries out at the Red Sea, and what happens? The sea is divided, Pharaoh enters and is drowned, and the people of Israel escape in wonderful fashion.

Therefore it would be of real benefit if we learned the habit of consoling ourselves by examples of this kind and concluded for certain that the Lord is both able and willing to gather together a great heap of good from such evils. Let us only do His will for the time being and not murmur against God as the Jews did in the desert, concerning whom it is stated in Ps. 106:13: "They soon forgot His works; they did not wait for His counsel." He was prepared to give them help, but they could not wait for it but wanted to have it immediately. Therefore they fell in the wilderness and did not enter the land of Canaan, for "they despised the pleasant land; they did not believe His Word. They murmured in their tents, etc." (cf. Ps. 106:24-25).

In this manner the saintly patriarch Jacob found himself in much grief and great perplexities, and he could not have surmounted these difficulties, had he not heard consolation from his father Isaac and from the rest of the members of his household, who reminded him of the promise and encouraged him in this way until he recovered his son, blessed with great glory and dignity. By far the greatest thing was that Joseph was raised to the rule of Egypt. If God had revealed this to Jacob previously and had said: "I will take care that the loss of your son will become the occasion of the greatest advantages," he

[W, XLIV, 264, 265]

would have let his son go with the greatest of willingness and joy. But He covers and hides this so that He may mortify the old man and fill and inebriate the new man with new and infinite blessings.

Meanwhile, however, his heart had to be aroused to faith, hope, and the expectation of divine help according to the teaching of the Psalm (27:14): "Wait for the Lord; be strong, and let your heart take courage, etc." God knows the end and outcome of trial, which you do not know. "Hold on! I want to mix in the sugar in such a way that, even though you die, you are overwhelmed with perpetual joy in the resurrection of the dead." For these exercises are useful to this end, that we learn to understand the mercy of God and the mystery of faith and hope and in some manner comprehend the inscrutable plans of God concerning us, as is stated in Ps. 4:3: "Know that the Lord has set apart the godly for Himself," and likewise in Ps. 16:3: "As for the saints, they are the noble, in whom is all My delight," and in Ps. 17:7: "Wondrously show Thy steadfast love, O Savior of those who seek refuge from their adversaries at Thy right hand." Mercy, grace, and the promise are certainly present, but it is wonderfully fulfilled beyond all our thoughts, desires, and wishes.

Therefore one must say with Job: "Though He slay me, yet will I trust in Him" (cf. Job. 13:15), and with Paul in 2 Cor. 4:8-9: "We are afflicted in every way, but not crushed; perplexed, but not driven to despair; persecuted, but not forsaken; struck down, but not destroyed." Our life is most wretched and full of great evils and disasters, but we are not forsaken. And so the godly heart concludes: "I know that I am not confounded; my hope and my faith will not deceive me because God, the promise, the sacraments, and absolution do not deceive, inasmuch as they are of God. Accordingly, in death I shall live, and in perishing I shall be preserved."

For Jacob is also cast off in this way, as it appears, but he is not forsaken; he is tempted but not deserted. Finally, he remains a son of God, and God is in him, but in a hidden and wonderful manner. At last, when the climax is reached when Jacob sees that his son is alive and reigning, he congratulates himself and rejoices over his former vexations and ills and thinks: "Never would such great joy have been offered to me if my home and church had been administered according to my own wishes and plan! Joseph would have remained a shepherd with the rest of my sons. But now he is raised to royal dignity and becomes the author and cause of salvation to many."

Therefore when we are afflicted and disciplined, our heart must be aroused against the feeling of evil, and we must say (cf. Ps. 118:17): "I shall not die, but I shall live, however different it may appear. Although I may, indeed, be compelled to despair of myself, I shall nevertheless hope in Him who made all things out of nothing and can restore me intact after being reduced to nothing, to my very great benefit and that of others." Therefore the fiercer our sufferings are, the greater and more wonderful are the things that are worked in the saints. It is a proof of grace and God's goodwill when they are disciplined by the cross and afflictions. For when they persevere by faith in the promise and endure, great and incredible blessings follow according to the statement in James 1:12: "Blessed is the man who endures trial, for when he has stood the test, he will receive the crown of life which God has promised to those who love Him," and in John 12:24 we read: "Unless a grain of wheat falls into the earth and dies, it remains alone; but if it dies, it bears much fruit." From the rotting and mortification of the grain there arises a very beautiful stalk, in one place bearing thirtyfold, in another sixtyfold.

This is the continuous teaching of the entire Holy Scripture and also God's will, namely, that we are mortified according to the flesh and made alive according to the spirit. Paul means to say the same thing in 2 Cor. 4:11: "For while we live, we are always being given up to death for Jesus' sake, so that the life of Jesus may be manifested in our mortal flesh." He also goes on to say (vv. 16-18): "So we do not lose heart. Though our outer nature is wasting away, our inner nature is being renewed every day. For this slight momentary affliction is preparing for us an eternal weight of glory beyond all comparison, because we look not to the things that are seen but to the things that are unseen."

This is the true and only knowledge of Christians, to which we have been called and chosen by Christ, as He says to His disciples in John 15:16: "You did not choose Me, but I chose you and appointed you that you should go and bear fruit and that your fruit should abide." Therefore He also disciplines and mortifies them that their fruit may be richer.

In this manner He treats these holy patriarchs as if He did not know them, and yet He also pours His grace and mercy on the grandfather Isaac, the father Jacob, and the son Joseph. For they are without any doubt most acceptable and pleasing to God. But this love and goodwill is so hidden that God did not even punish any of His enemies more severely and not even those parricides who had sold Joseph nor the Ishmaelites and Midianites who bought him.

So He certainly arouses and accustoms the saints to meditate on the wonderful purposes of God. But He allows the rest to grow, to live lives of pleasure, and to practice usury and robbery of every kind in the greatest smugness. He indulges their desires; He does not chastise them; He does not check their smugness and ungodly endeavors. But what a sad and unhappy indulgence! Those are far happier whom He hurls into grief, misery, and death! And yet He adds the promise, saying: "You have the promise: be content with it! If you had been cast off, I would not have given you a promise, and I would not have ordered you to trust Me. If I had wanted you to be condemned in eternity, I would not have absolved you, baptized you, and called you into fellowship with My Son. But because you have the Sacrament and the Gospel, remember My words (Matt. 5:4): 'Blessed are those who mourn, for they shall be comforted' and likewise (Matt. 5:11-12): 'Blessed are you when men revile you and persecute you and utter all kinds of evil against you falsely on My account. Rejoice and be glad, for your reward is great in heaven, etc.' "

But Jacob received not only heavenly and eternal rewards but also temporal wages exceeding all hopes and powers of thought. For through this momentary and slight temptation (cf. 2 Cor. 4:17) he was made the father of the king of Egypt, and he was also a bishop and teacher of many peoples. This is also a bodily and outstanding reward for patience and steadfastness in adversity. Accordingly, God is accustomed to hide His face and to withdraw His hand from His saints and loved ones, and He allows them to mourn, to be sold, to be thrown into prison, and to die, just as if they were the enemies of God, for whom He seems to care more than for them not because He really feels as He appears to be outwardly but because He is delighted in the works of His hands on account of this game, so to say. For He says: "Those whom I love, I reprove" (cf. Heb. 12:6).

Let us consider these matters carefully so that, after we have begun to believe and have hope in the future life that has been granted us through the Word and Baptism, we may learn to endure patiently whatever evils ensue and come to the conclusion that all things take place for our salvation not haphazardly but according to the Father's plan. This is the understanding which we eventually have when the trial is ended. When one is in the very throes of trial, this is not understood, for the feeling of the flesh tears us away from the promise. When a man is involved in tribulation and anxiety, it does not enter his mind to say: "I have been baptized; I have God's promise," but his heart is quite overwhelmed by complaints, grief, and tears according to the flesh. However, the flesh should be crucified and mortified, for it hinders the understanding of the promise and the truth of God's Word, which is perceived in temptation if one clings to it in firm faith. What is stated in the psalm (34:8) follows: "O taste and see that the Lord is good!" God allows us to be tempted that He may have an opportunity for satisfying, comforting, and filling those who have been emptied of all strength and stripped of all help. Otherwise we are sluggish and hear the Word with loathing and become quite torpid. Souring encourages eating, it is said. Hunger is a good cook!

18. *They saw him afar off, and before he came near to them, they conspired against him to kill him.*

19. *They said to one another: There comes this dreamer.*

20. *Come now, let us kill him and throw him into one of the pits; then we shall say that a wild beast has devoured him, and we shall see what will become of his dreams.*

God is silent over against the ungodly and bloody plans of these brothers. He does not disturb them or hinder them. He is blind and deaf; He neither sees nor hears, nor feels, and yet He said: "I will be your protector, etc." (cf. Gen. 15:1).

But it is a very unhappy situation to see such disgraceful and monstrous progeny in this house and church which was unique at that time and the holiest church in the whole world. In this church, with Isaac the foremost patriarch as its teacher, the Word and the promise concerning Christ were in a specially flourishing condition, the Holy Spirit was reigning, and the most beautiful examples of godliness, discipline, and domestic life were shining forth; and yet from this such horrible monstrosities arose. For Jacob with his whole church is subjected to the devil and all his angels to such an extent that it is not strangers, not enemies, not heretics but sons born from himself and educated and taught in the Word who kill their innocent brother.

It is assuredly a strange happening, exceeding all human eloquence and thought. I am of the opinion that it is even worse than Cain and his brother! In cruelty they seem to me to surpass the first parricide Cain. In such an unrighteous and monstrous manner, without any cause or guilt on his part, so many brothers hate the one youth Joseph, who had not yet reached the years of manhood. For what sin is this, to have had two dreams, to have been especially dear to his father, and to have reported to him the infamy of his brothers? Here there is sheer innocence, godliness, and simplicity, and all are very just causes for love. How can he help having dreams, etc.? Yet the brothers born and reared in the saintly home and very severe discipline of the patriarch are so bedeviled that they kill this godly brother and along with him their aged father. These men, to be sure, are the patricides, matricides, and fratricides concerning whom Paul speaks in 1 Tim. 1:9.

The father sits at Hebron with a quiet heart free from care; he thinks that all is tranquil and safe. While he is in this state of security and hope, his son Joseph perishes through the hatred of his brothers, and the father with him. What, then, must we wretched men not expect in this life if a greater burden of evils comes from the members of one's household, from sons and one's own flesh, than from neighbors or strangers? In Luke 1:71 [25] Zechariah sings of being "saved from our enemies, etc." Here it would have been more correct for Jacob to desire to be saved from friends and sons. Our life, too, is described as being subject to vanity, the devil, and all evils to such an extent that it is also necessary to be afraid of our friends, sons, and domestics that they may not be a cause of death and perpetual grief to us, for this is sadder than death.

Thus the sons of Jacob had the most distinguished teachers of the church and prophets from whom they daily heard the Word of God, the promise, the Law, etc. They saw the most excellent morals and numberless examples of honorable conduct. Yet those spiders sucked nothing but poison from the most beautiful blossoms and roses. But if they had not allowed themselves to be corrected by warnings and examples and to be deterred from their monstrous crime, they should nevertheless have spared their excellent father and saintly grandfather. But the god of the world blinded them so that they might not be able to hear or see (cf. 2 Cor. 4:4).

To this must be added the very grave scandal which arose from

[25] The original has "Luke 2."

this outrageous crime among the neighboring Ishmaelites, Midianites, and the rest, to whom this report had to spread of necessity. For Joseph is sold to them by his brothers, and so they could not help thinking: "Behold, these men are sons of the blessing; we are cast out of the church of Abraham, as though we were spurious and strangers to the promise and the church. These men who have perpetrated such a crime are the heirs."

This, to be sure, was a very serious and heartfelt offense for them, from which they could only conclude that the boasting about the blessing was vain and that they themselves with their own were rather the true church, in which such foul examples of disgraceful crimes did not arise. For a tree is recognized from its fruits. Moreover, the offense which arose from the defilement of Dinah was no less serious. These matters were undoubtedly a greater affliction for Jacob than the evil itself. Today also we are more pained and more grieved at the scandals that have been perpetrated in our churches than at the persecution of the papists and tyrants. For the papists do not harm the church as much as the false brethren do who boast of the same faith, doctrine, hope, and invocation and use the same sacraments as we do and are like us in every way. Because of such scandals the papists laugh at us, saying: "They are scoundrels through and through! They bite themselves and in turn are destroyed by each other."

Jacob, then, is an example of patience and thoughtfulness in regard to God's wonderful purposes concerning us. God wants this to be written and read and taught in the church that we may learn how God leads His saints in a wonderful manner (Ps. 4:3) and rules them in such a way that not even the saints themselves can comprehend the plans of God by which they are led. All this is for no other reason than that the flesh, our own senses, understanding, and wisdom may be mortified and that we may accustom ourselves to trust His promises with simplicity and with eyes shut, even though He pretends to be exercising no care for us and appears to be quite different. It is as the bride says in Canticles (Song of Sol. 2:9): "He stands behind our wall." He creeps into a corner, He hides behind the curtain, and like the 12-year-old boy in the temple withdraws from His parents (Luke 2:43). He conducts Himself in the same manner toward the godly, so that it seems that He does not know us at all. Even after the promises which have been given, even after the covenant which has been most certainly concluded with us, He nevertheless allows us to perish as if He had forgotten His promise and as if He did not care for us but regarded us as being rejected.

This is therefore the wisdom of the Christians, to endure the plans of God and to persevere by faith in the promise that has been given, for it is indeed sure and firm, and the Lord's covenant is faithful, according to the statement of Ps. 121:4: "Behold, He who keeps Israel will neither slumber nor sleep." But human reason replies: "These things are indeed excellently and beautifully spoken, but I am experiencing the contrary. He is not only sleeping but even snoring; to be sure, there is plainly no God at all to care for us and have regard for us." Thus Jacob is free from care and sure of the promise of God and also of the immovable agreement and covenant, yet he is treated by God in such a way that neither he nor his son seems to have guardian angels to resist the fury of a brother. All are silent and allow the devil to rage against the holy church. Where is God now?

We are often reminded and taught by examples of this kind that the promise must be apprehended by faith and that one must not doubt God when He makes promises. For as God cannot lie (Titus 1:2), so it is impossible for Him not to exercise care for us, especially if we adhere to the promise. For if this is firmly apprehended, it is impossible for us to be forsaken, because God is true. Accordingly, when He allows us to be tried, to be led down to hell, to be mortified, as we learn in this example of Jacob, we must always turn back to the promise, and that horrible scandal by which we are being crucified must be removed from our eyes.

Jacob and Joseph are submitted to a very hard trial in a manner plainly different from and contrary to the promise. Nothing at all can be seen of God's care and concern. He does not send an angel and, to be sure, not even the leaf of a tree by which the devil is checked, but He even opens the window for him that he may rage against the father and the son.

Jacob indeed has a very ample promise and also its fulfillment in living experience in the blessing implemented through 12 sons. But he comes into conflict with difficulties which are put in his way as if he had neither God nor any promise. However, we should not conclude that he is wholly forsaken. For the promise of Is. 49:15 remains immovable: "Can a woman forget her sucking child, that she should have no compassion on the son of her womb? Even these may forget, yet I will not forget you. Behold, I have graven you on the palms of My hands, etc." Why, then, are such awful experiences thrown in our path at the hands of our flesh, sons, and offspring? My reply is that this is the manner of God's government, and such is the life of the saints in this world. Therefore there is need of wisdom and doctrine exceeding the whole grasp of human reason, by which I am able to say: "I have been baptized; I have been absolved from my sins; I have eaten the body and drunk the blood of Christ; I have the most certain Word of God; He will not lie and not deceive me, however much all things seem to be carried in a contrary direction."

Jacob thinks: "I seem to be deserted, since my son of whom I expected the promise is carried off. This promise is now being called into doubt, but it is only a trial." But how many are there who could take up this attitude? Therefore the flesh and the understanding of the flesh and reason must be mortified, and all human wisdom must be reduced to nothing. It must finally come to this! All things have been made and are restored through the Word; we are created from the Word, and we must return to the Word. The sophists also spoke in this way, but without understanding, saying: "We must return to the beginning from which we proceeded." This is easily said speculatively, but practically it is work and toil to be reduced in this way, to die, and to pass away into nothing so that nothing seems to be left either of life or of carnal feeling except the Word. When I die, I descend into hell; I perish! What am I to do? No help remains except the Word: "I believe in God, etc." To this I firmly cling, however angry He may be, however much He may forsake, kill, and lead me down to hell. Why? Because I have been baptized and absolved; I have made use of Holy Communion. I believe this Word. God grant that even though heaven and earth break apart, etc., the promise and the sacraments are not on that account rejected or denied, even if I should be cast down into hell!

These are not speculative matters, but they are taken out of the midst of the real experiences of life, and they should not only be heard or contemplated once in life but should be repeated and practiced often. I have been baptized once; I have been received into God's promise; daily I am absolved and hear the remission of sins anounced to me; I am encouraged by the Word of God; I am in the kingdom of grace and salvation! What happens? So many great evils and monstrous experiences are my daily lot that if I had no other help or counsel than reason and my flesh, I would end my life immediately either with a noose or with some other weapon, so infinite are the tricks of the devil. All corners are full of a thousand kinds of death, snares, swords, etc.; and yet, whatever clouds and darkness may stand in our way, we should break through into the light of the Word and the promises and say: "In the name of God I confess that I have sinned, but I still believe that I have been baptized and that Christ is sitting at the right hand of the Father."

This is that groaning which God wants to arouse in the hearts of the saints so that they do not become smug and dull and perish ἀκηδίᾳ ("from indifference")[26] and from sluggishness of spirit. For if the spirit is aroused, faith is sharpened, the knowledge of God grows, and the new man is renewed from day to day and is taught what is the good and perfect will of God (cf. Rom. 12:2). So it has also come to pass in this man's case. The saintly man will now die; this was his last temptation which without a doubt consumed him, for he spent the rest of his life in the greatest sorrow, in darkness, and the shadow of death. For such a life spent in constant grief of the saddest kind is not life but death, where the sun turns black and there are neither sleep nor sweet foods nor any of those things which usually make a man joyful and give pleasure. This is certainly unmitigated and continuous death! Therefore Jacob goes under here! Jacob endures his last trial, which kills him, for his most beloved son is lost, his firstborn from his chief wife. At the same time also the wound resulting from the slaughter of the Shechemites and the defilement of his daughter breaks out again, and there is also the recent grief from the very deplorable death of Joseph's mother. Finally, Reuben defiles Bilhah. These four trials followed each other continuously, one after the other, within a period of three years. He is certainly a wretched man in whose saintly house, where the Word and the Holy Spirit reign, the devil prevails with such great power that sadder acts could hardly have befallen any heathen criminal. I wouldn't know how things could be worse even for a heathen. If these things had happened to Julius Caesar, Octavius, or Alexander the Great, they would certainly be undeserved and atrocious enough!

These are quite powerful and horrible themes, which I cannot handle according to their true worth. They are too high for me! Therefore let us not fear. Come what will, things cannot go as badly

---

[26] One of the seven deadly sins and a special temptation for monks.

for us as for this saintly man; harder experiences than these cannot befall us! We have not yet attained to the sufferings and crucifixions of this patriarch, and even though the Turk were to ravage, devastate, and kill us, the disaster would not be comparable with the troubles of Jacob. Indeed, even the torments suffered by the martyrs are not comparable, because they suffer full of the Spirit and joy, without sorrow and grief and, in addition, even hurling taunts at the tyrants. Their suffering is only for one moment. This was a perpetual killing which endured for 22 years, right down to the descent into Egypt.

The purposes of God by which the saints are ruled are wonderful, with Satan raging in a monstrous fashion and with the Holy Spirit present, guarding, teaching, exhorting, and preserving the church. For although the father and the son are forsaken, nevertheless, as I stated previously, they retain the Word for a whole 20 years during which both lived in death, that is, in the promise alone and in the Word.

This is a most wretched life according to the flesh, for in actual fact the father dies and sees nothing except the son's death and his own death. So he says below (Gen. 37:35): "I shall go down to Sheol mourning." But Joseph, in addition, will be thrown into prison and accused of adultery, as though there were not enough evil in exile and servitude and in the fact that he was torn from his dearly beloved father and family; and so death upon death and hell upon hell assails him. And still Joseph lives. Why and how did he live? Because he had heard the promise of God and the sermons of his father. "God promised to Abraham and Isaac my father," he said to himself, "that He will be the God of his seed and sons forever." These promises preserved and encouraged the father Jacob and the son Joseph, who was like good tinder, easily receiving the fire, and never departed from the words of his father. "I am Jacob's son," he thought, "to whom God has promised that He will care for me. This I firmly believe, although all things are being borne in a contrary direction."

The wretched papists, however, do not understand these lives and examples of the fathers. They hear that Jacob had a wife and cows, and they scorn these things as being carnal things. But come, consider this example more closely! What a wretched man Jacob was according to the flesh! But consider that torch which shines in a dark place before the eyes of Joseph and Jacob! They stay and live here for a long time, 22 years, in exile and hell itself. Although

Joseph is raised from hell 10 years before, he is nevertheless compelled to forego his most pleasant association with his father. Accordingly, in the fathers consideration must be given to the promise and to faith in the promise, inasmuch as they were able to endure such great troubles with no other aid except that they had this Word: "I am the Lord your God, your Protector! Do not fear! Have confidence! I am with you, I will defend you."

To us it is also said in Baptism, in Absolution, in Communion: "I am the Lord your God, do not be troubled! I will care for you! Cast your care on Me! You have a God who has promised that He will care for you." "And yet I see the contrary," do you say? "You do, indeed, see the contrary, but it is a trial which is useful for this purpose, that you may learn and experience how kind the Lord is. For if this trial were not added, you would remain in the flesh, stupid and senseless, and would never understand what I mean when I say: 'I am the Lord your God.' So it is necessary for you to be instructed and by the actual experience of various trials to learn that I am the Lord your God." Thus it is written in Deut. 8:4: "He fed you with manna that you might know that it is not only by bread, etc."

This is not done that you may perish, because Baptism is certain, and the promise and absolution are reliable. What for, then? This is done that you may learn what powerful life there is in the Word and that you may come to this conclusion for youself: "However harshly I am disciplined and afflicted and come to nothing, it is nevertheless done with this end in view, that I might remember my Baptism and God's promise; for I have God, who is taking care of me, and about this I am in no doubt at all, even though all things seem to be against me. They are only temptations and testings of my faith, to see whether I believe that God is my Protector."

These are the examples of the fathers in which I have stated that the promise and their faith in the promise should be observed, and afterwards also their cross. For these are the chief points in the stories of the saints. Then, too, God also tolerates domestic affairs and those servile duties which the world and the papists despise. The fathers were men just like other men, and they will perform works similar to the works of other men, works which are also done by ungodly men, so that there is practically no difference between Jacob and any other shepherd. But there is this difference which is not evident to any carnal viewpoint, that Jacob has the promise; he is

God's son and under the care and protection of Him in whom he trusts. Therefore all that he does in generating children and milking goats is pleasing to God and acceptable to Him. Why? Because the promise rules here; he is under the heaven of the promise, and he believes.

But when trials assail them, then the true virtues of the saints come into evidence, just as here, for example, no goat is milked but the father and son are killed, and the whole house is thrown into confusion, and the church is disturbed. What happens then? Cries and wailing arise! "Alas! We are nothing; we are done for!" But faith, on the contrary, says: "You have not perished; remember that you still have the promise which has been spread out over you just like a very broad heaven. God is taking care of you even if you do not see it or feel it. Only a little cloud has been drawn up, which seems to have swallowed God." These matters in the stories of the fathers should be mentioned and emphasized often that we may learn to stand boldly in faith and to think highly of our promises. Do not underestimate yourself, since you have been baptized and since you have God's Word, have been absolved, and called! Think that the kingdom of heaven has been spread out over you and that not only God but all the angels have their eyes fixed on you. Therefore, even if all things are in confusion, heaven and earth are merged, all the gates of hell (cf. Matt. 16:18) are moved, and the pope, the emperor, and the Turk rage in most cruel fashion, all you have to say is: "I am baptized." Then all is well with you; in this confidence you will conquer, for God is taking care of you; He will not forsake you, nor will any disadvantage happen without regard to your salvation.

I commend the word נָכַל to the Hebrews that they may investigate and search out its meaning. As far as I can gather, it means to do something astutely, to practice trickery, as we commonly say, to carry on unusual intrigues such as are practiced today at the courts and are characteristic of nearly all peasants. The brothers laid their plot with a cunning plan. With fraud and trickery they made it their aim to kill Joseph with trickery and cunning so that their father might not discover the deed and so that they themselves might not bear the blame. In Mal. 1:14 we read: "Cursed be the cheat who has a male in his flock, and vows it, and yet sacrifices to the Lord what is blemished." נוֹכֵל means astute, cunning. The Bishop of Mainz and similar old foxes devise stratagems and involve all things in their frauds, but they astutely cover them with their craftiness. We say in German: *"Wischen das Maul,* etc." ("They wipe their mouth, etc.!") Who did it? Mr. Nobody![27] "Nobody" is the one who disturbs and ruins everything in the home and state.

That is how these men act. They kill a saintly young man, in such a way, however, that they may appear to be models of innocence and beyond all blame. To be sure, they even pretend to be deeply affected by their father's grief. They cannot kill him with open violence, for their father would discover it, and they want to conceal the deed from him. Therefore they enter upon a malicious plan to destroy him, and yet they themselves do not appear to be the authors of the murder. They think: "We will act in this way and kill him and say that he has been torn to pieces by wild beasts, a lion, a bear, or a wolf. We know nothing of his death. Let us say that we found his bloody clothing on the road. We will send it to our father that he may see whether it is Joseph's clothing or not. We certainly do not know where or when he perished."

But this is a very beautiful mystery and image of the people of Israel. For the Jews are such נוֹכְלִים, as is evident in the case of Saul and in the case of the Jews before Pilate, who said (John 18:31): "It is not lawful for us to put any man to death." These are the נוֹכְלִים and that Mr. Nobody who do harm and yet earnestly desire praise for innocence and justice. This seems to me to be the force and meaning of the word.

But consider whether these brothers were not possessed by the devil, inasmuch as they plotted destruction for their brother so astutely and mocked their father so wickedly. Yet I could in all innocence believe that not all of them were so abandoned but that Simeon and Levi were the foremost leaders in the crime. Judah and Reuben do not seem to have given their consent willingly, as Reuben is absolved in the account of Moses and Judah advises that he should rather be sold. But those two brothers above had the fixed purpose in their hearts to kill and destroy their brother. But their age excuses the rest, Gad, Asher, Zebulon, Naphtali, and Issachar. For these events took place when Joseph was 17, Judah was 20, Levi 21, Simeon 22, and Reuben 23. The rest below Joseph were younger. Those two, then, were the leaders and masters. Simeon and Levi are the Junkers at the court, the plagues of this house! The rest do not resist and

---

[27] Cf. *Luther's Works,* 13, p. 203.

are involved in the same sin through those pestilential scoundrels. To be sure, dear Lord God, it often happens that a scoundrel can make a whole city go wrong.

Reuben resisted the abominable endeavors but was disregarded by his brothers. For he lost his authority through his act of incest, and the others were so much the more confident inasmuch as they insisted that they were righteous and saintly men and that for this reason the government of the house and church belonged to them.

It is helpful for the correction and consolation of the church that these matters be strongly emphasized. The sons of such a great man plan such an atrocious crime in such smugness, and at the same time they also seduce and implicate the other brothers in the same crime so that they enter into a conspiracy to kill Joseph for the sole reason that he recounted his two dreams and was dear to his father. Here all the duties of the First and Second Table are completely abolished and annulled. Nothing is left but the most heathenish barbarism. God is not feared, indeed, He is mocked and crucified. Secondly, with every right they can be called murderers of their mother, father, grandfather, and great-grandfather, for I believe that Isaac could have lived much longer had he been spared this disaster. If the honorable matrons Rachel, Rebecca, and Deborah had still been in the land of the living, they would have died of heartache, and it must be attributed to their good fortune that they were removed from the human scene before this disaster. For if they had lived during this year, they would not have been able to endure such great grief. In tears they would have torn their hair and perished of constant sorrow and grief. Therefore by this one sin these disobedient sons are involved in many very serious crimes.

Therefore, young men, learn to obey your parents, teachers, and elders! For disobedience of children is a great and horrible sin and the cause of infinite evils, for it kills parents, brothers, grandfathers, and a whole generation of men and crucifies the Son of God. Take heed!

In what manner Simeon and Levi did penance is not certain from Holy Scripture. But I believe that a large part of their penance and punishments was that drowning of the males in Egypt. It could be that God punished and afflicted them individually in His own time so that they in turn wept, howled, tore their hair, and perhaps endured more serious sufferings than we think of, sufferings that have not been recorded in writing. It seems likely, however, that God exacted a punishment equal or similar to their sin when the order was given by the king of Egypt to cast the male Israelites into the river, as if God meant to say: "You hurled your brother Joseph into a pit without water: I, in turn, will have your sons be hurled into the river to drown."

At length satisfaction follows sin, not that papal satisfaction, but the vengeance of God. God indeed pardons and remits sins, but let the sinner not fall asleep; let him not become smug and boast as though of something well done. For God comes with a rod of iron and visits the iniquity of the fathers upon the children to the third and fourth generation (Ex. 20:5). Why? Not because He is satisfied for sin through that punishment, for He is not satisfied by punishments. Nor does He have regard for our satisfactions, but He punishes so that the sinner may not smugly snore away or glory in his evil way but so that sin may bite us, mortify, and compel us to acknowledge its magnitude, to weep, to sigh, and to implore grace and the gracious pardon promised to those who weep and mourn and who repent of their sins and acknowledge them.

But if God did not punish, not only would we overlook sin and snore, but we would daily accumulate other far greater sins. "Sin is couching at the door," Cain is told (Gen. 4:7), but at length it will unexpectedly awake and crucify you, yet not for your perdition and damnation but for your repentance and change of heart, so that you may acknowledge your sin, groan, cry out, and invoke the mercy of God. They will have paid well for their sin! The Israelites, to be sure, paid quite a heavy penalty for their sins, as is set forth in the story of Exodus, chapter 1. For just as they killed their brother, father, and mothers, so in their turn they suffered infinite evils in Egypt under the tyranny of Pharaoh. Pharaoh really takes their measure in Egypt so that they may remember what a great sin they have committed and not regard sin as a light matter.

If we do not carefully and correctly estimate the magnitude of sin, God Himself will do so; if we do not judge ourselves, the Lord will judge us. But it is a great blessing that He judges and punishes for salvation and not for damnation, as Judas and Saul were judged. But if you idly think and say: "Even though I have offended my parents, what of it?" Then sin is of course asleep, but it will awaken and drive you to say: "How wretched I am! What have I done? Why have I despised God in my father, mother, and teacher? Why have

I not obeyed their admonitions?" This will eventually take place; it cannot be otherwise!

Similarly, we often give severe warnings concerning clandestine bethrothals that they should be avoided on both sides, by girls and youths.[28] But you can see many under the blind impulse of love rushing into ruin even contrary to conscience, the young men seizing wives by force, not marrying them, and the young women not becoming married contrary to the will of their parents. What else do these people do but pollute themselves with horrible and mortal sin? This, to be sure, sleeps for a time. The girl pleases him, and his heart burns with love for her so that he thinks and dreams of nothing else day and night. But after one or two months are past, there follows sighing and groaning, as Abigail says to David in 1 Sam. 25:29-31:[29] "The life of my lord shall be bound in the bundle of the living in the care of the Lord your God, etc. . . . my lord shall have no cause of grief, or pangs of conscience, for having shed blood without cause, etc." Such scruples continually harass conscience, namely: "I married her against the wishes of her parents." Then follows the itching of the neck, the bad little black dog Remorse, who bites you all your life without ceasing, even though your sin is forgiven.

But grief of conscience becomes even heavier among those who now know God's will that marriages should not be contracted without the consent of parents. For previously, when we did not know God's commandment, ignorance in a way had an excuse. But rather than trying to find pleasure in a secret and clandestine union, how much better would it be now to enter into marriage with the consent and will of parents so that in sleeping with the girl you may embrace her with joy and a good conscience without any scruple and sobbing, with God as well as the parents smiling on you and bestowing favor upon you? In the former case, the heart conscious of its abiding guilt would keep on murmuring: "I could have obtained and enjoyed her with the goodwill and joy of her parents; why, then, have I grieved God and men?" That little black dog of repentance which is too late does not cease barking and biting, however much you know that your sins have been forgiven.

Those of us who are in the church's ministry often have much trouble with such consciences that are troubled and burdened with

---

28 See, for example, *Luther's Works*, 5, pp. 193—194.

29 The original has "1 Sam. 15"

this kind of sin until we encourage and console them. Therefore we are rightly angry with the jurists and their canons, inasmuch as they are the authors of these disturbances. They set fire to houses and then leave them to us to put out. But we do what we can; we absolve and console those who are burdened by such sins. But the little black dog continues to act up! Grief breaks out afresh as often as any misfortune strikes in the household, when a son takes sick, a wife has a miscarriage or dies, etc. The cause of the whole evil is manifest, namely, contempt of parents, and the little dog immediately barks at this. If this cause is absent, we endure difficulties of every kind with more equanimity, and the heart is quiet and tranquil and knows that this kind of life is pleasing to God. It plays with a wife free from care and is certain that all its doings are approved by God, nor is it easily moved or terrified even if something of an adverse nature happens.

I say these things for the sake of example. They should be applied to all other sins upon which grief of conscience is bound to follow, even in those who are most smug and most fierce. For a habit of this kind is removed from its subject only with difficulty. Therefore, dear children, be circumspect! This sort of thing comes: take heed! You are still young: you do not know what a cruel beast a bad conscience is! Accustom your hearts to render obedience towards your parents and teachers. It is a very fine thing, as Juvenal says, "not to grow pale as a result of guilt." [30] Nothing is more desirable than living a life pleasing to God and agreeable to parents, and I could adduce many examples from personal experience and from what I have seen in others, showing what a great evil the knowledge of sin is. I omit them for the sake of brevity.

It is necessary simply to come to this conclusion, that sin is death and damnation to death. But damnation is twofold, of wrath and of grace. If it is the damnation of wrath, such great might of sin is felt that it overwhelms and destroys conscience without any remedy or consolation, as happened in the case of Judas, Saul, and all who have been led into despair. May the Lord free and preserve us from this! The other damnation is that of grace, concerning which Paul says in 1 Cor. 11:31: "If we judged ourselves truly, we should not be judged" by the Lord. Here God preserves the condemned through the Word and the promise, through the comfort and ministry of the

---

[30] The passage is not from Juvenal, but from Horace, *Epistles*, I, 1, 61.

Word. When a pastor of the church is present, or any minister of
the Word, and he cheers up this conscience, still, no matter how
much it is cheered up, a groaning contrary to the will and all experience of consolation repeatedly returns. I know what happens to me
when I call to mind the previous actions of my whole life. For even
though I know that my sins are forgiven to me, that פּוּקָה ("qualm
of conscience") still returns. I cannot be without sobs, without shame
and blushing. "Shame on you!" "What have I done? etc." I am certainly not conscious of defiling another man's wife, of murder, or
similar enormous crimes. In this respect the little dog cannot bite
me, but he bites me again in respect to other sins, even though conscience has been healed and the scar closed up.

For some, then, sin is an awakening to damnation but for others
an awakening for chastisement and repentance so that they are instructed and converted, so that they cry out and are saved, as sin
was aroused in Manasseh (2 Chron. 33:10-16), but for grace and salvation, and similarly also in the case of Peter, Paul, and the Magdalene.
But those are still more fortunate who live without sobs and sighs
like godly spouses who are certain of the consent of parents. They
endure and overcome any evils whatever with a joyful and good
conscience much more easily than others who have despised the
authority of parents.

But the sin of these נוֹכְלִים is now quiet while they perpetrate
a monstrous and abominable crime, and this example is set before us
both for our consolation and for the terror of the ungodly and the
smug. These brothers indeed obtained mercy so that they eventually
groaned, sighed, and made satisfaction, not with papistic satisfaction
but with God's, which is damnation to death in such a way, however,
that the sinner is aroused to cry out and to implore the mercy of
God set forth in Christ. In this way the Ninevites were converted and
fasted, but this fasting was not their repentance and satisfaction, but
that groaning — "so that we perish not" (Jonah 3:9) — was for salvation, lest there be a damnation to death.

But to their fierce plan they added also very bitter words: "Here
comes this dreamer." He indicates very bitter contempt. For their
heart and tongue is full of diabolical malice and bitterness. A bishop
in our neighborhood is to be compared with these נוֹכְלִים. He supported a good and godly preacher, Master George, and heard him
preaching at his court. Later he had him killed in secret and after

the murder had been committed pretended that he was ignorant of this crime and put on a show of great grief on account of the unjust murder.

Therefore as soon as they spy their brother, whom they should have loved, received with joyful countenance, and, in particular, defended at this age and seeing that he was innocent, they forthwith speak about him in a hateful and malicious manner, saying: "Behold this בַּעַל of dreams," for that is how the Hebrew runs, that is, "this lord and master of dreams." "The miserable fictionist, the dreamer is coming." They fix this blame on him, that he is the author and inventor of dreams.

בַּעַל means "lord," properly, "husband," "master of a house." In Is. 1:3 we read: "The ox knows its master, etc.," and in Deuteronomy: "If you see an ass straying, return it to its master" (cf. 22:1). From this the cult of Baal derived the most renowned name of idolatry. For those idolatrous people chose a more extraordinary form of worship than the usual method of worshiping God. They wanted to have a husband, one who would be their lover. בַּעֲלָה means a beloved woman. "We are not content," they said, "that he should be our master, as he is the master of others, but we want him to be our בַּעַל, our lover; we want to be better than others." So they instituted festivals and fixed sacrifices as the monks had among us; for they are not content with spiritual acts of worship consisting in faith, love, hope, etc., and they have thought up in addition new forms of clothing, distinctions of food, times, and places. And this they call perfection, just as though they were not common Christians but angels placed far above the common crowd of Christians.

We see, then, how bitterly they interpret the dreams of the simple and excellent youth as though they had been skillfully invented by him to seize the kingdom and priesthood from the others. In this way they increase the flames of their unjust hatred. Simeon and Levi could not endure this. Reuben had been rejected on account of his sin; Judah was too young. So they said: "The dominion belongs to no one but us two. When I, Simeon, die, Levi will be the successor." These two are the shameless masters and actors of this tragedy, and below they will be painted in their true colors by the patriarch Jacob with appropriate punishments when he says (Gen. 49:5-7): "Simeon and Levi are brothers; vessels of iniquity are in their tents. O my soul, come not into their council; O my glory, be not joined to their com-

pany, etc. I will divide them in Jacob and scatter them in Israel."
The whole tribe of Levi had nothing of its own; in the tribe of Simeon
there were only poor scribes and schoolmasters. As the Jews say even
now: "There is no scribe in the whole people except in the tribe of
Simeon." Therefore this punishment of poverty and beggary came
upon both tribes, even though their sin was pardoned through
repentance.

Accordingly, although they were treading the path to the topmost
position and royal pinnacle, they were cast down in wretched fashion
and reduced to perpetual poverty. For strife concerning the birthright
and the royal and priestly dignity is the cause of these great conflicts
and hatreds by which the brothers are impelled to a monstrous crime
which far exceeds Cain's murder, for he killed his brother Abel for
the same cause, namely, because his sacrifices were approved by God
but his own were rejected. Therefore he had to die! In this way
Joseph dreams that he will be a ruler and a priest, and the meaning
of the dreams is manifest. Therefore they are seriously moved so that
they say: "Are you, indeed, to have dominion over us?"

It is still common for the same thing to happen among brothers,
who very rarely have concord in the division of inheritances. Among
strangers agreement is easier than among brothers. Joseph, to be sure,
dies for the sake of the prerogative which was his due by every right.
For he was the firstborn of the chief wife, who had been sought first
and dearly loved by Jacob. Leah was foisted on him by fraud after
this one although she had never been sought nor loved. These two
scoundrels, however, try to snatch away a dignity owed to Joseph
both by their father's wishes and by the right of birth. They are
assuredly worse than Cain, and their sins are far more atrocious than
the murder he committed. For they do not reflect that they will shatter
their poor old father, who had been tossed this way and that from
the beginning of his marriage with so many evils on their account.
No sense, no power of reflection remains in them! They simply let
themselves go! He must die! This comes from the devil.

Later, their descendants, the Jews, did the same thing. Paying
no regard to the many great miracles performed by Christ, they kept
on repeating: "We do not want this Man to reign over us; He wants
to teach us; He wants to be our pontiff, priest, and king. He says
that He is God's Son: away with Him; crucify Him" (cf. Luke 19:14).
The same obstinacy is to be found at all times in those who fight

against the truth and the ordinance of God, for today the papists also sound forth the same thing, saying: "We do not want to be ruled or taught by anyone, etc."

The rest of the brothers are not the authors of this Satanic plan but are nevertheless implicated together with them, as usually happens in the world. After they have set their hearts on killing their brother, they go on to form a very crafty plan by which they may conceal both their own crime and the body of their dead brother. But behold, I ask you, how horribly blinded they are and possessed by Satan, for they join lying to murder, and so they omit no sin, especially against the Second Table but also against the First, except adultery.

Therefore if anyone wishes to enlarge on their sin, he will have material in great plenty. For they sin against the whole Decalog. They deprive their father of his whole posterity, possessions, reputation, and even the promise, had that been possible for them. They do not sin against the Sixth Commandment, but they are plunged into and completely overwhelmed by all the rest of the sins forbidden in the Decalog. Likewise, they upset the whole household and throw it into wretched grief. They sin, in particular, against their father and grandfather, who sees disaster befall his grandson and does not know who its author is. But the Ishmaelites and Midianites know, and this involved the whole church in the greatest of scandals.

They give themselves airs in a very crafty manner and say: "Let us throw him into one of the pits, and we will say that a wild beast has devoured him." Here there is no consideration or concern for the claims of brotherhood. Even to the most cruel enemy it would certainly have occurred that this was his brother and that he should have been spared by brothers, but they kill him and bury him in a pit and invent an excuse for the crime before their father and others, saying: "We did not kill him, a beast devoured him."

Here again is a passage for reflecting upon the wonderful plan of God, which we either do not perceive at all or, at all events, only slightly and obscurely. For if God is angry, as it appears, He is not angry from the heart but keeps His mercy and truth over us, as Holy Scripture testifies concerning Him. Such promises shine forth in this darkness and in a very gloomy place. Then, too, it is another plan of God that He allows the brothers of Joseph to set up stratagems and with great wisdom to conceal their murder, just as Cain thought that Abel's murder was concealed and unknown to God and men. So they did not doubt that it was possible to take precautions to prevent their father from finding out, but they were completely deranged and blinded by these cunning plans and stratagems on which they congratulated themselves so much.

So also today God allows the Turk and the pope to be wise and to weave plots, and He grants them wonderful successes, but in the selfsame way He reduces them to madness when they seem to themselves to be very wise. But who sees this? For we rather tend to be weak, foolish, and despised in the world; we mourn and are sad, whereas they rejoice and exult in the glory of their wisdom and power and, in short, in ruling over the whole world. But those who have the Holy Spirit and know the mind of the Lord come to the conclusion stated in Ps. 73:18: "Truly Thou dost set them in slippery places; Thou dost make them fall to ruin." Accordingly, all who rely on their own wisdom and cunning err in their thinking. Bishops and cardinals are very foolish with their smart practices, but no one sees it. We see them quite mad and raving in all their plans and deliberations, but we shall not convince them.

Therefore, when the ungodly threaten us with death, the cross, sword, and fire by which they plan to kill us and bury us, let us know for certain that God, who said (Gen. 15:1): "I will be your Protector," is laughing at their folly and setting the opposite in motion. For Joseph's brothers say: "Come, let us kill Joseph!" God, on the contrary, says: "Let him live and preserve him unharmed." They say: "We will bury him in a pit." He says: "Raise him up." They promise themselves praise for justice and innocence; He, on the contrary, says: "Accuse yourselves and hurl yourselves into eternal damnation." In this way God changes and overthrows the plans of men, and those who have the Holy Spirit and have experienced God's help and liberation from dangers understand this.

This is the teaching of the Second Psalm, which depicts the plans and endeavors on both sides. The kings of the earth and the princes rage and shout: "Let us burst their bonds asunder, and cast their yoke from us" (Ps. 2:3). "We do not want to recognize their Christ," they mean to say. But He who dwells in the heavens laughs at them, and the Lord has them in derision (Ps. 2:4). "Your rejecting and bursting asunder," He says, "is My exaltation, raising, crowning, and appointment as King." This is their gain! "Your burial is My raising from the dead, and the release of your crime is eternal damnation."

Accordingly, what they say in great confidence: "And we shall see what will become of his dreams," they did see later to their great detriment when they had glutted their hatred for their brother with an abominable crime. For God also saw their mad acts, even though they thought that their brother could be concealed. Let us learn, then, to despise the threats and cruel plans of our enemies and conclude for certain that God in the heavens has decided on quite different things and is already laughing at them but playing with us so that He may prove our faith and hope and discipline us. And although the game is very unpleasant to us and bitter, to those whom He derides His decision will be most bitter and gloomy!

21. *But when Reuben heard it, he delivered him out of their hands, saying: Let us not take his life.*

22. *And Reuben said to them: Shed no blood; cast him into this pit here in the wilderness, but lay no hand upon him — that he might rescue him out of their hand, to restore him to his father.*

Moses makes an excuse for Reuben for not conspiring with the rest of the brothers to kill Joseph and for opposing their rage in a manly manner. Although he was not able to liberate him completely, he nevertheless did his best that he should not be killed. For he did not even want him to be thrown into a pit, although he seems to advise it, but in a way he tried to preserve his brother's life. Accordingly, it was accounted to him by God as a complete act and a perfect rescue to the best of his ability, inasmuch as his will was ready to give perfect consideration to his brother and would have gladly hindered both this murder and throwing him into a pit. On this viewpoint Augustine says: "God crowns the will inwardly where He does not find an outward opportunity," [31] and Christ interprets the Fifth Commandment in this manner (Matt. 5:22): "Everyone who is angry with his brother shall be liable to judgment." "Anyone who hates his brother is a murderer" (1 John 3:15). For the whole will is present when it wishes that the brother be removed. When the will is perfected either for good or evil, the work is perfected.

Reuben is innocent of his brother's blood, although this innocence does not free him from the incest which he previously committed. It seems, moreover, that he wanted to escape or mitigate this punish-

[31] Augustine, *Enarratio in Psalmum 103 [104]*, I, 19, *Patrologia, Series Latina,* XXXVII, 1351.

ment with this deed, to see if he might possibly insinuate himself into his father's favor again. But his father took no notice of his efforts and this humble attitude, and although he forgave Reuben's sin, the punishment remained, as is stated in the German proverb, "Old guilt does not rust," a debt however old it gets, does not contract rust.

Thus by the very hard servitude of their descendants and the slaughter of the male infants, the rest of the brothers at length paid their due punishment for the sin of murder, but the two tribes of Simeon and Levi were especially cursed by their father in a singular manner, for sin is not forgiven and remitted without having the punishment of sin and of an evil conscience remain. Thus in the case of David's sin, although he heard from Nathan the words: "The Lord also has put away your sin" (2 Sam. 12:13), a very severe punishment from God still followed, the rebellion of his son Absalom, who stripped his father of the kingdom and all his property and defiled all his wives.

We must be on our guard against sins with all zeal and watchfulness, for they never depart with impunity unless the punishments are removed by very earnest repentance and God's mercy. Otherwise it is a case of old guilt not rusting. Moreover, when dangers are impending, we pray: "O God, do not avenge old guilt; do not remember our iniquities, O Lord." Simeon and Levi sin quite freely, and for a time the sin lies dormant. But it is sleeping at the door (cf. Gen. 4:7) so that sometime later it may be aroused for punishment. Then it is suddenly present and bites so that the sinner cries out: "O wretched man that I am! I have merited this punishment by some sin or another. Alas! This is what I learned thereby." Here sin is a horrible and sad matter, carrying punishment from God with it, especially if we do not judge ourselves, just as, on the other hand, our good deeds never lack their own rewards.

Thus, to be sure, Reuben's incest is still dormant, and now he wishes to enter into favor with his father. But it is not the time for placating his father, and so he obtains nothing. Previously, when he could have abstained from sin, he did not contain himself; now when he wishes to benefit his father, it is unacceptable. Before God, however, it was a good work because he tries to liberate Joseph, and he could have been excused like Judah too. But Simeon and Levi, the very worst of scoundrels, are the authors and leaders of the crime, and therefore Simeon pays the heaviest penalty of all of them. For he was later thrown into prison because he was the chief author of this outrageous sin (cf. Gen. 42:24). Nor do I think that Christ was killed by any others excepting these two tribes, the rulers and the scribes. The chief priests were from the tribe of Levi, and the scribes from the tribe of Simeon. Therefore just as they tortured Joseph, so their posterity crucified Christ, and they were completely abandoned to crime together with their whole posterity.

Jerome says somewhere that in the enumeration of the Twelve Tribes Simeon is omitted because of the traitor Judas.[32] Of the chief priests it is certain that they were of the tribe of Levi, but Annas and Caiaphas are descended from Simeon and also Judas, their guide, as Peter says in Acts 1:16. This, then, is an excuse for Reuben, who intercedes for Joseph and prays that they should not take his life. "You must not take his life." Similarly Issachar, Zebulon, Gad, and Asher were also innocent, but induced by the authority of the older brothers, they gave their consent. In the time of Christ also the chief priests drew the people to themselves and brought them over to their opinion so that they ordered Him to be crucified. Now the real climax follows.

23. *So when Joseph came to his brothers, they stripped him of his robe, the long robe with many threads that he wore;*

24. *and they took him and cast him into a pit. The pit was empty, there was no water in it.*

The brothers follow Reuben's advice and throw Joseph into an empty pit which did not have water in it. In this passage this is described by Moses in a few words, but below, when they have come into Egypt, it is repeated at length by Reuben with a very severe censuring of the brothers, saying (Gen. 42:22): "Did I not tell you not to sin against the lad? But you would not listen." Joseph was undoubtedly a very handsome youth of 17, which is the flower of a man's life and the most pleasant time of life. But suddenly, at a time when he has no such fears, he is dragged off to his death by his brothers, who make an assault on him, crying: "You traitor! You scoundrel, you have to die!" Although he became a suppliant on bended knees and with folded hands, groaning, wailing, and beseeching them by God, by all things sacred, and by the piety and respect owed to their parents, he sees that no place is left for prayers and tears, as they themselves acknowledge, saying (cf. Gen. 42:21): "In truth we are

[32] See p. 326.

guilty concerning our brother, in that we saw the distress of his soul, when he besought us and we would not listen; behold, his blood is required of us."

Reflect how wretched the face of the youth was as he raised his hands and eyes to heaven and with tears and groaning made supplication to his brothers, by whom he sees himself surrounded and about to be killed. For what great misery it is to fall not by the hands of strangers and enemies but by those of brothers! But they are harder than flint and diamond and are not moved by the distress, sighs, and wailing of the young man, and by such factors, it has been ascertained, as even enemies have often been moved.

The cruelty of the two brothers cannot be adequately emphasized, for they rage in such monstrous fashion against their own flesh and blood. Christ's passion is also sad and atrocious, although we know that it happened by His Father's will. But the ferocity of these brothers is far greater, for they should have been moved with natural στοργή ("affection") towards their brother. Reuben tries to arouse this completely extinct emotion and love in them when he begs for his brother's life. But he accomplishes nothing. For although they do not strangle the youth immediately, as they had decided, they still throw him into a pit, an act sadder and more cruel by far, for they plan to kill him in this solitude by hunger and thirst. How much more tolerable it would have been to be killed suddenly than to be exposed for such a long time to so many tortures! But their endeavors and plans were confounded by God, for we see that those who are rather harshly afflicted also desire present destruction so that they may be rid of the evils by which they are afflicted as soon as possible.

Accordingly, the devil wreaked his extreme cruelty on these brothers who were to become the high priests. For Joseph is a figure of Christ, and His descent into hell is indicated in this passage, or, as Zechariah says, into the lake in which there is no water that by the blood of His testament He might set free those bound in the lake (cf. 9:11).

But first they strip him of his tunic woven with many threads or unsewn, not because they found great delight in this item of plunder but to deceive and delude their excellent father, the very wretched old man. This tunic which was previously a sign of the father's love towards his son now becomes a hard and abominable sign to sadden and torment the father who has been especially delighted by it and with special zeal has adorned his son with this tunic. By the same he is now killed, for he will say later (cf. Gen. 37:33): "It is my son's robe; a wild beast has devoured him, etc."

Moreover, after stripping him of his tunic, they throw him into a pit. They let him lie there and think that now it is all over with him. For their plan is that he should die of hunger, thirst, and filth in that pit. Yet by God's providence it came to pass that it had no water so that he was not suddenly overwhelmed by the water. Otherwise he would have been suffocated in this moment of time. They take up Reuben's plan so that they may torment Joseph for some days and in this way [33] fill up their ill will and hatred against him.

Thus the devil reigns in the house of the saintly patriarch Jacob, among the sons of God, as Job says (1:6). Meanwhile, however, Benjamin, who was still a boy, was crying in his cradle, for all these events happened within a period of two years: the defilement of Dinah, the death of Rachel and Deborah, Reuben's incest, and the selling of Joseph. One misfortune followed upon the other. Reuben can be excused, as has been stated above, and I think that the rest of the brothers, Dan, Naphtali, Issachar, etc., were also innocent. But Annas, Caiaphas, and Judas are the real authors of these sins; and they were even wonderfully pleased with themselves and gave thanks to their master, Satan, for such a fortunate success in their plans and rejoiced and exulted in the basest of designs, having no regard for their aged father and brother Joseph, who in the meantime cries out, groans, and is tormented in death and hell without any comfort or hope of rescue. For no one is present to console him in his affliction and to tell him to trust in the goodness and presence of God, who will be his Protector in his worst and saddest troubles, but he remains in the extreme misery of solitude and hell. They take the tunic with them that it may become a poisonous bane for their excellent father, whom it had so often and so pleasantly delighted previously.

Incidentally, nothing is added about whether they tore up the garment before they dipped it in the blood. If they did not tear it up, they certainly acted foolishly and what usually happens befell them, namely, what is stated in the well-known proverb that folly is always joined to impiety. Hilary says: "If prudence were as thoughtful as wickedness is daring, it would be difficult to espouse the cause of truth." [34] Therefore a common saying tells us: "A liar must have

---

[33] The Weimar text has *in,* but we have read *ita.*

[34] Perhaps this refers to Hilary, *De Trinitate,* III, 24—25, *Patrologia, Series Latina,* X, 92—94.

a good memory and be intelligent." [35] But if they left the tunic intact to be dipped in blood, it was marked folly, and they betrayed themselves by this. For in this case the father could have inferred: "Behold, they say that Joseph was torn by a wild beast! How, then, did it not tear his tunic?" Or, if it had been torn, he would nevertheless have thought that it was necessary for a search to be made for some portion of bone and flesh which the beast had left. In this way, to be sure, wickedness and lying betray themselves. Moreover, if Jacob had retained his presence of mind, this would undoubtedly have occurred to him. But he was confused to the point of distraction, even as men are beside themselves in more violent paroxysms of joy or sorrow so that all their senses become benumbed and they neither see nor think anything. So Jacob is completely overwhelmed and absorbed by grief and sorrow at the first news of the death of his son. "O Lord God, can he be dead?" he would have asked. Otherwise, when the tunic was presented to him, he could have asked whether nothing was left of the body and how the garment had remained intact since, indeed, wild beasts usually tear to pieces a body with its garments. He could have also requested to be conducted to the place where some traces of this cruel destruction were in evidence. But his disturbed heart pays no attention to these matters and is not concerned about them.

This is therefore an illustrious example of stupidity in liars, who are never consistent with themselves and can easily be detected and reproved by those who are attentive. They think that they have discovered a beautiful and wise plan; but if you estimate it correctly, it is as stupid as can be and full of danger. They should have lost body and life on this account if their father had not been too credulous.

25. *Then they sat down to eat; and looking up they saw a caravan of Ishmaelites coming from Gilead, with their camels bearing gum, balm, and myrrh, on their way to carry it down to Egypt.*

They sit down to eat bread as though they had carried off a successful transaction. Their conscience is secure, and sin is asleep. But God attends to all matters in a wonderful manner. The wretched father sits at home, not knowing how matters stand with his son. Nor does Joseph discern any ending to his misfortunes. God is the only one who sees, and He plays with the father and son in a very kindly manner. For it is a game full of divine mercy and goodness,

[35] Quintilian, *Institutiones oratoriae*, IV, 2, 91.

very heavy and sad for us but working in us an eternal weight of glory beyond measure (2 Cor. 4:17).

Accordingly, as they are sitting there, an opportunity is offered to them by God to rescue Joseph from the pit and of recalling him from hell, although there still remains the unhappy status that he is a captive and dead on the civil plane, since, indeed, he is torn away from his dear father. The father also is undone by the same fate, namely, he is robbed of his son whom he loved in a special manner. Had he been preserved safe and sound, it would have made the loss of the rest of his sons and all his property easier. For Joseph was his firstborn, in whom all his hopes and resources were founded and from whom a posterity both of the church and state was expected. Therefore the whole household was affected by wretched grief and a great sorrow more bitter than death itself.

Furthermore, the Ishmaelites who bought Joseph were blood relations of Joseph and his brothers, for Ishmael and Isaac were brothers. They were brothers and cousins on their father's side in the third and fourth degree, cousins and close friends. The Midianites were also cousins on their father's side in the same degree. It appears also that the old hatred still endured among the relatives, for they were not slow to buy the youth Joseph and did so eagerly. And they were traders in spices, gum, and myrrh.

But what the force of these three words should be in Hebrew we could not understand unless we gathered it in some way or other from Exodus. They carried on trade in spices. That land, especially in those times, by the special blessing of God abounded in balsam, myrrh, and cinnamon, as can be seen in the description of the royal anointing oil in Ex. 30:23, 24, which was compounded from balsam, cinnamon, aromatic cane, and cassia. But how these were separated and which ones denote species and which genus, I am not sure.

Some interpret נְכֹאת as a spice, and others interpret it as a desirable, or precious article. Some even think it is wax.

צְרִי means gum. It is the general name for all the liquids dripping from trees, as is evident in our cherry tree. But this is wild gum. Frankincense and myrrh were very precious. Pitch is the crudest of all, with which casks are smeared. Our amber is also a gum, for it flows from a tree and gets hard. How many kinds they had we do not know. Balsam is the king of all resins or gums. Scripture calls it uncut balsam, as also the doctors and historians make a distinction, because it flows of itself with a kind of flowing abundance of the tree.

Opobalsam, or the first balsam, flows of its own accord from an uncut tree, and it is the most precious of all. In Canticles it is called chosen myrrh (Song of Sol. 5:5). It is the first balsam, not squeezed out but given off through the bark of the tree of its own accord and not forced out. The same word occurs in Jer. 8:22, where he says: "Is there no balm in Gilead? Is there no physician there? Why then has the health of the daughter of my people not been restored?" Others have translated it as a drop of frankincense or balsam. But he means the medicinal spices from the trees by which Jerusalem could have been healed as in chapter 51:8, where he mocks the Babylonians saying: "Take balm for her pain; perhaps she may be healed."

The meaning of the word לט is also ambiguous. For sometimes they interpret it as a musical instrument, a meaning which is often employed in the psalms; others say it means an acorn or a chestnut, etc. Whatever it was, we take it as a noble sap flowing from trees, and we are content with this general knowledge of these things, namely, that they were dealers in spices who imported precious gums and other fragrant articles into Egypt for which there was use in medicine. Our amber also has great power in the case of women in childbirth and against the stone and apoplexy. But if the power of our saps, which are cruder, is so great, how much more benefit was there to the health of men in the spices and saps of those regions! Below, Jacob orders his sons to take of the fruits of the land and take them to the governor of Egypt (cf. Gen. 43:11), inasmuch as these fruits did not grow in Egypt or grew in less abundance and so they were the more welcome. The three Magi offered the child Jesus gifts of balsam, frankincense, and myrrh (cf. Matt. 2:11). We in Germany have none of these things, or we have them in a corrupt or artificial form.

Now there also follows the vindication of Judah, who makes use of the opportunity offered and actually rescues his brother from destruction.

26. *Then Judah said to his brothers: What profit is it if we slay our brother and conceal his blood?*

27. *Come, let us sell him to the Ishmaelites, and let not our hands be defiled, for he is our brother, our own flesh. And his brothers heeded him.*

Judah in a way softens the anger of the brothers, induced perhaps by regrets that he had consented to Joseph's murder. However, his display of religious feeling is very slender. He acknowledges that Joseph is their brother and their flesh and by this rhetoric persuades them to treat him more mildly. "He is our brother," he says, "our flesh and our blood, the son who is especially dear to our father." These are certainly very strong and sound arguments, and there are hardly any stronger arguments than these in the world among men who are healthy and endowed with common sense, for they include the whole στοργήν ("affection") which is implanted in human nature.

By this rhetoric and dialectic, then, the brothers should have been moved and driven from their purpose. But they are moved even more by his statement: "Let us sell him, etc. Let not his blood be upon our hands!" It is not possible to placate them completely or to persuade them to change their viewpoint. They do, indeed, concede a change, but only of bodily death to death on the civil plane. The deportation remains, or the selling of a freeman into slavery and being torn away from parents. I think that it is often true that a man would bear bodily death more easily than death on the civil plane. For it is uncertain what evils will come to pass in connection with death on the civil plane, and it is a perpetual cross, infinite misery and servitude, and finally, being separated from parents, brothers, and the whole household. For me it would be far more tolerable to be struck on the head than to spend my life in perpetual slavery and exile.

Into these troubles the holy patriarchs Jacob and his son Joseph are now hurled. This cross was fabricated for them by the artifices and stratagems of the brothers. They are very poor carpenters who fabricate and forge this hard cross for their father and their brother Joseph. The only ones who can endure such a cross are excellent and saintly parents. God keeps quiet and makes out that He does not see, as though He were helping these carpenters, and yet He sees that they are setting these doings into motion. But why does He allow this? Why does He not hurl His thunderbolts at them and prove Himself the undoing of these wicked attempts with their authors? Or why does He not rather allow robbers, adulterers, and tyrants to be tormented and afflicted and spare such saintly men?

My reply is that God wants us to consider and learn how great the love of parents towards children is, that we estimate from this the magnitude of God's love by which He embraced us when He was willing to let His only-begotten Son suffer and be crucified for us. For Joseph is the image of God's Son.

However, the hypocrisy which is still found in Judah must not be covered up. For he advances a theological argument, but it is an unsuitable one and indeed a Pharisaical and diabolical one. "Let not our hands be upon him," he says. This Pharisaical theology has reigned from the beginning of the world. For Cain did not want to seem to have killed Abel when he said (Gen. 4:9): "Am I my brother's keeper? Indeed, who would want to do such a thing to a brother?" Similarly, Saul says concerning David in 1 Sam. 18:17: "Let not my hand be upon him, but let the hand of the Philistines be upon him." So also in Christ's passion the Jews do not enter the praetorium so that they may not be defiled or be regarded as the authors of an unjust murder (cf. John 18:28).

Accordingly, these Talmudic and Pharisaical opinions remained from the beginning in this saintly home and church of Jacob. There were such theologians here who thought that a man was not a murderer if he withheld his hand from actual murder. But they hurled him into the pit with their hands. Why then did they concoct consolation for themselves and assume a great show of sanctity because they did not lay a hand on their brother but sold him? Beautiful justice, to be sure, not to kill with the hand but to do so with the will, with one's desires, and with counsel, help, and consent! "Let us sell him," they say, "and we will be innocent." O Judah, you are not yet clean! This is simply Talmudic! But so it usually happens in the world. There must be hypocrites also in holy churches. Therefore it is in no way strange that there is such a large number of them today, too. And in the Gospel history Christ hardly attacks any other class of men more sharply, saying: "Woe to you, hypocrites, etc." (cf. Matt. 23:13). With sinners He drinks, eats, speaks, lives, and performs miracles, but with hypocrites He has nothing to do at all. "Behold, You have loved truth and hated hypocrisy," David says in Ps. 45:7.[36] Later Christ was killed by hypocrites.

In this way these holy fathers repent, namely, they change a bodily murder into a civil one, and they draw a kind of Mosaic veil over their eyes under the pretext that they have not laid their hands on Joseph, although they sin far more grievously and increase the wretchedness and misfortune of Joseph. This is the experience of the

[36] The original has "Ps. 51."

ungodly when they want to make themselves look good; they make matters seven times worse. For they are wise in their own judgments alone. God does not understand or discern so acutely! Their father also does not see it, nor will he ever ascertain it. So they are flattering themselves, and the more they make themselves look good and make efforts to cover the atrocity of their sin, the more emphatically they publish abroad their own cruelty.

Moses says nothing about what Joseph did and said in his great peril. He speaks of him just as if he were dumb or a stone or a tree trunk who said nothing, asked nothing, did not cry out, and plainly did nothing that he could have done to placate his brothers. But he leaves it to the reader to imagine all these things which cannot be expressed or described in words. Therefore let each one imagine for himself how sad his gestures were and how mournful his words, groans, and sighs were as he made supplication. For there was in him a very tender nature and outstanding στοργή ("affection") towards his father. From him he is suddenly and unexpectedly torn away, and his garment given to him by his father is stripped from him. He is cast into a pit and then dragged out again and sold and taken far away from the sight and embrace of his dear parents, nor is any hope of return left to him. What sighs and tears were his! "O my dear father, how are you faring? How you will cry out and make lamentation!"

These are very tragic features in this story of Joseph, and they should have been brought out into the light of day. But Moses passes over them and signifies that God also kept silent. Below they are related by the brothers themselves with great grief when they say: "We saw the distress of his soul when he besought us, and we would not listen; therefore is this distress come upon us, and his blood is required of us, etc." (cf. 42:21-22). He really assumed a pitiable attitude and did not laugh or keep silent. It was a horrible tragedy to be without help and hope of rescue. His father Jacob was absent, ignorant of all that was being done, but this whole disaster would at length overwhelm him. So the evil increases and Joseph dies in many ways. "Behold, I am dragged off and compelled to leave Hebron and my wretched father bereaved," he said. He already foresaw his father's grief and sorrow then. In this way, then, God overwhelms His saints with great troubles and those whom He regards as His dearest ones. These features are to be referred to Christ so that we may reflect what it means to hand over a son for us, to be cast into a pit, into a lake

without water, as we read in Zech. 9:11. The prophets did not celebrate these matters to no purpose and wondered that a son is handed
over into the hands of the Egyptians.

Secondly, a grammatical question in this passage must also be
dealt with, namely, whether the Ishmaelites are the same as those
called Midianites. These matters have been dealt with by Augustine [37]
and others irrelevantly. I would certainly prefer that questions should
be raised about more serious and useful matters, about God's will and
wonderful works, the cross and faith of the fathers, and for what purpose God disciplines His saints with such great troubles, namely, for
our consolation and to foreshadow the passion of Christ. But let us also
look at these matters! Lyra says that according to the view of the
Jews Joseph was sold three times, first to the Ishmaelites by his brothers, secondly, to the Midianites by the Ishmaelites, and thirdly, to
Potiphar the Egyptian.[38] This emphasis on Satan's ill will to look down
on the hypocrites and to produce hatred for the envy of the brothers
appeals to me. But I think that he was sold only twice, as is plain
from the story, which testifies that Potiphar bought Joseph from the
Ishmaelites. And still I do not reject the opinion about the triple
selling, for it will also be stated about the Midianites that they sold
him to Potiphar. But the question about Keturah and Hagar, whether
they are the same woman, has been explained above.[39]

Moses sometimes names Midianites and at other times Ishmaelites
indiscriminately. I think that there was one community called by two
names, as sometimes happens in commercial transactions. I am especially influenced by this reason that Moses stated previously that they
saw not Ishmaelites but a crowd of Ishmaelites. For the word אֹרְחַת
means travelers, or, speaking abstractly, rather a company of travelers,
a train, as is said concerning Christ in Luke 2:44 that they supposed
Him "to be in the company." Often men of different ranks and nations
come together and make a journey together. Such also was the company of Ishmaelites and Midianites, who were joined together in business transactions, commercial relations, and agreements, as is common
also among very different and remote nations. Whether these or those
sold Joseph is of little import. This much is sure, that he was sold.

Nor is there as much importance in a grammatical question as in

[37] Augustine, *Liber quaestionum in Heptateuchum*, I, 124, *Patrologia, Series
Latina*, XXXIV, 582.

[38] Lyra *ad* Gen. 37:26-27, p. 103 recto, note "f."

[39] Cf. *Luther's Works*, 4, pp. 301—302.

the matter that comes up for consideration in this passage, namely, how the Ishmaelites or Midianites bought Joseph from his brothers. Then there is the question whether they first made investigations and questioned Judas, that is, the traitor Simeon, and Levi, that is, Caiaphas and Annas, as to who the youth was whom they wanted to sell, or from where he had come into their hands, whether by theft or plunder. For there is no doubt that they made inquiries not only about price but also about the quality and quantity of their merchandise, in the manner of merchants. But if that was so, Judas, Annas, and Caiaphas undoubtedly broke out into a very severe accusation against their brother Joseph. To their question, "He is your brother, why are you selling him?" they replied (John 18:30): "If this man were not an evildoer, we would not be handing him over to you." So they heaped up crimes of every kind against him as the Jews did against Christ in the presence of Caiaphas. In the same manner they also shouted that he was the worst of scoundrels, opposed to his brothers, disobedient to his parents, disturbing and confusing all things at home, and, in short, plotting against the property and dominion of his father and the success of his brothers and wanting to reign alone after they had been crushed. If the Ishmaelites and Midianites heard this and approved of this false and unjust accusation, they certainly conspired against the blood of Jacob.[40]

But the brothers were undoubtedly highly pleased with such buyers who were enemies of the house and church of Jacob. For in their neighborhood there were Canaanites and Amorites to whom they could also have sold Joseph. But they prefer to push him on to those who after taking him far away from the sight of their parents would treat him more unkindly and harshly than neighbors would. In this manner I would be quite glad to emphasize Satan's works and their unheard-of ill will. "If we sold him to neighbors," they thought, "even though they are also hostile to our family, and would have been no less eager buyers, there is nevertheless the risk that our father may discover it and bring him back home." Therefore it is an excellent opportunity for deporting a turbulent and rebellious man into distant parts so that he may not be able to cause trouble in the future and aspire to dominion in his father's house!

This is the conspiracy of Pilate and Caiaphas against Joseph, and if I am not mistaken, the Holy Spirit through David composed the

[40] This is how the original reads, but perhaps Joseph is meant.

Second Psalm from this passage when He says: "The kings of the earth
set themselves, and the rulers take counsel together, against the Lord
and His Christ" (v. 2). The nations and the Jews enter upon a common plan — the Midianites and Ishmaelites, Herod, Pilate, Caiaphas,
and Annas, who had previously been bitter enemies. Above we heard
that Ishmael was driven out of Abraham's house, and the Midianites
and sons of Keturah were also sent away with gifts and did not enter
upon their father's inheritance. As a result of this a continuing hatred
arose among those peoples, although they were descended from one
and the same blood.

In this way all the nations and peoples were burning with undying
hatred and rage against the illustrious and saintly house and family
of Abraham, which retained the promise, as the pitiable complaint and
burning prayer of Ps. 83 testifies: "Yea, they conspire with one accord;
against Thee they make a covenant — the tents of Edom and the Ishmaelites, Moab and the Hagrites, Gebal and Ammon and Amalek,
Philistia with the inhabitants of Tyre; Assyria also has joined them;
they are the strong arm of the children of Lot" (vv. 5-8). Here also
in the same manner the brothers of Joseph conspire with their own
and their father's enemies, and they are wonderfully pleased with this
covenant.

But if no discussions occurred between them and no conspiracy
was made, the Ishmaelites and Midianites in a way can be excused.
But I think that they entered into an agreement and conspired with
them; otherwise they would have censured and avoided such a monstrous crime on the part of the brothers. Joseph was therefore sold
to relations and brothers on his father's side, to whom he undoubtedly
raised suppliant hands, imploring, beseeching, and entreating their
mercy and help so that they might spare him and lead him back to
his father on the basis of that very close tie of blood. "Dear friends,
I am your cousin, help to rescue me! I am the brother of these men
who have sold me to you." But he found them to be no milder than
his brothers. In this way the Ishmaelites and Midianites conspire with
Israel and kill the son of God, as is described in the Second Psalm.

Moses in this passage does not mention the crying and the tears
of Joseph, but there is no doubt that he gave vent to pitiable lamentation and with the humblest of voices begged that he might be
rescued and that the anger and hatred of his brothers might be mitigated. "O dear no!" "Protect me from my brothers!" Here, to be

sure, the Ishmaelites and Midianites should have opposed the brothers and prevented them from venting their rage in such a cruel manner on the excellent young man, or they should not have bought tainted merchandise, or at least they should have sent him back to their father to be redeemed for a price. "What are you doing, Simeon and Levi?" it would have been right for them to say. "Why do you want to harm your own blood, an unworthy crime and foreign to all feelings of humanity and to your way of godliness?" It would have been fitting for the Ishmaelites to say this, but this is not the way of the world. This would have been right for the Ishmaelites, but the world is not constituted to do something good but is rather intent on harming others per se, or it connives at crimes done to others and foments and assists them that it may render perfect service to its own master, the god of this world (cf. 2 Cor. 4:4). Therefore the brothers do not listen to Joseph as he makes mournful supplication, nor do his relatives, the Ishmaelites and Midianites, nor does God Himself. This example, as has been often stated, is for our consolation, that we may confirm and strengthen ourselves by it in our afflictions and that we may not be immediately broken in spirit if any disadvantage and dangers are put in our way. For we cannot fear more atrocious evils from the Turks or any other enemies. Those who endure attacks from the Turks do not experience anything similar to the disasters suffered by these fathers, and to them we are still much inferior. For it is one of the most bitter evils of all for children to be torn from parents and contrariwise. This is death itself and far harder than the most atrocious punishments suffered by the martyrs, which lasted for one hour, or at the most for two.

But God wanted His saints and church to endure such horrible trials that their hearts might be aroused to reflect what a great thing it was that the Son of God was on our account also torn away for a time, so to say, and sent into exile and cast into hell that He might rescue us from the exile of the most obstinate sin and eternal damnation.

Therefore it is not without purpose that the Midianites and Ishmaelites are mentioned by Moses by name. He does not say traders, Amorites, etc., concealing the names of relatives, but he purposely names the relatives to signify that all agreed on the destruction of their cousin, and from this example it is possible to learn how great the ill will of the world is. Later on, too, the Jews, although they themselves were also relatives and cousins of our Lord Jesus Christ, savagely raged against Him, moved by no prayers and by no mercy, and they, to be sure, were not Ishmaelites but Israelites, so that what was spoken by the prophet was fulfilled: "A man's enemies are the men of his own house" (Micah 7:6). Pilate and the heathen feel pity for Jesus, are sympathetic toward Him, and judge Him to be innocent, but we see that His cousins are more cruel than asps and monstrous beasts.

This is a picture of the church of all times, which God has set forth in His Son and His saints. If you want to be Christians, adapt yourselves to it! Therefore let us learn to obey God in such troubles and adversities and to keep our eyes fixed on heaven. For God is not delighted with our destruction, exile, and the other evils we suffer, but the consolation which He announces in Ps. 36:5, 8 is steadfast and abiding: "Thy steadfast love, O Lord, extends to the heavens, Thy faithfulness to the clouds, etc. Men will feast on the abundance of Thy house, and Thou givest them drink from the river of Thy delights," and likewise in Ps. 37:18: "The Lord knows the days of the blameless, and their heritage will abide forever."

This, then, was God's purpose in what befell Joseph and Jacob. "My dear Jacob and Joseph, I see what evils are bearing down on you; I am not sleeping, but I do not want to remove them and comfort you at present. For the time of rescue is not yet at hand, but you must first experience and learn what the devil, the world, sons, brothers, and death are, so that My grace may become even sweeter and that you may see that you were under My care in tribulation and death. For not even a hair of your head will fall without My nod and will, provided you are not broken in spirit but learn to endure and to bear the cross. I will certainly keep what I have promised. I have promised that I will bless you; I will keep that promise and I will not lie. The flesh indeed murmurs, but resist it and rule over it by faith and the expectation of rescue!"

28. *Then Midianite traders passed by; and they drew Joseph up and lifted him out of the pit, and sold him to the Ishmaelites for twenty shekels of silver; and they took Joseph to Egypt.*

Joseph was sold for a smaller price than Christ was, and I think that the price was about 20 thalers. I am not inclined to engage in rather minute discussions on silver coins. But from this passage Zechariah undoubtedly derived his prophecy concerning Christ (Zech. 11:12): "They weighed out as my wages thirty shekels of silver." For facts and circumstances agree excellently, and there cannot be a greater similarity than that between Christ crucified and Joseph; the selling and death of both are in agreement. For as Isaiah (53:8) says of Christ, "He was cut off out of the land of the living," so also Joseph is removed from the land and sight of his father, just as if he would never return to his father or see him again.

29. *When Reuben returned to the pit and saw that Joseph was not in the pit, he rent his clothes*

30. *and returned to his brothers, and said: The lad is gone; and I, where shall I go?*

יֶלֶד signifies a child, as in Is. 9:6: "to us a child is born." This is another admonition given through Reuben, who certainly seems to act seriously and to be worthy of pardon, for he does not fear the hatred of his brothers at all and defends the lad Joseph with all his powers and regards it as wrong that he has been removed. "Where is the boy?" he says. "He is not here!" But it also occurred to him that he had perhaps been carried off by others after his brothers spared him and were unwilling to kill him. This might have been done by the devil or by robbers or by the neighboring Amorites or Canaanites, who had also laid plots for Jacob's household previously, or he may have been found by some shepherd and may have been handed over to be slaughtered by the Shechemites or other heathen in the neighborhood. So he suspects that the lad had perished from the time that he had been thrown into the pit by the brothers. He seems to fear harm and acts of hatred from the neighbors, and yet he confesses that he wished to keep Joseph alive and condemns the deed of the brothers. Indeed, he also accuses himself, saying, "And I, where shall I go?" and below he will repeat the same reprimand. Not that he expiated his own sin of incest in this way, for he is still held fast in quite heavy punishments, having lost his birthright and very great privileges. But because he acknowledges his sin and wants to avoid partnership in another's sin, he makes an effort to testify that Joseph is innocent and in this way to rescue him. But Simeon and Levi despise him on account of his disgraceful act of incest and force the issue.

The reprimand is just and true: "What have you done? The lad has now been removed from our hands and power, and if we all wished him to be safe and free, we could not redeem him at any price. If the Canaanites happen to fall on him, they will undoubtedly take him into distant parts and kill him, or they will slay him with wretched and perpetual slavery."

Moses therefore excuses Reuben; he does not say what the brothers replied, but in a veiled way he seems to indicate that Simeon and Levi persuaded him to keep quiet and to give his consent to the horrible act of fratricide along with his brothers. But all of this is the product of the accursed theology which the Jews also retained later, namely, that one who does not kill with his hand is not a murderer. With this argument they persuaded him to keep quiet, lest he cause another far greater disturbance by his intercession in case his words and cries might chance to be reported to his father, and they threatened him that unless he concealed this deed along with them, he would experience the same violence or perpetual hatred of his brothers. Nor would it have been strange if they had become involved in mutual violence against each other with blows and slaughter — the very thing to which the devil without a doubt pays constant attention, and he would have brought it to pass had God not prevented it. Accordingly, Reuben keeps quiet and agrees with the others who keep quiet and conceal the matter so that he may not be the author of a greater disturbance for his father or of brotherly dissension. But by this agreement he makes himself a partaker of parricide and fratricide.

Although this is not expressly written by Moses, it is quite clearly hinted at. For he tears his garments and is greatly troubled about the danger and destruction threatening his brother, but out of fear for a greater disaster and the rest of the brothers he is silent. Master Iscariot, Simeon and Levi, Caiaphas and Annas could well have struck him on the mouth and ordered: "Keep quiet and help to conceal the matter, or something will happen to you! Take care to conceal the deed from our father, lest we seem to have killed our brother. For if he discovered it, he would cast us all out of his home and church on the spot and excommunicate us." This he will do later.

It was great wisdom, then, which we see conceded to them by God, that they conceal this deed from their father. Everything else in this story is evil in the extreme. This one suggestion is good, if there can be any good in so great a crime, that the father is persuaded that his son has been torn by a beast. Accordingly, they approached their father and pretended that they, too, were overcome by grief and sorrow for him. They made a show of great longing for their dead brother, but falsely and hypocritically. And yet there is considerably less evil in this pretense than if they had disclosed the whole business to their father.

But Reuben seems to have an excuse, although it is very weak, even as he expostulates on his own with the rest below, saying, "Did I not tell you not to sin against the lad? But you would not listen, etc." (Gen. 42:22). It also seems that he gave them wise and correct advice, but beneath this statement there is that hypocrisy about which I spoke previously, that they concluded that what was not perpetrated with one's hand was not murder. But if he had wanted to be free from all blame, he should have fled in secret to his father to tell him to conduct an inquiry among his sons in regard to the one responsible for the murder. But overcome either by fear or their threats, he agrees with Master Simeon and Levi and the traitor Judas and Caiaphas, who were ruling the others and issuing orders to them.

Judah and Reuben and all the rest are compelled to be quiet about this outrageous crime, and in this way Reuben together with the others pollutes his soul and conscience with the horrible slaughter of his father and Joseph. Their own case, however, they gloss over in excellent fashion meanwhile and make a smoke screen for their father so that he may not get a clear view of things.

I, for my part, greatly wonder what went through the minds of the brothers during all of these 22 years. For that is how many years intervened between the selling of Joseph and the descent into Egypt. It was assuredly a very great scandal, and I am fully persuaded that they did no good during all that time, nor could they with a good conscience have raised the slightest groan of invocation and prayers to their Father in heaven. This is quite certain, for Joseph's blood, their father's death, and the grief of the whole household remained fixed in their hearts. Moreover, a conscience overwhelmed by such a huge mass of trouble cannot in any way pray to God. I, indeed, would not be able to pray if I were conscious of the slightest offense or ill will. Therefore the heart which wishes no one ill but desires what is best for all and is ready to pardon must be free from all ill will, hatred, and envy towards its neighbor. For if ever official duty demands that we censure the faults of men whom we try to lead to repentance by chastising them, it should not be thought that the duty of love in any way ceases in such a case. For it is not out of hatred or the desire to harm but out of zeal for amendment and correction that such rebukes are administered.

In the matter of prayer our heart should be quite indifferent to all hatred even though we should hate and detest the faults and sins of men. So, for example, it is right for us to pray for ungodly bishops, for we should not be so minded that we call down evils or destruction upon them. But I censure and reprove their ungodliness and their disgraceful acts with this end in view that they may be corrected.

Hence I really wonder what the brothers did during these 22 years in which they saw their father sitting in sackcloth and ashes, weeping and wailing on account of the death of his son. I, to be sure, could not have been a spectator of such great and such pitiable grief nor could I have kept myself from saying: "O wretched men that we are! What have we done?" But they hear their father teaching daily and are regarded as members of the church and house of Jacob, and yet none of them can pray to God or do any good, or if they do anything well, it is still wicked and rejected because they remain enmeshed in mortal sin and the murder of their father, brother, and grandfather. Hypocrisy can initiate and perpetrate such disgraceful acts! Hypocrisy can commit such abominable sins and persevere in such great evils.

If Reuben had died in that space of years, he might perhaps have acknowledged and confessed his sin to his father and sought his pardon. But the rest of the throng would have perished with their sin concealed. For in such a long period of time none of them repented, and they gradually became more and more hardened to the feeling and scruples of conscience. Therefore although their terrors of conscience returned repeatedly inasmuch as they could not completely lull them to sleep or bury them by forgetfulness of their crime, seeing that the grief and tears of their father was before their eyes and hearts daily, the sons, who were harder than flint and diamond, still despised them. They were plainly possessed and hardened by the prince of demons since, indeed, they were able to endure the consciousness of such a great sin for such a long interval of time.

Nor is there any doubt, since Holy Scripture attests it elsewhere, that God was very deeply moved and that He denounced the guilty authors of the extreme and atrocious crimes of parricide and fratricide. It is a hard and horrible thing to read and understand such things of these men in the highest station and of princes of the church and of sons and heirs of the promises of God which they had heard taught with great diligence and care by their grandfather and father in the home of their father from their earliest years. But it still happens.

We also, being corrupted by original sin, are inclined to sin. But in such great weakness of human nature, let us still make an effort to retain a heart and brotherly and filial στοργήν ("affection") so that we do not summon punishments and destruction upon ourselves. For these brothers in their eagerness to crush innocent Joseph, whom they regard with a burning hatred, become their own fiercest enemies and devils, and so they harm themselves more than Joseph would ever have harmed them if he had obtained the rule over them.

31. *Then they took Joseph's robe and killed a goat and dipped the robe in the blood;*

32. *and they sent the long robe with many threads and brought it to their father and said: This we have found; see now whether it is your son's robe or not.*

33. *And he recognized it and said: It is my son's robe; a wild beast has devoured him; Joseph is without doubt torn to pieces.*

They add another piece of deceit by which they may both cover their deed more easily and afflict and torture their father more severely. For they take Joseph's robe and dip it into the blood of a goat and send it to him to persuade him that Joseph has been torn to pieces by a wild beast. But how far God is from their sight! How smugly and without all fear they do everything! They take no thought how their aged father may be affected by such an unexpected and sad message. They might at least have taken this precaution not to terrify him by the unusual and atrocious sight of a bloody garment, the saddest object with which the wretched and decrepit old man could have been confronted. It would have been milder to indicate to the father that the son had been intercepted on his journey by robbers and abducted and that they had not seen him and did not know how he had perished and that he had perhaps fallen into the hands of enemies in the neighborhood, the Ishmaelites and Midianites to whom they had sold him. But none of these suggestions enters their minds, and they do not spare their father but augment his grief of heart with a sad and horrible object.

It is a case of outstanding and diabolical ill will by which Satan delights to pour out all his cruelty and savagery upon an excellent old man. They are plunged into horrible sins, and they remain entangled in them against their conscience and without any repentance, without any feeling of godliness. For throughout the 22 years that followed, they lived without prayer, the fear of God, and all the spiritual exercises without which they were not able to have godly aspirations. First it was necessary to acknowledge their sin and to make a reconciliation with their father and brother.

In the meantime, what does God do? What does our Lord God do about this matter? Where are those magnificent promises: "I will be your Protection and Reward, etc." (cf. Gen. 15:1) and "Grow and multiply; I will be with you" (Gen. 35:11; 31:3)? Do not all things appear to be quite different from such great promises? For He does not seem to know them or care for them but rather to have thrown them to the devil since, indeed, He allows a holy father to be tortured in such a wretched manner by the furious ragings of his sons. Or shall we say that God was mindful of His promises? Indeed, no statement or judgment has less right to be made. But David saw this and proclaimed after the deed was done what cannot in any way be discerned in the critical time of trial. For he says (cf. Ps. 105:17): "He sent a man ahead of them to save Jacob."

But of what kind is this mission? What is this idiom, to send a savior into Egypt to save Jacob and his whole house? How is he sent? He is thrown into a pit; he is sold; his father is killed. Is this sending a savior? It is, indeed, but in accordance with God's idiom. For he is appointed king, but God alone sees it. Jacob and Joseph do not see it inasmuch as they are involved in the greatest trouble and grief. This, then, is a special and heavenly language, to send a savior and to appoint a king by hurling him into a pit and hell. We should therefore accustom our hearts to this language so that we may learn to understand what David says elsewhere (cf. Ps. 37:12, 13): "The wicked plots against the righteous and gnashes his teeth at him; but the Lord laughs at the wicked, for He sees that his day is coming on which he will perish, etc." This we cannot do. We cannot look forward and retain faith, excepting a very weak faith. But God holds very fast to His promises, so to say, and so far is He from forgetting them that He even looks forward and laughs at His adversaries, and, indeed, He even casts His vote against them, as is stated in Ps. 2:4 in the words: "He who sits in the heavens laughs; the Lord has them in derision."

"And yet I do not see." Quite correct! These examples are set forth so that in our trials we may reflect that our adversaries are being laughed at and that punishments are being decided on for them, but that we, however much we are afflicted, are chosen, loved, cared for, and regarded, but in a hidden manner, as Isaiah says (Is. 45:15): "Truly Thou art a God who hidest Thyself, O God of Israel, the Savior."

It is therefore sufficient for us to have the Word and the sacraments, in which God appears to us, but the fruit and the end of the signs will follow in His own time. In the meantime, we sustain ourselves by this thought: "I have the sign and the Word; I shall firmly cling to these, however much the world and Satan rage against me and overwhelm me with calamities of every kind." Let us only make it our business to suffer whatever it is with a good conscience, for there is no doubt that we are in high favor with God and precious to Him but that our adversaries are being kept for very heavy punishments and tortures under the bitter derision of God. For the laughter of our Lord God bestows the fire of hell, as is stated in the following words of the psalm (Ps. 2:5): "Then He will speak to them in His wrath and terrify them in His fury." Indeed, be on your guard against such laughter!

Jacob and Joseph are sons of grace before God, but those who did the selling are sons of derision, damnation, and wrath. Would that we could learn these matters and in some way hold fast to them! For the flesh offers opposition, and yet it is certain that a life of suffering is the best and most precious life, and so much so that it does not need the remission of sins because it is without sin. I am saying these things of the godly, that is, of those who suffer in their faith in Christ. These do not sin, but they endure and bear the sins of others. There is an excellent statement indeed from Socrates which says: "It is better to bear injustice than to commit it," [41] for he who bears it does not sin, but he who commits it sins. He who is conscious of doing right and feels that he is being afflicted unjustly, relies on his innocence and at the same time looks to the promise of rescue. So he does not fall into a panic and is not broken in spirit. For he knows that he is harming no one but is bearing the injuries and sins of others. When the solid rock is standing there, namely, a good conscience, nothing can harm us; even though Caiaphas and Iscariot should come and rage, we nevertheless carry off the victory. A good conscience is like the firmest rock, on which the godly rely in their affliction, and with great and high courage they despise the threats of all adversaries, as is written in 1 Peter 3:13-14: "Now who is there to harm you if you are zealous for

[41] Plato, *Gorgias*, 469.

what is right? But even if you do suffer for righteousness' sake, you will be blessed. Have no fear of them, nor be troubled."

On the contrary, when those who have inflicted wrong are afflicted, they quake with fear and fall into a horrible panic and, as the poet says, they plainly turn pale at every thunderbolt.[42] "Woe is me!" they exclaim, "I have merited this punishment by my wickedness and arrogance! What shall I do? Where am I to turn?" This is assuredly a wretched torment of the conscience accusing and condemning itself.

Therefore things go well with Jacob and Joseph, although they do not laugh or acknowledge their good fortune in this critical condition. For he is truly a blessed man who in temptation is so constituted that he can come to this conclusion: "Even though heaven and earth should be thrown into confusion and the world should crash into ruin,[43] and the world with its prince and all the gates of hell (Matt. 16:18) should vent its worst madness, what is that to me? I have a good conscience, for I bear the cross and the wrongs inflicted by others; I do not harm anyone; I do not sin. Besides I have my absolution and the sacraments. Come what may, I shall not be moved and fall into a panic. Woe to those who sin and afflict me!" For it is the mark of Christians not to be angry and not to be indignant in regard to evil inflicted on themselves. Although the flesh is accustomed to grumble after its own fashion, the spirit is not angry, but rather thinks: "Woe to you! You have not done this to me, you have done it to yourself. You have offended yourself in particular, not me!" In this way Jacob and Joseph were able to say: "You do not sell, cast off, and kill me, but yourselves." The flesh, indeed, thinks otherwise, but this is how the spirit feels.

But now someone will ask: "What, then, is to be done? Is the rein to be loosened to ungodliness and no curb to be placed upon the fury and ill will of men by laws or punishments, but, in addition, should thanks be rendered to a wicked man for injury inflicted on us, and must we say: 'You have done me no harm. Do what pleases you, and I shall be glad to suffer it!'? Will not evil men in this way be invited to increase and augment their outrageous sins when, indeed, we teach that troubles placed in our way by others should be borne with joy and a good conscience?"

My reply is that to us there has been entrusted the ministry of the Law and the Gospel according to the direction of Paul: "Rebuke, be

42 Juvenal, *Satires*, XIII, 223.
43 Cf. p. 9, n. 6.

urgent in season and out of season, be confident in reproof and blame, and even be angry and indignant with sin" (cf. 2 Tim. 4:2). This pertains to the ministry of the Law and the duty of fathers, teachers, magistrates and, indeed, private citizens also for the sake of brotherly reproof and admonition which has been entrusted by God to individuals so that as far as possible we may resist evil, each one in his own station, and take precautions that evil men do not rage with impunity either against us or against others. If that is done and nothing helps, I must be content and say: "You will punish not me, your teacher, but yourself." [44] When we have made no progress by all these means, the only thing left for us to do is to be content at heart and wait for the vengeance of God. For they will experience to their great loss that they have gravely injured not others but themselves. The devil will be able to attend to their tortures!

But we have this consolation, that the more they vex, afflict, and torment us, the more they increase our glorious crown in heaven. In the meantime, however, they must be reproved, not in such a way that we harm them but that we may bring evildoers back onto the right way, lest they run up against the hatred and wrath of God, who is a consuming fire (Heb. 12:29) for those who do not repent. In this manner we resist evil with the ministry of Word and sword, and yet, the evils which cannot be averted we bear to our great advantage but to their detriment and destruction.

This is the theology and wisdom of Christians; and although we have not yet attained thereto, we should nevertheless be exercised therein and accustomed thereto daily so that in a crisis and the disasters which we endure we may be able to say with steadfast and tranquil heart: "You cannot harm me; I am a Christian. You are not harming me but benefiting me. Take heed to yourself!" What harm does the selling and exile do Joseph? Indeed, for what did it not benefit him? Or how could the brothers have provided him with greater honor and dignity? For in the very thing by which they try to hinder and crush him, they most conveniently raise him to that pinnacle and peak of sovereignty which he had dreamt of a little while ago.

In regard to this line of thought there is also a celebrated dictum of Gregory: "The ungodly do good to us by doing evil." [45] And Augus-

---

[44] Cato, *Disticha*, II, 26.

[45] Cf., for example, Gregory, *Moralia in Job*, XI, 2, *Patrologia, Series Latina*, LXXV, 954—955.

tine says of the infants slain by Herod that an enemy with his whole
strength and all the resources of his kingdom could not have benefited
the children more than by killing them.[46]

Accordingly, God humbles those who are His to exalt them; He
kills them to make them alive; He confounds them to glorify them;
He makes them subject to raise them up. This is the art of arts and
science of sciences which is not usually learned or discovered except
with great toil and by a few; but it is nevertheless sure and certain,
as this example testifies, for what is stated in Ps. 105:21 is true: "The
Lord appointed Joseph king of Egypt and lord and savior of many."
How? By having him sold, cast off, killed. These are works of God
which are not understood unless they are fulfilled and completed. In
the meantime, however, while they are being carried out, they cannot
be grasped except by faith alone. For it is necessary simply to hold
fast to this: "I BELIEVE IN GOD THE FATHER ALMIGHTY,
Maker of heaven and earth, etc."

In the same manner, when I am about to depart from this life,
I support myself with this consolation that I believe in God's Son.
And yet I am buried; I am eaten by worms; I am consumed by the
most foul rottenness, as Job says (Job 17:14): "I said to the rottenness,
'You are my father,' and to the worms, 'My mother,' or 'My sister.'"
Here I do not discern God's plan, that although I die and rot away,
I must at some time be revived. But God has promised and said (cf.
John 14:19): "You will live, for I live, and you will live. I am the Lord
your God!" How? In eternal life and with a more beautiful and
brighter body than the body of the sun. At present I do not see or feel
this, but I believe it and suffer this very short delay. For this life has
already been prepared, and in the meantime the crown of the kingdom
and glory is being prepared "which the Lord will give me on that
Day, the righteous Judge," as Paul says (2 Tim. 4:8), "and not only
to me, but also to those who love His coming."

But all these things are done in a hidden manner, and so the wonderful concealment of God must be borne and endured. Jacob and
Joseph do not see the crown of the kingdom, nor do the brothers adore
him on bended knees, as will happen later in Egypt, but by this selling
future events are being prepared, and before God they are regarded
as past and over. With our God this is as if it had already taken place.
It certainly comes to pass!

[46] Augustine (?), *Ad catechumenos sermo alius,* 4, *Patrologia, Series Latina,*
XL, 655.

These matters, then, have been written for our instruction (cf. Rom. 15:4), that we may learn to understand and exercise this faith which can bear death and all evils and yet in the midst of these can hope for life and rescue, which endures the violence and wrongs of others, although for duty's sake it severely rebukes and reproves them; which for all that hates no one but pardons gladly, prays, hopes, wishes, and does good without desire of vengeance. We see this clearly in the example of Joseph, who does not remember the wrongs done to him and is not desirous of vengeance but does good to the basest of murderers who sold him.

In this manner those who have the power of chastisement and punishment either with the Word or the sword or the rod should accustom their heart to patience, faith, and love. "Let patience," says James (1:4), "have the perfect work." For he who is patient does not sin; "he who has died is freed from sin," we read in Rom. 6:7. He who is patient in faith in Christ is truly holy. No sin remains in him. For whatever he suffers is sheer righteousness as pure as it can be.

These things are both written and carried out in the stories of the saints, but very weakly and imperfectly, as appears in the case of Jacob and Joseph. They did not, to be sure, call down any evil upon their sons and brothers or do them any evil, but it is likely that in both there was a great struggle against the weakness of the flesh. How often Joseph must have looked with tearful eyes in the direction of Hebron, where his father lived when he was taken away! With what sorrow he must have suffered this! Suddenly and unexpectedly he was taken from the sight of his father and from his home and led away to the authority of others! It was impossible for the flesh not to murmur, but the spirit conquers as it struggles in opposition and groans, enduring unjust violence without desire for vengeance, while these unmitigated scoundrels rage and indulge their hatred.

Moses also adds how they tormented the wretched old man in a most unworthy manner by a fictitious account of what took place, how pitifully they tortured that grand old man. His wretched and mournful complaint attests this: "It is my son's robe; a wild beast has devoured him, etc." He assumes this from the words of his sons and from what they point out when they exhibit the garment soaked with blood. Here he adds that it is proof of the mangling by a wild beast. And yet it was much more likely that a man was responsible for this, and if the father had inquired into the individual circumstances more carefully, he would have detected the deceit immediately. "Why has the robe remained intact?" he would have asked. "Where did you get it? No traces either of the teeth or claws of a wild beast are in evidence. If a beast had mangled him, it would not have stripped him of his garment nor would it have left it whole, but it would have torn it in pieces along with his body." But these thoughts do not enter the father's mind. He is completely submerged and absorbed by heartache and grief. And so it is an easy matter to persuade him in such great grief and heavy temptation.

34. *Then Jacob rent his garments, and put sackcloth upon his loins, and mourned for his son many days.*

35. *All his sons and all his daughters rose up to comfort him; but he refused to be comforted, and said: No, I shall go down to the grave to my son, mourning. Thus his father wept for him.*

36. *Meanwhile the Midianites sold him in Egypt to Potiphar, an officer of Pharaoh, the captain of the guard.*

Now these Junkers have really done things well! By selling and killing their brother they also become responsible for perpetual grief and ruin for their father. They actually torment him more cruelly than their brother. They compel him to mourn for 22 years on end, and [47] during this long period of time they see him going about in sackcloth and wretched grief; they see his groans, sighs, and tears; nor do I think that he later ever assumed a bearing or countenance that was inclined to be joyful. What an amazing thing it was, and what barbarism to look upon a father grieving in such an unworthy manner and for so long! Alas, that men could be such complete devils!

I would never have believed that such an outrageous sin could befall a man that he could knowingly and purposely see his father, consumed by old age and in addition also harassed by his sin, die and descend into hell without any pity and without all feeling of humanity and στοργῆς ("of affection") such as has been implanted by God in all living creatures towards a father and a grandfather. Is this honoring father and mother? And old Father Isaac is also compelled to look upon this. The grief and sorrow of Isaac must also be added here, for he lived for 12 years after the selling of Joseph and at last was undoubtedly brought to his end by heartache on account

---

[47] The Weimar text has *a,* but we have read *ac.*

of his lost grandson. This ornament of the world had to weep and grieve himself to death!

And certainly nothing is more strange than that they heard the word of promise and blessing for so many years and yet not even one of the brothers bettered his ways when admonished by the very serious doctrine and godly standards of his father and grandfather. Nor were they led to pity by the exceptional sorrow of the excellent and saintly old men. You are real hard customers, and this is the way to serve the devil! But they do not harm their father, grandfather, and Joseph most, but themselves.

Simeon and Levi were impelled by the hope and desire of the birthright. Simeon was a pope, Levi a cardinal. Judah was somewhat more sincere but feared the might and power of his two brothers. Reuben had no authority with them but was despised because of the disgrace of the crime he had committed, and so he was compelled to keep silent for the sake of Iscariot and Caiaphas. It would not have been surprising if our Lord God had made a case of Sodom and Gomorrah out of it! Nor would it have been strange if they had been destroyed with fire sent down from heaven after the examples of the Sodomites. They would undoubtedly have perished in the same manner if it had not been for the few godly people and the famous pillars of this family, the grandfather Isaac, the father Jacob, and the son Joseph. These men were the three Atlases of this age. These three men were their support, otherwise God would have struck with brimstone and pitch.

In this way the sins of these men must be emphasized and enlarged upon as much as possible for our consolation. For since they obtained their pardon and remission, there is no need at all to despair on account of our sins. But see that you do not tempt God, for Judas in despair ended his life with a noose! See to it that you do not bring this evil end upon yourself! But if a case occurs that "a man is overtaken in a fault," as Paul says (Gal. 6:1), then there is need of such examples so that you reflect that even the holy patriarchs were sinners and had most disgraceful lapses. I, for my part, am not conscious of such an atrocious sin, except that I served the Antichrist for 15 years, performing the abominable sacrifice of the Mass daily. But I sustain myself in terrors of conscience with examples of this kind and with the promises of the Gospel. Even an act of incest would have been more tolerable than a crime so unworthy of these brothers by which they slay their father, brother, and grandfather with sorrow and grief of heart. But there is no doubt that they still experienced horrible terrors of conscience when they stood in fear before their brother, who was the king of Egypt. To be sure, even all the ills which they with their posterity endured under Pharaoh were a punishment imposed by God on account of this sin. In Egypt they really had to feel it!

So far, then, we have heard that Joseph was taken down into Egypt and sold by the Ishmaelites and Midianites to Potiphar, the king's cook, the master of the kitchen, the controller of the king's household. This God permits to be done while He is silent, asleep, deaf, and insensitive without any mercy and recognition of such a beloved son. All the angels are silent, and such a great treasure, such a great patriarch, prophet, and future monarch is carried away into Egypt for such a trifling price, being sold for 20 pieces of silver. What is our Lord God doing with His elect? What sort of government is this for the elect of God? Why is it that He forsakes and afflicts them in this way?

Unhappy Joseph is carried off by those who bought him and compelled to pass by Hebron; and then, to be sure, the thought enters his mind: "Behold, my father is living here, and he does not know what is happening to me, nor am I permitted to speak to him, to look upon him, and to leave him my last farewell." This was assuredly a great and wretched misfortune! I forbear making mention of the father, who, after he had discovered the deed cried out: "I shall go down to Sheol; I shall be buried with my son. After losing him, this life will never be pleasant and welcome to me." But fine merchants indeed are these, who convey such a precious treasure past Hebron and take him down to Egypt, a man who will later be the salvation of the whole kingdom, a savior of bodies and souls alike. For he will restore the church and the doctrine of God and will administer matters of greatest importance and value for the whole kingdom. But first he must be crucified and mortified before the day of resurrection and glorification comes, so that he may not be proud but remember who he was and whence he rose to such high rank.

That is our Lord God, and these matters are written for our consolation. Meanwhile, during this horrible cross of the father and the son, God is deaf and dumb, taking no thought of the things that are done and not knowing them. But faith is present, and God is still speaking to his heart, saying: "O Joseph, wait; be patient; believe! Do not despair! Cling to the promise which you heard from your father!" In this way God speaks to him through the word of his father. "God promised seed to your great-grandfather, your grandfather, and father. Persevere in that promise with firm faith!" But He speaks with him in a wonderful silence, in which he sees nothing and hears nothing. For God, so to say, is blind and dead; he only lives by and relies on the general promise: "God promised to Abraham, etc. I believe in God, in whom my fathers believed." Later, He will really speak with him in a wonderful manner when He appoints him king and savior of Egypt. But now Joseph is buried and dead, and he has his Preparation and Sabbath; his father is also dying, but they will both rise again by the power of God, which makes the dead alive. The heart of a believer must live in spite of everything and rise again even though 10 worlds were lying on him. The heart of the believer must live again and be raised from the dead even if it were buried under the incalculable weight of the whole world.

These examples, therefore, are set before us that we may accustom ourselves to endurance in afflictions so that we may not be impatient and murmur, no matter by how many great disasters we are overwhelmed. It certainly hurts, as it undoubtedly also must have hurt the tender heart of Joseph. Certainly, the human heart cannot endure and overcome these hardships without great grief and pain. Thus Joseph was no doubt deeply stricken and disturbed and thought that he was being torn from his father in an unworthy manner, thrown to strangers, and consigned to perpetual slavery, where he could never obtain anything that was his own or hope for liberty but would be compelled to be a slave of slaves. For slavery, even of itself, is burdensome and wretched enough even when other difficulties are not added to it. But it is more troublesome for the excellent youth because he is deprived of parents and all the advantages of this life in the flower of his youth. Therefore if our Lord God lets such experiences come upon His children, we should not murmur when things do not always turn out for us just as we want them to. If God lets His saints, whom He loves dearly, be so afflicted, then let us too, bear it patiently if at some time sad and adverse experiences fall to our lot.[48] For these matters are not signs of wrath and of being forsaken but rather proofs of grace for the testing of our faith.

---

[48] The Weimar text has *abiiciuntur,* but we have read *obiiciuntur.*

Such a life, then, was the saintliest of lives, and it was a mark of the greatest patriarchs, with whom our monks and bishops cannot even stand comparison. The fastings and miracles which are recounted in the legends of our saints, Francis, Ambrose, Augustine, etc., are nothing. They have really demonstrated what life is. What is read in the legends of the saints is pure child's play. These are examples which show what the Christian life is and what the true exercises of godliness and patience are. Very well, then, Joseph is gone! So we must let him rest in hell. Joseph is already buried; let us permit him to rest in שְׁאֹלָה, as his father says, in his school.[49]

[49] A play on the words *Sheol* and *Schul.*

Index

By JOHN H. JOHN

to be restrained 198
concern of mothers for
15
Esau's inquiry con-
cerning 167
of Jacob 66, 124, 161,
175
and rod 153
scared by terrifying
objects 239
slaughter of 210, 211
teaching of 186
Christ
called Righteousness
and our Lord 249
commands hatred 29
crucifixion of, signi-
fied 153, 379
deity of 185
doubt reproved by 101
and Fear of Isaac 72
Guardian of oppressed
311
influenced by glory of
49
Jewel enclosed in
bodily blessing 73
killed by two tribes
378
Mediator 230
monstrous hatred of
Jews for 326, 373
not promised to Gen-
tiles 113
one Shepherd 9
our fear 85, 86
portrayed in Joseph
153, 342, 379, 385,
386, 387, 392
promised Seed 72, 73
standing on Jacob's
ladder 126
sweating blood 103
tortured and crucified
by Jews 351, 391
walking on sea 151
Wrestler 125, 130,
138, 144, 185
Christian(s) 76; *see also*
Saints
from, to apostate 18
masters of God 142
name of 258

obtain knowledge of
Scripture from New
Testament 181
Christmas Gospel from
Isaiah x
Christopher, St. 230, 238
Chronology ix, x, xi, 179,
187, 188, 282, 314,
340
Church
of Abraham 359
where altars were
raised 185, 186
bears disgrace of be-
ing heretical 52
devil hurls threats at
38
disciplined by tempta-
tion 90
fellowship with 284,
285
God has need for 23
God hides 146, 147,
149
holy because ministry
is pure 34
in idolatrous house 32
mystery of 71
not to be governed by
women 60
purpose of 234
scandals in 358, 359
spoils conferred on 20,
21
subjected to devil and
his angels 357
support of 20, 21
universal 81
wheat of, mixed with
tares 32, 34
world continues for
sake of 217, 218
Cicero
De divinatione 90 n.
Circumcision 10, 204,
205, 209, 210, 263,
283, 289, 307
Citizen(s) 206, 211, 216
one who goes out of
gate 209
slaughter of 210, 211
Civility 169
Clara, St. 230

Claromontanus 331 n.
Claudian
De raptu Proserpinae
304 n.
Claudius Claudianus
*De quarto consulatu
Honorii* 195 n.
Color 4, 12, 13, 14, 15,
305, 323, 324
Comfort; *see also* Con-
solation
God's, against fury of
Satan 95
of Word in dangers
22, 116
Commanded; *see also*
Orders
through angel 37, 42
to pray 111
virtues, by God 114
Commandments of men
85, 86
Communication of prop-
erties 126
Company 106
dividing of 118, 120,
160
of travelers 387
Complaint(s)
in danger 102
of Jacob to wives 11,
12, 13, 14, 15, 19
of Laban 42
of Rachel and Leah
15, 16, 18, 19, 22
of saints 90
Compostela, Spain 128
Concepts 182
Concern
God's, for all who hear
and believe Word
74
God's, for household
matters 9, 74
for government of
kingdoms 9
mother's, for children
15
for temporal matters
346, 347
thank God for knowl-
edge of His 9
Concupiscence 133

INDEX TO SCRIPTURE PASSAGES